Indian Literature and Popular Cinema

This book is about the popular cinema of North India ("Bollywood") and how it recasts literary classics. It addresses questions about the interface of film and literature, such as how Bollywood movies rework literary themes, offer different (broader or narrower) interpretations, shift plots, stories, and characters to accommodate the medium and the economics of the genre, sometimes even changing the way literature is read. This book addresses the sociopolitical implications of popular reinterpretations of "elite culture," exploring gender issues and the perceived "sexism" of the North Indian popular film and how that plays out when literature is reworked into film. Written by an international group of experts on Indian literature and film, the chapters in this book focus on these central questions, but also cover a wide range of literary works that have been adapted in film. Each part of the book discusses how a particular genre of literature has been "recast" into film. The individual chapters focus on comparisons and close studies of individual films or film songs inspired by "classics" of literature. This book will be of interest to those studying Indian film and literature and South Asian popular culture more generally.

Heidi Pauwels is Associate Professor in the Department of Asian Languages and Literature at the University of Washington in Seattle. She teaches both Modern and Old Hindi language and literature, and courses on Hinduism. Her publications include two monographs on sixteenth-century *bhakti: Kṛṣṇa's Round Dance Reconsidered: Harirām Vyās's Hindi Rās-pañcādhyāyī* (1996) and *In Praise of Holy Men: Hagiographic poems by and about Harirām Vyās* (2002) and various articles in scholarly journals and conference proceedings, including comparisons of medieval and contemporary film and television retellings of the stories of Krishna and Rama.

Indian Literature and Popular Cinema

Recasting classics

Edited by
Heidi R.M. Pauwels

LONDON AND NEW YORK

First published 2007
by Routledge
2 Park Square, Milton Park, Abingdon, Oxon, OX14 4RN

Simultaneously published in the USA and Canada
by Routledge
270 Madison Ave, New York, NY 10016

Routledge is an imprint of the Taylor & Francis Group, an informa business

Transferred to Digital Printing 2009

Typeset in Times New Roman by
Newgen Imaging Systems (P) Ltd, Chennai, India

British Library Cataloguing in Publication Data
A catalogue record for this book is available from the British Library

Library of Congress Cataloging in Publication Data
A catalog record for this book has been requested

ISBN10: 0–415–44741–0 (hbk)
ISBN10: 0–415–57660–1 (pbk)
ISBN10: 0–203–93329–X (ebk)

ISBN13: 978–0–415–44741–6 (hbk)
ISBN13: 978–0–415–57660–4 (pbk)
ISBN13: 978–0–203–93329–9 (ebk)

Dedicated to Nasreen Munni Kabir

A pioneer in promoting the study and appreciation of Indian popular cinema, and an inspiration to all of us.

The Contributors

Contents

Figures

Contributors

Vidyut Aklujkar is Research Associate at the Institute of Asian Research, University of British Columbia, Vancouver. She is an award-winning Marathi author and editor as well as a scholar. Her work has been published in several international journals and anthologies. Her books in Marathi include *Śabda-vedha*, a collection of essays on language (Mumbai 2005), a novella (1998), and a collection of travelogues (1991). One of her scholarly publications in English is "Haroun and the Sea of Stories: Metamorphosis of an old Metaphor," *Commonwealth Novel in English* 6:1–2 (1993).

Mandakranta Bose is Emeritus Professor at the Institute of Asian Research, University of British Columbia, Vancouver. Her research on Sanskrit texts on dance, the *Rāmāyaṇa*, and women's issues has led to many publications, including *Movement and Mimesis* (Dordrecht 1991), *Ramayana Revisited* (New York 2004), and *Faces of the Feminine in Ancient, Medieval and Modern Times* (New York 2000).

Gayatri Chatterjee is Independent Scholar of Film Studies. Based in Pune, she has taught and lectured widely in India, Europe, and the United States. She is the author of *Awāra*, which won the President's Gold Medal (*svarna kamal*) for the best book on cinema in 1992, and *Mother India* (London 2002), part of the prestigious Film Classics Series of the British Film Institute. She also works in Indological studies and her articles are included in several edited volumes.

Cecilia Cossio is Researcher of Hindi Language and Literature and Teacher of Indian History at Ca' Foscari University of Venice, Italy. She has done research on contemporary Hindi Literature and on Hindi cinema. Among her publications is *Cinema in India. Lo strano caso di Shashi Kapur* ("The strange fate of Shashi Kapoor"; Venezia 2005).

Corey K. Creekmur is Associate Professor in English and Film Studies at the University of Iowa, where he also directs the Institute for Cinema and Culture. He has recently coedited *Cinema, Law and the State in Asia* (New York 2007), and has published a number of essays on popular Hindi cinema.

Alain Désoulières is Maître de conférences, Urdu Language and Literature, and Political History of Muslim India in the South Asia Department, at the

National Institute of Oriental Languages and Civilisations (INALCO), Paris. His publications include *Anthologie de poésie ourdou* (Paris 2006), "Images of a historical character: Mirza Ghalib," in *Heroes and Heritage* (Leiden 2003), and "The three lives of Umrao Jan Ada," in *Narrative Strategies* (Leiden 1998).

Naseem Hines is Preceptor Hindi-Urdu at Harvard University, Cambridge. Her publications include "In Quest of the Correct Combination: The Homecoming Episode in Maulana Daud's Cāndāyan," in *The Banyan Tree: Essays on Early Literature in New Indo-Aryan Languages* (New Delhi 2000). She is working on a translation of the important medieval Sufi text Cāndāyan.

Philip Lutgendorf is Professor of Hindi and Modern Indian Studies at the University of Iowa. His book on the performance of the *Rāmāyaṇa, The Life of a Text* (Berkeley 1991) won the A. K. Coomaraswamy Prize. He received a Guggenheim Fellowship in 2002–03 for his research on the popular Hindu "monkey-god" Hanuman, which has appeared as *Hanuman's Tale, The Messages of a Divine Monkey* (Oxford 2007). He maintains a website devoted to Indian popular cinema (www.uiowa.edu/~incinema).

Ali Mir is from Hyderabad. He is Associate Professor of Management at William Paterson University, Wayne, New Jersey. He is co-author of the book *Anthems of Resistance* (New Delhi 2006) a part-critical, part-celebratory examination of the Urdu poetry of the Progressive Writers' Movement. For his songs in the movie *Dor* (for which he also co-wrote the story and penned the dialogue) he was nominated for Best Lyricist of 2006 for several awards. He is currently working on an annotated translation of Faiz's poetry and the songs/scripts of a few forthcoming Hindi films.

Heidi Pauwels is Associate Professor in Hindi and Indian literature at the University of Washington, Seattle. Her research on sixteenth-century Krishna *bhakti* was published as *Kṛṣṇa's Round Dance Reconsidered* (London 1996) and *In Praise of Holy Men* (Groningen 2002). Currently, she is working on comparisons of medieval and contemporary film and television retellings of the stories of Sītā and Rādhā.

Preface and acknowledgments

This book grew out of an enthusiastic encounter in Seattle in March 2004 of several of the contributors with London-based documentary filmmaker Nasreen Munni Kabir of Hyphen Films. Munni has been an inspiration for all of us in her untiring and enthusiastic research on popular Indian cinema, the study of which she pioneered unapologetically years before this now popular topic was even touched by academia. Through her insightful writings and documentaries, she has recorded a history that would otherwise have been lost and at the same time brought Indian popular cinema to the attention of a large audience. For that reason we wholeheartedly dedicate the book to her.

The symposium about the interface of Indian literature and popular film was held at the Seattle Asian Art Museum and was made possible thanks to the support of the South Asia Center and the Simpson Center for the Humanities at the University of Washington in Seattle. It created great enthusiasm in audience and participants alike. Soon we came up with the idea of producing a volume on the basis of the papers of the initial participants from Iowa, Harvard, and Vancouver. We were extremely lucky in bringing aboard more excellent scholars working on related subjects from Pune, Paris, Hyderabad, and Venice. Vidyut Aklujkar even kindly agreed to do a second paper, to "fill a gap."

Among the colleagues at the University of Washington who made the symposium happen, I want to thank first Kalyanakrishnan Sivaramakrishnan (Shivi), Director of the South Asia Center, who was the major *shakti* behind the symposium, and Keith Snodgrass, Associate Director of the Center, who superbly coordinated it all. Special thanks to Carol Salomon who helped as respondent, as well as Shantha Benegal and Ramesh Gangolli who illustrated the talks about film music with a splendid performance. Thanks are also due to Kathleen Woodward of the Simpson Center for financial support of the symposium as well as for the indexing of this book, Sarah Louden of the Seattle Asian Art Museum, and Charu Gupta of Motilal Nehru University, Delhi, who was a thought-provoking respondent. Finally, we owe a special thanks to our enthusiastic and inquisitive audience who made it all worthwhile.

For the transformation of the papers into a published volume, we gratefully acknowledge the anonymous peer reviewers from whose comments we benefited much and especially Dorothea Schaefter of Routledge for believing in the project right from the start and seeing it through to publication. I am also grateful to

Jameel Ahmad of the University of Washington, who helped out with diacritics for the Urdu papers in this volume. Thanks are also due to Susan Miller and Nanette Cardon for their superb work on the index.

For the pictures reproduced in this volume we gratefully acknowledge the kind permission for reproduction given by Mr. Shyam Benegal for the stills from *Kalyug*, and by Mr. Boney Kapoor for the stills from *Hum Paanch*. The reproduction of the illustration of Anarkali is printed with kind permission of Arif Rahman Chughtai, Chughtai Museum, Lahore, holder of copyright to all Chughtai material. Special thanks to Munni Kabir and Alain Désoulières in securing these permissions.

Transliteration and abbreviations

The transliteration policy of this book is to refer to all titles of movies in the conventional Romanized spelling. Likewise, names of persons involved in the making of the movie do not have diacritics, but are given as they appear in the movies' credits. Names of movie characters don't have diacritics either, following the convention in the popular press, with the exception of works based on Sanskrit literature, for which characters, authors and technical terms are given with diacritics. I have also given diacritics for the film dialogue quotes and the transliteration of the songs. I realize this may have a bewildering effect on readers used to the transliterations of the popular press. However, those transliterations are often unclear on whether vowels are long or short, which renders significant differences in meaning, and the same for the consonants and nasals that may be dental or retroflex. Native and near-native speakers of Hindi, who have seen the movies and heard the songs, will have no difficulties filling that in, but not so non-native speakers. Since this book is also aimed at the latter, I provide this aid for better understanding by giving the reader a precise transliteration.

Thus I have followed the Hindi-Sanskrit transliteration conventions that are standard in scholarly literature: macrons on top of vowels indicate that they are pronounced as long (for instance *ī* is pronounced as what is popularly transliterated as *ee, ū* as *oo*), dots under dental consonants indicate the consonants are to be pronounced as retroflex (with the tongue curled back, touching the top of the mouth), but *ṃ* stands for nasalization of the previous vowel, *ṛ* stands either for a vocalized *ri*, or for the flap, and *ḥ* stands for a *visarga*. Further, *ñ* is a palatal nasal, similar to Spanish, *ḥ* is a velar nasal (as the last sound in English "king"), and *ś* is a palatal sibilant (often transliterated as *sh*). For the Urdu characters, q stands for a voiceless uvular stop (*qāf*), *kh* stands for a voiceless velar fricative (*khe*, sometimes also transliterated as *x*), and *gh* for its voiced counterpart (*ghain*), *f* for a voiceless labial and *z* for a voiced sibilant. I have not tried to reproduce the other distinctive spelling variants of consonants of Urdu, as they do not make a difference for the pronunciation.

In transliteration from Sanskrit and old Hindi, I have given the inherent –a-, which is pronounced and important for metrical correctness. For modern Hindi, however, this –a- is dropped. For names in languages other than Hindi, I have generally followed the individual author's transliteration choices.

It is always a bit of a subjective decision to determine which Indian-language names and terms are to be italicized and given diacritics and which ones can be deemed part of the English language. I've tried to follow the individual author's preferences in this matter, except for words that occur throughout the book, where I had to make decisions for consistency.

Finally, another matter of convention: throughout the volume, references are made to EIC, the influential *Encyclopaedia of Indian Cinema* by Ashish Rajadhyaksha and Paul Willemen, first published in 1994 and revised in 1999 (London: Oxford University Press), without repeating the citation in the lists of references each time. I also follow the EIC's convention of abbreviating d. for "directed by."

Introduction*

Heidi Pauwels

Why this volume?

This book is about the ways in which the popular Indian cinema of North India recasts Indian literature, from epics and classical drama, over devotional songs, Urdu poetry and drama, to colonial and contemporary novels. While the relation of "film and fiction" has been studied extensively for Western films (see, for example, the bibliographies in McFarlane 1996, Stam and Raengo 2005), that is not the case for Indian popular cinema. Our focus is on the Hindi-language cinema of Bombay/Mumbai.[1] We counter the stereotype that this cinema, recently (and controversially) labeled "Bollywood,"[2] is a rip-off from Hollywood, by foregrounding its extensive engagement with Indian literary traditions.

The volume presents case studies of film versions of "timeless classics," bestsellers, and lesser known recent literature. It has a special focus on gender issues and looks for the sociopolitical implications of popular reinterpretations of "elite culture." Studying the interface of literature and film has a wider relevance: adaptation is after all the retelling of important stories of a culture, which provides a way of negotiating cultural heritage and betrays much about the postcolonial project of coming to terms with modernity.

"Bollywood" takes root in the West

Why focusing on "Bollywood"? For decades, the Hindi popular cinema has had an appeal well beyond South Asia. It has an enthusiastic following in the so-called South Asian diaspora, the communities of South Asian origin residing all over the world, including in the West.[3] Recently, Indian popular cinema has come to extend its traditional audience beyond this ethnically specific group to the mainstream, as witnessed by the Western press coverage generated by the Oscar nomination in 2002 of the Indian movie *Lagaan* by Ashutosh Gowariker (2001, with Aamir Khan, Gracy Singh, and Rachel Shelley) and the appeal to mainstream audiences in the West of recent "Bollywood"-inspired movies, for example, *Monsoon Wedding* (2001, d. Mira Nair), *Bend It Like Beckham* (2002, d. Gurinder Chadha), and *Bollywood/Hollywood* (2003, d. Deepa Mehta).

In other words: "Bollywood" is in the news. In 2003, the Freer and Sackler Museum in Washington DC hosted major Indian movies and the film series

"Cinema India!" toured several cities in the US during the following year. Major newspapers and magazines have carried reviews of the aforementioned movies and series. Popular culture has been quick to appropriate the appeal of Bollywood: in London, Selfridges department store organized its 2002 summer season around a Bollywood theme. There was much publicity surrounding the Andrew Lloyd Weber/A.R. Rahman musical "Bombay Dreams," which came to Broadway in 2004 and toured the United States. To turn things topsy-turvy: some "Hollywood" movies now carry references to "Bollywood" song and film (e.g. Terry Zwigoff's 2001 movie *Ghost World* with its clip from Raja Nawathe's 1965 *Gumnam*[4]). In short, Bollywood has begun to take firm root in the West.

Does this interest in popular Indian cinema go beyond the appeal of the exotic? A typical "masala movie" may seem naïve and simplistic to the untrained Western eye and ear. Film audiences in the West, long weaned from the musical, are so steeped in Hollywood's tradition of "realism" and (alleged) innovation, that they may have difficulties in appreciating this decidedly "other" cinema with its predeliction for song and dance, its self-conscious camera work, and its (supposedly) "formulaic" approach. South Asian diaspora viewers may feel exposed when their cinema is compared to the mainstream fare in the West. There is a need for serious work that helps understand the popular Indian movies on their own terms without unhelpful value judgments dictated by "Hollywood" pundits.[5]

Academia turns to "Bollywood"

After decades of neglect by academic scholars, popular Indian cinema has recently become the subject of lively inquiry and analysis by both Indian and Western scholars. A landmark for research in this area is the impressive *Encyclopaedia of Indian Cinema* by Ashish Rajadhyaksha and Paul Willemen (EIC; first edition in 1994, revised edition in 1999). In its wake, at least eight major studies have appeared (e.g. Ganti 2004, Gokulsingh and Dissanayake 1998, Gopalan 2002, Kabir 2001, Mishra 2002, Pendakur 2003, Prasad 1998, and Vasudevan 2000, to name only the most accessible, general works). A new journal published by Routledge, called *South Asian Popular Culture*, was launched in spring 2003, in part to provide a forum for this dynamic field of studies.

These recent works have opened up the field for serious academic study and provided the stepping-stones for others to build on. A lot of headway has been made in studying the movies for their political relevance and their impact on popular culture. Most of the contributions have focused on socioeconomic issues of the industry and the sociopolitical implications of its products. On the other hand, meta-issues, such as the glamorous star system, fan clubs, film posters and film magazines also have received attention from popular culture scholars (see, for example, Dickey 1993, Dwyer and Patel 2002, Gandhy and Thomas 1991). Ironically, although many of these studies argue for and see themselves as part of a rehabilitation of popular movies as a serious object of study, little sustained attention has been paid to detailed analysis of the films themselves. Sometimes, scholars seem mainly interested in the way films may be invoked to address larger debates over theory within specific academic disciplines.

This volume seeks to contribute to the scholarly literature on popular North Indian cinema in three ways: by widening the academic discussion to a broader audience, by focusing on the films themselves rather than theoretical and contextual issues, and by foregrounding neglected interdisciplinary approaches. First, the volume is aimed at a nonspecialist audience. While a lot of new studies make excellent contributions, there is a tendency towards theorization and an abstract (and sometimes jargon-ridden) discourse that is difficult to follow for the uninitiated. This leads to a gap between the narrow world of the academic theoreticians and the wider cosmos of consumers of popular cinema—which includes many thoughtful viewers who are interested in insightful analysis of mainstream films—provided that it is in accessible idiom. This book consciously seeks to return to straightforward language and focus on concerns intelligible to the makers and viewers of these movies.[6]

Second, this book strives to provide detailed analyses of representative films. The authors have, so to speak, done away with their "fast-forward" button in order to pay close attention to details of image, song, and dialogue. Our premise is that Indian popular movies deserve serious attention on their own terms, and not merely as illustrations of theoretical issues. It is appropriate to start a new field at a general level, staking out the major issues and their broader relevance. In a second phase of inquiry, though, the generalizations need to be examined at the level of individual films. There is a need for close readings of influential popular films. Surprisingly, there are very few monographs on individual movies that go beyond the format of glitzy coffee-table "making of..." books. The only exceptions are for a few truly landmark movies *Mother India*,[7] *Awara* (Chatterjee 2002, 1992), and *Sholay* (Dissanayake and Sahai 1992).[8] Also lacking are balanced evaluations of the work of influential individual directors. There is only one serious study on each of these major directors: Mehboob (Reuben 1994), Bimal Roy (Bhattacharya 1994), Raj Kapoor (Dissanayake and Sahai 1988), Guru Dutt (Kabir 1996), and Yash Chopra (Dwyer 2002).[9] Of course, such studies require a great deal of on-site research, as well as access to films, production records, and ephemeral publications which are unavailable outside India (and which may be very difficult to obtain even there; see Pendakur 2003: 3–4). A positive trend in the United States is that several major universities have recently hired specialists in South Asia in their Film Studies departments. Hopefully, a new generation of graduate students will push forward research on popular cinema beyond the level of theory and generalization.

Third, this volume broadens the range of disciplinary approaches that are brought to bear on popular Indian cinema. At the same time that the focus can now be narrowed to individual movies, the pool of researchers working on the topic needs to be broadened. Input from beyond film studies and social and political sciences is necessary.

Contributions from many disciplinary angles are to be encouraged and solicited. Studying Indian popular movies requires interdisciplinary cooperation, including input from the other side of the divide, from the humanities. Religion and literature specialists can make worthwhile contributions in dialogue with what is going on in departments of film studies and popular culture. The need is particularly pertinent for a genre of films that has remained vastly understudied: films that are based on literature, in particular on religious literature.

Forgotten foundations of films: after amnesia

In India the connection between film and literary classics/scripture was evident from the start and has endured till the present time. This is most obviously true for the cinema's link with the classical epics *Rāmāyaṇa* and *Mahābhārata*. One of the earliest Indian feature films, Phalke's *Raja Harishchandra* (1913, remade in 1917), was based on a legend included in the *Mahābhārata*.[10] This inaugurated a persistent trend of epic-derived films.[11] Such early examples may give the false impression that epic-based movies are old-fashioned, reactionary, and/or irrelevant for contemporary cinema, an attitude manifested in the sad neglect of the so-called mythological in academia. However, that the epics are an abidingly popular source of inspiration is made clear by the spectacular success of the televised epic serials *Ramayan* by Ramanand Sagar and *Mahabharat* by B. R. Chopra, which were aired between 1987 and 1991 on the Indian state television network, Doordarshan. These serials, now in their DVD avatars, have remained popular ever since, as is witnessed also by the many new mythological films and serials that followed in their wake. Obviously, given the political use to which the epics are being put, the mythological should be of great general interest, and a careful study of epic-inspired movies against their literary and religious background has much to offer.

Another neglected genre—and one that should be of great interest to understand contemporary South Asian politics—is that of the "historical." Here too, literary studies can contribute significantly, but it is not always known that major historical films are based on literature. The classic *Mughal-e-Azam* (1960) by K. Asif was based on the earlier film *Anarkali* (1953 version) by Jaswantlal (EIC 329), itself a remake of earlier versions—all ultimately traceable to the (unacknowledged) "archetype" of Imtiaz Ali Taj's 1922 Urdu play. In this case, the ultimate film version has been so successful as to obliterate the memory of its source of inspiration in the popular mind. Still, the study of such movies against the background of their literary sources may reveal more precisely which aspects are period-specific for the movies (as opposed to what was stressed in the literary source), and thus historically significant for that period. If we ignore the sources, we may end up marking features of the original as typical for the period of the movie. In short, this promises to be a fertile field of studies that will contribute to the ongoing debate over the link between cinema and the construction of national history.

Other films that are landmarks of Indian popular culture have roots in literature too, but again these are understressed. There has been much discussion in the popular press about the successful recent movie *Devdas* (2002) by Sanjay Leela Bhansali, which was a remake of the classic 1955 movie by Bimal Roy. Little was said though about the 1917 novella by the Bengali writer Sarat Chandra Chattopadhyay on which the movies were based. Yet the novella was celebrated in its day, and its success among Bengali readers led directly to its remarkable cinematic career. A thorough study of the now-prolific *Devdas* phenomenon surely requires grounding in the knowledge of its textual component.

Whether the connection is well-known or forgotten, it is clear that many movies are inspired by or directly based on literature. Academic study of such movies should of course not be limited to the literary angle. However, there is no doubt that to counter this amnesia a worthwhile contribution can be made by scholars of literature and religion. A start of this was made in the seventies, in an insightful article on the Hindi film in relation to Indian Literatures by Edward Gerow (1974). Unfortunately, hardly any contributions in this direction have been made since.[12]

The value of such contributions seems obvious and one wonders why up till now this field has remained so underexplored. One reason may be that film and literature are sometimes viewed as two mutually exclusive, even antithetical institutional fields (for some possible reasons for the perceived rivalry between film and literature, see Stam 2005: 4–8). This may be understandable in the West with its general bias of privileging the written word, but does not make sense in India. Moreover, in the Indian popular film industry, authors collaborate closely with filmmakers or have turned to film making themselves. To name only two successful contemporary directors: Ramanand Sagar started out as a writer of novels and plays and proceeded to film script writing, before becoming a producer (Tully 1991: 134), and Gulzar has kept up publishing poetry and literature, while writing film songs and dialogues and directing films (Gulzar 1983: 193, 195, 203). Already in the early period there was a symbiotic relationship between the worlds of drama and literature. Interestingly, this has been very strong in leftist circles: many famous directors were involved in the Indian People's Theatre Association (IPTA) and screen play, dialogue, and song writers in the Progressive Writers' Association (PWA) of the 1930s.

Another reason why scholars do not bring the insights of literature studies to bear on popular cinema may be the myth of the unsophisticated audience. It is often asserted that these popular movies are intended for the masses, who are overwhelmingly illiterate and thus are imagined not to have access to "the classics." That is however a misunderstanding as being illiterate in the sense of being unable to read does not necessarily mean illiterate in the sense of not knowing one's literature. Many in the audience are actually well versed in the vernacular versions of the epics and in devotional literature via oral transmission. They know their classics by heart. The fact that popular Indian movies abound with sophisticated references to this literature, both obvious and subtle, is a clear indicator that the directors know their classics and assume their audience does too. The critic who remains unaware of this dimension misses much of the delight that Indian popular cinema provides.

A further obstacle in the crossbreeding of Indian Film Studies and the disciplines of religious and literature studies is the prejudice against "Indology" as backward from one side and an equally arrogant looking down upon popular films as hardly worth attention from the other. This volume demonstrates that there is much to be gained by religious and literary approaches to popular movies. Of course, their focus is limited in that it is strongly focused on the narrative, but still they can make worthwhile contributions. The different disciplinary angles do not need to be antithetical, but can be complementary. Scholars in all disciplines can draw inspiration from each other's insights. The challenge remains to forge a way forward in true dialogue and interaction.

Contents of the volume

Questions asked

As this volume is focused on the interface between film and literature, the general question is basically what happens when classics of literature get taken up in popular North Indian movies. I use the term "classics" broadly in a nontechnical sense, basically referring to texts that are well-known. In this volume we discuss both narrative texts and songs, both traditional texts and more recent ones, both popular narratives and novels that have become "canonized" as part of "Great Indian Literature." I first elaborate on how it is important to study in detail how such texts are made into movies, before breaking down the topic into more specific questions.

Especially at this point in time, it is important to analyze how "Bollywood" recasts the tradition by reworking classics. The screen image has a powerful impact on the imagination. It is capable of drastically shaping the spectator's memory. The literary classic is easily conflated with the movie based on it. Specialists of the literature, through careful analysis, can alert the public to what the differences are and the political implications. This is especially pertinent at a time in India where a new hegemony of religious interpretation is taking over the public sphere, including cinema. The Hindu Right seems to have embarked on a project of reconstructing memory and history. This affects audiences both in India and in the diaspora communities. The latter communities are often crucial for the fundraising efforts of the political parties concerned. Thus, such reshapings are not innocent and as scholars we need to bring our expertise to bear on these issues.

We start out the volume by looking at religious classics. By this, we do not intend to perpetuate the myth of India as "lost in myth," on the contrary we wish to carefully lay out the historical fluctuations and machinations in this perceived ahistorical mythic consciousness. Although most of the contributors to this volume are trained as scholars of literature, we are careful not to privilege the book over the movie. We have studiously avoided going "by the book," and have worked to abandon the "tyranny of fidelity analysis" (see, for example, McFarlane 1996: 8–11), which always ends up finding fault with the film for differing from the book. Rather, we want to uncover the rich ways in which the movies add to and go beyond the interpretation and reading of the text (Stam 2005: 24–31). We have paid attention to the movies on their own terms. Scholars of religious texts are preeminently placed to do so, because their training has familiarized them with the fluidity of religious texts in the subcontinent. They are well aware that there is not just one Ur-text of, say, the *Rāmāyaṇa*, fixed for all times. Sensitized to the panoply of voices interpolating, erasing, and expanding on traditional texts, textual scholars are in a wonderful position to help understand Bollywood's creative transformations.

The questions we are asking start at the level of the individual film and focus on narrative and thematic. Close readings and comparisons of the films with the literature they are based on reflect on several issues. We study how the film broadens or narrows the interpretation of the literature it is based on. Which parts are foregrounded, which ones are cut out, and which are substantially edited? How are lacunae filled? How does the movie deal with breaking points and contradictions in the literature, and where are its own moments of discontinuity? Does the director acknowledge his source texts, explicitly problematize his approach, or suggest in more subtle ways departures from the literary source? To what extent can such changes be attributed to the medium? How might these choices be determined by philosophical, historical, sociopolitical, economic, and other agendas?

More insights are to be gained from comparing different screen versions of the same literary work, as several of the chapters in this volume do. What is the significance of similarities and shifts in stories, plots, and characters? To what extent can these be said to accommodate the medium and its economics or represent a uniform ideology of the Hindi film? Do we distinguish differences that fall along the lines of different periods during which the movies were made, along the different film genres, or maybe according to different genres of literature on which they were based?

At a more general level, questions informing the discussion are how Indian popular cinema changes the way literature is "read" (better: "perceived") in India. Given the long history of adaptation of classics in Indian arts (theater and dance), is Indian popular cinema doing anything new? Does the modernity of the medium carry an inherent ideological message, and if so, what may that be?

A related instructive question is how "Bollywood" differs from Hollywood. If the medium of film has its own agenda, how can we account for differences in Indian and American popular cinema? It has been argued that Bollywood has a distinctive heterogeneous mode of production, wherein the screenplay is relatively looser and less dominant than in some Western cinema (Prasad 1998: 42–57). How do we understand the prevalence of movies based on literature in that light?

From a different angle, we might ask why certain literature seems so popular as material for moviemakers. Why are certain texts remade as film over and over again, while others remain neglected? Can we distinguish some themes of particular preoccupation in the cinema that are better treated by literature from certain periods than others?

Finally, many of the chapters in this volume grapple with issues of gender in Indian popular cinema. The Censor Board is supposed to forbid "visuals or words depicting women in ignoble servilitude to man or glorifying such servility as a praiseworthy quality in women" (as quoted by Pendakur 2003: 75). Yet, most Bollywood movies seem to fly in the face of such noble intentions. What are we to make of this? Popular movies at the same time reflect gender values and help construct or reconstruct them. When we compare with the supposedly normative texts on which the movies studied are based, do we find a continuation of a reactionary element and maybe even a stiffening of attitudes, or do we detect contestation? What drives the differences? What seems successful and what not? How much can boundaries be pushed? Is there something inherent in the genre of popular film that fuels certain gender constructs? Such questions are of major interest to gender studies beyond India.

Working towards answers[13]

In order to focus the reader on the interface between literature and film, the chapters in this volume have been organized by literary genre. Such organization may seem unusual at first sight: it is based not on the chronology of the period the films discussed are made, but by the type of literature they treat. What is kept constant is the subject matter, whereas the variants may be the different eras, genres, or modes of cinematic adaptation. This is indicative of the focus of the volume on literature, seeking to analyze how literature of a similar genre is appropriated by North Indian commercial cinema.[14]

There is an underlying narrative running throughout the volume. The genres represented are organized roughly chronologically and move approximately from more to less religious literature and from poetry to prose. The first part studies film versions of the all-influential great epics of the classical period, the second of the great classical Sanskrit dramas,[15] and the third of popular medieval devotional songs. The fourth part of the book looks at what for lack of a better term is called "Indo-Islamic" literature.[16] This in itself had a strong religious element, but, as we shall discuss at length, this aspect has been secularized in its popular film versions. The fifth part concentrates on film versions of colonial literature. The preoccupation of this literature included themes of religious reform that were important in the growing nationalist movement. Here, the transition is made from poetry to novels. The theme of nationalism continues into the sixth part, which focuses on "agenda"-driven literature, mostly of the postcolonial period. We have contributions on the PWA and on chauvinist Hindu literature dealing with Partition.

Within the scope of a single volume, the chapters cannot exhaustively deal with each of the literary genres singled out for analysis. Still, the chapters represent major streams of literature in each genre. For the epics there is representation of both *Rāmāyaṇa* and *Mahābhārata*; for Sanskrit drama, of course Kālidāsa and his much-hailed *Abhijñāna-śākuntalam*, and also a play that is less known in the West but very popular in India: *Mṛcchakaṭikam* by Śūdraka. For devotional literature, we were unfortunately able only to address the influential Northern (Hindi) streams of *bhakti*, but at least by looking at the pan-Indian saint Mīrābāī. For "Indo-Islamic" literature, there are contributions focusing on the early and late Mughal period, with the story of Anarkali set during Akbar's time, and the life of the poet Ghalib contemporary with the takeover by the British Crown. That brings us to the colonial period, which has a focus on Bengali literature, justifiable because that is where reactions against colonial rule were voiced first and most strongly. There is both the much-beloved Tagore and the classic theme of *Devdas*. In the part on agenda-driven literature, the chapter on the PWA deals with a host of famous poets of the period and the chapter on communalism focuses on a minor Hindi novel by Catursen transformed into film by one of the most influential contemporary directors, Yash Chopra.

To zoom in on the individual parts: the first part of this book studies how the great Indian epics, *Mahābhārata* and *Rāmāyaṇa*, have been transformed as they are "recast" in film. Both epics have served for more than two millennia as a rich source of inspiration for Indian visual artists, poets, playwrights, and storytellers, who have often exercised remarkable license in their representation of characters, episodes, and chronology. The vast and often self-reflexive corpus of epic-based storytelling has, during the twentieth century, been supplemented by numerous film and television productions. As with earlier enactments of the story, these productions have variously chosen to represent either individual well-known episodes from the oceanic saga, or to offer condensed or (in the case of television serials) expansive retellings of the "complete" epic story, notably Babubhai Mistry's 1965 feature film in Hindi, *Mahabharat*, and B. R. Chopra's massive 1990 television serial of the same title, and of course Ramanand Sagar's *Ramayan*. In addition, several movies have taken the epic characters and events as the basis of contemporary reworkings. Both chapters in this part look at such reworkings, and each compares two contemporary examples.

In the first chapter, Philip Lutgendorf focuses on two feature-length Hindi film reworkings of *Mahābhārata* with well-known actors and aimed at mass audiences. Both appeared in 1980: *Hum Paanch* ("We five") by Telugu director Sattiraju Lakshminarayana (popularly known as "Bapu"), and *Kalyug* ("Age of discord"), by Hindi art film director Shyam Benegal. Each film is interesting in its own right as a radically modern recasting of the main *Mahāhārata* story, but Lutgendorf's pairing them is provocative, since they offer strikingly different interpretations of the story's message. In examining the two films and their innovative and nearly opposite readings of the *Mahābhārata*, Lutgendorf also endeavors to place them in the context of contemporary sociopolitical events, and within the broader lineage of postcolonial reenactments of the epic.

The second chapter by Vidyut Aklujkar similarly compares two successful recent mainstream Hindi movies that draw heavily on *Rāmāyaṇa: Hum Saath Saath Hain* by Sooraj Barjatya (1999) and *Lajja* by Rajkumar Santoshi (2001). Both remakes select only some incidents of *Rāmāyaṇa*. The chapter analyzes the contrast in their respective interpretations of the epic characters, and in the messages they project. Aklujkar argues that these are rooted in contrasting ideologies, in one case, the traditional ideal of the joint family based on sacrifice and in the other, the modern ideals of feminism based on equality and individualism. She concludes that common formal elements such as the star-studded cast, the routine of song and dance, excellent photography and technical expertise make each one a box-office success, but the final outcome of each film is directly dependent on the initial outlook and conceptual framework of the filmmakers.

The second part focuses on film reworkings of classical Sanskrit drama. This is an important part of the book as Sanskrit dramatic theory and its conventions are highly instructive in understanding the aesthetics of the popular Indian film (Gerow 1974)—filtered as it may be through a multiplicity of folk dramatic traditions. Each chapter in this part draws attention to the multiple mediations these dramas have undergone by the time they make it onto the screen.

In Chapter 3, Gayatri Chatterjee studies Kālidāsa's classical drama *Abhijñāna-śākuntalam* and V. Shantaram's film adaptations. First she demonstrates that visuality is one of the organizational and narrative principles of Kālidāsa's play with its numerous references to the act and circumstance of looking, gazing, and eavesdropping—underlined repeatedly by the characters verbalizing their doing so—and also by the references to pictorial art and image making and the act of looking at representations. The fact and act of looking becomes a recurrent motif binding the narrative; this has been one main source of pleasure of reading this play and seeing it performed, so it is but natural that the story of Śakuntala has been through several film adaptations. Chatterjee then focuses on V. Shantaram's film adaptations, mainly *Shakuntala* (1943), but also *Stree* (1961). The first film is an interesting hybrid. Chatterjee argues that in the beginning it centers around creating the "gaze" and visual pleasure, which is in keeping with the Orientalist reception and excitement over Kālidāsa's play. Later on, though, the heroine undergoes a transformation and here the filmmaker follows the critique of the play launched by the nationalist writer Bankimchandra Chatterjee and aspires to the nationalist goal of the empowerment of women. The later remake, *Stree*, looses this subversive element. Thus we see the complexity of the filmmaker's "reading" informed by a multiplicity of previous readings and performances.

In Chapter 4, Vidyut Aklujkar focuses on *Utsav*, the 1984 film produced by Shashi Kapoor. The movie's script writer and director, Girish Karnad, uses two classical Sanskrit dramas *Cārudattam* of Bhāsa (CE 300) and *Mṛcchkaṭikam* by Śūdraka (CE 400) to recreate the story of the impoverished and artistic hero Cārudatta and his love, the courtesan Vasantasenā. Aklujkar goes well beyond comparing these Sanskrit dramas with the movie. She discusses the innovations introduced by Karnad in the light of the popularity of *Mṛcchakaṭikam* on the Indian and international stage, tracing influences from vernacular Marathi theater, and internationally staged English translations. This chapter also deals with the portrayal of courtesans from Sanskrit literature in film and compares with Urdu literature. Aklujkar's main interest is Karnad's treatment of Eros and gender, examining the reinvention of the female characters in the movie, the courtesan Vasantasenā and her rival, the wife of Cārudatta. She also draws attention to Karnad's caricature of Vatsyāyana, author of the *Kāma-sūtra*. Aklujkar shows why *Utsav*, in spite of having received passionate criticism from some quarters and being a commercial flop, remains an important recreation of a time-treasured classic.

The third part, Saints on the Screen, returns to the issue of film and religion by looking at the understudied yet popular genre of the devotional movie. Interestingly, many devotionals contain outspoken social criticism, foregrounding the revolutionary potential of *bhakti*'s discourse of equality of all castes in the eyes of God. At the same time, there is a striking absence of similar messages for the uplift of women. This genre certainly deserves more attention. The literary material recast by these movies is of two kinds: devotional songs by and hagiographic writings about the saint featured.

In Chapter 5, Heidi Pauwels studies the devotional songs. She focuses on the link between devotional songs and gender through a case study of the famous woman-saint, Mīrābāī of Rajasthan, as represented in the popular 1979 movie *Meera*, directed by Gulzar. This chapter analyzes how the songs excerpted in Gulzar's movie relate to the popular *bhajan* tradition of Mīrā. By the contextual placement of the song, the director invites the viewer to read in meanings that may undermine those of other performance contexts, while at the same time capitalizing on the songs' popular appeal. Pauwels introduces the concept of "inter-aurality" to understand the phenomenon and presents an intertextually sensitive close reading of the movie's songs. In terms of the treatment of gender, the analysis shows disparate forces at work simultaneously: there is advocacy of women's resistance to patriarchal norms, as well as reinforcement of a status quo. The chapter illustrates that there is no simple way to characterize the modernity of the movie: it is a site of contestation.

The fourth part deals with some ways "Indo-Islamic" literature is represented in the popular cinema from Bombay. Much has been made of the "Muslim" contribution to this cinema in terms of actors, directors, writers, and other personnel, and of its possible decline in the current climate of increasing Hindu-chauvinism. Here, the focus is not so much on the religious identity of the contributors, but on the representation of "Indo-Islamic" literature and history. It would be a worthwhile project in itself to map out the subtle reworkings of Indian history in popular culture, in particular the shifting interpretations of "foreign Muslim" rule. One chapter here deals with a narrative set in Mughal times, and the other with poetry from the late Mughal period.

In Chapter 6, Alain Désoulières focuses on the famous saga of Anarkali, the tragic love story of a slave girl and the Mughal prince Salim (later emperor Jahangir). It has been filmed several times, most famously in K. Asif's *Mughal-e-Azam* (1960; re-released in a colorized version in 2005). This is a case where the literary source has been nearly obliterated by the success of the movie to the point that some later movies do not even acknowledge the source text, the Urdu historical drama *Anārkalī*, which was written in Lahore by Sayyad Imtiaz Ali Taj in 1922 (rewritten in 1931). Désoulières analyzes the drama and adds a further layer of complexity by investigating in turn the sources of the play, which are both oral folk traditions in Urdu and Punjabi, and late-nineteenth-century Urdu historical writing. He discusses in detail some of the literary techniques of the Urdu playwright, who was writing for the then new "talking cinema," and whose work shows cinematic influence. Thus, this study shows the fallacy of seeing the transformation of literature to film as a one-way street. It also shows how the romantic story of the ultimate sacrifice of love came to be recast as a parable for the sacrifice of private considerations for the public good of the nation, upholding the politically correct version of Akbar's reign as that of the enlightened Indo-Islamic monarch.

In Chapter 7, Naseem Hines studies popular film representation of Urdu poetry. Her project is to investigate how popular Indian cinema has preserved the memory of the Indo-Islamic contribution to North Indian classical music traditions by introducing influential Muslim poets and singers to the general public. Hines here presents a case study of the poet Ghalib, comparing Sohrab Modi's 1954 Minerva Movietone film with the 1988 TV serial directed by Gulzar.

She shows how both recast Ghalib's life and poetry in the same way: downplaying religious elements in favor of romantic ones. In the process, Ghalib's—sometimes difficult—poetry is edited substantially for a general public.

The fifth part asks how literature produced in the colonial period is recast on the screen. One might expect such literature to be "dated," colored as it is by the concerns of specific political circumstances and issues of religious reform in response to colonial challenges. Yet, the popularity of its film adaptations makes for a fertile ground to study the postcolonial struggles to come to terms with the colonial past. One chapter focuses on a "bestseller" and its enormously popular narrative, which also as a film became a blockbuster. The other looks at an art film representation of a somewhat lesser-known Tagore novel.

In Chapter 8, Corey Creekmur looks at the multiple versions and references to the popular narrative of *Devdas* through a century of adaptations of Sarat Chandra Chattopadhyay's novella. He pays particular attention to the concept of repetition within the narrative of *Devdas*, including the continual returns to the city and to the village, and how that is underscored in the film versions by the repetition of specific camera movements.

In Chapter 9, Mandakranta Bose concentrates on issues of colonial and gender oppression by studying Rituparno Ghosh's film based on Rabindranath Tagore's novel, *Chokher Bali.* She shows how the director imagines the novel as an opulent setting for two liberation movements, one seeking release from the harness of gender and the other from that of coloniality. Ghosh renders Tagore's understated representation of passionate self-reflection into a visually breathtaking spectacle whose opulence transforms its presumed location in a historicized India into an imagined community. This chapter shows that while Tagore's story attempted to grasp the psychological authenticity of a period of socially realized tension, Ghosh's romantic makeover seizes upon the original's implied politics of gender and nationalism, yet transforms it into an aesthetic confined to postures, whereby the narrative and ideological processes of the film are left unresolved.

Finally, the sixth part deals with postcolonial agenda-driven literature and how this fares on the screen. This is an excellent place to study ways of coming to terms with modernity, including progressive and regressive ideologies. How do literary products driven by political agendas fare in a market-driven popular culture? One chapter focuses on leftist while the other on Hindu chauvinist politics. The first one returns to song lyrics and the second discusses the adaptation of a novel.

In Chapter 10, Ali Mir looks at the period when the PWA had a hegemonic hold over Urdu poetry and dominated the landscape of Hindi film lyrics (roughly from the 1920s till 1950s). Preeminent lyricists, such as Sahir Ludhianvi, Majrooh Sultanpuri, Kaifi Azmi, Ali Sardar Jafri, Shailendra, Jan Nisar Akhtar and others, penned songs inflected with their politics and the politics of their movement. Mir examines the trajectory of progressive lyrics in Hindi cinema from the early days of the independence struggle through the period of the PWA hegemony to the present time.

In the last chapter, Cecilia Cossio looks at a narrative of the traumatic Partition of the Indian subcontinent in 1947. She compares a Hindi novel and its film version: the movie *Dharmputra* ("Son by Faith"), directed by Yash Chopra, based on the 1954 novel of the same name, written by Catursen. The story poses an interesting problematic: in the midst of the Delhi riots following Partition, a young Hindu militant discovers that he is in fact Muslim by birth. Cossio lays bare the diverging representations of the same historical event in the two narratives: what the novel understands to be a war won by the "Indian people" (read: "Hindus") over the "foreign invaders" (read: "Muslims"), the film shows as a political vivisection of the common "motherland." The chapter investigates how the filmmaker takes a more progressive political stance than the author.

While this volume is very rich in covering a large area and many genres, it reveals only the tip of the iceberg. I regret that many significant authors and works do not figure at all. This volume is indeed just a beginning, hoping to inspire more research in this line. While our focus is only on films in Hindi (and a couple in Bengali), there is a whole fertile field out there of early film adaptations of regional literary classics in Marathi, Gujarati, and Bengali,[17] and in Punjabi, Rajasthani, and so on in more recent times. And that is only the North of India; obviously South India's popular film has reworked to great political effect not only the classical epics, but classics of Tamil and other literature, often in a "revival" spirit (for instance, well worth studying is M. Karunanidhi's contribution to P. Neelakantan's 1964 film *Poompuhar* and comparing with Shyam Benegal's 1988 TV series, also based on the Tamil epic *Cilappatikāram*).

In addition, there are a number of literary genres that we have left unrepresented. I especially regret the absence of folk literature, in particular the folk tale. A beginning has been made by investigating the applicability of categories from Indian folklore in film (Booth 1995). In addition, there is Pendakur's analysis of two Nāginī, or "snake woman" movies, including the 1997 Kannad movie *Nagamandala*, which was based on a play written by Girish Karnad that was in turn based on a folk story (2003: 173–98). The Urdu *dāstān* tradition too has been a major source of inspiration, which awaits further analysis (see Sreenivasan 2005). Generally, the continuity between movie and folk tale in the Indian tradition, in terms of motives and tropes is also a fruitful category to study. It is hoped that this volume will inspire more studies on the interface of film and literature.

Notes

* I am grateful to Philip Lutgendorf for his incisive comments on earlier drafts of the Introduction.

1 Not all of the films included in this volume fit the label equally well; some Bengali films and several older, Hindi art films are also discussed.

2 The term "Bollywood" was first coined in the 1980s (see Kabir 2001: 21–2). Notwithstanding the objections of many, it has caught on widely. The term is nowadays often used loosely, as shorthand for North Indian commercial cinema. That is the way it is used in this volume, without wishing to evoke any of the pejorative connotations the term is sometimes understood to imply. By no means do we wish to detract from the value of those movies or equate them with the Hollywood rip-offs of later cinema. I should also note that the term "popular" is equally problematic (Kazmi 1999: 22–49).

3 In addition, Bollywood movies have been popular with non-South Asian audiences in Russia, the Central Asian republics, Africa, and several South East Asian countries.
4 I wish to thank my Hindi student, Dawn Neil, for drawing my attention to this movie.
5 One excellent article that can serve as an introduction to understanding Indian popular cinema on its own terms is Thomas 1985.
6 Ashish Nandy has repeatedly expressed frustration with academic literature on popular culture: "formal film theory and trendy hermeneutics of the kind that, for reasons of academic correctness, sucks all life from one of the most vigorous expressions of the selfhood of the Indian" (Nandy 1998: 16–17). He has recently pleaded for more ethnographically grounded studies (Nandy 2003), as a result of which the journal *South Asian Popular Culture* called for and published papers on Bollywood audience response.
7 For the importance of this movie and its female star, Nargis, see Rosie Thomas 1989.
8 There are some longer articles on individual movies, notably Lutgendorf's and Veena Das's on *Jai Santoshi Maa* (Das 1980; Lutgendorf 2002). Further, Kathryn Hansen's articles on *Tisri Kasam* and *Sara Akash*, as well as Hueckstedt's also on the latter were featured in a special section called "Literature to Film Studies" of the *Journal of South Asian Literature* in 1981.
9 For the "new cinema" there is more material, in particular from the National Film Development Corporation in New Delhi and the National Film Archive of India in Poona (see, for example, Hood 2000).
10 At least this important early film has been subject of a recent detailed study (Schulze 1998), which has shown that it was neither produced nor consumed as a nationalist movie at the time. This case illustrates the danger inherent in generalizing before careful study of individual films has been done.
11 That the *Mahābhārata* narrative was used as a metaphor for political events early on is clear from the reception of the 1921 movie *Bhakta Vidur* (*Dharma Vijay*) by Kanjibhai Rathod. This movie was banned in Karachi and Madras because Vidur appeared clad in Gandhi-cap and *khaddar* shirt and because it was performed with a music score that included a strident nationalistic song in praise of the *charkha* (EIC 244; see also Mir in this volume).
12 Some studies of films based on literature have appeared in a recent volume edited by Vasudha Dalmia and Theo Damsteegt 1998. This volume juxtaposes articles exclusively focused on literature and others taking into account film versions of literature. All of the articles feature quite innovative approaches. The present volume builds on and is a continuation of the trend in the articles on film in that volume.
13 The description of the individual chapters and their introduction is largely based on the authors' own summary, often using their turns of phrase.
14 I hasten to add that in no way do I wish to replicate a problematic periodization of Indian history (see also note 16).
15 This term is a bit of a misnomer, as of course the classical drama was multilingual, with different characters speaking in different forms of Prakrit, and Sanskrit being reserved for the higher-class male characters and the stage directions.
16 This term has come in for some criticism and some prefer now "Islamicate." However, I find that term unfortunate as it seems to imply something derivative. An alternative would be "Indo-Persian," yet that may also be confusing with Indian Persian.
17 To name just a few outstanding examples, Baburao Painter's 1923 *Sinhagad* was based on a Marathi classic novel by Hari Narayan Apte, and several early Bengali movies were inspired by Saratchandra Chatterjee and Tagore (e.g. 1927 *Balidan*).

References

Bhattacarya, R. (1994) *Bimal Roy: A Man of Silence*, New Delhi: Indus.

Booth, G.D. (1995) "Traditional Content and Narrative Structure in the Hindi Commercial Cinema," *Asian Folklore Studies* 54.2: 169–90.

Chatterjee, G. (1992) *Awara*, New Delhi: Wiley Eastern.
—— (2002) *Mother India*, London: British Film Institute.
Dalmia, V. and Damsteegt, T. (eds) (1998) *Narrative Strategies: Essays on South Asian Literature and Film*, Leiden: CNWS.
Das, V. (1980) "The Mythological Film and its Framework of Meaning: An Analysis of Jai Santoshi Ma," *India International Centre Quarterly* 8: 43–56
Dickey, S. (1993) *Cinema and the Urban Poor in South India*, Cambridge: Cambridge University Press.
Dissanayake, W. and Sahai, M. (1988) *Raj Kapoor's Films, Harmony of Discourses*, New Delhi: Vikas Publishing House.
—— (1992) *Sholay: A Cultural Reading*, New Delhi: Wiley Eastern.
Dwyer, R. (2002) *Yash Chopra*, London: British Film Institute.
Dwyer, R. and Patel, D. (2002) *Cinema India: The Visual Culture of the Hindi Film*, New Brunswick: Rutgers University Press.
Gandhy, B. and Thomas, R. (1991) "Three Indian Film Stars," in C. Gledhill (ed.) *Stardom: Industry and Desire*, London: Routledge.
Ganti, T. (2004) *Bollywood: A Guidebook to Popular Hindi Cinema*, New York: Routledge.
Gerow, E. (1974) "Epilogue: The Modern Film," in E.C. Dimock *et al.* (eds) *The Literatures of India: An Introduction*, Chicago: University of Chicago Press.
Gokulsingh, K.M. and Dissanayake, W. (eds) (1998) *Indian Popular Cinema: A Narrative of Cultural Change*, New Delhi: Orient Longman.
Gopalan, L. (2002) *Cinema of Interruptions: Action Genres in Contemporary Indian Cinema*, London: British Film Institute.
Gulzar (1983) "Interview, January 1982," in A. Vasudev and P. Lenglet (eds) *Indian Cinema Superbazaar*, New Delhi: Vikas Publishing House.
Hansen, K. (1981a) "Hindi New Cinema: Basu Chatterjee"s *Sārā Ākāś*," *South Asia* (Australia) 4.1: 15–21.
—— (1981b) *"Tīsrī Kasam:* The Story and the Film," *Journal of South Asian Literature* 23.1: 214–22.
Hood, J.W. (2000) *The Essential Mystery: The Major Filmmakers of Indian Art Cinema*, New Delhi: Orient Longman.
Hueckstedt, R. (1981) "Equivalents in the Two Forms of *Sara Akash*," *Journal of South Asian Literature* 23.1: 204–12.
Kabir, N.M. (1996) *Guru Dutt: A Life in Cinema*, Delhi: Oxford University Press.
—— (2001) *Bollywood: The Indian Cinema Story*, London: Channel 4 Books.
Kazmi, F. (1999) *The Politics of India's Conventional Cinema: Imaging a Universe, Subverting a Multiverse*, New Delhi: Sage.
Lutgendorf, P. (2002) "Jai Santoshi Maa and Caste Hierarchy in Indian Films" and "A 'Made to Satisfaction' Goddess: Jai Santoshi Maa Revisited," *Manushi* 131: 10–16; 24–37.
McFarlane, B. (1996) *Novel to Film: An Introduction to the Theory of Adaptation*, Oxford: Clarendon Press.
Mishra, V. (2002) *Bollywood Cinema: Temples of Desire*, New York: Routledge.
Nandy, A. (1998) "Introduction: Indian Popular Cinema as a Slum's Eye View of Politics," in A. Nandy (ed.) *The Secret Politics of Our Desires*, Delhi: Oxford University Press.
—— (2003) "Notes Towards an Agenda for the Next Generation of Film Theorists in India," *South Asian Popular Culture* 1.1: 79–84.
Pendakur, M. (2003) *Indian Popular Cinema: Industry, Ideology and Consciousness*, Cresskill, NJ: Hampton Press.
Prasad, M.M. (1998) *Ideology of the Hindi Film*, Delhi: Oxford University Press.

Reuben, B. (1994) *Mehboob, India's DeMille: The First Biography*, New Delhi: Indus.

Schulze, B. (1998) "The First Cinematic Pauranik Kathanak," in V. Dalmia and T. Damsteegt (eds) *Narrative Strategies: Essays on South Asian Literature and Film*, Leiden: CNWS.

Sreenivasan, R. (2005) "Genre, Politics, History: Urdu Traditions of Padmini," in K. Hansen and D. Lelyveld (eds) *A Wilderness of Possibilities: Urdu Studies in Transnational Perspective*, Delhi: Oxford University Press.

Stam, R. (2005) "Introduction," in R. Stam and A. Raengo (eds) *Literature and Film: A Guide to the Theory and Practice of Film Adaptation*, Oxford: Blackwell.

Thomas, R. (1985) "Indian Cinema: Pleasures and Popularity–An Introduction," *Screen* 26.3–4: 116–31.

—— (1989) "The Mythologization of Mother India," *Quarterly Review of Film and Video* 11.3: 11–30.

Tully, M. (1991) *No Full Stops in India*, New Delhi: Viking.

Vasudevan, R.S. (ed.) (2000) *Making Meaning in Indian Cinema*, New Delhi: Oxford University Press.

Part 1

Indian epics in film

1 Bending the *Bhārata**

Two uncommon cinematic adaptations

Philip Lutgendorf

Introduction

The prominent cultural role of the two classical Indian epics *Mahābhārata* and *Rāmāyaṇa* can hardly be exaggerated. Both remain highly visible in contemporary society both as multiform texts and as bodies of visual art and performance. Moreover, in the voluminous scope of their Sanskrit redactions, with their complex main plotlines and baroque profusion of subsidiary tales, each seems to aspire to a sort of encyclopedic or "mother-of-all-stories" status; indeed the *Mahābhārata* is quite brazen in claiming this in its famous boast, "No story is found on earth that does not rest on this epic" (1.1.240; van Buitenen 1973: 43). Given that such hyperbolic assertions are sometimes echoed within the Hindi film industry—as in Rosie Thomas' observation that "It is common to hear filmmakers say that every film can be traced back to these stories, and even that there are only two stories in the world, the *Ramayana* and the *Mahabharata*" (Thomas 1995: 182, n.35)—the comparative rarity of treatments of these epic stories, either in whole or in part, in the copious output of mainstream Bombay cinema might appear surprising. To be sure, allusions to the epics, especially through dialogue and the names of characters and less commonly through narrative situations, abound in popular Hindi films, and there have periodically been successful send-ups of the basic stories as spectacles of the "mythological" film genre, such as Babubhai Mistry's *Sampoorn Ramayan* (1961) and the same director's *Mahabharat* (1965), made in the ornate and comic-book-like visual style standardized by decades of popular illustration. But although "mythological" films dominated the first decade of indigenous feature film production, their output rapidly diminished during the 1920s, yielding to action-packed "stunt" and "historical" films, crime dramas, and later to the "social"—a loose designation referring to any melodrama with a contemporary setting. With the coming of sound in 1931, the dominant Hindi film market would itself be dominated by this omnibus genre, and mythological films, though they would remain robust players in regional and especially southern cinemas, would generally be confined, among Bombay productions, to occasional low budget "B-grade" releases aimed at niche markets of pious grandmothers and rustics, although occasionally such a film would become a hit with a broader audience (e.g. the unexpected success in 1975 of the goddess film *Jai Santoshi Maa*;

Lutgendorf 2002). The relative absence, during the post-independence period, of films directly based on the classical epics, and indeed of films with "historical" subjects, is even more surprising given the remarkable prominence during the same period of epic themes in Indian fiction writing and of mytho-historical plays on the urban Indian stage.

The year 1980, however, saw the release of two unusual feature films that were inspired by the central narrative of the *Mahābhārata*: Shyam Benegal's *Kalyug* ("Kali Yuga," or "Age of Discord") and Bapu's *Hum Paanch* ("We Five").[1] Although they represented contrasting aesthetic and marketing strategies within Hindi cinema, both films were commercial releases that featured well-known actors and that incorporated musical numbers by established composers and lyricists. Neither was "mythological" in visual presentation: rather, both presented the *Mahābhārata* in a modern setting—urban in the case of *Kalyug* and rural in *Hum Paanch*. Both films made striking departures from the traditional story, while still emphasizing their derivation from it and alluding to it in readily recognizable ways. Together the two films constitute a notable cinematic meditation on and intervention in the *Mahābhārata* storytelling tradition. In the sections that follow, I will first introduce each film and offer a synopsis of its plot. I will then discuss their respective aesthetic and narrative strategies, both in the context of their historical moment and against a wider background of ongoing traditions of *Mahābhārata* performance and interpretation.

Kalyug

After an early career in advertising and documentary filmmaking, Shyam Benegal emerged as a nationally recognized director following the modest commercial success of his first feature films *Ankur* ("the sprout," 1974), *Nishant* ("the calm," 1975), and *Manthan* ("the churning," 1976), all of which dealt with themes of peasant oppression and mobilization. These films were widely hailed by urban critics as exemplars of an Indian "new cinema" movement (a.k.a. "parallel cinema"), that was seen as rejecting the timeworn clichés of the "dream factories" of Bombay in favor of shorter films with more "linear" narratives, little or no song and dance, a "realist" mode of representation, and a focus on social issues viewed through the lens of progressive leftist politics. Another label sometimes given to these films, many of which were made with the financial assistance of the Indian government, was "middle cinema," ostensibly for their location between mass-market entertainment films and the aggressively non-commercial avant-garde—though the designation might equally well point to their target audience being primarily the educated urban middle class. The "failure" of this supposed revitalizing movement by the mid-1980s—reflected in the mass audience's continued preference for big-budget melodramas and the turning of even such celebrated directors as Benegal toward more accessible and marketable films—has occasioned much subsequent critical analysis (e.g. Chakravarty 1993: 235–41). A more commercial turn is perhaps already suggested in *Kalyug* by the choice of a celebrated pan-Indian narrative as the template for the screenplay, by the casting of prominent stars like

Figure 1.1 The women of *Kalyug* mourn their dead; courtesy Mr Shyam Benegal.

Shashi Kapoor and Rekha in principal roles, and by the seemingly gratuitous inclusion of a disco scene and a romantic song set in an exotic locale. Nevertheless, the film's short running time (by Indian standards) of 143 minutes, subdued acting style, linear narrative, and overwhelmingly serious and indeed ominous mood, unbroken by the comic subplots that are normally expected in Bombay films, all serve to mark this as a departure from mainstream cinematic fare. The fact that the screenplay was co-authored by Benegal and Girish Karnad—the latter likewise a famous "middle cinema" actor and director, as well as one of the most celebrated playwrights of post-Independence India—further confirms this.

The title itself suggests a dystopian vision, since *kalyug*—colloquial Hindi for the Sanskrit *kaliyuga*—names the fourth and most degraded era of cosmic time, when *dharma* falls to its lowest strength. Since this "dark age" is widely believed to have begun around the time of the war celebrated in the *Mahābhārata* (precise datings for this event vary, but many modern astrologers favor 3102 BC) and will continue beyond the imaginable future, it refers to our present-day world or even to the human condition, and in everyday speech the label is most frequently invoked to remark on such endemic problems as individual dishonesty, family disharmony, communal violence, inflation and unemployment, bureaucratic corruption, and so on.

The fact that, in Benegal's film, this title is displayed during a credit sequence super-imposed, to the accompaniment of a tense, driving orchestral score, over images of factory interiors, in which elegantly suited managers watch workers operating giant machines for the forging and shaping of metal parts, suggests the further association of moral turpitude with the age of industrial capitalism. Though this will remain no more than a sub-theme in a film largely preoccupied with family dynamics and interpersonal conflicts, its invocation helps to position the film temporally and politically as an implicit critique of the more optimistic view of industrialization characteristic of films of the 1950s and 1960s (cf. the credit sequence of the iconic 1957 hit *Mother India*, which unambiguously celebrated hydroelectric dams, power lines, and rumbling tractors).

The credits to *Kalyug* are preceded, however, by a brief and unusual sequence introducing, through a terse voiceover narrative and a gradually built genealogical chart illustrated with black and white photos, all the principal characters in the film's two clans of rival cousins. Bewildering as this may appear to non-Indian viewers, it serves the obvious purpose of identifying the film, for its target audience, as a *Mahābhārata roman à clef*, in which actual epic names, colloquialized according to normal Hindi practice (Bhisham for Bhīṣma, Kishan Chand for Krishna), are artfully combined both with epithets (Dharam Raj for Yudhiṣṭhira, Bal Raj or "king of strength" for Bhīma) and with commonplace names that lack *Mahābhārata* associations yet carry ironic or allusive weight in this context (e.g. Dhan Raj or "king of wealth" for the acquisitive Duryodhana, the morally and nationalistically resonant Bharat for Arjuna, Supriya or "beloved

Figure 1.2 Factory scene accompanying credits; courtesy Mr Shyam Benegal.

one" for Draupadī, and Savitri—the paragon of the chaste Hindu wife who rescues her husband from premature death—for the sexually compromised and widowed Kuntī).

The patriarchs are, on the "Kaurava" side, the elder brother Khubchand, who like Dhṛtarāṣṭra is handicapped—here, as an apparent stroke victim confined to a wheelchair—and on the "Pāṇḍava" side, the deceased junior brother Puranchand, who is survived by Savitri and her three sons (the epic's twin junior sons are dispensed with, as is, in this age of mandated Hindu monogamy, Pāṇḍu's second wife Mādrī). Other names are identifiable only by their placement within this matrix: thus Khubchand's brooding wife Devaki represents Gāndhārī, and their younger son Sandeep, who suffers from a heart condition, suggests Duḥśāsana. A few characters are apparently inserted simply to normalize the family scenario—for example, Dhan Raj's wife Vibha, and their young daughters Dia and Keya (played by the children of Victor Banerjee, who himself acts the role of Dhan Raj). Other non-family characters will be introduced in due course, and their names allude to the ethnic milieu of Bombay during this period, with Marwari

Figure 1.3 Part of *Kalyug*'s genealogical chart; courtesy Mr Shyam Benegal.

entrepreneurs (Puranchand, Khubchand) running industries that were staffed by both (reputedly) placid Maharashtrians (e.g. the workers Mhatre and Kulkarni) and more aggressive recent immigrants from Uttar Pradesh (e.g. the tough union boss Pandey).

The story turns on the rivalry between two family firms. Khubchand and Sons Ltd is led by the elderly bachelor Bhisham Chand (A.K. Hangal), called *Dādā* or "grandfather," who devoted himself to raising his two fatherless nephews, Puranchand and Khubchand. He retires midway through the film after failing to make peace between his feuding grand-nephews, and is supplanted by Dhan Raj (Banerjee) and his friend and advisor Karan Singh (Shashi Kapoor), an orphan of unknown parentage raised by Bhisham. Puranchand Dharamraj and Brothers Ltd is led by the three Puranchand sons, whose names, dress, and deportment all convey epic allusions.

The senior brother, Dharam Raj (Raj Babbar), is reserved, bookish, and soft spoken; he dresses in immaculate *kurta-pajama*, yet we learn early on that he has a passion for race horses—suggesting Yudhiṣṭhira's "gambler" alter ego. His frequent absences from the office infuriate his junior siblings and his wife, all of whom regard him as "soft" and ineffectual; as the corporate rivalry heats up, he invariably recommends conciliation and moderation. Bal Raj, the film's Bhīma (Kulbhushan Kharbanda) is portrayed as lusty and energetic; he favors safari suits with shirt unbuttoned to display his hairy chest, is frequently shown eating or drinking (recalling Bhīma's epithet of "wolf belly"), and makes love energetically to his shapely wife Kiran (Rima Lagu), who likens him to a bear.

Bharat Raj (Anant Nag) is, like his model Arjuna, temperamentally situated between the two poles of his senior brothers; a hard-drinking workaholic, he favors stylish western suits and ties and appears to be the most astute in business matters; unmarried as the film begins, he soon weds the beautiful Subhadra, who is many years his junior and the daughter of his friend and cousin Kishen Chand (Amrish Puri). Kishen's sister, Supriya (Rekha) is already married to Dharam Raj, in a match that has clearly gone sour, leaving her frustrated and irritable.

Since even the large cast of the film represents a drastic compression of the epic's sprawling *dramatis personae*, some characters allude to multiple epic roles. Thus the two youths Sunil (son of Bal Raj) and Sandeep (younger brother of Dhan Raj), both of whom die tragic deaths in the escalating family conflict, seem to represent all the epic's doomed junior characters—Abhimanyu, Ghaṭotkaca, the five sons of Draupadī, and the ninety-nine brothers of Duryodhana—although Sandeep's succumbing to heart failure while being violently shaken by the angry Bal Raj makes an obvious reference to Duḥśāsana's slaying by Bhīma. And the creepy Swami Premananda ("love's bliss"), who is eventually revealed to have been the biological father of the three Puranchand brothers and of Karan Singh, at once suggests all the absentee Brahmin and divine progenitors in the *Mahābhārata*: Parāśara, Vyāsa, and the five gods who sire the Pāṇḍavas. That the film's only clearly "religious" character is revealed to be a profligate and bogus holy man—he is clearly hated by Savitri, whom he first molested while he was living in her father's house—is in keeping with its radically secularized and de-mythologized reading of the epic.

Indeed, since "Kishen Uncle" (Amrish Puri) is merely an avuncular business partner, the only "gods" left in this saga are the numerous *objets d'art* displayed in the elegant mansions of the two families—huge Nathdwara *pichwai*s, tastefully mounted folk bronzes, and museum quality sandstone sculptures—all expressive of both authentic elite taste and perhaps a certain directorial irony (thus a large *caturbhuja* Vishnu adorns the sitting room of the Khubchand/Kaurava clan, and a silver *panch-mukhi* Shiva lingam that of the Puranchands/Pāṇḍavas). Grimly allusive humor is evident as well when Bharat and Subhadra, on a pre-nuptial date, attend a Kathakali performance of the slaying of Duḥśāsana and leave in disgust as the Bhīma-dancer drinks his cousin's blood, or when Savitri pays a desperate visit to the hermitage of the retired Bhisham Chand and finds him reading what appears to be an ochre-bound popular edition of the *Bhagavad-gītā*.

The "kingdom" over which the two families are struggling consists of a series of massive government contracts, presumably defense-related, on which both have bid, and which, in the course of the film, they attempt to "steal" from each other, assisted by the unethical tricks of bought-out union bosses and hired thugs. The film thus effectively evokes the business climate of pre-liberalization "license raj," when imported raw materials and technologies were strictly controlled, as well as the endemic labor unrest of the 1970s and the ensuing period of autocratic rule by Indira Gandhi (the Khubchand and Sons factory sports inspirational signboards of the sort that proliferated during the Emergency; for example, "Prosperity Through Productivity"). Its equivalent of divine weapons are precision foreign machines, obtained by Bharat and Karan as a result of sojourns in the West (the "heaven" of the modern Indian elite), and its version of the Kaurava-instigated humiliation of the Pāṇḍavas takes the form of an income tax raid on the Puranchand brothers' mansion to uncover suspected "black money," during which agents rifle through the enraged Supriya's wardrobe, fingering her jewelry and undergarments. Although the film's carnage is mild by *Mahābhārata* standards—claiming a mere (though perhaps symbolic) five victims by its end—the manner in which these deaths come about, as escalating commercial hostilities lead to a series of deceptions, misunderstandings, and acts of self-destruction, and their devastating impact on family members, combine to produce a chilling sense of moral and material collapse that effectively evokes the holocaust of Kurukshetra.

But just as, in the *Mahābhārata*, the realpolitik of clashing kingdoms is grounded in the dynamics of dysfunctional families (both human and divine), so in Benegal's film the conflicts of clashing corporations—which in India are characteristically family owned and managed—are shown to be intertwined with the similarly strained relations between extended family members. Special attention is given to sexual tensions and issues of legitimacy. Dhan Raj/Duryodhana despises the Puranchands as "bastards" because he knows their father was impotent, and he engineers a humiliating reunion, during Bharat and Subhadra's marriage, between their mother Savitri and the lascivious Swami Premanand. The Puranchands likewise scorn Karan Singh as a bastard foundling who has schemed his way to a position of power in Khubchand and Sons, discovering too late that he is their own elder brother. Bharat/Arjuna's hatred of Karan is augmented by his discovery that the latter had once courted Supriya/Draupadī prior to her marriage to Dharam Raj—an allusion to the epic Karṇa's unsuccessful participation in Draupadī's *svayaṃvara* and his subsequent sexual harassment of her during the dicing match. Draupadī's own preference for Arjuna, suggested at several points in the epic, is here transposed into a sexually charged *bhābhī-devar* bond, heightened by Supriya's obvious frustration with her arid marriage to Dharam Raj and her jealousy of Bharat's young "trophy wife" (and her own niece) Subhadra.

Indeed, in the film's disturbing penultimate scene, she comforts the drunken and grief-deranged Bharat (who, having engineered the murder of Karan, has just learned that his victim was his own eldest brother) by taking his head on her lap and fondling him in a manner that is at once maternal and erotic. The inner torment of Savitri/Kuntī (Sushma Seth) in concealing her own history from her sons is also effectively explored in the film, conveying both a renewed sympathy for Kuntī's shame, and her suppressed longing to acknowledge Karṇa as her firstborn son—here strikingly portrayed in the scene (one of the very few in the film that directly parallels a familiar epic episode)[2] in which Savitri reveals to Karan that she is his mother.

That Karan Singh/Karṇa emerges as the most sympathetic character in the film (and the role claimed and sensitively played by its producer Shashi Kapoor) will come as no surprise to those familiar with folk and vernacular retellings of the *Mahābhārata*, for epic audiences have always identified with this tragically disinherited hero—a princeling abandoned to conceal his royal mother's indiscretion, and later scorned as the son of a lowly charioteer—and have generally admired him, despite his moral lapses, for his unwavering loyalty to the doomed Kaurava cause. Kapoor's Karan Singh is a bachelor intellectual and aesthete, a former Rhodes scholar turned corporate strategist, who keeps a photo of Supriya/Draupadī on his bedside table and devotes his leisure to solitary golf games or to pondering the world from the balcony of his high-rise flat while listening to somber baroque airs on his stereo system. A lonely outsider scorned by the Puranchands, he is fiercely loyal to his only friend Dhan Raj and properly unscrupulous in advising him on business matters. Yet the screenplay endows Karan not merely with nobility, but with an innate morality that, as the conflict escalates, gradually estranges him from the desperate Dhan Raj, whom he (in a striking departure from the epic scenario) ultimately abandons. His successful effort to save Bharat's life from an "accident" orchestrated by Dhan Raj lends especially tragic irony to his own hit-and-run murder, planned by Bharat (as misdirected revenge for a killing in which Karan had no part) and executed (of course) at sunset, while Karan is changing a flat tire on his car.

The complete absence from Benegal's film of any sense of redemptive divine design makes its plausible human tragedy the more numbing and senseless. Blame for its escalating series of disasters is evenly portioned out between both clans, and even the suicide of Dhan Raj—who has eventually pursued the most ruthless tactics in the conflict—is staged to evoke viewers' maximum sympathy. The Puranchands' final, empty victory is achieved through a Kishen-brokered buyout of the stock in Dhan Raj's ruined company.

The devastated family elders, retiring to a Himalayan ashram, have no hope of a comforting vision of their dead sons, and the little boy Parikshit—the son of Dharam Raj and Supriya, who has been away at boarding school in Darjeeling during much of the film (and is played by future star-heroine Urmila Matondkar)—returns to a grieving household, innocently unaware of being the sole surviving junior member of two devastated clans. The final long shots of the smoggy Bombay skyline, awash in ambivalent gray, underscore the message that the bleak *kalyug* is indeed our contemporary age.

Hum Paanch

Like Shyam Benegal, the director of *Hum Paanch*, Sattiraju Lakshminarayan (better known by the nickname "Bapu," which alone appears in the film's credits) was born in the Telugu-speaking state of Andhra Pradesh and had worked in advertising before breaking into filmmaking. Though trained as a lawyer at Madras University, he soon turned to creative pursuits and became an illustrator, working for a time as a political cartoonist for a leading Telugu newspaper. His first films were also in Telugu, and he continued to direct films in his mother tongue throughout his career, though his growing reputation enabled him to increasingly work in the more widely distributed and lucrative Hindi film industry—frequently through directing Hindi remakes of successful Telugu pictures. *Hum Paanch* was such a remake, based on his own *Manavoori Pandavalu* ("The Pāṇḍavas of Our Village," 1978), which was itself inspired by the earlier Kannada film *Paduvarahalli Pandavaru* ("The Pāṇḍavas of Paduvara Village") by S. R. Puttanna Kanagal. For the Hindi version, Bapu received the backing of Bombay producer Surinder Kapoor.[3] Unlike Benegal, who was influenced by Italian neorealism and by the Bengali art cinema, Bapu frankly embraced the aesthetic and narrative strategies of mainstream Hindi film and longed to produce full-blown *masala* pictures. However, he seldom had the budgetary means to engage the biggest-name "A-List" stars, and his casts, as in *Hum Paanch*, usually featured comparative newcomers or "B-List" stars as heroes and heroines (e.g. Raj Babbar, Gulshan Grover, Naseeruddin Shah, and Shabana Azmi), backed by seasoned character actors (e.g. A.K. Hangal, Sanjeev Kumar, and Amrish Puri). Nevertheless, within the constraints of a "B-film" budget, Bapu's ambitious vision is readily apparent; quite apart from its literally epic theme, *Hum Paanch* boasts a score of seven songs with music by the well-known team of Laxmikant-Pyarelal and lyrics by Anand Bakshi. The film's dialogues were penned by Dr Rahi Masoom Reza, a Muslim screenwriter who, a decade later, would achieve national prominence as author of the Sanskritized script for the wildly popular ninety-four-episode Doordarshan television serial *Mahabharat* directed by B.R. Chopra. Whether due to budgetary constraints or to Bapu's own sensibility, *Hum Paanch* mostly eschews soundstage sets in favor of locations in and around a village in Melkote

Figure 1.4 The reborn Pandavas inspired by Krishna; courtesy Mr Boney Kapoor.

District, Karnataka, that is marked by magnificent Vijayanagara-period ruins, which are used to great effect by Bapu and his talented cinematographer Sharad Kadwe. Large numbers of local people serve as willing (and sometimes visibly gawking) extras. The pillared halls and immense tank of a classical Dravidian-style hilltop temple, as well as the recurrent use, as prominent backgrounds, of sculpted friezes of *deva*s and *apsara*s, underscore the story's mythological resonances, and the presence, in such a setting, of Hindi-speaking characters (including such North Indian stereotypes as zamindars, *pehelwan*s, and Kayasths), and of a mélange of regional dress styles, contributes (no doubt intentionally) to the film's dislocatedly pan-Indian character.

The title "We Five" immediately suggests a rousing call to collective action, as does the cartoon image of a driving fist that accompanies the opening credits. Indeed, *Hum Paanch* is a magical-realist parable about the overthrow of an oppressive feudal order through the unification of a broad spectrum of caste groups, instigated and inspired by an incarnate divine agent and his chosen instruments: five young men of diverse backgrounds, who gradually come to identify themselves as the avenging "Pāṇḍavas" of the *Mahābhārata*. Their enemy, of course, is "Duryodhana," here reborn as the heartless *zamindar* ("landlord") Veer Pratap Singh (Amrish Puri), who rules his village from a mansion stuffed with hunting trophies and Victorian statuary. That Singh is evil is already evident from the casting of Puri, who regularly played arch-villainous roles, but is confirmed by the opening scene—in which he benignly feeds pigeons, only to pounce on one, announcing to his henchmen, "Breakfast!" His mock-penitential prayer for his avian victim ("May its soul find peace!") displays his cynical use of the trappings of Hindu piety to mask his personal rapacity.

Subsequent scenes will further develop this portrait of a ruthless tyrant operating under the cloak of a paternalistic discourse of compassion, protection, and pious humility, backed up by the iron fist of a corrupt constabulary and a private army of thugs. He extracts revenue from the villagers in the form of handloom cloth and agricultural produce, cheats the more prosperous out of their inheritance by plying them with liquor and engaging them in card games, and claims (when in the mood) the sexual favors of their sisters and daughters. With his ill-gotten gains he lives like an old-style raja while sending his "modern" son Vijay to the big city to attend college and learn the urban arts of cheating via government "rural development plans."

Yet the Thakur's neighbors seem initially not only unaware of his crimes but positively adoring of him as a benevolent "giver of grain." Their celebration of his birthday features obsequious speeches by his merchant-class toadies, and ecstatic drumming and dancing by the lower classes, including the untouchable brothers Swaroop and Mahavir (Uday Chandra, Gulshan Grover), and the landlord's low-caste servant Bhima (Mithun Chakraborty), who leads the reverential song *Ātī hai pālkī sarkār kī*, "Here comes the Master's palanquin!" His other indispensable crony and constant advisor is Lala Nainsukh Prasad Shrivastava (Kanhaiyalal)—a groveling buffoon character soon to be identified as the film's scheming "Uncle Śakuni"—who epitomizes the comparatively low but "clean" scribal castes (such as the Kayasthas in northern India) and whose self-interest was tied to the feudal order. Also among the celebrants is the beautiful Sundariya (Shabana Azmi), Swaroop and Mahavir's sister, with whom the Thakur is having a secret affair on the pretext of having "married" her with private vows before the village goddess. The only sour note is sounded by the Thakur's own nephew, Arjun (Raj Babbar), who confronts the procession near the village temple and sings, "What kind of 'master' is he? This is no service, it's slavery!" We learn that he is angry over the suicide of his father, provoked by shame over having gambled away the family estate to his greedy brother-in-law. Yet, though the villagers reject his message, Arjun will soon find an ally in Suraj (Naseeruddin Shah)—his name, meaning "sun," is an apparent reference to the epic's Karṇa, who is sired by the sun God and becomes an ally of the Kauravas. This "Karṇa," however—a Bania or merchant-caste youth whose own father is in the process of being ruined in the Thakur's gambling den—will be quick to embrace the "Pāṇḍava" cause. Unable to complete his studies in the city because of the family's waning fortunes, Suraj has returned to the village as an "angry young man." Both Arjun and Suraj wear urban (i.e. "western" style) shirts and trousers that mark them as educated youth, and although they recognize the criminality of the Thakur's regime, they are initially unable to convince the *dhoti*-clad villagers to join them in opposing it.

Figure 1.5 The evil Thakur with his sidekick Lala; courtesy Mr Boney Kapoor.

Watching the scene with seemingly detached amusement is Krishna (Sanjeev Kumar), the Thakur's junior brother. Clad in spotless white, he haunts the village temple and receives daily rations of food and country liquor sent from the family mansion to keep him in a contented alcoholic fog so that he will not demand his share of the estate. Yet, from his trenchant comments delivered in the form of periodic song-sermons ("When both man and God fear the rich . . . who will save the powerless from the powerful?"), as well as from the camera's reverent juxtaposition of his swaying form with icons and emblems of Vishnu and the soundtrack's provision of a solo flute whenever he appears, it soon becomes clear that Krishna's wastrel ways are mere *līlā*, disguising an acute awareness of his brother's crimes, which he is both cataloging and counting, waiting for their number to reach a fateful one hundred. This is, of course, a reference to the epic Krishna's delaying his revenge against the wicked king Śiśupāla until the latter's offenses reached that number.

Veer Pratap Singh, however, has no fear of divine or fraternal retribution. He invokes "our immemorial traditions" when convenient, lies under oath before the village deity (a folksy-looking mustached *murti* of Vishnu surrounded by a frieze of his ten avatars), and neglects the festival of its large-eyed patron goddess for dalliance with a prostitute. Yet, the film shows the hypocritical manipulation of religion by the powerful, and is careful not to ridicule faith itself, especially the conviction that providential justice will eventually catch up with a tyrant. Like Krishna, the pious temple Brahmin (A.K. Hangal) sees through the Thakur's lies,

Figure 1.6 Krishna drinking in the temple; courtesy Mr Boney Kapoor.

and after Lala Nainsukh taunts him that both he and his God owe their living to the Thakur's benevolence, the priest prays to Vishnu to "cease being a stone" and come down to relieve man's suffering. Although the human Krishna's timely interventions are an obvious answer to this prayer (and he will display a kind of *Gītā*-like apotheosis by the film's end) the director will not resort to the overtly miraculous *deus ex machina* found in many Bombay melodramas. Instead, the Thakur's comeuppance, as Krishna himself announces, will come about through the "awakening" of the entire village, catalyzed by the consciousness-raising of the young untouchables Swaroop and Mahavir and the Shudra Bhima, and their uniting with the Kshatriya and Bania youths Arjun and Suraj to become the unstoppable fist of "we five Pāṇḍavas"—a symbol of a caste-liberated collectivity.

As in the *Mahābhārata*, the decisive event in turning the film's Pāṇḍavas into avengers is the violation of a "Draupadī," a role here divided between two women, appropriately named "beauty" and "modesty," two traits of the goddess Lakshmi, whom Draupadī incarnates. The pregnant Sundariya, humiliated and abandoned by the deceitful Thakur, attempts suicide but is rescued by Arjun, who also stops her brothers from killing her to hide their shame. She lives—to wander demented and wraithlike through the village temple where she is fed and comforted by Krishna—as a constant reminder of the Thakur's hypocrisy. Then there is Lajiya (Deepti Naval), Bhima's sweetheart, for whose sake he requests a golden marriage necklace from his adored master, but receives only a beating in return. When Bhima turns against him, the Thakur then attempts to rape Lajiya after

Figure 1.7 Lajiya's disrobing; courtesy Mr Boney Kapoor.

having her disrobed by his henchmen. Krishna, of course, intervenes to save her modesty—but not before the Thakur's crude slapping of his left thigh, inviting Lajiya to have sex with him, has led her to declare that Bhima will shatter the offending limb, an oath that will be fulfilled (in the best overdetermined epic fashion) not once but twice.

The film's *Mahābhārata* allusions are densest in its second half and are increasingly acknowledged by the characters themselves. The rebellious heroes, united at last, inform Lala Nainsukh that "The Pāṇḍavas have taken birth again!," and then taunt him with the song, "*Ham pānc Pāṇḍav, yah Śakuni māmā*," the chorus of which declares, "We five are the Pāṇḍavas and he is Uncle Śakuni; Now just watch the drama of *Mahābhārata*!" Lala too, coming upon the five being lovingly fed by Arjun's widowed mother, cynically remarks, "Amazing! A scene of *Mahābhārata* right before my eyes: Mother Kuntī feeding the Pāṇḍavas.... It seems like some religious film is running!" He appears to embrace his assigned Śakuni-role gleefully, goading his master into ever more dastardly deeds, and the Thakur, preparing to rape the disrobed Lajiya, gloatingly equates himself with Duryodhana. There is a *Gītā* of sorts, delivered by Krishna—though not to Arjun but to the dejected Suraj when he is on the point of giving up the struggle ("Oh coward, why do you flee the battlefield?")—as well as an "exile" of the heroes, when the Thakur forbids the villagers to feed or house them and then engineers their lockup by the police on charges of disturbing the peace. When they return, they first humiliate the Thakur's son Vijay, whose jeep tire has gotten stuck in a rut (alluding to the scene of Karṇa's chariot wheel sinking into the earth). With the aid of Lala Nainsukh, Vijay retaliates by setting fire to a thatched hut in which they are sleeping together with Arjun's mother (recapitulating the episode of the "lacquer palace"), and for a time everyone believes them dead, though in fact they have escaped through Krishna's vigilance. The fact that such parallel incidents transpose epic characters and reshuffle epic chronology only contributes to the delight of recognition experienced by a knowledgeable viewer of this *film à clef.*

The Thakur's ultimate crime—and the equivalent of the Kauravas' theft of their cousins' kingdom—is a scam directed against the village as a whole. While his young enemies languish in jail, Singh joins his son Vijay and the latter's fiancée Nishi, daughter of a "high government official," in the Big Bad City (Bombay, of course). This allows for an obligatory disco-cabaret number (in the course of which the Thakur, like Duryodhana in the royal assembly of the *Mahābhārata*'s Book Five, sees an enormous image of Krishna staring at him above the strobe-lit dancers). More importantly, it draws him into an elaborate scheme to bleed the villagers of their remaining wealth for the ostensible purpose of helping finance the construction of government-sponsored textile mills that will make everyone rich. This plot twist allows for an astute satire on top-down "development" projects, the collusion of urban bureaucrats with rural landed interests, and the mystifying power of the English language (which Vijay admonishes Nishi to speak to his father because "We Indians are so easily charmed by English!"). When the poor villagers manage to assemble the requested two lakhs of rupees, chiefly in the form of women's wedding jewelry, it becomes a prize over which the Thakur, Vijay, Nishi, and Lala Nainsukh all squabble, in scenes cleverly engineered by Krishna to provoke inadvertent confessions that the village elders overhear. A final effort is made by the now-wounded Thakur to shoot the "Pāṇḍavas". Krishna brings the tally of the landlord's crimes to the fateful one hundred, and provokes a mob attack on Thakur's mansion. We soon see Singh and his cohorts in desperate flight, pursued by a horde of villagers armed with clubs and farm implements, while Krishna approvingly declares, "An awakened village is like God's cosmic form (*virāṭ rūp*), and no one can equal its strength." Indeed, he makes no effort to check the frenzy of the mob, and such vigilante justice is further endorsed by a final scene in which the assembled populace, now evidently free of the tyrant and his family, worships with Krishna and the Pāṇḍavas in the hilltop Vishnu temple while a voiceover intones *Bhagavad-gītā* 4:8, "For the protection of the virtuous and the destruction of evildoers, and in order to securely establish *dharma*, I come into being in age after age."

Re-dressing the *Mahābhārata*

The performance tradition of the *Mahābhārata* is now at least two millennia old and encompasses a spectrum of re-enactments that may be conveniently classified, in terms of their textual basis, predominant patronage, and intended audience, as relatively more "elite/literary/classical" or more "popular/oral/folk" in nature, albeit with the caveat that these categories, particularly in India, often overlap and cross-pollinate. To the former we might assign, for example, the set of *Mahābhārata*-based Sanskrit dramas attributed to the playwright Bhāsa (*c.*second century CE?) that were rediscovered early in the twentieth century, as well as pre-modern vernacular literary epics, such as the tenth-century *Bhāratam* in Kannada by the poet Pampa, or Villiputur Alvar's *c.*fourteenth-century Tamil *Makaparatam*, and more recently a series of plays (to be further discussed) mounted in urban theaters in the half century since Indian independence. In the latter category we might place open-air folk theater traditions of uncertain (though possibly long) historical pedigree such as the *Mahābhārata* plays of Tamil *Terukkuttu* drama (Frasca 1990) and the *Pāṇḍav Līlā* of the Garhwal Himalayas (Sax 2002). Both these regional performance genres feature in local festivals of community renewal through ritualized propitiation of divine protectors, and also involve the periodic possession of actors and sometimes spectators by the divine characters being portrayed. The distinction between relatively "elite" and relatively "popular" performance genres suggests one way to conceptualize the striking differences in both performance style and in narrative interpretation between the Benegal and Bapu films.

I should begin by noting, however, that in all forms of *Mahābhārata* performance, beginning with the earliest surviving dramas and including both ends of the elite–popular spectrum, radical reinterpretation of the Sanskrit epic story, often involving the omission, invention, and transposition of events and characters, has been the rule rather than the exception. Indeed, right from the era of Bhāsa—who in *Urūbhaṅgam* ("the breaking of the thigh") permitted Duryodhana to die a peaceful and noble death in his palace, surrounded by his family members and magnanimously forgiving the Pāṇḍavas and Krishna for their role in his downfall, and in *Pañcaratnam* ("the five gems") went so far as to effect a reconciliation of the feuding cousins without recourse to war—to the modern *Terukkuttu* players' fascination with extra-epic characters like Pottu Raja, the earthy and demi-demonic bodyguard of Draupadī-as-local-goddess (Hiltebeitel 1988: 333–67), the history of *Mahābhārata* retelling through performance has been characterized by a narrative fluidity and an interpretive freedom that makes even the innovations of Benegal and Bapu appear, in a sense, quite "traditional." Yet I would like to move beyond the generalization that these two films bear witness to the extreme adaptability of the *Mahābhārata* story and attempt to more specifically locate each within a lineage of epic interpretation and performance.

The naturalistic and understated acting style of *Kalyug*, its "realistic" locations, lack of significant music and dance episodes, and "invisible style" of camerawork (emphasizing temporal and spatial continuity to produce the illusion of a voyeuristic glimpse into private realities) all serve to link Benegal's film with the conventions of Hollywood filmmaking and international art cinema. However, its choice of the *Mahābhārata* as narrative source and its interpretation of that narrative reflect the apparent influence of India's urban theater tradition as it developed in the decades after independence. The most influential play of this period was Dharmavīr Bhārati's *Andhā Yug* ("blind epoch"), composed in Hindi verse and first presented as a radio drama in 1954. Though not actually staged until 1962 in Bombay, the play then saw nineteen major productions prior to 1980, including versions translated into Bengali, Manipuri, Assamese, and Marathi, and mounted by virtually every major director of the period. Its story, which begins on the evening of the eighteenth day of the battle of Kurukṣetra and concludes thirty-six years later with the death of Krishna and the bleak dawning of the *kaliyuga*, presents, in Aparna Dharwadker's words, "a radical reworking of the *Mahābhārata*" focusing on "the failure of all forms of authority and political power" and "the dissolution of moral certainties" (Dharwadker 2005: 191–2). Bharati's implicit, Marxist-influenced critique of Congress Raj would come to appear especially prescient given the stagnating economic conditions, worsening unemployment, labor unrest, and regional secession movements that marked the 1970s and 1980s, and this contributed to his play's acquiring the status of a "classic" for urban theater companies and their middle class, college educated audiences. By focusing on the defeated Kauravas rather than the victorious Pāṇḍavas, depicting Yudhiṣṭhira as a failed monarch, and giving voice to "victims" like Gāndhārī, Aśvatthāman, and Yuyutsu as critics of Krishna, *Andhā Yug* assailed the nationalist triumphalism and optimism of the early Nehru era, even as it brooded on the fate of humanity in a post-nuclear age. The play was certainly known to Girish Karnad, co-author of the screenplay for *Kalyug*, whose own ongoing fascination with *Mahābhārata* episodes resulted in two plays (*Yayati*, written in 1963, and *Agni Mattu Male* or "The Fire and the Rain," in 1994), as well as to noted Hindi playwright Satyadev Dube, who penned the dialogues for *Kalyug*.

Apart from restagings of *Andhā Yug*, one of the most notable developments in urban theater during the 1970s and 1980s was the revival by renowned directors of the ancient *Mahābhārata* plays of Bhāsa, with their focus on "antiheroes, outsiders, and victims, notably Duryodhana, Karna, Ashvatthaman, and Abhimanyu" (Ibid.: 180). K.N. Panikkar in 1978 staged *Madhyama vyayoga* ("the middle one" depicting the relationship between Bhīma and his half-*rakshasa* son Ghaṭotkaca), followed by *Karnabharam* ("the burden of Karṇa," 1984) and *Urubhangam* ("the breaking of the thigh," 1985). Habib Tanvir in 1979 presented *Duryodhana*, his own version of *Urubhangam* in the dialect and style of Chattisgarhi folk drama. A Manipuri version of *Urubhangam* directed by Ratan Thiyam was mounted in 1981, followed by *Chakravyuha* ("the circular formation," 1984), Thiyam's original meditation on the death of Abhimanyu, which was widely interpreted as a critique of secessionist violence in the Manipur region (Ibid.: 181–4). These prominent *Mahābhārata* dramas share several features with Benegal's 1980 film: a broad sympathy for the losing Kauravas and especially for the "outsider" Karṇa, a de-sacralized reading of the epic as a meditation on the failure of traditional social institutions—the patriarchal extended family, and the modern family businesses (and by implication, the nation) built on its model—and on the futility of violence, and an attempt to link the epic's mytho-historical narrative with contemporary issues.

Of course, in contrast to the stage dramas, *Kalyug* transposes the *Mahābhārata* into a contemporary setting. In this choice too it mirrors a modern international theatrical convention: that of reinterpreting classical dramas by transposing them in time and space, often with the intent of conveying a pointedly political message. This approach has been especially used for Shakespeare and the Greek classics; for example, Orson Welles' "brown shirt" production of *Julius Caesar* (1937) as a parable of the rise of fascism; Richard Schechner's Yale University production of Euripides' *Bacchae* (1969) as an exploration of hippie counterculture; or Baz Luhrmann's film of *Romeo + Juliet* (1996), that sets the star-crossed lovers of Verona amid youth gangs in south Florida. In a more radical departure—as in *Kalyug*—the text itself is rewritten to suit the new setting, though its basic plot remains discernible; for example, Jean Anouilh's rewriting of Sophocles' *Antigone* (1944) as an indictment of the Vichy government of occupied France; or Akira Kurosawa's *Throne of Blood* (1956), that applies the samurai ethos and the conventions of Noh drama to the themes of *Macbeth*. Such radical "translations" not only offer viewers who are knowledgeable of the archetype the pleasure of recognizing its contours in an unfamiliar guise, but deliberately de-familiarize it in order to inspire fresh interpretations. They wrench it out of its "classical" frame and insist on its radical contemporaneity. This too appears to be part of the intent of the makers of *Kalyug*.

Despite its similarly modern setting, however, Bapu's *Hum Paanch* belongs to a different aesthetic lineage. As a Bombay-produced "*masala* picture," it has its roots in folk and popular operatic theatrical traditions such as the *Nautanki* of the Hindi belt, the *Tamasha* of Maharashtra, the *Yakshagana* of Karnataka, and the *Terukkuttu* of Tamil Nadu, as well as the European-influenced traveling "Parsi Theater" companies of the late nineteenth century. Popular films have largely supplanted these earlier genres, but have inherited from them a preference for histrionic, declamatory acting, spectacular sets, sharply drawn divisions between good and evil, characters who are fixed and idealized types rather than psychologically complex or evolving individuals, and storylines that, regardless of their plot and theme, are regularly expected to be interrupted by interludes of song, dance, slapstick comedy, and fisticuffs. Further, directors and actors generally ignore the realist theater convention of the "fourth wall" and its cinematic descendant, the "invisible style" of camerawork and strictly observed continuities, in favor of a flashy visual technique that deliberately calls attention to cinematic artifice and that favors a "frontal" display of actors who sometimes directly address the camera, or who even discuss being in a film. All of these strategies, observable in *Hum Paanch*, are also found in Indian folk performance genres, and the film's manic exuberance is likewise suggestive of the rowdiness and bravado of street theater. Indeed, the film itself depicts a deliberate restaging and reclaiming of the *Mahābhārata* story in which, as in some ritual performances, its heroes let themselves become increasingly "possessed" by epic characters as they move toward a violent climax—for example, just before Bhima's first public assault on the Thakur, he smears his forehead with the vermilion of the village goddess, takes up a club, and roars in exultation, surrendering his former servile identity to the newly claimed archetype of Pāṇḍava strongman.

Applying the *masala*-film and folk-theatrical style to the template of the *Mahābhārata* yields some interesting results. Although a literary scholar might be horrified that an epic tale grounded in the sacerdotal-martial elite of ancient India is here retooled as a paean to subaltern and middle-caste rebellion against authority, the director appears to take this transformation in stride. A former political cartoonist, he sketches in broad strokes a *Mahābhārata* that is both political and cartoon-like, yet faithful in its own way to another strand of popular epic interpretation. He reminds us that, for all its moral murkiness, the *Mahābhārata* has also been revered as the *Jaya*, the "song of victory," that celebrates the triumph of (relatively more) virtuous over (relatively more) villainous people, and that it ends with a restoration and revival of the moral order represented by *dharma*. The film's inspiration thus lies closer to popular *bhajan*s and aphorisms that pointedly contrast, for example, "dastardly Duḥśāsana" (*duṣṭa Duḥśāsana*) with "stainless Draupadī" (*vimala Draupadī*), and its united heroes resonate with folk concepts in which the collective will and wisdom of the village community is embodied in the number five (as in the Hindi saying *pāñc parameśvar*—implying "Where there are five, there is God"—or in the tradition of the *panchayat* or juridical council of five elders).

For all the film's exaggeration and stylized melodrama, the kinds of social inequities it depicts have remained part of the everyday experience of many Indians, especially in rural areas. If its character portrayals lack psychological complexity, they nevertheless resonate with perceived realities. In its historical context, the film displays a striking, even extreme instance of what M. Madhava Prasad has termed the "aesthetic of mobilization": a turn toward angry, working-class heroes rebelling against corrupt and oppressive bosses, exemplified by the massively successful Amitabh Bachchan "Vijay" films released during the tumultuous decade of the Emergency and its aftermath (Prasad 1998: 138–59). It thus exemplifies the spirit of labor unrest, youth discontent, and lower-caste and Dalit assertion characteristic of its era.

Its heroes do not merely oppose their high-born oppressor; they repeatedly taunt, abuse, and humiliate him and his henchmen, displaying the crude antics of uppity subalterns—as when they smear Lala Nainsukh's face with mud and beat him with sweepers' brooms, or when Bhima strips off the loincloth of the goonda who disrobed Lajiya, and then hurls the discolored undergarment in the landlord's face.

Taken together and viewed retrospectively through the lens of a scholar who is a fan of the *Mahābhārata* and of Hindi cinemas—both popular and "parallel"—the Benegal and Bapu films, with their very different agendas, complement and compensate for one another in telling ways. Ironically, the "parallel cinema" of the 1970s was known especially for its depiction of the "real India" of rural inequities, a theme that Benegal had explored in his early feature films that received critical acclaim and enjoyed modest commercial success among urban, middle-class audiences. In *Kalyug* he turned to an urban setting, a mytho-historical theme, and a moral universe that was, in parallel cinema terms, less clearly coded. For the film depicts a systemic corruption that infects both capitalists and workers, and that is rooted in individual ambition, family loyalty, and domestic sexual tension. This turn may have reflected Benegal's collaboration with Karnad, a drama scholar as well as a playwright, actor, and director, but it appears to have contributed to the film's lukewarm reception from its target audience (Datta 2002: 129). The film has also been criticized for its fidelity to the epic story ("to the point of sometimes strained ingenuity," as critic Iqbal Masud noted in his *Indian Express* review),[4] so as to appear, in Sumita Chakravarty's more recent assessment, "self-consciously 'academic' " (Chakravarty 1993: 252). At the same time, in its radical secularism, it is neglectful of other *Mahābhārata* elements that have always been important to audiences: the great epic's sincere conviction, despite its own moral complexity, that there are degrees of evil, as well as a providential (albeit sometimes mysterious and "dark") cosmic power that ultimately guides humanity toward a greater good. In draining the story of mythos, the film provides no pivotal event—comparable to the dicing match and disrobing of Draupadī—to explain the bitterness and jealousy between the cousins; just a series of escalating rivalries and misunderstandings, which may reflect its writers' conviction that such is, indeed, more truly the way the world (and the extended family) actually ends. It is also noteworthy that the two important characters who are missing from the film are precisely those who, in most *Mahābhārata* retellings, come closest to personifying "good" and "evil": Krishna and Śakuni. The former is only vestigially present, as a rarely seen uncle and corporate ally of the Puranchand brothers. The latter's role as adviser to Duryodhana and architect of the Kaurava *coup d'état* is here assumed by the wily Karan Singh, yet he is, of all the film's characters, the most sympathetically developed. Indeed, the film's most glaring liberty with its epic source seems intended to render Karan even more appealing: his desertion of the Khubchand cause at the eleventh hour in an attempt to save Bharat/Arjuna from death. Finally, one may observe that the film's pretext, within its "realist" frame, of depicting a conflict-ridden extended family whose members are *unaware* that their situation recapitulates that of the *Mahābhārata* itself appears strangely "unrealistic" in the Indian context.

The very elements absent from *Kalyug* are, of course, present in *Hum Paanch*, and in spades. Within its unbridled *masala* fantasy, it depicts a set of people who come to recognize (as Indians often do) that their situation parallels that of epic characters, and who then consciously model themselves on these archetypes. Evil is present from the get-go, in a ruthless *zamindar* who ruins several good men through gambling matches, disrobes and molests not one but two virtuous young women, and revels in the advice of a "Śakuni Māmā" who, true to many popular epic stagings, is at once a villain and a buffoon.

The power behind the reincarnated Pāṇḍavas is a Krishna who is playful and slightly dissolute, yet fundamentally just and benevolent: a patient and apparently omniscient strategist who counts the accumulating crimes that will eventually spell the tyrant's doom. The one conspicuous absence from this film's epic cast is Yudhiṣṭhira, the pensive "dharma-king," for there is little scope for the most cerebral and Brahmin-like of the Pāṇḍava brothers in this action-adventure emphasizing violent retribution—the work of a director raised in the mostly anti-Brahmin political milieu of twentieth-century South India. Yet the Pāṇḍava line-up must be complete, and so in a characteristically imaginative move, Bapu fills Yudhiṣṭhira's empty slot with Suraj/Karṇa—thus restoring the disqualified but much-admired senior-most Pāṇḍava to his mother and brothers. Indeed, both *Kalyug* and *Hum Paanch* bear witness, in their very different ways, to the popularity and staying power of this outsider and antihero who has long fascinated *Mahābhārata* audiences.

In its narrative strategies, Bapu's freestyle *Bhārata* is more akin to the adaptation of the story in recent centuries by folk poets of the North Indian *Ālhā* cycle, whose sanguinary epic songs, set in the twelfth century, constitute a highly fluid "text" that appears to have been orally circulating and growing for several hundred years. This cycle has come to be widely interpreted, at least during the past century, as "the *Mahābhārata* of the Kali Yuga" (Hiltebeitel 1999: 121–52). This designation does not, however, indicate an authorial strategy of retelling the Sanskrit epic (à la *Kalyug*), but rather a claim that its characters literally reincarnate those of the older tale and carry their struggle forward in time; a transposition more akin to that found in *Hum Paanch*. In doing so, not only are the heroes re-dressed in the chivalric culture of Rajput of North India on the eve of Muslim conquest, but certain of their longstanding wrongs are redressed as well: in the *Ālhā* poets' *Mahābhārata*, the Kauravas triumph over the Pāṇḍavas in the end, and the unfortunate Karṇa finally succeeds in slaying the overconfident Arjuna.

In the prolific world of Hindi cinema, directors and screenplay writers continually search for stories that will seem both original and acceptably familiar to audiences, and their borrowings from other national cinemas—of stories that are then invariably "Indianized" in setting, theme, and emotional texture—are notorious to the point of being overstated by some critics, who see virtually every *masala* film as a shoddy "remake" of a Hollywood picture. Bombay directors also regularly allude to Indian myth and epic within the framework of modern "socials," but this usually takes the form of minor themes or subplots (e.g. echoes of the Śakuntalā story in Raj Kapoor's 1984 hit *Ram Teri Ganga Maili*, or the teasing *Mahābhārata* allusions in the successful 1994 film *Karan-Arjun*). Both Benegal and Bapu deserve credit for their ambitious projects of re-dressing the "world's longest epic" in the highly condensed timeframe of a feature film, but assessing which director's effort is more successful will depend on the viewer's own understanding of the *Mahābhārata*, and on his or her taste in entertainment. *Kalyug* reportedly failed to engage even art-cinema audiences, whereas *Hum Paanch* achieved a "decent run" on the mainstream distribution circuit. Chakravarty's broad assessment of the "parallel cinema" seems pertinent here:

> In its ideal-typical mode, the new cinema leans toward the intellectual-rational rather than the emotional-mythical. As such, its links are more with the Brahmanic tradition in Indian culture and less so with the popular or little traditions.... India's art cinema is wedded to a mimetic view of life that resonates inadequately with the general population.
>
> (Chakravarty 1993: 240)

Despite its ingenious screenplay and fine acting, Benegal and Karnad's intellectual meditation on the inevitability of competition and conflict is, among other things, the *Mahābhārata* at its most ominous: the scripture you revere, but which you do not want to keep in your home lest it provoke family quarrels. Bapu's optimistic and populist parable, on the other hand, reminds us that the Sanskrit text that academics and art cinema auteurs privilege is only one of many *Mahābhārata*s in circulation. In *Hum Paanch*, the audience's understanding that they are watching a transposed *Mahābhārata* actually comes to be shared by the filmic characters themselves, who embrace their own incarnation of myth even as they boldly proclaim their right to re-write it. This empowerment of lower-class characters, potentially shared by audience members, is in stark contrast to the trapped fate of the upper-class principals in *Kalyug*, who are condemned to recapitulate a woeful myth, drained of all redemptive value, that they themselves no longer know.

Notes

* I use the term *Bhārata* both for alliteration and because it refers, within the Sanskrit *Mahābhārata*, to the "core" or principal story of the epic, which is sometimes said to comprise roughly a quarter of its hundred thousand couplets. It is this "main story" that has inspired the two films considered here. I am grateful to Heidi Pauwels for the conference invitation that has occasioned this chapter. I also thank Swarnavel Eswaranpillai, filmmaker, film connoisseur extraordinaire, and graduate student in the Department of Cinema and Comparative Literature at the University of Iowa, for helpful insights into the Benegal and Bapu films.

1 There is disagreement in printed sources over the date of *Kalyug*. The *Encyclopaedia of Indian Cinema* assigns it to 1980 (EIC 416), as does Sangeeta Datta in her recent study of Benegal's films (Datta 2002: 125; but note that she cites an *Indian Express* review of the film dated August 3, 1979; 228, fn. 4), whereas Sumita Chakravarty gives its date as 1981 (Chakravarty 1993: 252). The censor certificate that appears at the start of the film on its Eros Multimedia/B4U DVD bears the date of March 1981. Since that of *Hum Paanch* is dated November 1980, it would in any case appear that the two films were approved for release within a few months of each other.

2 In my own breakdown of the film into seventy-four scenes, I find that although nearly all of them contain epic allusions of one kind or another, only about a half dozen portray readily recognizable *Mahābhārata* episodes. Significantly, three of these involve Karṇa (Kuntī informing Karṇa that he is her son; Karṇa's slaying by Arjuna while attempting to free the wheel of his chariot; and Kuntī revealing to the Pāṇḍavas that Karṇa was their elder brother).

3 Kapoor is better known to Hindi cinema aficionados as the father of star Anil Kapoor, whose own breakthrough film *Woh Saat Din* ("Those seven days," 1983), was likewise a Bapu-directed remake from Telugu. Anil Kapoor's name appears in the credits for *Hum Paanch* as part of the filmcrew.

4 According to Sangeeta Datta, Masud's review, under the title "The Epic as Trap," appeared in *Indian Express* on August 3, 1979 (page not cited); Datta 2002: 128, fn. 4, 228.

References

Chakravarty, S.S. (1993) *National Identity in Indian Popular Cinema, 1947–1987*, Austin: University of Texas Press.

Datta, S. (2002) *Shyam Benegal*, London: British Film Institute Publishing.

Dharwadker, A. (2005) *Theatres of Independence*, Iowa City, IA: University of Iowa Press.
Frasca, R. (1990) *The Theatre of the Mahābhārata: Terukkuttu Performances in South India*, Honolulu, HI: University of Hawaii Press.
Hiltebeitel, A. (1988) *The Cult of Draupadi, vol. 1, Mythologies: From Gingee to Kuruksetra*, Chicago, IL: University of Chicago Press.
—— (1999) *Rethinking India's Oral and Classical Epics: Draupadi Among Rajputs, Muslims, and Dalits*, Chicago, IL: University of Chicago Press.
Prasad, M.M. (1998) *Ideology of the Hindi Film, A Historical Construction*, Delhi: Oxford University Press.
Sax, W. (2002) *Dancing the Self: Person and Performance in the Pandav Lila of Garhwal*, New York: Oxford University Press.
Thomas, Rosie (1995) "Melodrama and the Negotiation of Morality in Mainstream Hindi Film," in Carol A. Breckenridge (ed.) *Consuming Modernity: Public Culture in a South Asian World*, Minneapolis, MN: University of Minnesota Press, 157–82.
van Buitenen, J.A.B. (trans.) (1973) *The Mahābhārata*, vol. 1, Chicago, IL: University of Chicago Press.

2 Family, feminism, and film in remaking *Rāmāyaṇa*

Vidyut Aklujkar

Introduction

The *Rāmāyaṇa* has appeared on screen since the cradle days of the Indian film industry, starting with *Lanka Dahan* and *Setu Bandhan* by Dhundiraj Govind Phalke in the early twentieth century, followed by many more partial or whole renderings throughout the decades. Quite a few of these retellings have sought to suggest bold improvements to the well-known epic storyline. In this chapter I am particularly concerned with issues of gender and family in the *Rāmāyaṇa*, and how they get transferred in film. While taking stock of the major innovations, I shall focus on two successful recent mainstream Hindi movies, *Hum Saath Saath Hain* by Sooraj Barjatya (1999) and *Lajja* by Rajkumar Santoshi (2001). Both movies attempt to remake some incidents of *Rāmāyaṇa* with the goal of rewriting the story in totally different outcomes. The first movie addresses the traditional ideal of the unity of a joint family based on sacrifice and the second modern ideals of feminism based on equality and individualism.

Rāmāyaṇa in film through the decades

Rāmāyaṇa has served as the formula on which the Indian film industry was nourished since its infancy in the early twentieth century. Every decade since has produced many movies on *Rāmāyaṇa*, most of which are simple retellings of the ever-popular epic through the newly found medium of film (see Appendix). Just as *Rāmāyaṇa* has provided a ready cultural context to Indian films, the medium of film, in turn, has offered a lot to the continuation and interpretation of *Rāmāyaṇa*.

The significance of *Rāmāyaṇa* for Indian films as a rich cultural context has been multilayered. *Rāmāyaṇa* has all the necessary ingredients for entertainment: the poetry and romance, the drama, the adventure and miracles, in addition to the moral and philosophical ideals. I shall illustrate the richness by citing a few examples. Mythology means miracles, and film was the most suitable visual medium to create magical scenes with the help of technological special effects. The pioneer filmmaker D.G. Phalke was a special-effects genius. He explored a vast range of techniques, including animation (Barnouw and Krishnaswamy 1980: 19). These special effects were used to enhance the story in film. Naturally, the most popular events in the movies on *Rāmāyaṇa* were the transfer scenes of a golden deer turning into Mārīca or the bearded beggar turning into Rāvaṇa, and the motion scenes of the flying chariot of Rāvaṇa and of Hanumān flying across the ocean.

The transfer of the oral epic or the written scripture to the visual medium of the silver screen gave rise to some wonderful sequences, which utilized the medium creatively and memorably. For example, Homi Wadia's 1961 film, *Sampoorn Ramayan* included a clever and original interpretation of the ten heads of Rāvaṇa. It showed the multiple heads of Rāvaṇa as an outward expression of his internal conflict. While Rāvaṇa is being introspective, each of his extra heads materializes on either side of his face as his distinct mental attitude and these appear to be at war with each other.

For our purposes, the treatment of gender issues is most important. It is a popular saying that Sītā's trials are not over in present day India, and the heroine's suffering at the hands of her spouse in any movie always brings to mind a comparison with the epic heroine. More often than not this is made explicit in the movie in a variety of ways.

One example of a conservative interpretation is *Gumrah*, a 1963 B.R. Chopra film about the emotional conflict of a modern married woman. This movie begins with a quotation from the *Rāmāyaṇa*. It shows the narrative sequence of the golden deer incident. Rāma goes on the deer chase, leaving Lakṣmaṇa to protect Sītā. The well-known sequence ends in the drawing of the famous line by Lakṣmaṇa (*Lakṣmaṇa Rekhā*) around the hut to protect Sītā. The informed audience knows what happened when Sītā disregarded his admonitions and crossed the protective line. The movie begins by saying that it is a story of just such a transgression. The filmmaker presents here a moralistic interpretation of the golden deer scene of *Rāmāyaṇa*, implying that a woman's place is safe within her home, and that the transgression of the limits of the four walls (*cār dīvareṃ*) is nothing but to court disaster.

On the other hand, the tradition is also questioned. Indian filmmakers have been partial to Sītā, and following the lead of the Sanskrit poet Bhavabhūti, have found ways of expressing their disapproval of her treatment at the hands of her righteous husband. *Sītā-tyāga*, or the abandonment of Sītā, is an often replayed theme. In the classic 1952 film *Awara* by Raj Kapoor, the pregnant heroine is thrown out of her house by her husband. The reference to Sītā is made explicit in a song sequence while she goes from door to door in search of support. The male singers actually sing about the similar plight of Sītā, the favorite daughter of Janaka and also the beloved of Rāma. The words of the song are "You punished the virtuous mother Sītā with an exile in the forest. Why didn't the heart of the earth break? Why did the sky not burst open?"[1] The refrain of the song is "She endured a lot of injustice. The favourite daughter of Janaka, the beloved of Rāma endured so much injustice!"[2]

The traditional use of *Rāmāyaṇa* as a reference context to enrich a modern story is not limited to the early days of cinema, but found even in the works of contemporary filmmakers. The most recent example of such a use can be found in the 2003 film called *Pinjar*. Interestingly, here the *Rāmāyaṇa* is mediated through a literary adaptation, as the film is based on a short story by Amrita Pritam.[3] The movie *Pinjar* uses *Rāmāyaṇa* as a contextual background which permeates the narrative through songs and allusions. Throughout the execution of the storyline based on the incidents of the bloody partition of India in 1947 we hear echoes of *Rāmāyaṇa*. *Pinjar* is a story of a Punjabi Hindu girl, Pooro, and her kidnapping by a Muslim man just prior to her wedding. Her initial resistance and fight, her subsequent trials, unwilling reconciliation to her fate, and her final choice of identity are portrayed in this powerful film with great sophistication and sensitivity. One explicit link to the *Rāmāyaṇa* is the name of Pooro's betrothed husband, Ram Chand. Interestingly, the film shows him to be a scholar who is translating Vālmīki's *Rāmāyaṇa* into Urdu. He sings a song about Sītā's fire ordeal that ends by saying that although Sītā survived the fire ordeal to be united with Rāma, who stood on the other side with outstretched hands, her real exile began since that day.[4] A few more such allusions to the exile follow, resulting in our understanding that the story of a woman's ordeal is, in a sense, a reenactment of the age-old story of Sītā of the classic *Rāmāyaṇa*. The *Rāmāyaṇa* is thus explicitly evoked to make sense of the trauma of partition.

Even movies that present themselves as faithful retellings of *Rāmāyaṇa* have found ways of expressing disapproval of the treatment of Sītā. Thus, Homi Wadia's *Sampoorn Ramayan*, a faithful retelling of *Rāmāyaṇa* in film, already mentioned above, introduces at the end an incongruous scene that critiques its source. The young lads Lava and Kuśa, sent by Vālmīki to Rāma's palace to recite the *Rāmāyaṇa*, arrive at Rāma's horse sacrifice and sing a totally outrageous song. The two boys begin by saying, "There are blemishes even on Rāmacandra's lustre/glory." They say, "We are here to recite this *Rāmāyaṇa* written by the teardrops of women. We sing the fiery songs of injustices against women." They tell Rāma that "as long as the miseries of all Sītās belonging to this land of Bhārat are not ended, O Rāma, your *Rāmāyaṇa* will not come to a conclusion." They go on to say that "as long as the man is entitled to test a woman, he will go on finding faults with her. Without trusting a faithful woman, he will order her to jump into fire. As long as the scandals raised against the woman do not burn to ashes in fire, O Rāma, your *Rāmāyaṇa* will not come to a conclusion." King Rāma is shown unable to take these accusations of injustice and he leaves the court in shame whereupon sage Vālmīki is shown to address the people of Ayodhyā to consider the truth of the accusations.

I call this scene incongruous, because right after this outburst of emotions and modern sentiments against the injustices of Rāma, the film goes on to show all the events culminating in Sītā's final entrance into mother earth: the repeated accusations of the washerman, the people of Ayodhyā beating up the washerman, Rāma continuing with his horse sacrifice, the twins obstructing the sacrificial horse sent by Rāma, the defeat of Rāma's army in battle, Rāma's recognition that the two singers/warriors are his own children, and the last meeting of Rāma and Sītā when she proclaims her purity and her final entrance into mother earth. Then we hear the last stanza of the earlier song, which somehow declares, "Now the tragic tale of Vālmīki's great epic is complete. Now that Sītā has entered the Earth, *Rāmāyaṇa* is complete." We notice that the filmmaker has not changed the progression and ending of the *Uttara-kāṇḍa* of the classical *Rāmāyaṇa* in any way, but has expressed his own modern sensibilities against the injustices for the benefit of the audience through the mouths of the children. That results in an uneasy compromise between tradition and modernity.

Having discussed so far the filmmakers' traditional uses of *Rāmāyaṇa* as a contextual background, and an occasional incongruous innovation within the storyline, I would now like to concentrate on some other, more adventurous remakings of *Rāmāyaṇa*. Contemporary filmmakers find novel ways to address the issue of injustices in the old epic.[5] In fact, *Rāmāyaṇa* themes crop up and surprise us in the most unlikely contexts. I would like to discuss now two recent movies which have used *Rāmāyaṇa* in innovative but distinctly different ways. One of them is the box-office hit of 1999 by Sooraj Barjatya called *Hum Saath Saath Hain* [*HSSH*]. The other is *Lajja* by Rajkumar Santoshi in 2001, which also made waves in Indian and overseas movie houses.[6] The two films are quite apart from each other in the director's approach, the mood, the execution of the theme each chooses to emphasize, and the final message that each one projects. Nevertheless, the fact remains that both are mainstream Hindi movies, both boast a stellar cast, both were successful in terms of box-office revenues, and both seek to recast some of the issues of *Rāmāyaṇa*. I wish to analyze the films and their different treatments of *Rāmāyaṇa* themes in detail, to see how their initial ideologies and subsequent compromises affect the final outcome.

Family struggles rewritten

HSSH, released in 1999, was called "The movie of the Millenium" by the newspapers such as *The Daily* (October 30, 1999). Its story and dialogues were written by its director, Sooraj Barjatya, the man nicknamed "Mr. Box Office" by critics. Sooraj Barjatya, a young director/story writer had produced three successive box-office hits, the earlier two being *Maine Pyar Kiya* and *Hum Aap ke Hain Koun?*[7] His film was a joint family venture as is usual with the Barjatya clan, the oldest family making movies in India for fifty years. Dedicated to their mother, and in memory of their father, Tarachand Barjatya, the production was carried out by the three Barjatya brothers, Kamal Kumar, Rajkumar, and Ajit Kumar, with the grandson Sooraj as one of the two associate producers. It had a cast of Mohnish Bahal, Tabu, Salman Khan, Sonali Bendre, Saif Ali Khan, and Karisma Kapoor along with older and renowned actors/actresses such as Sadashiv Amrapurkar, Rima Lagu, Aloke Nath, and so on.

Sooraj Barjatya is famous for making clean, wholesome family entertainment once again a profitable enterprise. Like Barjatya's other two movies, *HSSH* also centers around the ever-present theme of idealized extended family in the context of a super-rich modern industrialist, Ramkishan, of Rampur. The first half of the movie is simply a long celebration of the seemingly seamless extended family beginning with the twenty-fifth wedding anniversary of Ramkishan and Mamta, who have a married daughter and three sons. The movie portrays them from being in love, to arranged engagement, dances, stage-shows, wedding, another engagement, honeymoon Indian style, more dances, parties, picnics, Satyanārāyaṇ Pūjā, and third engagement. All throughout this first half of the movie, allusions to *Rāmāyaṇa* abound. For example, in the wedding song, the elder brother Vivek about to marry his bride is compared to Rāma about to marry Sītā.[8] We see the family gather every morning to a daily recitation of Tulsī's *Rāmcaritmānas*, in front of the huge idols of Rāma, Sītā, and Lakṣmaṇa with Hanumān in their temple room, and we hear some of the *caupāī*s recited by the mother of the family. She recites verses from the end portion of the work of Tulsī "One father had many sons . . . the father loved all of them equally" (*Uttara-kāṇḍa*, *saptama sopāna*, 86: 1–4).[9] I think that they are selected here to stress that no matter how different the characters of the brothers, the parents' love for them knows no difference.

In the second half of the movie, which is surprisingly devoid of any music or dance sequences, this parental love is put to test. In a sequence that echoes the *Ayodhyā-kāṇḍa* of *Rāmāyaṇa*, the aging industrialist father, Ramkishan, announces that he is going to make the eldest son, Vivek, the managing director of his factories and corporate industries. The mother, Mamta, who is actually a doting stepmother to Vivek, is happy at first because she loves all her children equally. However, other characters around her start to wag their tongues, and finally convince her how this is detrimental to the well-being of her own sons, Prem and Vinod. The Mantharā types in this movie are three female friends of Mamta, who are unmarried social butterflies—or rather, stinging wasps, reinforcing the sexist belief that women cannot live together under the same roof without quarreling with each other. They tell Mamta to divide and conquer her daughters-in-law. The father of her (future) youngest daughter-in-law also is of the opinion that the decision to offer the managing directorship to Vivek is detrimental to the interests of the other two sons, and especially to the well-being of his daughter, when she marries the youngest son of this family.

In addition to their combined advice instigating the rift in Mamta's family, another unhappy situation develops in her married daughter's family. Mamta's son-in-law Anand is deprived of his share in his father's estate and factory, by his elder brother Anurag. In this side-story, we witness a tension between two brothers somewhat like Sugrīva and Vāli of *Rāmāyaṇa*. However, instead of fighting for his rightful share of the family property, the son-in-law decides to give it up, leave his position in the factory, and go to another city to start a new life. In this, he imitates Rāma's attitude of resignation rather than Sugrīva's impulse to fight. Mamta is upset at the plight of her darling daughter, robbed of her right to hereditary property and decides to prevent this kind of injustice from happening to her younger sons. Mamta presses her husband, Ramkishan, to divide the property among all three sons. He resents this suggestion, as it goes against the very foundation of the ideal of a united, extended family. The problem is resolved by the eldest son Vivek. He proposes to renounce the position offered to him, and goes with his young bride to live on the lesser family estate, the factory in the remote village of Rampur. The youngest brother Vinod decides to accompany Vivek into his voluntary exile, reminding us of Lakṣmaṇa accompanying Rāma.

The "foreign-returned" middle son, Prem, criticises his mother's actions in a manner reminiscent of Bharata criticizing Kaikeyī. Prem then goes to Vivek in exile, to bring him back to his rightful position, the chair of the managing directorship, but Vivek refuses it in the manner reminiscent of Rāma's refusal to return to Ayodhyā. A reluctant Prem returns to the industrial empire and carries on the affairs in a resigned manner, refusing to sit on the chair of the managing director, saying, "It belongs to the elder Bhaiyā and he shall have it when he returns."

While we brace ourselves to witness the new incarnation of *Rāmāyaṇa* in this industrial day and age, the matter is resolved in an abrupt manner and the movie ends. This modern day *Rāmāyaṇa* never proceeds to go toward the next chapters, the *Araṇya-, Kiṣkindhā-, Laṅkā-*, and *Yuddha-kāṇḍas*. There is no Rāvaṇa here, no kidnapping, no need for a Hanumān and no battlefield, let alone the abandonment and the fire ordeal of Sītā. The initial exile, the *vanavāsa* of the eldest brother itself is brought to an end by a happy turnabout. How does this happen? It is the change of heart, and repentance of the Vāli-like figure in the side-story that triggers the turnabout in the core family. Anurag, the unfair elder brother of Anand, comes to realize his mistake in driving away Anand from his inheritance. Anand is found to be indispensable to manage the complaints and outbursts of the workers in his factory. Anurag's children also are much attached to Anand and his wife, Sangita, and they have become miserable at home without their auntie and uncle to pamper them. Anurag's wife then arranges for the return of Anand and Sangita, and they readily comply. Anurag repents and accepts them with open arms, and order is restored to that joint family. This turn of events prompts Mamta to understand that even wronged brothers can be united, and that she has committed a sin in separating the three loving brothers in her own family. She repents and goes to bring her stepson Vivek and his wife home. They all rejoice in the recent birth of their grandson, and it all ends well.

The overall effect of this movie is so sweet that we may want to call it "*Rāmāyaṇa* in a Rabḍi bowl." Since it has more than the usual mix of beautiful settings, lavish houses, fashionable clothes and stunning jewelry, exuberant dances and songs, prayers and picnics, and since the talented actors and actresses have given their best natural performances to complement the director/story-writer's vision and conviction, this movie has become a favorite of the masses. Apart from some cynical reviewers, most critics have found something worthwhile in it. The film strives to suggest that the initial exile of Rāma and later misfortunes of Rāma and Sītā could have been avoided, had Kaikeyī shown the maturity not to listen to the separatist advice of Mantharā.

In order to realize this conviction in a contemporary context, Sooraj Barjatya has introduced some novel ideas. He has united the three mothers of *Rāmāyaṇa* in the sole character of Mamta, thereby suggesting perhaps, that a single person is capable of both good and bad attitudes of motherhood in her character. The stepmother-hood in this movie is not simultaneous as in *Rāmāyaṇa*, but linear, in that Mamta has married Ramkishan, a widower with a young son, Vivek, whom she raises with great love and care. The name Mamta selected for the mother in this film is significant, not just because it means "love of motherhood," but because it also means "possessiveness," showing the two sides of the same coin. On the other hand, Sooraj Barjatya has split the character of the poison-tongued Mantharā into three shortsighted, garrulous female friends, and also extended it across the gender line to include the greed of a poorer father of a bride. These deliberate changes to the old characters are significant not just because they add spice to the storyline, but because they distribute the blame of the wrongdoing between both sexes, however unequally it may be. The resolution of the conflict by essentially effecting a change of heart and restoring order is more in line with the traditional ideal of nonviolence and faith in the slogan, "united we stand." The message is that, with the proper upbringing that teaches the children values, such as respect for elders, selfless love and unity of the family, any sacrifice is possible. It reflects the director's firm conviction that sacrifice and love are the foundations on which the future of the family resides, and that they will bring about the change of heart even in misguided characters. As Ramkishan says, "The family that eats together, laughs together and prays together, stays together."

Sītā's travails retold

In its patriarchal framework, *HSSH* is mainly concerned with the injustice done to Rāma by his stepmother. Sooraj Barjatya does not attempt to address the larger, more vexing issue of the multiple injustices heaped upon Sītā by society, and especially by her own husband, Rāma. That is precisely the issue tackled by the other director/scriptwriter/producer, Rajkumar Santoshi,[10] in his memorable, powerful film, *Lajja*.[11] The two movies are worlds apart in their respective moods, directing styles, and ultimate messages. If in *HSSH*, we get more of the light-hearted entertainment peppered with just one-fourth of the diluted conflict of the epic, in *Lajja*, we concentrate on the Sītā story. The movie begins on a serious note of the cracks in a marriage and becomes increasingly grim. We are presented with four faces of Sītā, in the intertwined stories of four women, suffering various kinds of injustices, familial and societal.

Unlike Sooraj Barjatya, Rajkumar Santoshi dares to tackle the pressing issues of the wrongdoings against women of present day society. His heroines in *Lajja* are intelligent and brilliant, some timid, some with spirited defiance, and other with outright rebellion. He has tried to achieve a believable blend of idealism and realism in this film. Although feminism and an acute awareness of social injustice are infused into the whole movie, they are tempered with a wonderful sense of humor and astute sensitivity to dramatic balance. With a few melodramatic exceptions, his characters are multifaceted and lifelike.[12] The dialogues are witty, the storyline is fast-paced, and the overall acting is superb.

The main narrative of the film is Vaidehi's story. She is on the run from her abusive, rich and influential husband, and stumbles upon and enters into the lives and stories of the other three women, Maithili, Janaki, and Ramdulari. All these women are Sītā's namesakes.[13] Although they are quite differently raised, some urban, some rural, differing in education, wealth and courage, they each share with the epic heroine that they are suffering on account of the men in her life. Vaidehi's husband, Raghuvir, rendered unable to have children due to an accident, wants to reclaim Vaidehi just to have possession of her unborn child to continue his line. Maithili, a middle-class bride is faced with humiliation at the hands of her prospective father-in-law who doubts her chastity but is willing to accept and "purify" her at an exorbitant cost exhorted from her already impoverished father. Janaki, the third woman is a dancer/actress, a heroine in a small town dramatic group, who has to resist the unwanted advances of her director/mentor, Purushottam. Janaki finds herself put to a test by her lover/hero Manish who doubts the paternity of her unborn baby. Lastly, Ramdulari is the fourth heroine, a socially conscious Dalit woman, a midwife, and a helper of other women, who has to suffer atrocities of kidnap, captivity, and much more committed by the village headman, who is worse than Rāvaṇa, with no redeeming qualities whatsoever. All of these stories are interwoven amazingly well to create a rich tapestry. Struggle against injustice strings together every one of these stories, and in each one, success is coupled with sorrow, and sacrifice is rewarded with hope.

In the women's stories in *Lajja*, Rajkumar Santoshi has shown different nuances of the injustices against Sītā. Maithili's chastity is in doubt. Janaki's child's paternity and her loyalty to Manish are in doubt. Janaki, an unwed mother-to-be, is abandoned by her lover, and Vaidehi who had married with all due ceremony into a respectable family is also destitute while she is expecting. "Exiled with child in the womb" (*Kokh meṃ baccā liye vanvāsī*), in these words Janaki describes the plight of herself, of Vaidehi, and of the Sītā of *Rāmāyaṇa*. Janaki and Vaidehi are the two heroines who voice the most scathing commentaries on the plight of women through allusion to Sītā. At the end of the film, Vaidehi bursts into a passionate and moving speech which links all the heroines with the epic Sītā and blasts the society for its lip-service to feminine goddesses while committing all its injustices and atrocities against women.

The most eloquent incident in *Lajja*'s take on *Rāmāyaṇa* is Janaki's rebellious stand on stage while acting the role of Sītā in the fire ordeal scene in a *Rāmāyaṇa* play. Janaki is upset by the accusations of her real life lover Manish, who is also playing Rāma's role opposite her in the play. In a preceding scene, Manish as Rāma is shown stringing his bow off stage while he rejects Janaki and refuses to marry her, thereby bringing to our minds the *Rāmāyaṇa* scene of Rāma stringing the bow of Śiva to win Sītā. While acting the part of Sītā, Janaki brings those frustrations to the surface, and instead of humbly accepting Rāma's decision to abandon her for staying in Rāvaṇa's captivity, Janaki/Sītā starts to question Manish/Rāma about whether he really loves her or not. She demands that he stand by her if he really loves her. She upsets the other actors by her improvised speeches, and asks poignant questions as Sītā that are at once doubly significant to her role in the play and her own life. Janaki/Sītā belittles Rāma's valor by saying that she had single-handedly combated and conquered Rāvaṇa by resisting his sexual advances. She considers her own spiritual victory over Rāvaṇa superior to that of Rāma and his army of apes and bears. When the actor playing Lakṣmaṇa tries to intervene to save the situation, she brushes him off by saying that he is the root cause of all her miseries. She was kidnapped by Rāvaṇa due to Lakṣmaṇa's mistreatment of Rāvaṇa's sister, Śūrpaṇakhā. When Lakṣmaṇa tries to coax her into entering the fire so as to purify herself and thereby lead the play to a happy ending, she refuses to comply. She says that she does not want to prove anything to anyone who doubts her in the first place. She refuses to enter the fire alone, saying that both she and Rāma have stayed away from each other, and so Rāma should enter the fire as well. The audience, which is becoming more and more agitated throughout this scene, breaks into a riot at this point, and they have to bring down the curtain.

In real life, it was this very scene in *Lajja* that resulted in similar demonstrations by the BJP workers in Bhopal, who burnt an effigy of Rajkumar Santoshi and also burnt posters of Madhuri Dixit, playing Janaki, playing Sītā. They protested against the film's "objectionable dialogues." In Delhi, the Shiv Sena also led a demonstration against the movie, and sought an immediate ban on its screenings saying that it has an "insulting portrayal of the Hindu goddess Sītā."

Rajkumar Santoshi may have anticipated such a reaction from the Indian public. We find that he has actually answered it at this point in the film. The rioters sloganeer that "Janaki is a sinner, we will not suffer the insult against our religion" (*Janakī kulaṭā hai, dharam kā apmān nahīṃ saheṃge*). Janaki declares to Purushottam—who propositions her on the path to incarceration—that she has not insulted anyone, she has only given voice to the age-old question in the minds of millions of women. I think that Rajkumar Santoshi deserves credit for giving voice to more than just a question. *Lajja* is not just a film portraying the atrocities against women, nor just remaking *Rāmāyaṇa* in jest. It is a film that has a strong message to deliver. "Women's plight can be changed only when women take their fate in their own hands." It is to Santoshi's credit that the message is delivered not through sermons or simplistic situations but through the totality of complex characters and real-life-like situations.

We saw earlier how incongruous was the addition of the Lava-Kuśa song accusing Rāma in *Sampoorn Ramayan*. The bold attempt to remake *Rāmāyaṇa* in *Lajja* stands out by being artistic and sophisticated in that it uses the "play within a play" mode to introduce the change in its perspective. As a skilled director, Santoshi knows how to mix humor with serious issues and how to balance the pace with the content. All the questions asked by Janaki as Sītā are relevant in women's lives today. Although they articulate the feminist reaction to the epic, they may not seem in character for the epic Sītā, in her times and society. It is not easy to try to change the characters in *Rāmāyaṇa* that have become larger than life, and assumed godliness in the minds of people. Santoshi has found a way out of this by employing the embedded frames and succeeded in making the scenes effective because they operate at once on different levels of truth.

Conclusion

To sum up, different filmmakers with different agendas approach *Rāmāyaṇa* at different points, and attempt to remake it in their own inimitable styles, resulting in such different movies. In *HSSH*, Sooraj Barjatya upholds the traditional values of unity of the family, respect to elders, and selfless love and sacrifice to bring about a change of heart, to show how Kaikeyī can be redeemed and familial conflict avoided. Since he starts from this traditional standpoint, Barjatya has no place for feminism. The good women in the movie are those that cook for the family, sacrifice for the family, and pray for the family and the bad women are the ones that remain unmarried, smoke, play cards, and do not like to cook. The bad women are also those that seek to break a joint family. In *HSSH*, Barjatya succeeds in making a family-centered happy movie, and within that framework he only redresses the injustice done to Rāma.

In *Lajja*, Rajkumar Santoshi magnifies the injustices done to Sītā from the point of view of Indian feminism, and delivers a powerful, memorable and rebellious remaking of the abandonment (*Sītā-tyāga*) and the fire ordeal (*agni-parīkṣā*) incidents of *Rāmāyaṇa*. Apart from the abrupt surprise ending of *Lajja*, which shows a change of heart in Vaidehi's husband Raghuvir, and her instant acceptance of Raghuvir, both of which go against the expectations of the audiences, Santoshi has not compromised much in the artistic integrity of the movie. Perhaps, in that somewhat happy ending, he was trying to accommodate the ideology of traditional family into feminist parameters.

The star-studded cast, the routine of song and dance and excellent photography and technical expertise make each one a box-office success, but the final outcome of each film is directly dependent on the initial outlook of the filmmakers. If Tulsidās would have been able to watch both these films, he would probably have said, *jākī rahī bhāvanā jaisī, prabhu mūrati dekhī tina taisī* or, in other words, "to each his own *Rāmāyaṇa*."

Appendix: films on *Rāmāyaṇa*

The earliest films of D.G. or Dadasaheb Phalke included *Lanka Dahan* in 1917 and *Setu Bandhan* in 1931, based on major incidents of *Rāmāyaṇa*. These were followed by recurring renderings of *Rāmāyaṇa* throughout the decades of the last century. To cite a few, in 1933, there was the *Ramayan* of Madan Theatres, directed by Debaki Bose and featuring Pyare Sahib, Mukhtar Begam, Leela and Namrata Shankar. In 1943, another *Ramayan* was produced by Bharat Laxmi Rao, directed by Sudarshan and Prafulla Roy, featuring Prithviraj Kapoor, Rajkumari, Devbala, and Nayak. Right on its heels, came the *Ramayani* in 1945 of Purnima Productions directed by S. Badami, with Pahadi Sanyal, Nargis and Chandramohan. The most popular movie in North India in the sixties was the *Ramayan* of ALS Production, in 1960, directed by K. Somu, with a stellar cast of Shivaji Ganeshan, Padmini, N. T. Ramarao, V. Nagaiah, and G.Varalakshmi. This was followed in 1961 by *Sampoorn Ramayan* in Hindi, produced by Homi Wadia of Basant Pictures. The director was the famous Babubhai Mistry, and the cast included Anita Guha, Mahipal, Sulochana, and Lalita Pawar. In 1987, Babubhai Mistry had one more go at directing *Kalyug aur Ramayan*, which was produced by Shashi Goswami.

Along with these more or less complete *Rāmāyaṇa*s on the silver screen, there was no dearth of partial *Rāmāyaṇa*s based on some aspect of the popular epic.

For example, there were *Seeta Haran* (1936), *Sita Svayamvar* (1976), *Sati Seeta Lav Kush* (1983), and so on. Vijay Bhatt's trilogy starting with *Bharat Milap* (1942), *Ram Rajya* (1945), and *Rambaan* (1948) featured Shobhana Samarth as Sītā and Prem Adeeb as Rāma. This pair became extremely popular and appeared on popular calendars as Rāma and Sītā despite the fact that Prem Adeeb was a Muslim. Another most popular topic from the classic epic was Hanumān's exploits. A cursory search via the Internet revealed that there were 11 films on Hanumān in the interval of 1948–1981. These are *Jai Hanuman* (1948), *Sri Ram Bhakta Hanuman* (1948), *Hanuman Patal Vijay* (1951), *Hanuman Janam* (1954), *Pavan Putra Hanuman* (1957), *Ram Hanuman Yuddha* (1957), *Ram Bhakta Hanuman* (1969), *Hanuman Chalisa* (1969), *Hanuman Vijay* (1974), *Jai Hanuman* (1974), and *Mahabali Hanuman* (1981).

Notes

1 *Pativratā Sītā maiyā ko tūne diyā vanvās. Kyūṃ na phaṭā dhartī kā kalejā, Kyūṃ na phaṭā ākāś?*
2 *Julama sahe bhārī Janaka-dulārī, Janaka-dulārī Rāma kī pyārī.*
3 An English translation of the story *Pinjar* can be found as the first story in Khushwant Singh's 1987 translation of a collection of short stories by Amrita Pritam.
4 *Sītā ko dekhe sārā gāṃv, āg pe kaise dharegī pāṃv.*
Bac jāye to devī māṃ hai, jal jaye to pāpan.
Jiska rūp jagat kī ṭhaṇḍak, agni uskā darpan.
Sab jo cāhe, soce, samjhe, lekin vah Bhagvān.
Vah to khoṭ kapaṭ ke vairī, vah kaise nādān?
Agni pār utarke Sītā, jīt gaī viśvās.
Dekhā donoṃ hāth baṛhāye, Rām khaṛe the pās.
Us din se saṃgat meṃ āyā, sacmuc kā vanvās.
5 Here I must mention films that make marginal use of the old epic, if only to set them aside. Several films simply use the names Rāma or Sītā for their characters, or refer to them as, for example, *Rampur ki Seeta*, or *Doosri Seeta*, or *Radha aur Seeta.* Innumerable film heroines are given names echoing one of Sītā's epithets. Often this is a meaningful reference to the *Rāmāyaṇa*, though sometimes it can be just a representation of the real life names given to Indian children.
6 Santoshi's film *Lajja* broke all records in its opening week in the UK and grossed 126,160 pounds.
7 *HAHK* made it to US Top Ten which no other Indian film has ever managed to do. It has grossed Rs 200 crore, which is the record collection of any Hindi film in the history of Indian cinema (see Ramesh Sippi's article in *Hindustan Times* of December 26, 1999).
8 *Choṭe bhāiyoṃ ke baṛe bhaiyā, āj baneṃge kisī ke saiyā.*
Jacte haiṃ dekho kaise baṛe bhaiyā, Rāmjī bihāne cale Sītā maiyā.
9 *Eka pitā ke vipula kumārā, hoṃhi pṛthaka guṇasīla acārā.*
Koū paṇḍita koū tāpasa jñātā, koū dhanavaṃta sūra koū dātā.
Koū sarvajña dharmarata koī, saba para pitahi prīti sama hoī (Poddar 1942).
10 Rajkumar Santoshi is one of the most versatile directors of present times. He has made many memorable movies, including *Damini, Barsaat, The Legend of Bhagat Singh,* and *Khaki.*
11 Santoshi has employed in it a stellar cast of Manisha Koirala, Madhuri Dixit, Mahima Chaudhuri, and Rekha, with Jackie Shroff, Anil Kapoor, and Ajay Devgan.
12 While the men who have married or are in love with these women fail to stand by them, the women find support with other male characters in *Lajja*. A thief on the run helps

Vaidehi in her escape from her husband, and also helps Maithili by giving her the money to complete her dowry. There is the character of the armed rebel, Bulwa, who fights against injustices and rescues many oppressed people and who also helps Vaidehi in her flight from Raghuvir. Vaidehi's husband Raghu at one point accuses Bulwa of keeping in custody another man's wife and likens him to Rāvaṇa, but Bulwa is the anti-Rāvaṇa character in *Lajja*, in that he never raises his weapons against a woman, always considers every woman his mother, and never compromises her security. Bulwa incorporates some of Hanumān's aspects in his character, in that he lives in the forests, and swings into action by jumping from any tree or boulder to rescue the woman. Crossing the epic boundaries, as it were, Bulwa, the bandit, at one place takes on the significance of Krishna of the *Bhagavad Gītā*, when he assures Vaidehi that "Bulwa does not die. Bulwa is immortal. Whenever a voice is raised against injustice and atrocities, rest assured that Bulwa is there."

13 All the names are well-known epithets of Sītā: "Maithilī" means "princess of Mithila," "Jānakī" means "Janaka's daughter," "Vaidehī" refers to Sītā as "the princess of Videha," and "Rāmdulārī" as "beloved of Rāma." The choice of these names reflects the regional style of naming girls. Two of the male names are reminiscent of Rāma: the husband of Vaidehi, who is concerned with the continuity of his line called Raghu, or Raghuvir, reminding us of Kālidāsa's poem called *Raghuvaṃśa*, and, ironically, Janaki's aggressor, is called Purushottam, which means "the excellent hero," also an epithet of Rāma.

References

Editions

Poddār, H.P. (ed. and comm.) (1942; 1990) *Śrīmadgosvāmī Tulsīdāsjī viracita Śrīrāmcaritmānas*, Gorakhpur: Gītā Press.

Other

Barnouw, E. and Krishnaswamy, S. (1980) *Indian Film*, 2nd edn, Oxford: Oxford University Press.

Singh, K. (trans.) (1987) *The Skeleton and That Man by Amrita Pritam*, New Delhi: Sterling.

Sippi, R. (1999) "Big B," *Hindustan Times*, December 26, 1999. Online. Available HTTP: <http://www.rajshri.com/hssh-press2.html> (accessed September 2004).

Part 2

Casting classical Sanskrit drama

3 Śakuntalā

The look and the image in literature, theater, and cinema*

Gayatri Chatterjee

Introduction

It is well-known that Kālidāsa had based his celebrated Sanskrit play *Abhijñāna-śākuntalam* on a short story in the *Mahābhārata* (Bhat 1985; Kale 1957; Stoler-Miller 1984; Thapar 2000). The chapter begins with a synopsis of the Śakuntalā story in the epic, followed by a close look at the Kālidāsa play. Several scholars (the above ones and also Gerow 1979) have previously noted the thematic and structural changes and additions Kālidāsa made while creating the play. This chapter suggests other differences between the two works—one a short tale embedded in an epic and the other a full-fledged classical play. An epic is to be read or be listened to; a play is performative, a spectacle to be viewed (of course, it could also be read). The chapter exhibits how this difference is highlighted in the construction of the play by making the *acts of looking and image making* important organizational principles.

The *act of looking* is complex and tiered. Differentiating between the various circumstances and the attendant meanings and feelings the act involves, I have used three terms—looking, seeing, and gazing. "Looking" is an empirical act; it is someone spotting someone or something else, making the first acquaintance. It might be the initial stage of a dramatic narration or specifically guide some episode within. The *act of looking* here is not yet invested with de-ontological aspect or value.

The *act of seeing* is attentive and focused; it is attached to emotions or affects like desire and love, and to mental activities like cognition and knowledge. The play by Kālidāsa has been noted for being about memory (Malamoud 1998; Stoler-Miller 1984). The empirical act of seeing is connected with this abstract activity of the mind as well. Freud noted the tremendous pleasures attached to the act of seeing connected mostly with the sexual drive and called it *Schaulust* (Freud 1909: 7–55). The English translation "scopophilia" is widely employed in film studies, where it has *negative* value, in that here people are viewing subjects and submit the object of seeing to a controlling gaze. Many studies insist the members of the audiences identify with the aggressor. What the aggressor (and with him the audience) sees and takes pleasures in is not actually meant for viewing; it is a clandestine act and thus the term "scopophilia" gets connected with the term "voyeurism." In such cases, the act of looking is also conveyed through the word "gaze."[1]

The *act of gazing* involves someone looking at some other person (or object), purposefully over a prolonged period. The phrase is loaded with meaning and value as it is widely used in feminist criticism and film studies—synonymous there with male-gaze voyeurism and sexual politics (Mulvey 1975; Willemen 1986). The drive to gaze, control and consume (sexual or other ways) has been linked to psychological reasons (family disorder, childhood trauma, feeling of lack in early life) or sociological reasons (environment, urban dystopia). However, the act also belongs in religion, where it is connected with adoration or feelings bereft of carnality. It fulfils the spectator's desire for sublimation of desires. The prolonged act of looking, in these cases, is linked to transcendence into any field of idealization. And ultimately the visual extends towards greater meaning making—towards the realms of the symbolic. In India, the term used for all of this is *darśana*.[2] What all this means is that the gaze could be perceived as invested with positive *or* negative values (it is usually seen as an either) or a mélange of the two (a more fruitful way, for the studies of texts, performances, and cinema).

Through a close reading of the play, this chapter demonstrates all the aspects of the Look—the term standing for all of the above—are fully employed in *Abhijñāna-śākuntalam*. Edwin Gerow has established the relationship between the structure of this play and the *rasa* that flows out of the experience of watching it (Gerow 1979).[3] In addition to that, I suggest the Look indeed is the organizational principle of the play. It is spread over the entire play; it lies behind the construction of many scenes and dramatic moments. Different visual constructions and verbalizations (of the visuality) in terms of dialogue—as well as the playwright's stage-direction notes—all combine here to enhance the flow of the *rasa*.

This leads to the final section of the chapter, which discusses two films made by the same director. *Shakuntala* by V. Shantaram (1943) is adapted from both the epic and the classical play; it also introduces some new elements, thereby rendering itself thoroughly modern. Interestingly, the antecedent of the film lies in the history of the revival of the play during the colonial period and the Orientalist perception and excitement around it in the previous couple of centuries. The chapter briefly provides that history. One more crucial link in the chain of events that followed the first translation of the Kālidāsa play by Sir William Jones and the film versions, is the play's translation in regional languages and performance on stage.

The film is marked by the Orientalist habit of turning the figure of Śakuntalā into an allegory for India itself and by extension, the East (Figueira 1991). The film fully exploits the strong factor of visuality present in the play. But then again, made in the period of nationalism, the film also brings in a spirit of reform and does this precisely through the figure of the woman—now an allegory for a raised subjective consciousness. Indian films in all languages have often adapted the story of Śakuntalā; whether they reflect the contemporary spirit, carry the Orientalist construction or do something innovative with this traditional tale is the topic for a future study. I end the chapter noting Shantaram's own remake, *Stree* (Hindi, 1961), which shows a director bereft of his earlier certainty of the modernist project. *Stree* is all about the male gaze, elements of popular entertainment, and it is consequently regressive.

The story in the epic

Śakuntalā is conceived in a moment of passion between the *apsarā* Menakā and the sage Viśvāmitra (*Ādi parvan*, 1.65–6, all references are to Sukhtankar 1971). After her birth, her celestial mother abandons Śakuntalā (her father does not feature in the narrative). Till sage Kaṇva picks up and adopts her, a *śakunta* bird shelters her; and so her name becomes Śakuntalā.

Out on a hunt, The Puru king Duṣyanta sees and is instantly attracted to young Śakuntalā. She too is similarly attracted; but before agreeing to unite sexually she demands her son should be the crown prince. She tells him, "If that is so, O Duṣyanta, then let me unite in sexual union with you" (1.67.17). The king agrees and they enter into a mutual attraction-consent (*gāndharva*) marriage. Baudhāyana in his *Dharmasūtra* explains that the *gāndharva* marriage takes place when a man and a woman, both with desire, have sexual intercourse (*Baudhāyana-dharmasūtram*, 11.6).[4]

The king returns to his kingdom; Śakuntalā bears a child and carries it in her womb for three years. She gives birth to a son, who is named Sarvadamana. She is not in a hurry to make the king fulfill his promise and raises the child on her own for another three years. Maybe it was not difficult for a heroine in those times to be single mother and bring up a son without the father. Or perhaps as the daughter of an *apsarā*, the epic heroine could afford to be independent (*svādhīnā*). But eventually, she surrenders to societal laws for the sake of her offspring, who is a mortal and should rule as a king after his father. So six years after she married the king, Śakuntalā visits him in his court and demands he should now take charge of his son. But Duṣyanta ("the untamed one") is reluctant to acknowledge his past liaison with a poor anchorite woman; so, though remembering fully, he denies knowing her. Śakuntalā is about to leave; but a voice from the sky (*ākāśavāṇī*) enjoins the king to accept the boy as his own. The king obeys the heavenly command. The heroine gains victory as the *deus ex machina* acts on her behalf. And aided by an outside agency, the king is reinstalled in *dharma.*[5] Though the tale begins by a man approaching a woman and seducing her, later in the narrative the woman is the narrative agent. What counts is what she told him. The part-mortal, part-celestial heroine rebukes the mortal hero in strong terms. Epic fashion, the narrative pleasure here is derived out of ethical discourse, but linked to a love tale.

Chronicling the end an epoch (*yugānta*), the *Mahābhārata* paints a picture of various grades and shades of male sexuality and manhood befitting men from the warrior and other castes. This is a time of moral ethical dilemmas (Matilal 1989). So perhaps it is necessary for a Śakuntalā to put down some conditions before entering into a relationship with a king. Additionally, these stories perhaps carry vestiges of women's social importance and power in former times, when women had narrative importance (if not actual powers), endangered now in the epic times—when narrations, visuals and sociocultural symbols are bent to growing patriarchal rules and structures. The matter of inheritance of the male progeny had undergone many changes between the period of the *Dharmasūtras* and the Epics. All male issues of all the eight forms of marriages extant in the earlier periods were eligible to the father's identity and property. For example, an unmarried woman with a child could marry a man; the child (the son) would in that case inherit the new father's identity and property. Such widely spread out boundaries of inheritance and social identity were tightened at the time of the Epic.[6] Śakuntalā must extract a promise of material security for her future son before she unites sexually with Duṣyanta.

The play by Kālidāsa

Abhijñāna-śākuntalam highlights the *gāndharva* marriage between Duṣyanta and Śakuntalā, describing in detail their meeting and attraction for each other, their separation (the wedding is not shown) and sorrow. There is the drama of the curse, as a result of which Duṣyanta forgets his love of and promise to Śakuntalā. In this melodramatic narrative, the heroine does not decide her own destiny. On learning she is pregnant her foster-father sage Kaṇva sends her off to Duṣyanta's court. Śakuntalā does give vent to her anger at the betrayal, but her public degradation is pitiable. Repeatedly declared in the play as fully installed in *dharma*, the king is justified for all his actions. To make matters worse, the anchorites accompanying her decide to leave her at his mercy (her place is now in her husband's and not father's house). So, Sānumati (a friend of Menakā) takes Śakuntalā away and helps her give birth to her son. Later, Śakuntalā brings up her son in another *āśram*, that of sage Mārīca. A few years later, the signet ring (*abhijñāna*) Duṣyanta had given Śakuntalā (as her marker) is found and he regains his memory. Passing by the *āśram* one day, Duṣyanta sees his son and feels attracted—the family is united.

Kālidāsa was not writing an epic about civilizational debacles, but a play to provide performative-narrative pleasures to kings and nobles—his sponsors (Stoler-Miller 1984). The king he depicts here must be a hero and so, not deceitful or hypocritical (as in the epic). First, Duṣyanta actually suffers a loss of memory because of a curse; that he forgets his wife is not *his* fault and so not to be blamed for his behavior in the court. Second, his pursuit of Śakuntalā is fully explained, too. Though he has married several times, he is childless and in need of a male issue.[7] Third, scholars have seen Duṣyanta's refusal to believe and accept Śakuntalā as an example of his awareness of *dharma*. If she is carrying a son in her wombs: she is either his wife or someone else's wife. Since, he cannot remember his marriage to her, he prefers to be safe and refuses her. "It is a worse crime to touch another man's wife than to abandon one's own"(Bhat 1985). Both the man and the woman are victims of circumstances in this melodrama, but the heroine suffers rejection, shame, homelessness—and all this over a prolonged period. However, the play is constructed along the subjectivity of the king (the first dramatic persona to be introduced on stage); the book celebrates his union with his son-and-heir—and so do the audiences, traditionally.

Close analysis of the plot following the occurrences of the Look

The play is about the pleasure of looking. I do not problematize this pleasure in the beginning here—after all, a dramatic performance is about the joys of the visual. I suggest instead that this pleasure element is a crucial aspect of the play and the entire play is organized around the fact of the Look. I work into the full implications of the Look as I proceed into the study of the play, and then into the discussions of the two films.

The beginning of the performance and the Look

The traditional prelude to the play (*prastāvanā*) begins with a prayer (by *nāndī*) to Lord Śiva endowed with eight visible or manifest forms (*pratyakṣa*).[8] After the benediction follows a conversation between the manager/narrator (*sūtradhāra*) and his dancer-singer wife (*naṭī*). He announces that the evening's play is *Abhijñāna-śākuntalam* by Kālidāsa and wishes the actors would perform well and satisfy the audience. He then proceeds to sing about the season (the summer month of *jyeṣṭha*) that has recently set in. Introducing a synesthesia of touch, smell, and sight, he sings about the breeze made fragrant by the *pāṭala* flowers, the joys of a cool bath in this season, and a nap in the shade (I.3).[9] His wife is more specific and adds: the *śirīṣa* flowers stuck in the maidens' hair; the tips of the delicate filaments of the flowers; and black bees gently kissing the delicate flower tips (I.4).

Abhijñāna-śākuntalam opens into the empirical world—the world of the audience. Later, it would take many leaps into affective, imaginary, and representational worlds. Kālidāsa describes the audience as if inscribed into a painting, riveted as they are by the melody. The songs evoking the lazy turpitude of the season induce in the manager a short memory lapse; the presenter forgets the name of the play he has just announced. He tells his wife: "I was led away by your song just as king Duṣyanta was by the deer" (I.5). This serious lapse foreshadows the main dramatic event of this play—Duṣyanta forgetting Śakuntalā.

Looking at the hero

The king enters with his charioteer (in a chariot) chasing a deer. Looking both at him and the deer he is chasing, the charioteer says, "It is as if Lord Śiva has made himself visible (*sākṣāt*)." Heroes often are the first objects of gaze in Indian popular plays—and in films. The king's first appearance is while stalking an animal—as he would a woman soon after. Stalking is possible only when the object of prey is clearly visible.

Perspective—as attached to the act of looking

There follows a discussion involving moving objects, relative motion, and perspective. The king wonders, "How then has he (the deer) become faintly visible, though I have been pursuing him closely?" He elaborates, "On account of the speed of the chariot, that which is minute in appearance suddenly attains magnitude; that which is cut in the middle appears as if it were joined; that which by nature is crooked appears straight. Nothing is at a distance from me for a moment, nor is it near to me" (I.9). The king's chariot had been riding over uneven grounds and has lost speed. The driver will drive faster and the deer will become visible—it is easy to kill something when it is clearly seen.

This discussion could be linked to the Act VII, when Duṣyanta flies in a chariot driven by Indra's charioteer, Mātalī. Returning from the God's heavenly abode, the king is thrilled to see the mountains, trees, and houses, looking minuscule from the height of the *vimāna*. As the flying chariot descends, the earth becomes more and more visible; objects on earth gradually attain their true form and size. "The rivers whose waters had vanished in the narrowness, now become larger as they assume magnitude; behold the earth is being brought near to me as if some one is flinging it upwards" (VII.8). A third occurrence of the matter of perspective is when Duṣyanta paints a picture—the scene is discussed later in the chapter. The play abounds in realistic representations of event and emotions; and gradually added in it are heightened emotions, wondrous happenings, and fantastic beings.

Seeing, stalking, and killing

The hero is considered a superior being; at the same time, his actions might not be quite correct and then he must set himself right. A hero is one who can correct his path. The act of killing is to occur at this heightened moment of sight and perception. But the playwright brings about an ethical check—there is a cry from the wings, "Do not kill it" (*na hantavyo*). The deer belongs to the hermitage and is protected. An actual killing is staved off, but a metaphorical one will follow as the *āśram*-girl falls victim of the Look—and his looks.

Some anchorites enter and praise the king for not killing the deer; they bless him so he should have a worthy son. They also inform him that the sage Kaṇva is away from the *āśram* and that his (adopted) daughter Śakuntalā is there to represent him. Duṣyanta expresses his wish to convey her his respects for the sage. Wishing to enter the hermitage in a humble manner, he removes from his person all the signs of his royal status and walks off alone looking like a sage of some royal birth.

Dusyanta sees Śakuntalā

With a water pot resting on her hip, and accompanied by two friends Anasūyā and Priyaṃvadā, Śakuntalā comes to water the forest trees. Seeing them Duṣyanta muses, "these forest women have beauty rarely seen in the palace" (I.16). The king decides to hide and look at them in leisure. Women in villages continue to carry water pots on their hips or heads; what is an everyday arduous chore for many has been a perennial source of image-making and viewing-pleasure. Even so many centuries ago the village was as distant and exotic to the city-folk as it is today. This exoticization of the village/forest is more than a mere cliché, and important to the narrative (and to audience reception).

The king enjoys himself looking at the girls, discovering their beauty and identity. What the girls discuss accords him even greater pleasure. Anasūyā and Priyaṃvadā describe Śakuntalā's beauty, thus underscoring as it were the king's words of appreciation and praise (the conversation between the three women and the man's monologue are often inter-cut). Śakuntalā requests them to loosen her upper garment; Priyaṃvadā laughs: "Well, rather blame your youth which expands your bosom (and not me)." The king adds *sotto voce* "This slender-bodied lady is more lovely even with her bark-cloth" (I.18). The female protagonists' comments provide certain sanctions, as if it were, to the (male) gaze of the hero within the play and the audiences outside.

Voyeurism and dramatic pleasure

At this stage, the act of seeing-gazing is a clandestine act conducted without the knowledge of those who are being looked or gazed at, for which we could use the term "voyeurism." It is a clandestine act and one-sided, conducted without the knowledge, volition and agreement of the one being stared at. Not only the hero and the female friends contribute to this pleasure, as per convention, the heroine too repeatedly invites attention to her own person. The image to be looked at is so constructed as to invite the audience gaze. Śakuntalā speaks about and is compared (twice) to a creeper—implying the arrival of the hero, a tree around which the creeper would flourish (I.18–20).

The scene brings in synesthesia of the senses; there is a moment that accords primacy to touch (something seeing *must be* followed by). A bee sits on Śakuntalā's cheek and refuses to go away when she brushes it away (I.21–2). Duṣyanta "looks longingly" and versifies (or sings):

> Bee, you touch the quivering
> Corners of her frightened eyes,
> You hover softly near
> To whisper secrets in her ear;
> A hand brushes you away,
> But you drink her lips' treasures…
> (Stoler-Miller 1984: 96)

The gallant hero must save this damsel in distress, chased by a bee. There are similar scenes where the heroine is coy and artificial. Then again, she is free and bold, "When I see him, why do I feel an emotion that the forest seems to forbid?" (Stoler-Miller 1984: 97). A forest dweller, she has heard and read about such things, has discussed the same with friends—but has not yet had direct experience of sexual attraction and desire. The king's ardent gaze brings about stirrings of passion in her and she begins to be a willing "victim" of his willful "stalking." At the end of Act I, the women notice the royal signet ring on Duṣyanta's fingers. Pretending to be someone else he tells them it is just "a gift from the king;" he belongs to the royal clan, but is not the king. Act I ends but Śakuntalā and friends remain ignorant of his identity—"seeing" does not lead them to real knowledge.

One of the pleasures of reception in a popular form is when a character in a performance anticipates what the audience is thinking or feeling. The three women's talk and the king's many asides fulfill that function. Performance studies must concentrate on the audience as an individual as well a whole or group entity (or constituted of some pockets of individuals and wholes). In India (as everywhere), group reception is an important component of theater and film viewing—and this play shows the playwright's awareness in that regard. We do not fully know the nature of audience reaction in those days—did they speak out their reactions, as film audiences in India today do so liberally?[10] But we can see the playwright here weaving in the audience–performance relationship into his play.

In the third act, the king returns to hiding, looking, and listening to the women engaged in their private talk. Between the first and the third act, their separation has induced in the couple sorrow and suffering (*viraha*). Once again, the heroine's body is under minute scrutiny, first as it was in the throes of excitement of new love and now as the anxiety of separation. Śakuntalā also suffers because of her inability to do something about her feelings; other characters repeatedly remind her she is not independent (*svādhīnā*), but dependent on her foster-father and the rules of the *āśram.* She becomes emaciated and her upper garment sloth; her body burns as if in the throes of fever.

Indian melodrama (plays and films) is often very much about men suffering in love—they too become feeble. Similarly, the hero of this play has grown thin and pale on account of his as yet unexpressed and unconsumed desires. But Kālidāsa makes a distinction in the two cases. Śakuntalā's physical state is freely discussed and commented upon by her friends. The king describes in detail how her breasts, waist and arms have become slender; she is like the Mādhavī creeper shaken by the wind, causing its leaves to wither (III.8). However, it is he himself who describes his own state of suffering: hanging lose are his bracelets and amulets, signifying his stature and valor, for the thick skin formation on his former wounds no longer can keep them in place (III.11). His clothes or body is not mentioned otherwise. Duṣyanta wonders who would get Śakuntalā, this "flower no one has smelt yet," a "tender sprout no one has plucked with his nails, the fresh honey no one has as yet tasted." His court-jester friend jokes that they should then hurry and procure her, lest some greasy oily haired anchorite get her.

Seeing, stalking, and killing—analogy

The analogy of the king as a hunter is repeated in the context of his pursuit of Śakuntalā. After he has seen her, he cannot kill the deer that has taught her the sidelong glance (*kaṭākṣa*). He thinks: "When I remember Kaṇva's daughter, the thought of hunting disgusts me." Duṣyanta's friend the buffoon knows from convention that Śakuntalā must have looked at Duṣyanta in that particular way— "the sidelong glance." He wants to know, "Now, what kind of affection was betrayed towards Your Highness by her eyes?" (II.10).

The hero is happy to find out that the heroine has fallen hopelessly in love with him—he has met with his objective. In Act III Duṣyanta appears before the girls to make his claims upon Śakuntalā; and it ends with the king forcing her to stay and yield to his embraces and kisses. The heroine tries to resist, "O you belonging to the race of Puru! Please, guard and protect me." She still does not know whom she is attracted to, who is to protect her.

In the beginning of Act IV, Anasūyā and Priyaṃvadā announce Śakuntalā has got married in the *gāndharva* way. In this scene, the audience hears the voice of the sage Durvāsa putting his curse on Śakuntalā: the one she is thinking of, forgetting all else, will forget her. The friends discuss that before parting, the "royal sage" (they still do not know the real identity of the hero) has given her a royal signet ring; it would serve as a reminder of Śakuntalā. Visuality is indeed a chief ingredient in this play, the title of which bears the name of an object—a ring—meant to mark her as his wife or something to remember her by. The *deus ex machina* of the epic, a voice from the sky informs Kaṇva: "Know, O sage, that thy daughter holds, for the good of the world, the energy (*teja*) implanted by Duṣyanta, as the Śamī tree contains fire within" (IV.4). Now everyone knows the true identity of the man who has married Śakuntalā in *gāndharva* style.

Look, emotion, cognition—memory and recall

Some serious questions are attached to the act of looking and seeing in all the chapters. Do we see what we see? Do we always see well what is there in front of us? When we see something, we feel something—are those feelings always the right ones (that the sight invokes)? Finally, the play is about not knowing the true identity of a person and then knowing; remembering and forgetting; and then recognition.

Emotion might be straightforward and the dramatic personae might correctly assess the other people's feelings through the observance of the eyes; at times, seeing is the way of divining other people's thoughts and emotions. Duṣyanta correctly guesses: though Śakuntalā is looking elsewhere, her mind is entirely engaged in the thoughts of him. "She might not be facing me, but her eyes rest at no other object" (I.25).

The king questions one's deductions on the basis of seeing and makes the circumstance of gaze complex. He thinks Śakuntalā has reciprocated his feelings; and then he laughs at himself "Thus is mocked the suitor who infers the feelings of his cherished one from his own" (II.1). Duṣyanta cautions the audience that one must not measure the beloved's mind with one's own feelings. He looks for signs that will tell him Śakuntalā feels the same attraction as he does for her. She looks askance at him, but does that mean she is in love with him? Though her eyes were downcast she threw him sidelong glances; he felt it was all for his sake, but how could he be sure? For, "a lover sees his own self everywhere" (II.2).

Duṣyanta is back in his palace; one of his wives Haṃsapādikā sings a sad song, implying he has stopped loving her. Like a bee he has forgotten how he often kissed the mango-blossom, now that the lotus has satisfied him (V.1). He wonders why he should feel such strong emotions, even though not separated from anyone he loves. The curse is on the king and he has forgotten Śakuntalā. He muses (in a celebrated verse), "Seeing rare beauty, hearing lovely sounds, even a happy man becomes strangely uneasy…perhaps he remembers without knowing why, loves of another life buried deep in his being" (Stoler-Miller 1984: 134).

Śakuntalā arrives with people from the hermitage. Since the king has forgotten all about his marriage to her, he must look at her in order to recognize her; but he is reluctant, "One must not look at another man's wife" (V.16). While he feels strangely attracted to this (for him) unknown woman, he fails to be reminded of past events even after Śakuntalā assures him she is his wife and recounts incidents and exchanges that took place between them. The spoken word has ceased to be sacred; only the visible is of consequence.[11] He is annoyed, thinking these hermitage people are out to cheat him. And yet, he suspects on seeing her angry red eyes and knitted brows that she speaks the truth. Śakuntalā's companions leave her saying, if she will not be accepted as a queen, she must stay in her husband's house as a maid. At this point Sānumatī, an *apsarā* (a friend of mother Menakā) who had been eavesdropping on the proceedings, descends and takes Śakuntalā away with her.[12]

Some years later, the ring is found in the belly of a fish. As it is bears the royal insignia, it reaches the court and the king's memory is restored on looking at it. Duṣyanta is cast in deep sorrow and remorse.[13]

Pictorial art or creating the visible

Now I will jump chronology and allude to all the references to pictorial art and visuality in the play. The act of seeing, attached to different emotion and affects, produces further mental images, evokes different kinds of meditation and mental activity—it induces desires to give further rise to visuality.

The king tells his court-jester and friend, Mādhava, "It is as if God first painted a picture of hers and then infused life into it. When I think of the Creator's creative powers and her bodily form, I think that Śakuntalā is a unique creation of God" (II.7). In Act III, Śakuntalā is lost in sorrow due to separation. Priyaṃvadā tells Anasūyā, "Look at her with her face resting on her left hand. Our friend looks as if she is painted (*ālikhita*)." When Śakuntalā is being prepared for her departure, the forest nymphs and trees gift her ornaments and friends must put them on her. They explain, "We have never used ornaments; but we will put them on your limbs, from our knowledge of paintings" (IV, 6).

In the sixth act, Duṣyanta has painted Śakuntalā in order to get over his sorrow and remorse. We do not see him doing it, the painting is brought on the stage. The man who until now has been "the bearer of the look" (to use another phrase from feminist criticism) is now the creator of the visible as well. He has painted Śakuntalā and events connected with his meetings with her.[14] The buffoon discusses the technical details of the painting and comments how it evokes emotions, how one's glance glides easily over the undulating surface of the board. Sānūmatī—always a voyeur—watches unobserved (she has come to find out why there are no preparations for the approaching spring festival in the kingdom and has learnt the king is grieving for Śakuntalā). Sānūmatī remarks on the perfect simulacra, "I think my friend stands before me, in person" (VI, 13). According to traditional theories of dramaturgy every stylization, flight of fancy, and mythical allusion must weave in and out of verisimilitude and mimesis—we see very good examples of these in this play.

The king sits down to add more details in the painting. What follows now can be spoken of in cinematic terms: the painting is first described as if in a long shot. The king feels it is wanting of further details. He focuses on details: the river Mālinī, pairs of swans, hills. The description now adopts a panoramic view of the landscape in the way of a moving camera (something a painting cannot capture). And then the visual is a cut into an extreme close up; Duṣyanta says: "I wish to paint a doe, rubbing her left eye against the horn of a black buck."

The king and his jester-friend imagine that the picture in front of them is live—reality itself. Śakuntalā is scared of a bee that is attracted to a *śirīṣa* flower stuck to her ears. The king drives it away, but it returns and sits on the woman's lips. The spell is broken and the jester realizes his folly and remarks, "He certainly has gone mad and associating with him, I too am losing my senses." He reminds the king, "It is only a picture!" The king laments: "With my mind wholly wrapped up in her, she had become real. Now once again, she is transformed into picture" (*citrīkṛtakāntā*) (VI, 21).

In the seventh act, Duṣyanta (as mentioned already) visits the king of the gods, Indra; on his return, as mentioned earlier, he describes in detail how the earth looks painting-like from the flying chariot, how the perspectives change and things look natural when they begin their descent.

On his way back, he visits the forest-grove of the sage Mārīca, where Śakuntalā is bringing up Sarvadamana. Visible signs and actions the boy engages in make the king feel paternal affections towards the boy and then he realizes the boy indeed is his son. Duṣyanta and Śakuntalā are united—and the boy is renamed Bharata.

Orientalist and Nationalist imaginations

Abhijñāna-śākuntalam played an important role in unfurling Orientalist imagination about India (Cannon 1953; Figueira 1991). William Jones initiated this process with genuine admiration for the play and he carried out a comparative study of Indian and Western drama. Jones' translation in 1789 was so popular that it was reprinted three times in eight years. It was printed in Calcutta in 1901. In the preface, Jones expressed the wish that people would learn Sanskrit and read the play in the original. The play was translated in French in 1803 and German in 1815 (Cannon 1953). Goethe's enthusiasm for the play is well known.

American transcendentalist poets discovered the play in the mid-nineteenth century; ballet performances of the play became popular the world over. Jawaharlal Nehru wrote, "To Jones and to many other European scholars, India owes a deep debt of gratitude for the rediscovery of her past literature." He called Shakespeare and Kālidāsa "world-poets," but added: "It is however, well worth remembering that the Bard of Ujjain lived eleven hundred years before the birth of the Bard of Avon." (Nehru 1946).

The play began to be available in printed books in Devanāgarī and other scripts. There was similar adulation, analyses and criticism in India, as well. In the late-nineteenth century, Bankimchandra Chatterjee provided new comments and critique of the Kālidāsa play and its heroine. He wrote as a colonial subject, but reversed the gaze onto the West and compared Śakuntalā to Shakespeare's Miranda and Desdemona.[15] For Chatterjee Śakuntalā is fully socialized and artful; she is filled with coquetry and ruse (he uses the Hindi word *bahānā*)—as if to challenge the Orientalist reception. He explains that the conversation between Śakuntalā and Duṣyanta contains "sweet nothings, but not noble passions rising from the depth of their beings." He further elaborates: the Indian play is "lyrical" and not "dramatic" the way the two Shakespeare plays *The Tempest* and *Othello* are (Chatterjee [1887] 1974: 204–9). Astutely, he likens Śakuntalā to a painting (and the two Shakespeare heroines to sculpted figures).

The history of the Marathi Sangeet-Natak (opera style drama) begins with Annasaheb Kirloskar's translation of this Kālidāsa play. The first show of *Sangeet Shaakuntal* was on 31 October, 1880, in Anandodbhava hall, Budhvar Peth, Pune.[16] This article cannot pursue all the reasons for studying this history in detail, but will engage with how that history is connected with the two films by V. Shantaram to be discussed here.

Film versions directed by V. Shantaram

As a young boy Shantaram Vankudre had joined Kirloskar Natya Company. When famous actors Balgandharva, Govindaram Tembe, and Ganpatrao Bodas broke away and formed Gandharva Natak Mandali, Shantaram joined them (1913–15). He has provided some details in his autobiography of how he learnt acting, singing, and dancing under them (and other masters). And then he speaks of the king of Baroda, Sawajirao Gaikwad's request of a performance of *Sangeet Shaakuntal* in which he played the role of Priyaṃvadā (Shantaram 1987: 30).[17] Shantaram left the theater; and in 1920 he began his film career. In 1927, Prabhat film company was formed in Pune, and there he made many significant films. Our story begins when he broke away from the Prabhat Film Company and went to Bombay to become the Chief Producer of the Film Advisory Board in Bombay. In 1942 (the year of the Quit India movement), Shantaram left the British government job and founded Rajkamal Kalamandir. He announced that the first film of this studio would be *Shakuntala*.

After a search for a suitable heroine, he cast his wife Jayashree in the lead. A great box-office success, *Shakuntala* ran for one hundred and four weeks at the

Swastik Theatre in Bombay. 'A new hand-colored print of the B&W *Shakuntala*' was shown in the silver jubilee week (Shantaram 2003).

At first glance, the popularity of the film could be seen as stemming from images that are prototypes of the Orientalist imagination with the figure of the woman as object of the gaze. The dresses, gestures, and postures, and the set design are all borrowed from popular images of an ancient India available through pictures, posters, and films (Indian as well as foreign). Shantaram put in extra efforts in terms of money and imagination.

The film begins with young girls bedecked with flowers dancing into the frame towards the camera. They sit around a sage who tells them about the land of the Aryans (*Āryāvarta*)—a land of exceptional women—and proceeds to tell the story of Śakuntalā's birth. More visual pleasure follows, as the celestial dancer Menakā dances and sings, "Without love, all knowledge is useless." She rouses the sage Viśvāmitra from his deep meditation; the film suggests they make love and Śakuntalā is born. The father goes back to his meditation and the sorrowing mother is taken away by other *apsarās*. Birds protect the infant and then the sage Kaṇva picks her up to raise her.[18]

Śakuntalā makes a theatrical entry here; upset by the traditional narration she tells the sage, "You want to tell everyone Father-Kaṇva is not my real father?" The sage asks for forgiveness and promises he will never hereafter relate this story. Wrenching the narrative away from a sage, Śakuntalā becomes the active narrative agent. A long sequence hereafter depicts the girls playing, swimming, and teasing each other. There is the continuation of the conventional visual pleasure elements; at the same time, gradually the women are invested with a rare subjectivity (under a benign patriarchy) through narrative and visual means—something that is strengthened with the entry of the hero.

The sequence begins with Duṣyanta (Chandramohan) as a perpetrator of fear; Śakuntalā is compared to the scared and endangered hermitage deer. In one shot, the king's pointed arrow occupies menacingly the entire forefront of the frame, framing Śakuntalā in the background. The shot cuts back to her first close-up: her eyes open wide—the heroine's doe eyes are capable of flashing in anger. Śakuntalā rebukes the king for scaring the animals and disturbing the tranquility of the *ashram*. But of course, soon she falls under his charm and persuasive ways.

Chandramohan's large penetrating light-colored eyes had become famous since *Amritmanthan* (Marathi/Hindi, 1934), a former Prabhat film by Shantaram. He gazes at Śakuntalā; less sure of herself, she asks, "What are you looking at?" He replies, "The doe has run away; I am looking at the eyes of the doe." Later, when he will miss her, he will remember only those eyes. The film thus cuts back and forth between showing the heroine as delicate and coy, but also strong and free to pursue her wishes. She is timid and vulnerable (hence desirable) as well as in possession of a strong and positive personality (hence admirable and desirable).

Following the original story, the king hides and looks at the girls. But his gaze is consistently interrupted by the girls' Look—as they similarly eavesdrop (while following the heroine protectively and inquisitively). And then Śakuntalā begins to look back at Duṣyanta; and her gaze lengthens as she falls in love or is progressively trapped by the hunter—as the king is called repeatedly. So, Shantaram visually articulates the male voyeuristic aspect of the Kālidāsa play, only to constantly undercut it by the female gaze. We could find reformist spirit behind this manner of representation by a male director; we could also see a modernist spirit desiring better equity between men and women.[19]

This way of visual construction and editing pattern is linked to or drawing upon the Indian aesthetics and devotional performative tradition, whereby the audience or spectator looks on or gazes at the dual-figure of divine lovers or a god-devotee pair; *both* become the source of the gaze; the audiences are made to identify with both—with no one character chosen over another (Chatterjee 2005: 95). Also, love-tales traditionally are cast in the mold of a devotional film; the spectator gazes at the mortal couple, the lovers, in the same way they would at God (*Bhagavān*) and God's favorite devotee (*bhakta*). Film aesthetics in such cases follow a traditional spectatorial position—a triangular relationship forms between spectator, God, and devotee (Cutler 1987: 29).

Śakuntalā's adoptive father Kaṇva returns to the hermitage, but does not command her presence when the entire hermitage is gathered to welcome him back. He says instead, "I will go and meet with her." The sage sees the royal ring on his adoptive daughter's finger, as she shyly covers her face with her hands. Śakuntalā asks, "Father, have I done something wrong?" The sage says, "With the education you have received, you are incapable of any wrong." She sings, "My father has agreed to my wishes!" The sequence would have been revolutionary for the audiences, at a period when love tales were so often about generational conflict.[20] The first melodramatic episode occurs when Śakuntalā leaves the hermitage to go to her husband's house.

The court sequence then is long drawn, as Śakuntalā tries to argue and plead. Like a classical heroine she swoons on Duṣyanta's refusal, crying, "I have no father's home; I have no husband's home; so, I belong to no one!" However, then Shantaram turns his heroine into the epic heroine—and more. Bidding her to remain in the palace, the hermitage people (mother-Gautami, Śāraṅgarava, and others) leave. The king offers her shelter, addressing her traditionally as a "weak woman" (*abalā*)! Śakuntalā now flares up. "Who is weak! Who is pitiable?" Repeating several times to herself she would take care of herself and the child she is about give birth to, she leaves.

A series of images made up of dissolves and superimpositions show the young (pregnant) woman stomping over grass and gravel, crossing mountain passes and rivers. This is an enraged woman forgotten and abandoned after being desired and caressed, a woman who can look after herself without assistance, without dissolving into tears and grief. Her father calls out from the other side of a river; she asks for his blessings but carries on her journey. When she drops down with exhaustion, mother Menakā takes her to the heavenly abodes. Śakuntalā rebukes her, asking where she was when she most needed her. Again she is on her journey across the earth and stops when it is time for her child to be born. It is quite amazing to see Jayashree, Shantaram's second wife abandon the traditional stoop of the representation of a *good and docile* damsel and straighten up in these scenes.

She was well into her pregnancy (with her first child) when these scenes were being shot. One can see her get easily into the role of a mother determined to protect her child.

Śakuntalā seeks shelter in a hermitage that reminds her of home. The day approaches—sage Mārīca, the patriarch of the *āśram* asks the female anchorites why they are not with Śakuntalā; they report Śakuntalā has refused all help. Śakuntalā delivers her child all by herself and emerges out to show her newborn to the assembly outside and announces she has decided to stay and bring him up on her own—the sage assents. Śakuntalā raises and educates her son in this hermitage "where lions and deer play freely." Along with other lessons, the boy learns: "only when boys are unable to look after themselves, they need a father's identity." This is the reply Duṣyanta gets when he meets the boy. He is further stunned when Śakuntalā pretends she has forgotten him, "just as he had." Echoing his sharp words at the court, she tells him: "Why are you telling me you and I are related—men are full of deceit and they try to trick innocent women."[21]

Shantaram was asked not to make his first film in Bombay—an adaptation of the Śakuntalā story, as two previous ones had allegedly failed. Adamant to pursue this project and wondering why such a world-famous play should not yield successful films, the director began to read "all the versions in English, Marathi, and Hindi" (Shantaram 1987: 333–56). As he read the Kālidāsa play, he thought there was something "wrong." The mother of a valorous son must not be so weak and weepy—he thought. "And when I read the original story in the *Mahābhārata*, I realized how without any hesitation Kālidāsa had made many changes to the root-story by the creator of the epic, the great Vyāsa. Now, my road was open before me."

I suggest that while planning this film Shantaram had closely followed contemporary writings in Marathi, for example, the introduction to the printed versions of *Sangeet Shaakuntal.* The preface and two introductions of the ninth edition, which I have consulted, showcase the nature of contemporary discussions.[22] Some are totally Orientalist and the argument runs on these lines: a few decades ago, not many in India were well versed in Sanskrit and the country had forgotten this play; when William Jones translated it, Kālidāsa became world famous like Shakespeare; but then, though the play was first revived in the West, and it is possible the foreigner got the full flavor and understood every nuance—still it remains for Indians to show what the play actually is or stands for through their performances. Both introductions to the book carry some comparisons of various translations. Arguing Kirloskar's one to be the best, they engage in moralistic discussions of how the sexually charged scenes should be put into word and staged.

Shantaram's film is marked by these discussions and debates. By this period of cultural renaissance in Maharashtra (that began in the nineteenth century) and of social reform in the whole of the country, a film like *Shakuntala* might not be radical, but neither is it an average film fully dedicated to producing entertainment and mindless pleasure. This becomes even more apparent when compared to *Stree* (1961), Shantaram's own color remake of *Shakuntala.*

"*Stree* was unanimously panned by the film critics of the day because it failed to recreate the magic of the earlier film, and as expected failed at the box office"

(Shantaram 2003). The film made in color, with Sandhya[23] as the heroine and the director Shantaram as the hero, is all about male gaze. Explaining his reasons for making yet another adaptation of the Śakuntalā story, Shantaram repeats twice in his autobiography, "I wanted to make amends to the wrongs I had done to Kālidāsa's great creation, the *Abhijñāna-śākuntalam*" (ibid.). The only explanation to this, as I understand, is that earlier he had felt there was *something wrong* in the play, which was the portrayal of the heroine as weak. Trying to make amends, he makes this Śakuntalā coquettish, a typical representation of the Indian woman in the Orientalist-romantic mould. Śakuntalā walks over rocks by steep waterfalls and snow-clad ice peaks; but in this case, she soon becomes weary and her feet bruised. Śakuntalā does not go to any *āśram* but a lion's den—the sequence is quite over the top. Shantaram was impressed with Sandhya's professionalism and dedication and describes how she would go into the circus lion's den and train with the trainer. But then, the film is heavily marked by a director's desire to show himself as young and successful (this was the time when some were advising him to retire). I would further add *Stree* shows the excitement of the modernist project, which is extinguished in the heart of the director, who now wants to be popular somehow.

Important to this chapter is the fact that *Stree* fully employs the cinematic male gaze. The film begins with a song describing a phenomenally beautiful woman—whose beauty is all aspects of the nature gathered together. The song yields animated drawings, which at the end of the song combine to form the title of the film—the Woman. Duṣyanta gallops into the natural surroundings of the hermitage—into the narrative and film—hunting and killing animals. Soon, the anchorites plead with him not to kill and he reins in his chariot. While talking to the young sages, he spots a pair of eyes, which he mistakes initially as belonging to a doe and then realizes they belong to a woman. Thus, the gazing woman is turned into the source of pleasure. He returns to the palace and sings again, reviving his memory of those eyes. The song picturizations employ garish colors and huge sets, paper flowers, and other items of sheer entertainment.

Conclusion

The story of Śakuntalā has spawned innumerable literary, Lutgendorf forthcoming dramatic, and film versions. It has yielded many film remakes (Thapar 2000; Lutgendorf forthcoming). If not the entire story, popular Hindi and other language films continue to carry visual and narrative motifs from the tale. Besides recycling of old stuff, some remakes have yielded interesting reinterpretations and innovations in terms of visual or thematic motif; and *Shakuntala* is a good example. A search for further examples could be taken up and this study taken forward, throwing important additional light upon the studies of literature and culture, cinema and performance in India.

Notes

* I thank Madhavi Kolhatkar, David Smith, Urmila Bhirdekar, Park Kyongsook, and Aniket Jaware for helping variously at different stages of the writing of this chapter.

1 Filmmakers also use this stratagem of the gaze to create fearful or disgusting situations.

2 The term *darshan* is seen as a special feature of Indian cinema and is used widely in film studies around Hindi films made in Bombay. I have spelt the word as transliterated from Sanskrit.

3 Kālidāsa, it seems to me, chooses a specific motif, issue, or discourse in each of his plays and books of dramatic poems; those thematic concerns, visual motifs, and narrative units would then be organizational principle and leitmotifs of the narrative—for example, the concept of *prema* and *kāma* and the concept of friendship (*sakhya*) in love in his *Kumārasambhava.*

4 *Sa kāmena sa kāmāyam mithassamyogo gāndharvaḥ.* A later commentary adds: "such a marriage should later be formalized in the presence of the respective parents."

5 The boy, now named Bharata would become important: not only is the epic named after him, the land of the story too gets to be known as Bhārata.

6 And so Kuntī must abandon Karṇa. Though born with the signs (armband and earrings) of his father, the Sun God, he would be known only as the son of a charioteer (after his adoptive father). I owe these insights to various lectures by Gouri Lad in Pune.

7 While Duṣyanta is away, his mother is observing a fast so he would get a son and the lineage would continue.

8 (1) That which was created first or water; (2) oblation or *havi*; (3) the sacrificer or *hotṛ*; (4 and 5) the Sun and the Moon those that regulate time; (6) that with audio-quality and permeating the universe; (7) that which is the source of and has the quality of all seeds; (8) that, by which a living being has life, and possesses breath (Stoler-Miller 1984). It is tempting to suggest that this list opens up a discussion on the Indian concept of category. Probably, the logic is to assemble several systems while creating apparently one particular category (Kale 1957).

9 References are to Kale's translation (1957). Occasionally I have taken recourse to Stoler-Miller's translation (1984), in which case, I give the page reference to her book.

10 We do not know what kind of discipline was enforced in the days of Kālidāsa, whether only the king and representatives of the upper class were allowed to speak out loudly during a spectacle. We know that plays were staged in royal palaces—and that the king, his court, and the queens with their entourage would be watching. The simultaneity of so many comments could be a ploy to support audience reception. The comments mirror what the audience feels or says aloud.

11 The word is sacred; it is what has value (and coinage). So the word given as a promise is to be kept at all cost. When Duṣyanta gave Śakuntalā the ring, he seemed to indicate that more than his words the visible sign of his authority is of a lasting value.

12 An Indian narrative often has several members of audience and several narrators. This is important to the understanding of Indian cinema.

13 After all that is the intention of a signet ring—the king had given it to Śakuntalā when she was scared of the matter of oblivion that perennially casts a shadow on love. The king, it would seem, always wears one; he obviously is used to giving such rings to those who need to remind him of promises he must keep, of transactions for which he has promised future payment, or payback for services rendered.

14 What the king has painted could be like a *pat* painting, where different spaces are used for different representations, but in different image sizes. This allotment of the painting surface and the choice of image-size might mean many things: perspective, status of persons depicted, priority of people in the narrative, or the priority of the object being shown. But then again, since the question of verisimilitude has been raised in the text—more than once in fact—we cannot ignore the question of perspective. We can say that the question of perspective can be or must be raised, but "perspective" here is not the same as that in the case of the *camera obscura.*

15 A trend of teaching and analyzing this text in this fashion is still extant in Indian universities. Additionally, Śakuntalā is compared with Wordsworth's Lucy. Lucy, Miranda, Śakuntalā and Kapālakuṇḍalā—all these literary figures epitomize the male habit

of seeing woman as nature; the habit in turn is associated with the binary: nature versus culture.

16 In the first plays only the Sutradhāra sang; that was followed by purely prose plays (with neither songs nor instrumental background music). Kirloskar's assistant writes in the foreword (of the ninth edition): "Annasaheb Kirloskar had come to Pune to see such a play *Tara*—an adaptation of Shakespear's *Cymbeline*; but since the performance was delayed, they went and saw the famous *Indrasabhā*, a Parsi Natya Company style musical in Urdu. Kirloskar had a consultation with his troupe about staging such a play in Marathi. The next morning, Kirloskar began to write *Sangeet Shaakuntal*" (Kirsloskar 1921).

17 Govind Ballal Deval was invited to direct the play and Bodas himself trained the actors.

18 Śakuntalā is now fully reinstated in the patriarchal world—and history.

19 As his reasons for leaving Prabhat, he writes about the strong opposition others at the studio had to Shantaram's marriage to Jayashree. According to Shantaram, they would much rather have her live as Shantaram's mistress, but not allow her to continue acting as his wife.

20 This is in congruence with a generation of "father's daughters" at time of Indian Nationalism. While in Prabhat, Shantaram had represented a Nationalist woman in *Kunku/Duniya Na Maane* (Marathi/Hindi, 1939); the celebrated social reformist Shakuntala Paranjapey had played a small role, in which she casts a strong positive influence upon the heroine.

21 There is a period in Indian cinema that can be called *pre-melodrama*—and this film is one example. It is a period when the filmmakers made films with contemporary beliefs and practices and audiences hailed progressive films. Female characters were shown free to enjoy themselves, to follow their desires, and pursue their own happiness. Not that these films are free from iniquity of gender, generation, class, and caste. They are progressive for the time of their making. And they are relevant for our studies today. Interestingly and sadly, such films at times are more radical than films made today, when it is impossible to find a film in which a heroine walks boldly down cities, villages, or mountains.

22 The preface is by the publisher, Ananta B. Patwardhan; two introductions are by S. B. Muzumdar, the actor who played Śakuntalā and became in charge of the company after the death of Annasaheb, and Trimbak N. Sathe, the accountant and manager of Kirloskar Natya Mandali—who was also a practicing advocate.

23 Sandhya began to live with Shantaram in the studio premises after Jayashree divorced and left him. She continues to lead a very reclusive life there.

References

Sanskrit works: translations and editions

Kale, M.R. (ed.) (1957) *Abhijñānaśākuntalam*, Bombay: Bookseller's Publishing Company.

Pāṇḍey, U.C. (ed. and trans.) (1998) *Baudhāyana-dharmasūtram* with Hindi translation, Benares: Chaukhamba Sanskṛt Saṃsthān.

Sukhtankar, V.S. (1971) *The Mahābhārata*: *Text As Constituted in Its Critical Edition*, vol. 1, Pune: Bhandarkar Oriental Research Institute.

van Buitenen, J.A.B. (trans.) (1973) *The Mahābhārata*, vol. 1, Chicago, IL: University of Chicago Press.

Other references

Bhat, G.K. (1985) *Sanskrit Drama: Problems and Perspectives*, New Delhi: Ajanta Publications.

Cannon, G.H. (1953) "Sir William Jones and the 'Śakuntalā'," *Journal of American Oriental Society* 73.4: 198–202.

Chatterjee, B. (1969; 5th edn. 1974) "Śakuntalā, Miranda evaṃ Desdemona," in J.C. Bagal (ed.) *Bankim Racanabali*, vol. 2, Calcutta: Sahitya Sansad.

Chatterjee, G. (2003) *Awara*, New Delhi: Penguin.

—— (2005) "Icons and Events: Reinventing Visual Construction in Cinema in India," in R. Kaur and A. Sinha (eds) *Bollyworld: Popular Indian Cinema through a Transnational Lens*, New Delhi: Sage Publications.

Cutler, N. (1987) *Songs of Experience: The Poetics of Tamil Devotion*, Bloomington, IN: Indiana University Press.

Figueira, D. (1991) *Translating the Orient: The Reception of Śakuntala in the Nineteenth-century Europe*, Albany, NY: State University of New York Press.

Freud, S. (1909; 1966) "Five Lectures on Psychoanalysis," in J. Strachey (trans.) *The Standard Edition of the Complete Psychological Works of Sigmund Freud*, 11: 7–55, London: Hogarth Press.

Gerow, E. (1979) "Plot Structure and the Development of Rasa in the Śakuntalā," *Journal of the American Oriental Society* 99.4: 559–72.

Johnson, W.J. (2001) *The Recognition of Shakuntala*, New York: Oxford University Press.

Kirloskar, A. (1921) *Sangeet Shaakuntal Naatak*, 9th edn., Pune: Aryabhushan Press.

Lutgendorf, P. (forthcoming) "Sex in the Snow: The Himalayas as Erotic Topos in Popular Hindi Cinema," *The Journal of the Association for Nepal and Himalayan Studies.*

Malamoud, C. (D. White trans.) (1998) *Cooking the World: Ritual and Thought in Ancient India*, New Delhi: Oxford University Press.

Matilal, B.K. (ed.) (1989) *Moral Dilemmas in the Mahābhārata*, New Delhi: Motilal Banarsidas.

Mulvey, L. 1975 "Narrative Cinema and Visual Pleasure," *Screen* 16.3: 6–18.

Nandy, A. (1995) "Invitation to an Antique Death: The Journey of Pramathesh Barua as the Origin of the Terribly Effeminate, Maudlin, Self-destructive Heroes of Indian Cinema," in R. Dwyer and C. Pinney (eds) *The History, Politics and Consumption of Public Culture in India*, New Delhi: Oxford University Press.

Nehru, J. (1946) *The Discovery of India*, New York: John Day.

Ranade, A. (1986) *Stage Music of Maharashtra*, New Delhi: Sangeet Natak Academy.

Shantaram, K. (2003) *V. Shantaram: The Legacy of the Royal Lotus*, New Delhi: Rupa.

Shantaram, V. (1987) *Shantarama*, Bombay: Shantaram Foundation.

Stoler-Miller, B. (ed.) (1984) *Theatre of Memory: The Plays of Kalidasa*, New York: Columbia University Press.

Thapar, Romilla. (2000). *Śakuntalā: Texts, Readings, Histories*, New Delhi: Oxford University Press.

Willemen, P. (1986) "The Look, Voyeurism and Dwoskin," in P. Rosen (ed.) *Narrative, Apparatus, Ideology: A Film Theory Reader*, New York: Columbia University Press.

4 *Mṛcchakaṭikam* to *Utsav*

Re-creation of a Sanskrit classic by Girish Karnad

Vidyut Aklujkar

Introduction

Although Girish Karnad has been, for decades, one of India's internationally famous playwrights,[1] actor both on stage and screen, and esteemed director who has a plethora of awards and honors to his credit in every field he has ventured in, somehow his film *Utsav* (1985)[2] was not a commercial success. We are informed that a film based on the Sanskrit play *Mṛcchakaṭikam* (*Utsav*) was conceived by Girish Karnad as early as 1974 when he was the director of the Film and Television Institute in Pune,[3] that it was in incubation for almost a decade, and that earlier, it was to be produced in French by a French director, but finally it was produced by Shashi Kapoor in Hindi/English. It was a big budget film, released simultaneously for the Indian and international market. It had all the right publicity, and there were big names in the film industry associated with it. It had Girish Karnad as its scriptwriter and director, and Shashi Kapoor as its producer; it had a stellar cast including Rekha and Shashi Kapoor, both with many memorable roles to their credit. It also had consummate supporting actors like Shankar Nag, Anupam Kher, and Kulbhushan Kharbanda. The music was by the ever-popular duo of Laxmikant-Pyarelal, background singers were the legendary Lata Mangeshkar, versatile Asha Bhonsle, Anuradha Paudwal, and classical singer Suresh Wadekar; the film had authentic costumes and meticulously designed sets by Nachiket and Jayoo Patwardhan.[4] In addition, the film was studded with delicately erotic scenes, fresh humor, and the usual medley of songs, dances, and wonderfully choreographed sword-fights. In spite of all that, did the film neither last in theaters for long, nor did it succeed financially. Perhaps it fell right through the gap between an art film and a popular run-of-the-mill film, since it seemed to please neither the elite handful nor the masses of veteran hard-core Bollywood film-fans.

Why was this so? Was it too "artsy" for one group and "not enough" for the other? Did it fail to appeal to the public who was too far removed from the classical Sanskrit play *Mṛcchakaṭikam* and the world portrayed in it to appreciate it? Or did it fail to satisfy the cultural connoisseurs and theater critics because they felt that it was too far removed from their old favourite play of Śūdraka? Rekha has played a courtesan in *Umrao Jaan* (1981) and in *Utsav* (1985), but why is she more remembered for her role in the former than the latter? I do not know the answers, I cannot even claim that there are any correct answers for these questions. Instead, I would like to discuss *Utsav* as a re-creation of the Sanskrit play, by noting its significant original contributions, so I begin by analyzing the film first against the background of its sources and then move on to judging it on its own merits as any film finally should be viewed.

The credits at the outset claim that the film is based on two Sanskrit plays *Cārudattam* of Bhāsa (300 CE) and *The Little Clay Cart* by Śūdraka (400 CE).[5] They do not tell us on which one of the translations it is based; however, any one of the several available English translations may have helped.[6] In addition, its vernacular translation was also consistently being performed for more than a century on Marathi stage.[7] Girish Karnad is fluent in Marathi and Kannada. He had served as the President of the Karnataka Nataka Academy in 1976–78, and is fully informed about theater in the regional languages.

Mṛcchakaṭikam has been a popular play for centuries, both in its original Sanskrit and in other modern Indian languages. I shall elaborate on its popularity shortly. *Cārudattam*,[8] ascribed to Bhāsa is incomplete, consisting of only four acts, slightly compressed in diction, but in plot and main characters and dialogues it is essentially similar to the first four acts of the larger and more complex play, *Mṛcchakaṭikam.* Karnad's *Utsav* has taken from *Cārudattam* merely minor details such as the names of certain characters.[9] Therefore, my main discussion will concern *Mṛcchakaṭikam* and *Utsav*. Since *Utsav* refers to its classical sources, a comparison of its contents, characters, dialogues, and outcome with those of its sources seems warranted and perhaps, it may help us to understand the lukewarm reception of the film a bit more. More importantly, it will bring out the differences in the different genres and make us more aware of the need to judge each on its own criteria.

I remember the bewilderment I felt when I first saw the film some years ago. My initial reaction was a mixed one. There was a lot to be admired in the film, and yet there was a strong sense of loss. To a lover of Sanskrit plays, and especially a *Mṛcchakaṭikam* fan, there was a lot that was missing in the film that declared itself to be based on Bhāsa's *Cārudattam* and Śūdraka's *Mṛcchakaṭikam*. Certainly absent was the wealth of *subhāṣitā*s from the original Sanskrit, all those famous aphorisms on poverty, courtesans, women, rain, politics, theft, and so many other topics that we fondly remembered as said by this or that character, so revealing of their values and sophistication, so fitting the incidents, often vital for the progression of the dramatic action and many that have by now become the common cultural heritage of Indians. Without those proverbial wise sayings, which enhanced the audience's enjoyment of the Sanskrit play, but which were woefully missing from Karnad's screen production, the Hindi film appeared to be quite impoverished and lackluster. Then again, the film used none of the original linguistic jokes of Śakāra/Saṃsthānaka, the foolish villain of the play, who not only lisps, hence his name, Śakāra, but who horribly jumbles well-known mythological references so that he comes across as a ridiculously pompous but inimitable villain, the one and only of his kind in the entire Sanskrit literature.

The Saṃsthānaka perceived by Karnad and portrayed by Shashi Kapoor in *Utsav* was totally bereft of the original humor so that he appeared to be only vulgar and crooked, thus forming a darker, monolithic shadow of the memorable Śakāra of Śūdraka. Since *Mṛcchakaṭikam* is loved by Sanskrit scholars and theater-goers in many modern Indian languages alike, to all of them, this loss of the complex personality of Śakāra, who had remained just as complex in translations on Marathi or Bengali stage, was rather too much to swallow. And to top it all, anyone who cherished the original play as the happily ending romance of Cārudatta and Vasantasenā had the final blow to their sensibilities of seeing Cārudatta not united with his ladylove at the end of this so-called festival of love, *Utsav*. Not only that, they had to further accept that in the end of *Utsav*, Vasantasenā herself shuns her worthy lover Cārudatta and goes to Saṃsthānaka instead, the same villain who actually strangles her and leaves her to die in an earlier scene! This was akin to seeing "Sītā run away with Rāvaṇa," as one commentator quipped. With all these major changes, many introduced additions and some minor deletions, *Utsav* was seen as quite far removed from the original popular, complex and sophisticated play. I, and I am sure many others with me, initially felt then that if it was indeed an *Utsav*, a festival of love and arts as it claimed, it had some very discordant notes in the total festive orchestra.

I have since come around to a more balanced, more critical appreciation of *Utsav*. I have seen it many more times, and now regard it as a remarkable re-creation of the themes of the old play in a totally different genre, by a creative genius, just as whimsical and iconoclastic as Śūdraka. In order to understand the journey from my initial reaction to my present awareness, and to place the film in its classical context only to judge it against it, we have to start with the popularity and uniqueness of *Mṛcchakaṭikam* in Indian literature.

Mṛcchakaṭikam *ascribed to* Śūdraka *and its popularity*

Unique in Sanskrit literature is this *prakaraṇa* or social play with its ten acts choc-full of action, and a complex plot, which is a heady mix of politics (*vīra rasa*), Eros (*śṛngāra rasa*) and humor (*hāsya rasa*). It incorporates a multitude of Prakrits or dialects along with Sanskrit used by a cast of colorful characters from all walks of life, such as a scrupulously proud and passionate cat-burglar, a king's brother-in-law who is foolishly pompous and cruel, a former gambler-masseur who becomes a monk, a courtesan with a chaste heart, an impoverished but generous, culturally sophisticated hero, his kind but proud wife, and his loyal but blundering Brahmin friend. Even the minor characters in this play are individuals with memorable personalities. With the multitude of characters and eventful acts, the plot races ahead, at an enjoyable speed. The whole play emerges as a tapestry with each strand distinct and essential to the final outcome. As H.W. Wells notes,

> To any student of theatrical history, *The Little Clay Cart* must seem almost encyclopedic, so remarkably does it summarize what is known of the theater throughout the world. ... Incident after incident reminds the informed

> reader of outstanding passages in Aristophanes, Plautus, Lope de Vega, Shakespeare, Johnson, Moliere, Goldoni, Strindberg, Pirandello, Shaw, Brecht, or Tennessee Williams. …Western playwrights have quite unwittingly been traversing the same grounds as Śūdraka for over a thousand years. His play, which presents these innumerable analogues, is thus equally compendious and prophetic.
>
> (Wells 1963: 135–6)

Śūdraka, the traditional author of *Mṛcchakaṭikam*, was original not just in conceiving a complex and enjoyable world of down-to-earth and lovable characters. He was unique in showing his disregard to some established Nāṭyaśāstra conventions. Although he observed the usual structure of the *prakaraṇa*, had the introduction by a stage manager and the concluding *Bharatavākya* following the conventional happy ending, he took liberties with some other stage conventions. He introduced a *gaṇikā*, or a courtesan as a heroine along with a chaste wife, and showed sleep, death, and fights on stage against Bharata's stipulations (Raghavan 1993). He also disregarded linguistic conventions and introduced characters like a highly educated, Sanskrit-speaking Brahmin burglar, an uneducated royal relative who speaks only Prakrit, and an accomplished courtesan who speaks both Sanskrit and Prakrit as need be. Śūdraka's dialogues are crisp and humorous, his characters are lovable, his evocative poetic descriptions have been cherished by generations, and some of his sayings have become proverbial. As one major theater critic, Farley Richmond, notes,

> In design and scope it is one of the most ambitious works of Sanskrit dramatic literature. It paints a vivid picture of life in the ancient and culturally important city of Ujjain, in North Central India. …Each and every character emerges with a lively and distinct personality. *Thanks to Śūdraka's keen sense of humor the play is one of the easiest and best to stage in the Western world.* In fact, it reminds one of the more delightful comedies of Plautus. However, its essential moorings remain in Indian philosophy, religion, and social life.
>
> (Richmond *et al.* 1990: 57; italics are mine)

Subsequent stage productions of Mṛcchakaṭikam

No wonder then, that the play has been produced and enjoyed several times over the years both in India and abroad, in the original Sanskrit, and in translations, both in regional languages and in English, and is still being performed by new theater groups.[10] It was probably staged around 600 CE in India in its original Sanskrit. But 1300 years later, it was the first Indian play performed at UC Berkeley's Greek Theater (Wohlsen 2005). It became the first major production of an Indian drama on US soil. In 1907, it was staged "with two live elephants, two live zebras, and a caste of hundreds." Its director was a British actor, Garnet Holme, who "took pains to observe authentically Indian theatrical traditions," as reported in a contemporary review (quoted ibid.). The production used the text of Arthur William Ryder's 1905 translation for the Harvard Oriental Series. The same text was used for another American production of *The Toy Cart*, on Friday, December 5, 1924, staged at the New York Neighborhood Playhouse, presented by the National Theatre Conference (Lal 1964: 77). We are told that its cast was all American, but the background music was played by two Indians, on sitar and esraj.

In the two prominent theatrical traditions of India, Bengal and Maharashtra, *Mṛcchakaṭikam* has been cherished as a favorite play, perhaps more so in Marathi, than in Bengali. The troupe Bahurupee directed by Kumar Roy staged the play in Calcutta in the last century. In Maharashtra, *Mṛcchakaṭikam* was performed in 1887 for the first time in Marathi on Marathi stage in Pune, by Lalit-kalotsav Mandali. Since then, it has been performed by different theatrical companies continuously on Marathi stage till the present times.[11] The text for the first and all further performances comes from Govind Ballal Deval's transcreation of it as *Saṅgīta Mṛcchakaṭika*. In its *prastāvanā*, Deval notes his indebtedness to an earlier, and more authentic Marathi translation of the entire play by Parashuram Pant Tatya Godbole.[12]

Deval's version was created specifically for stage production, so he did introduce some changes to the structure but kept the essence of the original intact. He compressed the ten acts into seven by joining the third and fourth into one as well as the sixth, seventh and eighth into one. He also deleted some stage fights and added a few more words to Vasantasenā's speeches. However, his characters are true to the original, and the play culminates exactly as in the original. In place of the *śloka*s/verses in the Sanskrit original, Deval introduced *pada*s or songs set in appropriate *rāgas*.[13] These were sung by generations of musically blessed actors such as the famous female impersonator Balgandharva, and actresses Meenakshi, and Jayamala Shiledar. The mood-creating songs were so popular, that they became the signature of the play. Even today they are fondly remembered and sung on the Marathi stage, radio, in concerts, schools and households.

Mṛcchakaṭikam ***on the silver screen***

Since the play had been so popular with scholars and on stage, even after the advent of cinema in India since 1896, it continued to be adapted to the new genre and new technology. Although Indian movies are greatly indebted to classical Sanskrit theater, especially in adhering to the "happy ending" convention of Bharata and incorporating the song/dance repertoire to replace the mixture of verses and dialogues in Sanskrit plays, nevertheless not many Sanskrit plays have been produced in film versions. The only other play of the classical Sanskrit theater that enjoyed more popularity in the new genre was Kālidāsa's *Abhijñāna-Śākuntalam*, which was produced at least thirteen times with the title, *Shakuntala*, in different languages (EIC q.v.). Next to it, *Mṛcchakaṭikam* has had several incarnations on the silver screen in India. *The Encyclopedia of Indian Cinema* by Ashish Rajadhyaksha and Paul Willemen indicates it first appeared as *Vasantsena* (1929) in a silent film produced by the pioneer of film D.G. Phalke (1870–1944) in Mumbai. Another silent film named *Vasantsena* (a.k.a. *Mricchakatik, The Toy Cart*) was produced in 1930 by Mohan Bhavnani. B.D. Garg notes that "Bhavnani's film brought members of the educated classes (Enakshi Rama Rao, Kamaladevi Chattopadhyaya, Nalini Tarkhud, and Jaikishan Nanda) to the screen as actors and actresses, which helped break down prejudice against the profession" (Garg 1996). As the year 1931 brought sound to the movies, *Mṛcchakaṭikam* again appeared with its newly found voice on the screen. *Vasantsena* a.k.a. *Mricchakatik* in Hindi was produced by J.P. Advani in 1934, *Vasantsena* by P.K. Raja Sandow appeared in Tamil in 1936, *Vasantsena* by Ramayyar Sirur appeared in Kannada in 1941, *Vasantsena* directed by Gajanan Jagirdar, and produced by Atre Theatres, in Marathi appeared in 1942. *Vasantsena* by B.S. Ranga in Telugu in 1967, and *Vasantsena* by K. Vijayan in Malayalam in 1985 (EIC q.v.).

Girish Karnad's *Utsav* as a re-creation of *Mṛcchakaṭikam*

The title: original yet authentic

The fact that all of the film versions above have chosen the name of the courtesan heroine Vasantasenā as the title for the film speaks for the enduring fascination the character of Vasantasenā commands in the hearts of the audiences. As a contrast, almost all vernacular translations of the play retained the original Sanskrit title, *Mṛcchakaṭikam*,[14] showing their loving faith in the classic and perhaps, not wanting to part company with the magical aura of the original literary source. The title of the Sanskrit play, [*mṛt+śakaṭikam*] refers to the little clay cart which is given to Cārudatta's son to play, but which he dislikes as a poor substitute for the gold carts with which the other children play. It stands as a symbol of poverty of the child, and his household, but is converted into a precious toy by the generosity of the courtesan, who adorns it with her jewelry, so as to please the child. The little clay cart remains fragile, just like love or life, but it serves to please the one who possesses it, for the time being. The significance of the little clay cart and its transformation is picked up again, in an exchange of carts of the hero and the villain later on in the play, whereby fortunes are lost and won for the heroine Vasantasenā and the political rebel Āryaka who are found riding in them. The title shows Śūdraka's originality in that, instead of weaving the name of the hero or the heroine into the title of the play as was the convention in Sanskrit drama,[15] he chooses to focus on a little object in his play suggesting many nuances of meaning thereby.

Girish Karnad, following in spirit the Sanskrit playwright, chooses a different title, thereby revealing that he is producing a film from a different perspective. Unlike the title of the play ascribed to Bhāsa, *Cārudattam*, or *Daridracārudattam*, which centers on the hero, and unlike the previous motion picture titles, which give prominence to the heroine, Karnad chooses to call his movie, *Utsav*, which means "festival," thereby alluding to a mood of joyous exuberance, which he strives to capture in his film.

In selecting this title, he is not too far removed from his source, though. Sanskrit scholars will recall that the word occurs in the seventh verse of the prologue (*prastāvanā*) of *Mṛcchakaṭikam*, where the stage manager, or *sūtradhāra*, introduces the hero, the heroine, and the contents of his new production. Here I offer a translation of the verses:

In the city of Avantī, (there is) the young, poor Brahmin merchant, Cārudatta, and the courtesan (*gaṇikā*) Vasantasenā, like the splendor of Spring, who is attracted to him due to his qualities.

King Śūdraka has composed all this based on the *festival* of their passionate union, and also (to show) the politics, the flaws in justice, the behavior of the crooked, and destiny (verses 6 and 7).

Mṛcchakaṭikam is not just based on the festival of love between the hero and the heroine, its action also centers around the festival of Spring, *vasantotsava*, in which the courtesan named Vasantasenā ("the army of Spring") has to play a major role, but which in fact turns into a festival of political insurgence bringing in a fresh new order. Drawing upon all these aspects from the source, Karnad's *sūtradhāra* elaborates on the meaning of his title by saying, that his new play (*khel* is the Hindi word used) is "the festival of Spring, of beauty, color, taste, fragrance, it's a festival of the freshness of body and mind, a festival of the love of the courtesan Vasantasenā" (*vasant kā utsav, rūp raṅg kā, ras gandh kā, tan man ke yauvan kā utsav, veśyā vasantsenā ke prem kā utsav*).

Verbal to visual: a balance of loss and gain

The transformation of *Mṛcchakaṭikam* from stage to screen is, first and foremost, a transformation from the verbal to the visual mode of enjoyment. As the classical Sanskrit theater did not use scenery, or stage props, in most of the stage happenings, the mood, the time, the nature, the atmosphere and any other surrounding details of the action were conveyed to the audience by the verbal descriptions, or miming (bodily acting/*āṅgika abhinaya*) of the actors.[16] This is why we get all those verses in the play describing the rains, the darkness of the night, the festivities and many other scenes. All this changes to simply following the eye of the camera in the film. Such a transformation allows the director of the film freedom in two directions. He can expand a verbal expression to flesh out the theme, and also compress a lengthy descriptive scene into several short sequences. Here I cite examples of both ways Karnad has exercised in his film.

The first is one in which reported action is transformed by being directly shown. In the play, (Act VI, between verses 1 and 2), there is one sentence spoken by the rebel Āryaka, which means, "and thanks to the graces of our dear friend Śarvilaka, I am freed from captivity." Instead, Karnad uses a whole sequence of shots to actually show us the thief Śarvilaka/Sajjal being taken to Āryaka's jail cell by the nameless mastermind accomplice of Āryaka, Sajjal using his precious touch to carve out three artistic holes in three walls to enter Āryaka's cell, and finally break away all his chains to free Āryaka from his shackles. We also see that he has left the rope tied to the ceiling from which they have descended into the cell, for Āryaka who uses it to climb up and escape just in time before the guards can get to him. As eye-witnesses to all these events, we get to enjoy the thrill of the story unfolding right in front of our eyes.

On the other hand, half of the entire fourth act of the play is devoted to the journey of Cārudatta's friend Maitreya through eight fun-filled courts of Vasantasenā's huge mansion teaming with artisans practicing body-painting, singers singing, dancing girls practicing with their dance-teachers, and maid-servants rushing with their tasks, tame animals roaming, birds cooing, and garden flowers blooming in the background. The consecutive scenes where he goes on describing all that he sees as he walks through the mansion, get summed up in the film in the fluid movement of the camera through the mansion. The shots are spread out over different scenes as when Maitreya or the thief Sajjal, or the masseur enter the house. No words are wasted. Similarly for the poetic verbal descriptions of the tropical rain, or moonlight that are in the play, the eye of camera does the job in the film.

Although this change has its obvious advantages, in congealing action, and quickening the pace of the film, it also robs us of the wonderful poetry of the original, which is a major part of the attraction of the Sanskrit play. In the vernacular translations of the play, the poetic dimension is not lost totally, but retained through songs/*padas* in place of *ślokas*. Being a playwright or literary artist himself, Karnad is well aware of what is lost in the transition from verbal to visual. But he is more concerned with another loss. As he says about *Utsav*, "What I hoped to do was to revive the two qualities which ancient Indian literature had, but which we seem to have lost in the course of the last thousand years—sensuousness and humor. Not sex, but sensuousness, the poetic, tactile quality of it" (Karnad 1984). In *Utsav*, Karnad incorporates poetry in action, by filming some lyrical moments such as the first encounter of the hero and the courtesan, and he does compensate for the lack of verbal artistry by including some exquisitely sensuous sequences.

Lyrics and poetry: memorable moments

In 1986, the Filmfare award for the best lyricist was given to Vasant Dev for the song, *Dil kyoṃ Bahkā* in *Utsav*. The best playback singer (female) award for that year also went to Anuradha Paudwal for the song *Mere man baje mridaṅg* in *Utsav*. There are only four songs in this movie, far less than the usual Bombay cinema formula of songs per footage but they are tastefully placed. Cārudatta's song, at the beginning of the film, sung by Suresh Wadekar, a classical singer with good understanding of the power of diction and a husky voice, creates the lyrical, sensuous mood for the first meeting of the hero and the heroine. The words of the song are:

> *sāñjh ḍhale, gagan tale, ham kitne ekākī*
> *choṛ cale, nainoṃ ko kiranoṃ ke pākhī*

The song begins with a note of longing as Cārudatta voices his own lonesomeness at the darkening hour of dusk. He is lonesome for companionship, but not just any company would do. He is shown covering the bird-cage to muffle the sounds the annoying bird is making. His lonesomeness is not merely due to his wife's leaving him to visit her parents, and the absence of his friend and servants from his house, it may refer to the wistful lonesomeness an artist feels from time to time. In the next line, he comments on the birds of bright rays which have flown away, leaving the eyes lonesome. In that, he may be suggestively referring to his musician friends who have stopped visiting him now that they have found him lacking in funds. The repetition of these lines thickens the mood of lonesomeness of Cārudatta, as the melody and meaning of the words make the hiding courtesan stop in her tracks and listen. Enchanted by the notes, her slender fingers play the beat on the dark wooden pillar beside her. The camera moves from her ornate fingers beating the rhythm to his unadorned ones moving on the Bānsurī at his lips. As the song progresses, the hero's mood leans towards optimism, and he sings:

> Soon the night will approach, covered with a garment of fire-flies.
> She will tell every tale in the notes fragrant with the night-jasmin.

Just as he is singing these lines, beautiful Vasantasenā, covered in a dark garment, but adorned with bright firefly-like jewelry is seen approaching. The longing and the hope expressed in the song perfectly match the mood of the wistful hero and the approach of the heroine hoping to take shelter in his secure house, and generous heart.

The two heroines: on stage and on screen

As I mentioned before, Śūdraka had already introduced two heroines in his play, Dhūtā, the proud but compassionate wife of Cārudatta and mother to his young son, and the wealthy and beautiful courtesan Vasantasenā, who is attracted to Cārudatta because of his music, his generosity, and straightforward character. Śūdraka's Vasantasenā is an ever-popular literary heroine since she is an ideal woman combining beauty, talent, artistic sophistication, and loyalty in her love. She is seen avoiding the advances of the uncultured royal relative, but is attracted to the virtues and cultural sophistication of Cārudatta. She is the courtesan with a heart of gold, as she is genuinely in love with the hero even though he has lost his wealth. She is also herself very generous and appreciative of adventure and love in others, as she helps rescue the masseur from his debtors, and sets free her own servant so that she can live a respectable life as a lawfully wedded wife to her fiancé.

Generally, the impression one gets from the play is that Cārudatta's wife is senior to the courtesan and therefore a loser in the end to the inevitable conquest of the courtesan's beauty and youth. Karnad has infused more life into both his heroines, by one brilliant stroke of imagination. He has shown the wife of Cārudatta to be younger than the courtesan, played by Rekha, who is actually older than the actress who plays the wife, here named Aditi. This little change alters the situation, and introduces new possibilities, which Karnad carries out to their logical culmination, as we shall see shortly.

Cārudatta's wife, Dhūtā, in *Mṛcchakaṭikam* stands out by her grace, loyalty, and understanding. She finds a way to offer her precious pearl garland to help her husband compensate for the theft of the ornaments of Vasantasenā from their house. When Vasantasenā returns her the garland through their housemaid, Dhūtā is seen as a proud and polite wife, not accepting the handout, and sending the following message with the maid, "I cannot take back what is gifted to you by my husband. Please know that my husband is my ornament" (Act VI).

Karnad's conception of Cārudatta's wife is strikingly different. For one, he changes the name: instead of "Dhūtā" which means "cleansed, purified," Karnad chooses "Aditi," the Vedic mother of the Sun, thereby altering her projected personality. Further, Aditi is young, beautiful, happy in motherhood, but easily excitable. She chides Cārudatta for his domestic lapses, storms to her parents' house whenever she is upset, taking the child and the maid, but also returns home one time to meet Vasantasenā knowing that she will enter the house as soon as she finds Cārudatta alone. The meeting, which underscores the change in the respective ages of the two heroines, is a twist in the tale which is totally Karnad's own contribution. Although it does not alter the course of subsequent events in the film, which essentially follows the main plot of the play, Karnad uses his twist to develop the characters' respective reactions to the love triangle, and ties it neatly with another twist at the end.

The meeting of minds: reflections and role-playing

The first meeting of the two heroines in the film as envisaged by Karnad is not a confrontation as one would imagine. Instead, we see a refreshing exchange of courtesies, favors, garments, jewelry, honest views on intimate details and light-hearted questions and answers, played out in a song sequence that won the movie one of its Filmfare awards. Sumita S. Chakravarty's comment on this unusual meeting sums up the reaction of feminist criticism: "The female bonding shown between the good, understanding wife and the courtesan plays out the ultimate male fantasy: the freedom of a man to move without guilt between a nurturing wife and a glamourous mistress" (Chakravarty 1993: 284).

However, in view of further developments in the film, and keeping in mind Karnad's final twist where Vasantasenā is forgotten by Cārudatta in his liberating moment of regaining his life and his wife, I think that Karnad has done more than just indulge in the ultimate male fantasy. He has shown us the other side of the overused coins of the "silently suffering, pure wife" and the "heartless, unscrupulous other woman." Karnad shows his sensitive understanding of female psyche in creating the one-time role-playing in which both women indulge in this meeting, but from which they have to extricate themselves in the end. Both Aditi and Vasantasenā come across as real women, at once strong and vulnerable, willing to try to understand "the other," but subject to changes in their attitudes and actions in accordance with the reality of their changing circumstances. We see them awkwardly trying to exchange courtesies, slowly warming up and developing something close to sisterhood in a short while, to the bewilderment of the housemaid who cannot fathom the behavior of her mistress. But in the last, telling scene of the sequence we see them both framed against each other standing on the threshold of Cārudatta's house. Vasantasenā is about to get into the cart parked on the road, supposedly sent by him for her to come to their rendezvous in the garden, and Aditi is silently standing aside to see her off. Vasantasenā wants to reach out to her in her newly forged friendship, but whatever had developed inside the four walls seems to escape her outside. In that public sphere, as she stands on the threshold of her lover's house, she hesitates to touch his honored wife, and with a half-sure gesture towards her, silently moves on.

Karnad has presented the entire sequence of the heroines' meeting very carefully, by mounting actions and reactions in an intricate pattern, which shows at once his debt to his sources and his originality. Only the scene of Vasantasenā with the little clay cart and Cārudatta's son is the kernel derived from the sources, around which Karnad has wrapped his original scenes between the two heroines. After Aditi has offered a sandalwood-scented bath to Vasantasenā, we see the courtesan sitting with a mirror in her hand, admiring her bejewelled beauty, while Aditi stands behind her with another mirror in her hand, showing Vasantasenā her coiffure. Vasantasenā, who is pleasantly surprised at Aditi's lack of jealousy offers to adorn Aditi with all her fine gold jewelry, which gesture the latter accepts in her youthful curiosity and willingness. Vasantasenā removes her own garments to put on a simple sari, which makes her look like the unadorned wife, and then just like an older sister, she adorns young Aditi and offers her a mirror. The mirror reflects to the young wife an altered image of her self, beguiling just like the courtesan. Both heroines have thus crossed over their present states for a moment and seem to enjoy their altered appearances. The mirror now held by Vasantasenā offers us a view of Aditi's reflected glory, which is rather removed from her impoverished reality. As Aditi's child approaches, she returns to reality, and hastens to remove the ornaments, so that he does not get upset at her sudden transformation. At the same time, Vasantasenā's unadorned appearance reassures the child that she is a motherly woman, just like his own mother. He had recoiled from her in her earlier adorned appearance, but now he is happy to accept her jewelry for his little clay cart. The child's earlier rejection and later acceptance of Vasantasenā serve to remind us that appearances hide real persons behind them and that only by going beyond appearances can one get a glimpse of the entire person, an awareness quite in line with Śūdraka's perception of his characters. Karnad's direction succeeds in enhancing our understanding of the complex reality, in the sequence of the role-change by his use of the double gaze, that of the impartial mirror and the innocent, outspoken child.

Appearances and reality: rejection and acceptance

The interplay of appearances and reality is a constant of any self-reflexive artistic genre, especially theater and film. All actors/actresses impersonate others, they appear to be what they are not, and by imitating reality, their art confers reality on illusion. In art, illusion becomes the reality. In life, when real appears as an illusion, it inspires philosophers to speculate on the nature of *māyā* and *Brahman*. In Śūdraka's play, we have many instances of mistaken identities, showing cross-currents of appearances and reality. To Śakāra, when he is chasing the courtesan, Cārudatta's housemaid appears like Vasantasenā, while to Cārudatta, Vasantasenā hiding in his house appears like his housemaid in the darkness of the night. To Maitreya, who is under the spell of sleep, the thief appears to be his friend, Cārudatta, so he thrusts in the hands of the thief the very ornaments he is supposed to guard. To the judge, the innocent Cārudatta appears to be the culprit homicide/ thief due to the sudden appearance of Vasantasenā's ornaments. The cart sent by Śakāra appears like the cart sent by Cārudatta to Vasantasenā, so that she rides in it and falls in the hands of the villain. In addition to all these instances from the play, which Karnad retains in the film, he often ties the interplay of appearances and reality with the dynamics of rejection and acceptance as we saw in the jewelry exchange sequence above. It is a recurring twin-theme throughout Karnad's film.

Even in the introductory scene of Karnad's *sūtradhāra* and the *naṭī*, we see the actress wrinkle her nose at the mention of the prostitute, *veśyā* Vasantasenā, and sneer with her hand held sideways away from her. Karnad, through his *sūtradhāra* explains that the courtesan is just another artist, like them, practicing her art as her livelihood.[17] He appeals to the good sense of the actress and his audience to accept the reality of the courtesan's life by seeing through the appearances. The same goes for the art of theft, the art of practicing politics, or the art of love. Even a common thief can be an educated Brahmin, proud of his dexterity and agility, and practicing a code of strict ethics even in his act of stealing. Being deluded by outward appearance leads one to be rash and reject the complexity of life. A mature audience is more receptive and able to see the reality hidden behind appearances. In his introduction, Karnad has allowed another self-reflexive dig at the *sūtradhāra*, who can be viewed as the alter ego of the director as he is orchestrating the performance of the play. When the actress learns that the *sūtradhāra* is going to play Vātsyāyana,[18] the writer of the manual of love, *Kāma-sūtra*, she rejects the idea as unlikely and suggests that her experienced reality may be different from the proposed appearance, but finally comes around to accepting the transformation as something attainable through his art.

The most memorable and humorous sequence of scenes in the film where appearances alter reality and force a viewer to reject its legitimacy is an original creation of Karnad. It is where the sexologist Vātsyāyana is gazing from his elevated peeping position in the brothel trying to grasp what he believes is another posture of love-making when it is actually something quite different. We know what he doesn't know, and so we can laugh at him. The pedant is shown to be a captive of his own perspective, and unwilling to change his (physical and academic) position. Although circumstances would seem to force him to, he cannot accept what he sees as another posture, as it seems too farfetched, and unbelievable. So, instead of investigating further, he rationalizes his rejection of the witnessed event, and his suppression of his academic data, by saying that

"We are writing this manual for the consumption of the common person. But this is something extraordinary. It's quite beyond human imagination. It is better to pass over it in silence." To quote Phillip Lutgendorf's sharp assessment,it is "a scene that skewers, in one poke, both the pomposity and voyeurism of academic scholarship."[19]

The last link of this series of turnabouts is the final scene of the film, the crowning glory of Karnad's direction, where Vasantasenā's earlier rejection of Saṃsthānaka turns into an acceptance of his attentions. So far, Vasantasenā has tried her best to vouch for Cārudatta's innocence, and stand by Aditi in their ordeal of watching the impending execution of the man they love. But when he is finally set free, young Aditi runs to embrace him, he responds wholeheartedly and Vasantasenā watching their joyous reunion from far away feels that she is the odd one out. She runs away in tears, and perhaps in that moment of epiphany, comes to terms with the reality of her ultimately lonely position in the society as a courtesan. This scene contrasts with the initial scene of their meeting where the hero is lonesome, and the courtesan has been able to join him and thus, end his lonesomeness. She may not be so fortunate herself. Saṃsthānaka, the formerly pompous royal relative is now seen as a fallen and defeated person who is beaten up by the enraged people, and rejected by his former companion. However, he is still haunted by the beauty of the unattainable Vasantasenā, and troubled by his own insurmountable guilt at having strangled her in his fit of rage. Since Vasantasenā has now experienced the bitter taste of rejection, and the unattainability of *her* lover, she becomes more sympathetic to his plight and therefore, she is seen in the final frame of the film entering Saṃsthānaka's place and trying to uplift the fallen fellow. In contrast to the initial bejewelled vision of hers when she is followed by Saṃsthānaka, in this final frame, she is seen unadorned, sedate, and resigned. In Śūdraka's play, the newly crowned king issues a decree whereby he confers wealth upon Cārudatta and respectability upon Vasantasenā, but Karnad probably rejects such a conventional "happy ending" as highly contrived. He offers us the more mundane, more humane reality of solidarity in defeat, and shows a pairing of societal rejects. The last scene shows us the bruised and beaten Saṃsthānaka crossing over a threshold, with the help of Vasantasenā's outstretched hands, suggesting perhaps, his redemption and her disenchantment. Perhaps this is an instance of *ghāyal kī gati ghāyal jāne, dūsarā na koya* or "it takes one wounded soldier to understand the pain of another." Viewed in this light, the ending seems more uplifting.

The **uttarīya** *exchange: reversed direction, altered significance*

It is a mark of a creative genius that Karnad takes the themes or concepts that are significant in one sense in the play and presents them in a different pattern, or context thus managing to alter their suggestive nuances. Karnad often toys with Śūdraka's favorite concepts in such a manner that they take on a new life, but become just as memorable as in the play. Take, for example, the exchange of

Cārudatta's *uttarīya* or upper garment/cloak. In the play, it is a significant garment that plays a multiple role in different contexts. It is a cloak made fragrant with the essence of jasmine flowers and is sent to Cārudatta by one of his older friends. In the first act, when Cārudatta throws it at Vasantasenā in the darkness of his house by mistaking her to be his housemaid, its fragrance assures her that the owner of this garment, Cārudatta, is still young and passionate. For a moment, she holds it close to her heart and imagines future pleasures. [20, 21] Cārudatta tells her (or, as he believes, his maid) to cover his son with it, so that he does not catch chill in the evening breezes, thereby manifesting to the audiences, his love and caring for his son. The *uttarīya* again comes in Vasantasenā's hands later when she hears that it was bestowed upon a fellow by Cārudatta as a reward for his act of valor on the street. This action of the hero speaks to her of his generosity and appreciation of other people's good qualities.

In *Utsav*, the cloak is first seen on and off Cārudatta, as he prepares to go out, and then decides against it, several times as the film begins. So we come to identify it as his garment to go out with. Then when he sees Vasantasenā hiding in the shadows, he mistakes her to be his housemaid, and asks her to give him the garment so that he can then accompany her to go out to his wife's father's house. Vasantasenā spots an opportunity here to come forward and cover him with the cloak, thereby forcing him to take note of her so she can introduce herself.

The direction of the *uttarīya* exchange is deliberately reversed from the play to the film so that it becomes a link in the chain of many such images. Instead of Cārudatta throwing a fragrant garment at the courtesan as in the play, in the film, it is she who covers him with his favorite garment to comply with his request. It is at once a bold and coquettish action, suggesting her initiative in their ensuing relationship. This action of hers also results, at once, in her covering him from the chill outside, and the lonesomeness inside. It is a forerunner of many such actions whereby she covers him later with her love and warmth, covers his wife from head to toe with her own precious ornaments, covers his son's little clay cart with her gold jewelry, and covers for Cārudatta in the scene of his impending execution by appearing there in person, and thereby giving evidence of his innocence.

Vasantasenā's ornaments: from ethics to aesthetics

Another instance of Karnad's creative direction is seen in his handling of the ornaments of Vasantasenā. As it is, the ornaments are highly significant in the play. They go through many hands, and assume different significance for different characters. To begin with, they are a symbol of the courtesan's wealth and position in the society and they show the difference in her and the hero's financial status. Later on, they are a symbol of her trust in Cārudatta as she entrusts him with their safekeeping, when they become the cause of anxiety to his friend Maitreya who is told to guard them at night. They become the desirable loot in the hands of Sajjal, the passionate thief who thinks he can exchange them to buy his beloved's freedom. Finally, they become the unfortunate "evidence" to incriminate Cārudatta in his alleged crime.

Note, however, that the ornaments in the play mainly revolve around ethical issues. They are kept in trust by the heroine with the hero, so he and his wife feel responsible to compensate for them when they get stolen, and although it is the wealth that falls into the thief's hands by an honest mistake, he is forced to return it to its rightful owner, Vasantasenā, and she, in turn, shows the fairness to relieve her maid from her bondage in exchange of the ornaments. Thus they seem forever to give rise to finer nuances of the moral code of conduct of most characters in *Mṛcchakaṭikam*.

All the original significance of the ornaments and shades of moral conduct associated with them are preserved in the film *Utsav*, but Karnad has added some humorous and erotic/aesthetic dimensions as well. In the play, according to the classical theater's stage conventions, the exchange of ornaments would be shown through mime. But in the film, Karnad could add the essential, visual appeal to the ornaments. Hence, some of the most memorable moments in the movie are wound around the intricate and artistic jewelry.[22] There are two or three scenes in which we get to see the clever touch of the director. Out of these, I have already discussed how Karnad handles the jewelry exchange between the two heroines to bring out their subtle emotional exchange. Here I shall discuss how the ornaments are used to handle the erotic exchanges between Cārudatta and Vasantasenā.

The first full view of Vasantasenā we get in *Utsav*, along with Cārudatta is when she removes the dark, upper cloak to reveal her body covered with her exquisite jewelry in his halflit house. The camera imitating Cārudatta's gaze moves slowly from her head to toe, and back again to complete her vision or *darśana*, like that of an Indian goddess adorned in all her finery. The vision stuns the spectator with its breathtaking splendor enhancing Rekha's sculpturesque features. Vasantasenā uses the jewelry to entice the hero by requesting that he help her remove it, as she wants to keep the jewels in his house, so as to avoid being chased by thieves. But of course, all the numerous hooks that Cārudatta has to remove to get it off her, bring him closer and closer to her physical charm, and soon he finds himself hopelessly entangled in the *hooker*'s net. The scene is as humorous as it is sensuous, and the intricate interplay of gazes and golden chains from many angles as the camera moves around the pair is hard to capture in words.

The second time we see Vasantasenā come to Cārudatta is after the jewelry has exchanged several hands and come full circle, in her possession. She comes to him in torrential rain, and this time, Vasantasenā, fully covered in the same fine jewelry, is eager to be near her lover. But again, he faces the daunting task of its torturous removal. At this point, to his relief, she simply removes one little crucial hook, and all of it falls like a net-garment at her feet. When he is puzzled, she remarks coyly that "all those hooks were meant for the thieves!" He understands and they end up laughing together. All these highly original scenes around the ornaments serve to enhance the aesthetic appeal of Karnad's film and make it into a truly enjoyable re-creation.

In conclusion: re-creating a classic—constraints and liberties

In tracing the construction of Karnad's re-creation of a well-loved classic I have so far noted the major changes introduced by him to the characters, such as the relationship of the two heroines, the monolithic villain, and the hero lacking his poetic finesse and sophistication. I have also talked about Karnad's altered perception of the reality of the courtesan's life as reflected in the final outcome of the film. I recognize the strength of his re-creation to be his careful balancing of the poetic, the erotic and the humorous elements in the final production, and therefore, I have traced in detail his treatments of themes such as reality/illusion, garment exchange, and ornaments of the courtesan. In conclusion, I would like to sum up my observations by taking note of what is lost, and what is gained.

Karnad's portrayals of the hero and the villain remain somewhat lackluster due to his omission of many of the original dialogues and behavioral details. To cite one example, Cārudatta in the play is lovable because he is generous, considerate of others, and unaware of his own losses. He shows his appreciation of the fine art of theft by praising the beautifully carved hole in the wall of his burglarized house, and he is sad that the thief had to go empty-handed from his, a fine merchant's house. These and other such finer shades of his character are missing in the film. As I have noted earlier, since the gaze of camera replaces many of Maitreya's fine speeches, and Karnad has also skipped the initial dialogue between Cārudatta and Maitreya on poverty and friendship, we get to see just another stereotypical Brahmin friend of the hero in *Utsav*, in place of the kind, compassionate, observant, sensitive, and humorous character of Maitreya of *Mṛcchakaṭikam*.

Although Karnad's hero and his friend, Maitreya are somewhat lackluster, his heroines are more lively and original. What is lost in the characters of Cārudatta and Maitreya is balanced by Karnad's additions of the highly humorous characters of Vatsyāyana and his disciple. The other minor characters are more or less faithful to the sources and well presented. Karnad has introduced some minor changes that do not essentially harm the progression of the film. For example, the right-hand accomplice of Āryaka (who is Darduraka in the play) remains a nameless character in *Utsav*, for as Karnad's *sūtradhāra* remarks, anonymity and secret manipulation of masses is a mark of the art of politics. Or, the masseur (Saṃvāhaka in the play, *campīvālā* in the film) remains unacquainted with Cārudatta in *Utsav*, whereas in the play, he is formerly in Cārudatta's service, and is one more person to praise the hero to the courtesan, who is already attracted to him. Although in *Utsav*, the masseur simply pretends to know Cārudatta, in order to save himself, Karnad ties in this detail neatly with the renunciation of the masseur, very much in line with the play, by his comment, "if a name of a mere person can save my body (from being beaten by the debtors), the name of God will certainly give me deliverance."

In spite of making such changes to his characters, Karnad has retained authenticity in the film by retaining many stretches of original dialogues intact.

For example, the heated exchanges between the masseur and his debtors in the market, the thief and his beloved on the return of the jewels, Vasantasenā and the thief, the two assassins about to kill Cārudatta, and several such dialogues, although they appear to be quite contemporary and fresh, are in fact Śūdraka's original creations faithfully reenacted by Karnad in the film. These dialogues substantiate his claim of his indebtedness to the classical Sanskrit sources.

Another way in which Karnad manages to retain authenticity in his film, is by intertwining the multiple strands of action as in the original play, by weaving the personal lives of Cārudatta and Vasantasenā with all their friends and servants and the political life of the rebels like Āryaka and his accomplices with the antics of the villainous Saṃsthānaka and his companion. Karnad has deleted some incidents from *Mṛcchakaṭikam*, such as the incident in Act II where Vasantasenā's elephant is out of control, and attacks a monk, who is rescued by Vasantasenā's servant, who in turn is rewarded by Cārudatta.[23] However, such deletions do not hamper the flow of the main course of action, nor do they hurt the overall enjoyment of the film.

Re-creating a classic is always a challenge, where the director/scriptwriter has to achieve a fine balance between authenticity and originality. Offense can be taken by staunch purists and any change can be perceived as sacrilegious. Karnad's *Utsav* did face some such accusations. One erotic scene where the hero drinks the water dripping from the neck of the courtesan had to be removed from the Indian version of the film, thanks to the outraged protests of the religious zealots who were offended by it. However, the film did receive some very favorable reviews, and it continues to be enjoyed in video and DVD formats by worldwide audiences. Puritans and custodians of culture who are possessively overprotective of Sanskrit classics may raise a storm, but after the dust dies down, I believe that *Utsav* may be enjoyed by international audiences as a highly original re-creation of *Mṛcchakaṭikam*, remarkably authentic in reflecting the spirit and exuberance of Śūdraka's festival of love, art, and life.

Notes

1 A casual search on Google reveals 42,000 entries on him. Among his many credits and awards are a Rhodes Scholarship in Oxford, a Homi Bhabha fellowship for creative work in folk theater, the Karnatak Nataka Academy Award (1984), Padma Shri Award (1974), Padma Bhushan Award (1992), and Jnanpith Award (1999). Among his ten plays are *Yayati* (1961), *Tughlaq* (1964), *Hayavadana* (1971), *Nagamandala* (1988), *Taledanda* (1990), *The Fire and The Rain* (1994), and the most recent one, *Heap of Broken Images* (2005). In addition, he has acted in more than 40 films, directed 10 films, and written scripts for just as many films including *Agni Varsha, Utsav, Kalyug, Kondura, Samskara, Godhuli, and Bhumika.*

2 Although *Utsav* is listed sometimes as a 1984 film in filmographies of Girish Karnad, the copyright date for the Filmvalas production shown on screen is 1985.

3 As told by Nachiket and Jayoo Patwardhan, the architect couple in charge of the costumes, set designing and art direction for *Utsav*, quoted by Taksale 1984.

4 The couple had already produced an award-winning documentary on a freedom fighter revolutionary, Vasudev Balwant Patwardhan. They did thorough research and took

great pains to reproduce the time to which the movie addresses. They used only the unstitched, hand-tied garments and naturally available colors (using flowers, barks etc.) for the colorful scenes in the movie. The murals on the house walls also are reflective of the style of painting known to pertain to the period.

5 The credits only list the name of the English translation for *Mṛcchakaṭikam* and utilize mixed transliterations as above. Since the respective chronology of the plays and the indebtedness of the playwrights are topics still being discussed, I shall not go in those details, but assume the traditional ascriptions of the plays to the respective playwrights. For a summary of discussions on Śūdraka's date, see Chakrabarti 1999. The political upheaval described in the play pertains roughly to the fifth century. Karnad has, on the whole, tried to evoke that period in his film.

6 The English translations are by Ryder (1905), Kale (1924; 3rd rev. ed. 1972), P. Lal (1957, 1964), and van Buitenen (1964, 1968). The Hindi translations along with original Sanskrit and Hindi commentaries on the play are several. To note a few, Brahmānand Śukla and Kṛṣṇakānt Śukla (1953), Śrīnivāsa Śāstrī (1962, 4th ed.1976), Rāmaśaṅkar Tripāṭhī (1969; 3rd ed. 1975), Jagdīś Candra Miśra (1985), Madangopāl Bajpeyī (1998; 3rd ed. 2001) and many others.

7 The Marathi translation into a musical play called *Sangeet Mṛcchakaṭik* was by Govind Ballal Deval. It was first staged in 1887, and has since been staged continuously until now.

8 *Cārudattam* in Devadhar (1937, 1951).

9 For example, the thief is called Sajjal, based on Sajjalaka of *Cārudattam*, rather than Śarvilaka of *Mṛcchakaṭikam*.

10 One of its latest production was in the Bidesia style of folk theater, in Patna by Kala Sangam in 1996, based on *Māṭī Gāḍī* (1993) a translation by Hrishikesh Sulabh in Bhojpuri Hindi.

11 After Lalit-kalotsav Maṇdali, Patankar Sangeet Mandali produced *Mṛcchakaṭika*, when the actor playing Śakāra in the former joined the latter company. Then Kirloskar Sangeet Mandali started staging the play since 1895, where at first, Cāruḍatta was played by Bhaurao Kolhatkar, Vasantasenā by Krishnarao Gore, and Śakāra by Shankarrao Mujumdar. Later, when Gore left the company, the famous singer/actor Balgandharva started playing the role of Vasantasenā. He was legendary for his "natural acting as a female, and also for his sonorous voice," as noted by the publisher, Madhav T. Parchure (Deval 1962).

12 Godbole's Marathi translation of *Mṛcchakaṭika* was published in 1862.

13 For example, he used the night-time *raga*, Darbārī Kanaḍa, for the majestic description of moonlit night by Cārudatta (Act I, verse 57 in Sanskṛit *Mṛcchakaṭikam*, and Act 1, last *pada* in Marathi) in the song *rajaninātha hā nabhī ugavalā*.

14 The only known exception to this norm is the 1993 translation by Hrishikesh Sulabh into Bhojpuri mixed Hindi, called *Māṭī Gāḍī* Sulabh(1993).

15 Exemplified in titles of plays such as *Vikramorvaśīyam*, *Mālavikāgnimitram*, and so on.

16 On the conventions of Sanskrit theater, see for example, Bhatt 1983, Raghavan 1993, Ṣadashiv and Sindhu Dange 1963, and Wells 1963.

17 Śūdraka maintains an excellent tension between art and livelihood. Saṃvāhaka, the masseur, remarks "I had learned it as an art, but now it is serving me as a source of livelihood." For more elaboration on the theme, see Pati 1991.

18 Both these roles are played by Amjad Khan in the film.

19 See Lutgendorf's review of *Utsav*, http//www.uiowa.edu/ ~incinema/utsav/html (accessed April 2007).

20 This scene from the *Mṛcchakaṭikam* was so romantic and popular in Maharashtra, that it inspired a renowned poet, Indira Sant, to write a well-known poem called *Śelā* ("the cloak"), where she compares the exchange of the fragrant morning mist between the sky and the earth to the exchange of cloak between Cārudatta and Vasantasenā.

21 In Maharashtra, the kept mistress was called *aṅga-vastra* or "top-garment," suggesting her superiority in one (erotic, emotional) sense, as well as her superfluousness in another (legal, conventional) sense. Given this connotation, the action of Cārudatta's in the play was suggestive of his accepting Vasantasenā as his paramour to the Marathi audiences. However, this connotation of the word *aṅga-vastra* may be only regional, and may not be shared by everyone watching the play in any other language.

22 Apparently Shashi Kapoor had to allow a rather big chunk of his budget to get these ornaments made to the exact specification of the art and costume directors. Jayoo Patwardhan and Jennifer Kapoor literally combed through the old silversmiths shops in many places, to get some ideas and intricate designs of old, heavy ornaments to complement Jayoo Patwardhan's research from old texts. They got the ornaments specially made to order and also got them goldplated. The work of incorporating several tiny hooks was timeconsuming and using the one central hook to hold all chains was finally accomplished by Jayoo Patwardhan (Taksale 1984).

23 Although minor in the progression of the play, this incident has given rise to a controversy among scholars regarding the identity of the monk attacked by the elephant, whether it is the same as the masseur-turned-monk or another (see on that topic van Buitenen 1964 and Dange 1994).

References

Sanskrit works: translations and editions

Bājpeyī, M. (ed.) (1998; 3rd edn 2001) *Mahākavi-Śūdraka-praṇītam Mṛcchakaṭikaṃ* (with *Jayantī* Sanskrit and Hindi commentaries by R. Dwivedi and J. Pandey), Benares: Bhāratīya Vidyā Prakāśan.

Devadhar, C.R. (ed.) (1937; 2nd edn 1951) *Bhāsa-nāṭaka-cakram Plays Ascribed to Bhāsa*, Poona: Oriental Book Agency.

Kale, M.R. (1924; 3rd rev. edn 1972) The *Mṛcchakaṭika of Śūdraka* (with a commentary of Pṛtvīdhara, various notes, and a literal English translation), Delhi: Motilal Banarsidass.

Miśra, J.C. (ed.) (1985) *Śrī-Śūdraka-kavi-viracitam Mṛcchakaṭikaṃ* (with *Vimalā* Sanskrit and Hindi commentaries), Chaukhamba Surabhāratī Granthamālā 76, Benares: Chaukhamba Surabhāratī Prakāśan.

Śāstrī, S. (ed.) (1962; 4th edn 1976) *Śrī-Śūdraka-kavi-viracitam Mṛcchakaṭika* (with Sanskrit commentary, Hindi translation, and notes), Meerut: Sāhitya Bhaṇḍār.

Śukla, B. and Śukla, K. (ed.) 1953. *Śrī-śūdraka-kavi-praṇītam Mṛcchakaṭikaṃ nāma prakaraṇam* (with *Priyaṃvadā* Sanskrit and Hindi commentaries), Benaras: Master Kheladilal and Sons.

Tripāṭhī, R. (ed.) (1969; reprint 1975) *Mahākavi-Śūdraka-praṇītam Mṛcchakaṭikaṃ* (with *Ramā* Sanskrit commentary and Hindi translation), Delhi: Motilal Banarsidass.

Other references

Bhat, G.K. (1983) *Theatric Aspects of Sanskrit Drama*, Post-Graduate and Research Department Series 18. Poona: Bhandarkar Oriental Research Institute.

Chakrabarti, P. (1999) *A Treatise on Śūdraka's Mṛcchakaṭika*, Delhi: Pilgrims Books.

Chakravarty, S.S. (1993) *National Identity in Indian Popular Cinema 1947–1987*, Austin, TX: University of Texas Press.

Dange, S.A. and Dange, S.S. (1963; 2nd rev. edn 1994) *Critiques on Sanskrit Dramas*, New Delhi: Aryan Books International.

Devadhar, C.R. (1937; 2nd edn 1951) *Plays Ascribed to Bhāsa*, Poona Oriental Series 54, Poona: Oriental Book Agency.

Deval, G.B. (1887; new edn 1976) *Sangeet Mṛcchakaṭik.* Pune: Ramyakatha Prakashan.

—— (1887; new edn 1989) *Sangeet Mṛcchakaṭik.* Mumbai: Balwant Pustak Bhandar.

Garg, B.D. (1996) *So Many Cinemas: The Motion Picture in India*, Mumbai: Eminence Designs.

Karnad, G. (1984) "Doing a Double Take," *Express Magazine*, January 24, 1984 (as quoted in Chakravarty, S.S. (ed.) (1993) *National Identity in Indian Popular Cinema 1947–1987*, Austin, 282, TX: University of Texas Press.)

Lal, P. (1957; 1964) *Great Sanskrit Plays in New English Transcreations*, A New Directions Book, New York: James Laughlin.

Pati, M. (1991) "Mṛcchakaṭikam: Thematic and Tonal Patterns," in M. Pati (ed.) *Sanskrit Drama: Essays in Revaluation*, Delhi: Amar Prakashan.

Raghavan, V. (1993) *Sanskrit Drama: Its Aesthetics and Production*, Madras: R. Kalidas.

Richmond, F.P., Swann, D. and Zarrilli, P.B. (eds) (1990) *Indian Theatre: Traditions of Performance*, Honolulu, HI: University of Hawaii Press.

Ryder, A.W. (1905) *The Little Clay Cart*, Cambridge: Harvard University Press.

Sulabh, H. (1993) Māṭī Gāḍī [Śūdrak racit Sanskrit Nāṭak Mṛcchakaṭikaṃ par ādhārit] New Delhi: Prakashan Samsthan, 80pp.

Taksale, S. (1984) "Utsav," *Miloon Saryajani*, Diwali issue, Pune: Kirloskar Brothers.

Unni, N.P. (1978) *New Problems in Bhasa's Plays*, Trivandrum: College Book House.

van Buitenen. J.A.B. (1964; 1968) *Two Plays of Ancient India* (translated from Sanskrit and Prakrit with an introduction), New York: Columbia University Press.

Wells, H.W. (1963) *The Classical Drama of India: Studies in Its Values for the Literature and Theatre of the World*, London: Asia Publishing House.

Wohlsen, M. (2005) "The Greatest Show on Earth: The First Indian Play Performed at UC Berkeley," *Illuminations: Berkeley's Online Magazine of Research in the Arts and Humanities* October 2005. Online. Available HTTP: <http://illuminations.berkeley.edu/archives/2005/history.php?volume = 9.> (accessed April 2007).

For further reading

Barnouw, E. and Krishaswamy, S. (1963; 2nd edn 1980) *Indian Film*, New York: Oxford University Press.

Devasthali, G.V. (1951) *Introduction to the Study of Mṛcchakaṭika*, Poona: Poona Oriental Book House.

Keith, A.B. (1924; reprinted lithograph 1964) *The Sanskrit Drama in Its Origin, Development, Theory and Practice*, London: Oxford University Press.

Part 3

Saints on the screen

5 *Bhakti* songs recast

Gulzar's *Meera* movie*

Heidi Pauwels

Introduction

The genre of the "devotional" movie

The (sub)genre of the "devotional" movie[1] has been vastly understudied, notwithstanding its popularity from the beginning of Indian popular cinema and its interesting links with progressive ideology. In fact, arguably one of the very first Indian movies could be said to belong to this genre, namely the 1912 silent movie *Pundalik* (d. Tipnis and Chitre, EIC 243). This movie was based on the story of a famous saint, and directly inspired by a Marathi stage play of the saint's life.

We see that trend continue in the era of the talkies with a series of films from Prabhat Studios, which was famous for its "devotionals." Rajaram Vankudre Shantaram (1901–90), one of the most famous directors of the 1930s, is considered to have been a trailblazer in this respect with his 1935 movie *Dharmatma* on the sixteenth-century Maharashtrian saint Ekanāth (von Skyhawk 2001).[2] Barely a year later, the same studio produced *Sant Tukaram* (1936), directed by V. Damle and S. Fattelal, on another famous Maharashtrian saint-poet of the seventeenth century.[3] Given the background in Marathi theater of these directors it is no surprise that they highlight Marathi saints.[4]

What stands out is that these movies carry a progressive message and take an anti-Brahminical stance. They turn *bhakti* saints into spokesmen for socio-economic equality and the uplifting of untouchables, inspired by Gandhian ideals (*Dharmatma* was originally titled *Mahatma*, EIC 262). The devotional songs are cast so as to make the desired points (see von Skyhawk 2001). In the case of Tukārām, the movie even contributes a new *ovī* song in "Tukārām style," which was mistaken by the audience to be an original composition (EIC 270). The devotional-cum-Gandhian trend was continued by Ranjit Movietone, which brought out *Sant Tulsidas* (1939, Hindi and Marathi, d. Jayant Desai), featuring the same actor, Pagnis (who also scored the songs), and writer, Vashikar (EIC 281; also Chatterjee 2005: 104–8) as *Sant Tukaram*.

A similar preference for the progressive "devotional" is found in Gujarati cinema. Here, the first feature film was on the life of the fifteenth-century

Gujarati Vaishnava Saint, *Narasinh Mehta* (1932, d. Nanubhai Vakil). This movie too owed its inspiration to Gandhi, whose "realistic" interpretation of the poet's life influenced the moviemakers (EIC 256). It is no surprise that the movie includes one of Gandhi's favorites, Narsī Mehta's song *Vaiṣṇava jana to*, which underlines the importance of the casting of devotional lyrics.[5]

Bengal too was right in with the devotional trend: New Theatres's first hit was a movie on the famous fifteenth-century Bengali saint, *Chandidas* (1932, d. Debaki Bose). The movie was based on a theatrical performance (a musical by Aparesh Chandra Mukherjee, EIC 255) and was so successful it had a Hindi remake by cameraman Nitin Bose in 1934, which became the studio's first Hindi success (EIC 259). In 1937, the studio brought out a Bengali-Hindi double production *Bidyapati/Vidyapati*, on the life of the fifteenth-century Maithili poet-saint.[6]

In the South too we have in the 1930s and 1940s a plethora of movies like *Bhakta Jayadeva* (1938, Telugu, d. Hiren Bose; on the twelfth-century composer of *Gītagovinda*), *Kamban* (1938, Tamil, d. C.S.U. Sankar; on the ninth-century Tamil poet of the *Irāmāvatāram*), *Bhakta Potana* (1942, Telugu, d. K.V. Reddy; on the Telugu translator of *Bhāgavata Purāṇa*), the hit *Thyagayya* (1946, Telugu, d. Chittor V. Nagaiah; on the eighteenth-century saint, central in Karnatic music; remade by Bapu in 1981), and *Yogi Vemana* (1946, Telugu, d. K.V. Reddy; about the seventeenth-century Reddy saint Vemana who attacked social inequality; EIC 174, 276, 293, 307 and 308–9, respectively). In the 1950s, the genre takes on a new political meaning: for example, Gemini's *Avvaiyar* (1953, d. Kothamangalam Subbu, featuring the actress-singer Sundarambal), on the Tamil Saint-poetess of the Caṅkam period, was a celebration of Tamil cultural and political revivalism, and at the same time was intended to counter the anti-religious DMK movies (EIC 330). In the 1980s, we have G.V. Iyer's films inspired by an effort towards Brahminical revivalism, featuring major Sanskrit philosophers, and partly spoken in Sanskrit, including *Adi Shankaracharya* (1983 in Sanskrit), *Madhavacharya* (1986 in Kannada), and *Shri Ramanujacharya* (1989 in Tamil; EIC 457–8).

The production of devotional movies has not ceased, and they typically enjoy a long life, as they are often replayed for religious holidays and formal occasions, in theater, temple, and on television. Several of these movies are enjoying a new lease on life thanks to the ISKCON movement (International Society of Krishna Consciousness, popularly known as Hare Krishnas), who feature revamped editions with subtitles in English by ITV Productions (catalogue at www.itvproductions.net). One feature that most of these movies have in common is the focus on the *bhakti* message of equality and social uplift of lower castes.

How come that this interesting genre is so understudied? There is on the one hand a tendency to dismiss devotional movies as simple expressions of popular devotion, on the other as manipulation of presumably illiterate masses. The frameworks of such interpretations see popular culture as an expression of the culture of the masses or a capitalist homogenizer respectively. Neither of these approaches is productive. It may be more interesting to see these films as sites of contestation. Upon close study, it becomes apparent that these movies interact in highly complex and sophisticated ways with devotional texts, which are often well known to the "illiterate" audience. It is thus important to understand the interface of these religious texts with the popular film versions, and close readings of both are very fruitful.

To understand the processes at work in the devotional, we have to study the way they reference religious stories and songs. If the spectator of movies is "caught in an interocular field," he also functions in what we could call an "interaural" field. Indeed, tweaking the definition slightly, we could say that "each site or setting for the socializing and regulation of the public gaze" (read also: ear) "is to some degree affected by the experiences of the other sites" (Appadurai and Breckenridge 1995: 12). In the Indian context it is important to take account of such aural references, for two main reasons. First, Indian culture is to a large degree determined by the aural. Stories told in the movies evoke other stories, heard in other contexts. Dialogues are often constructed deliberately to echo other dialogues. Old stories hijack the scenario of new ones. This kind of intertextuality is now taken more seriously for references between movies, but it often goes unnoticed with regard to traditional texts. This aspect deserves serious study in its own right. It pays off to look at how the texts are used and transformed. Second, Indian cinema is dominated by the genre of the musical, and thus centered around songs. Songs evoke other songs. Tunes and words echo back and forth between different milieus, from temple and folk gatherings to movie hall (and back!). Here the interplay between devotional, folk culture, and popular culture is particularly relevant. Again, I think the intertextual approach has much to contribute: it offers a close reading of films against the background of their narrative and sung traditions.

Neglected equality: "Devotionals" about women-saints

In the light of the progressive agenda of so many devotional movies, it is remarkable that so few of them are centered on women-saints and/or promoting gender equality. True, several foreground the issue of love beyond caste lines, usually by the devotee-poet for a low-caste woman with whom intermarriage is forbidden. However, the focus is on the caste issue, not on gender.[7]

Only one woman-saint has attracted quite a bit of attention from filmmakers, namely the sixteenth-century Rajput princess-poetess Mīrābāī. Her story was up on the screen as a silent movie right from the start with other mythologicals and devotionals (directed by Kanjibhai Rathod in the early 1920s, EIC 197). In 1933 New Theatres produced a big budget film, *Meerabai* in Bengali (d. Hiren Bose and Basanta Chatterjee; with Chandrabati Devi and Durgadas Bannerjee) and simultaneously shot in Hindi as *Rajrani Meera* (d. Debaki Bose) with none less than Durga Khote and Prithviraj Kapoor (EIC 257). The interest in the Mīrā theme may be partially explained by the contemporary success of the genre of the "devotional" (see above), as well as by the fashion of Rajput costume dramas in the films of the 1930s. In any case, Mīrā's story was taken up again and again by cinema (among others in Tamil, Telugu, Punjabi, and Gujarati), most famously in Chandraprabha Cine's production in Tamil in 1945, directed by Ellis R. Duncan (or E.S. Tunda), with the lead role played by the Karnatic classical singer

M.S. Subbulakshmi who sang the lyrics to great effect. The movie was a hit with an all-India appeal and its Hindi version too was successful to the point of establishing a canon of eighteen Mīrā *bhajans* in Hindi. Apparently, that movie had political links, as Sarojini Naidu was featured in the introduction (EIC 304). Unfortunately, none of these movies is currently available commercially.[8]

One would expect films about Mīrā to deal with gender issues, since her story can be interpreted as "liberating" for women: her prioritizing devotion to Krishna over everything else got her into trouble with the Rajput family she had married in, yet she escaped persecution and managed to carve out a life of devotion for herself. Several songs attributed to Mīrā seem to be defiant of patriarchy, especially those in which she mocks or challenges her persecutor, designated as "Rāṇā."[9] Some have called her an inspiration for feminists (Kishwar and Vanita 1989a: 90–2), though other feminists have critiqued her (see especially Sangari 1990). Still, there is no doubt that her story remains a source of inspiration for ordinary women to negotiate alternative lives for themselves (for contemporary ethnographic accounts, see Mukta 1994 and Martin 1995).

Gulzar's Meera: much maligned

One influential movie on Mīrā's life dates from the late 1970s: *Meera* (1979) directed by Gulzar (Sampooran Singh, b. 1936), produced by Premjī, and starring the actress Hema Malini. This film was not judged to merit an entry in EIC. Indeed, it was not a success at the time of its release: the director ascribes the movie's failure to his personal psychological interpretation of the story and its being a "historical" rather than a "mythological" (Gulzar 1983: 200–1). Still, it is an influential movie that is regularly broadcast on Indian television and often screened in connection with religious functions and festivals, such as Krishna's Birthday Celebration (*Janmāṣṭamī*), especially in the Braj area, viewed and reviewed by locals as well as pilgrims to the area. Thus, while it depicts a 1970s interpretation of the saint, it is widely viewed and influential on how Mīrā is interpreted today.

Of interest to us here is that the movie is directed largely towards women and draws a large woman audience, even more than a typical devotional, because it is about a female saint. Thus, it makes for a good focus to study how *bhakti* and gender intersect. Also of interest is that the lead actress, Hema Malini, seems to have been the driving force behind the movie; she reportedly claims to have been inspired by her family guru from Poona, Mīrādāsī (Gulzar 1979: 32). To some extent then this movie is for women, by a woman, yet central is the influence of the director, Gulzar.

Gulzar's movie has been berated by many academics: it has been called "vulgarizing" (Kishwar and Vanita 1989b: 100), and is regarded as middle-class, which carries the stigma of "bourgeois" (Mukta 1994: 205). Whenever it is mentioned in academic studies about Mīrā, it is dismissed quickly. If one studies the movie in its own right, one finds that it is not simply a facile, superficial interpretation of an oversentimentalized romantic Mīrā, as is sometimes implied. Rather, it is a complex movie that represents an erudite and multivocal creative adaptation of the Mīrā story. One could expect an interesting angle on the saint from Gulzar, the director who had just before writing *Meera* brought out a daring movie about gender relationships. *Mausam* (1975) dealt with the fraught relationship between a young prostitute (Sharmila Tagore) and the man responsible for her mother's downfall (Sanjeev Kumar). Gulzar sympathetically portrayed the flawed hero and heroine, allowing the prostitute to angrily voice her view of men's exploitation in strong language. In short, Gulzar's portrayal of the saint Mīrā might be expected to touch upon some contemporary women's issues and make some strong points for women.

Moreover, Gulzar, as an Urdu poet himself, can be expected to give an interesting and sensitive depiction of Mīrā's poems and indeed of the saint as a poetess. As a filmmaker too, Gulzar pays special attention to the picturization of movie songs, as he has said himself (Gulzar 1983: 197, 199). In this chapter I am particularly interested in analyzing the way Mīrā's songs are contextualized, and what impact that may have on the transmission of the saint's message. I focus on the way her songs may be interpreted as potentially liberating for women. This is important, as the movie is directed at a women audience and may be influential that way.

My approach to the movie is intertextual and consists of a close reading of the film against the background of the narrative and sung traditions about Mīrā. I will not address the cinematographical depiction *per se*, nor the ethno-musicological aspect of the music, only the text and context of the songs. This analysis will be focused on the way Mīrā's voice comes through in the movie.[10] I will show the ways in which the director has redacted and contextualized her popular songs, and will map out the most salient differences with the tradition. This will allow us to draw conclusions about modern interpretations of gender and *bhakti.*

The poet-director at work: sensitive contextualization of songs

What makes analyzing this movie so worthwhile is that Gulzar and his team really know what they are doing: they are very knowledgeable about the hagiographic traditions as well as scholarly writing about Mīrā's life (see Bhūṣaṇ Banmālī's comments on how he worked on the story in Gulzar 1979: 33–59). They are well aware that their interpretation cannot aspire to telling "the truth" about the saint, but is a creative adaptation of the story as passed on to them (ibid.: 16–17). Gulzar creatively reinterprets the hagiographic stories of the tradition for the medium of the movie. He acknowledges that he does take liberties with the story, but points out that his goal is to make it look real and that thus he has to make decisions to fill in the blanks (ibid.: 13). Gulzar also reflects in a sophisticated way on how to treat the miracles inherent in the genre of the "devotional." He is aware that his audience wants to believe in them, though he says he himself searches for scientific explanations. However, such explanations often destroy the feeling (*bhāva*) of the miraculous, thus he tries to have it both ways (ibid.: 14).[11]

As far as the songs are concerned, Gulzar has carefully selected several of Mīrā's "greatest hits," her most popular *bhajan*s. He knows and appreciates them well and brings a poet's sensitivities to the portrayal of these much-beloved songs. It is done stylishly with surprisingly restrained dancing for a mainstream popular movie (compare to the *bhajan* scenes in for instance *Jai Santoshi Maa*). Although the actual musical realization of the songs had its practical troubles,[12] they are not an afterthought, nor a concession to the "Bollywood" convention of the musical, but very much part and parcel of the movie's backbone. One of Gulzar's artistic accomplishments in this movie is how he uses some songs as leitmotiv, as we will see below.

Naturally, since this is a Hindi movie, the language of the songs is "regularized" and further away from the Rajasthani versions (e.g. Harinārāyaṇ Purohit 1989), closer to the Hindi ones (e.g. Ācārya Paraśurām Caturvedi 1983). This is in line though with what we find in the manuscript versions of the songs, the language of which differs according to the region in which they are written down or the audience for whom they are performed.

Some of the *bhajan*s in the movie are actually combinations of different songs. Gulzar clarifies why he chose a composite character of songs: he wanted as many of Mīrā's songs as possible in his movie, but also sought to limit each song to one "emotion" or *bhāva* (Gulzar 1979: 14). This too is in accordance with the tradition: the centuries-old manuscript transmission of Mīrā's poems shows a comparable reshuffling of refrains and lines in different combinations in different songs. Because of the lack of an authoritative transmission of a Mīrā corpus, this is perhaps more strikingly the case for Mīrā than for other *bhakta*s, but it is a typical feature of the oral transmission of *bhajan*s. Gulzar follows suit by leaving out lines or shuffling them around as suits his purpose.

Most importantly, Gulzar brings to the table new interpretations of the songs through contextualizing them in stories. Again, this is nothing new, many hagiographies provide such contextualizations, a notable case in point is the *Pada-prasaṅga-mālā by* Nāgrīdās (Pauwels 2006). Gulzar has done this with a very high degree of sensitivity and brings out beautiful aspects of different songs.

Meet Mīrā, the other-worldly poetess

The refrain of the very first of Mīrā's *bhajan*s that is sung in the movie comes back later in several different contexts, as we shall discuss further. This song is a combination of two of her hits, the refrain is taken from the famous *bhajan:*

> *mere to giridhara gopāla, dūsaro na koī,*
> *jāke sira mora mukuṭa mero pati soī*
> (Gulzar 1979: 68–9)

I call Giridhara Gopāla my own, no one else,
The one who wears the peacock crown, that is my husband.

This refrain is followed by verses that actually are taken from a different song with refrain *maiṃne liyau govinda mola* ("I have bought Govinda for a price!"). The refrain is not sung here, but the lines selected for the movie are:

koī kahe kāro koī kahe goro, liyo hai aṃkhiyāṃ khola
koī kahe halako koī kahe bhāro, liyo hai tarājū tola
koī kahe chānai koī kahe cavaḍai, liyo hai bajaṃtā ḍhola
tana kā gahaṇā maiṃ saba kucha dīnhā, diyo hai bājūbanda khola
(ibid.: 69)

Some say he's dark, others, he's fair; I've chosen him with my eyes open.
Some say he's light, others, he's heavy; I've chosen him, weighing [carefully].
Some say secretly, others openly; I've announced playing the drum.
The jewels of my body, everything I've given away; I untied my bracelets.

Mīrā is singing this *bhajan* when the viewer first sees her, which provides a wonderful introduction to what Mīrā is all about. No doubt viewers immediately recognize the songs and respond positively. They get a glimpse of the purported "first performance" of the song: they see Mīrā in the act of composing, during her worship of her image, with her confidante, Lalitā, writing down her words. This lends an aura of authenticity to both the song and the movie. Further, as the song evolves, Mīrā receives a present from her just-returned cousin-brother, brought to her by her cousin-sister, Krishnā. This is shown just when she sings the last line of the song, about having given away all her jewelry. Indeed, instead of placing the beautiful ring on her own finger, Mīrā is shown putting the ring on the finger of the Krishna image. This adds an element of "real life" behind the lines of the song. It also works well to set up Mīrā's character: she does not care for jewelry or worldly goods, everything she receives, is simply put in service of Krishna.

The reluctant bride: tropes from popular cinema

Gulzar casts Mīrā's life in the trope of tension between arranged marriage and love marriage, a staple of the popular movie, to which Mīrā's story lends itself well. All sources agree that Mīrā had given her heart to Krishna, who was her true love and some specify that she had considered him her bridegroom from when she was little (as does the movie). When she comes of age, though, her marriage is arranged for political reasons, many versions specify to the neighboring Sisodiyā prince Bhoj.[13] Like many a film heroine's, then, Mīrā's marriage is arranged by her elders without regard for her personal wishes, but she does not protest. The viewers witness her feelings: we see her torn between her exclusive devotion to Krishna and her forced worldly marriage.

Gulzar brings this to the fore in his sensitive contextualization of one of Mīrā's *bhajan*s, which contrasts bridal imagery with that of the ascetic:

bālā maiṃ bairāgana hūṃgī
jina bheṣāṃ merā sāhiba rījhe, so hī bheṣa dharūṃgī
kaho to kusumala sāḍī raṃgāvāṃ, kaho to bhagavā bheṣa
kaho to motiyana māṃga bharāvāṃ, kaho chiṭakāvāṃ keśa
(Gulzar 1979: 96–8)

Friend, I'll be an ascetic
Whatever dress pleases my Lord, that's the dress I'll wear.
If you say so, I'll wear a red sari; if you say so, an ochre one;
If you say so, I'll have my hair-parting dressed up with pearls; if you say so, I'll let my hair grow wild.

Gulzar shows this song as playing in Mīrā's head when she is carried in her palanquin on her way to her in-laws'. This fits well: it evokes the genre of women's wedding folk songs, and Mīrā has adopted many folk songs for her particular *bhakti* purpose. Thus Gulzar hits it just right with this instance where one of her songs becomes her personalized wedding folk song.

Gulzar in turn uses the occasion to present his female viewers with a recognizable situation: the ambiguity about marriage that many a North Indian bride feels. On the one hand, there is the joy and auspiciousness of the occasion; on the other, it represents a total break with her "protected" life as a daughter in her father's house. It is a big jump in the unknown. The ambiguity is especially clear in the last two lines (taken from a different song):

Prāṇa hamārā vahāṃ basata, yahāṃ to khālī khoḍa
Māta pitā parivāra sūṃ, maiṃ rahī tinakā toḍa
(ibid.: 98)

My life lies there, here is nothing but misfortune.
With mother, father, family, I've broken all relations.

These lines can be interpreted in different ways as to where is the "there" where the young bride sees her life, and where is the "here" that she feels to be a curse. While few girls would actually consider the alternative of the ascetic (if at all viable), still there might well be a desire of remaining virgin (*virakta* in that sense), rather than have to go through such a potentially traumatic change. The song voices well these mixed feelings of the young bride. It also serves in a clever way to answer an objection (*śaṅkā samādhāna*) that the viewer may raise as to the why of Mīrā's wedding. If she really were married to Krishna, why did God let it happen that she was married to a human groom? The song implies the answer that her worldly marriage too was ordained by Krishna himself. Mīrā seems to say, that she will do as Krishna pleases, if he wishes, she'll be adorned in bridal gear and married off, and she'll have to agree with that. The message then is one of submission to patriarchal arrangements. However, as we shall see, Mīrā has a hard time functioning in this marriage and soon will get in trouble with husband and in-laws.

Filling in the blanks: a poet interpreting poetry

Gulzar is especially good at supplying real-life reasons for Mīrā's sorrowful songs. The director takes care to add contemporary relevance for his audience, in particular the women. A good example is the following song:

> *karuṇā sunī śyāma merī, maiṃ to hoya rahī cerī terī*
> *tumare kāraṇa saba sukha choḍyā, aba mohe kyauṃ tarasāo ho*
> *biraha vyathā lāgī ura antara, so tuma āye bujhāo ho*
> (Gulzar 1979: 106)
>
> Listen to my plight, Śyām, I've kept up being your servant.
> For you I've given up all happiness, why are you holding out against me?
> The pain of separation burns inside my heart, so please come and put out the fire.

While the song on its own seems to speak of Mīrā's longing for Krishna, a common theme in her oeuvre, Gulzar contextualizes this with reference to a mundane incident, instantly recognizable to the audience as a dilemma for many women. The song comes at the end of a scene where Mīrā, newly arrived at her in-laws', is asked to cook meat. She refuses on religious grounds. The problem of different dietary habits between a woman's natal and her marital family in real life often leaves women caught between a strict vegetarianism of their upbringing and the pressure to "make an adjustment" in their new home. Women often compromise by cooking the nonvegetarian fare but not eating it themselves. In Mīrā's case, the refusal to even cook meat is radical. It is all the more defiant, because the meat is actually sanctified by temple worship, as it came from a goat sacrifice (*bali*) to the goddess. Worse, she gets into an argument with the *mahant*, the temple priest, who had carried out the sacrifice. The outcome is disastrous: infuriated, he takes a vow not to eat any food at all. As a result of the family guru's fasting, no one can eat, and all the blame is on Mīrā. Even her husband refuses to eat. When Mīrā sings the second line of the song, the audience feels for her plight: she has stuck to her Vaishnava principle of vegetarianism and got in trouble for living up to her religious conviction.

There is more to the song, it helps to sketch the downward slope on which Mīrā's marriage is sliding. The third line of the song refers to *viraha*, or love-in-separation. If the song is read on its own, this may be taken to refer to Mīrā's *viraha* for Krishna, however, the director subtly suggests here that it can be taken to refer to her estrangement from her husband Bhoj. Exactly as this line is sung, Bhoj is shown through one of the *jharokhā*s as coming out of his room. He runs into his sister, who comments sarcastically: "You hear [what she sings], brother, don't you? The wedding was just yesterday, and already today there is lament of separation in the house." This is one of several cases in the movie where the characters react to Mīrā's poetry, and not always positively. They provide the other side of the devotional coin, so to speak. Gulzar manages here to bring out the conflict between sisters-in-law (*bahū-nanad*), which is part of the lived experience of the audience, and to link it with the reception of Mīrā's song.

The Rāṇā songs reinterpreted: defiance domesticated

Slowly things grow worse in Mīrā's marriage. Gulzar illustrates this in an interesting scene that contextualizes one of Mīrā's defiant protests against the "Rāṇā," here interpreted to be her husband. The scene starts when Bhoj finds Mīrā engaged in sewing a little turban for her Krishna image. He teases her: "You seem a real housewife today, ahem?" She answers in the same tone: "I am making Krishna into a Rajput. When in Rome, do as the Romans *(jis deś rahnā, vahī bheṣ pahnnā).*" Bhoj then asks her what relationship she feels she has with Krishna, and she answers "As I should have with my lord." "And with me?" "You . . . you are my Rāṇā." Bhoj then confesses he is jealous of Krishna and they both laugh about how they are both jealous, he of Krishna, and she of Radha (Gulzar 1979: 109).

However, there is something bittersweet in their thus joking together, and the spectator's heart goes out to Bhoj. Mīrā's sewing of the miniature turban evokes the domestic activity of preparing clothes for little babies to come. This is potentially a tender scene between future parents to be. However, Mīrā disappoints her husband with her fixation on Krishna. The contrast is set up to subtly underline Mīrā's failure to fulfill this major duty of all wives: to bear their husbands sons. Mīrā will be accused of this much during her final trial: one of the charges is that she has not fulfilled her duty as a wife, failing to provide her husband with offspring (ibid.: 147).

To return to the domestic scene, Mīrā next returns to Bhoj the keys of the household storerooms that her elder brother-in-law (*jeṭh*) had given her. This gesture serves to estrange the world-weary Mīrā from most women in the audience. For most women the household keys are a much-coveted possession because it affords power over the family's resources. However, Mīrā does not accept the keys and even asks Bhoj to give them instead to her rival, her sister-in-law, Ūdā. She adds that she will give Ūdā some jewelry too (ibid.: 109). Nothing could be farther from a "flesh and blood" woman's instincts. The tussles between *nanad* and *bahū* about jewelry are proverbial and the topic of many folk songs. Mīrā's actions here distance her from the viewer. Bhoj voices the audience's thoughts when he complains semi-seriously that he has married a *yoginī.* Mīrā here is portrayed as an exception, not an example to be followed for ordinary women and housewives, but someone who has made a radical choice to step outside the safe and happy world of domesticity.

At this point, Gulzar works in Mīrā's Rāṇā song. He introduces it as follows: Bhoj mentions that he has discovered that Mīrā writes poetry, but he has refrained from reading it, as he wishes not to intrude on her privacy. However, he would like for her to take him into confidence and asks her to perform some of it. She sings:

> *rāṇājī maiṃ to govinda ke guṇa gāsūṃ*
> *rājā rūṭhe nagarī rākhe hari rūṭhyāṃ kahāṃ jāsūṃ*
> (ibid.: 110)[14]
>
> Rāṇājī I will but sing Govinda's praise
> If the king is upset, let him keep his city, if God is upset, where can I go?

She puts the now-finished turban on Krishna's head, and when she turns around, Bhoj has gone. Understandably, he feels slighted and insulted. His kind gesture to his wife has been repaid with her refusal to open up to him due to her austere, exclusive devotion to her God. An opportunity for intimacy between the couple has been missed.

Gulzar here seems to make use of the hagiographic trope where the *bhakta* refuses to sing the praise of anyone but his God. Usually it is a king who requests the *bhakta* to sing his praise, and the *bhakta* refuses, forgoing great monetary rewards. However, in this case, Mīrā's song does not support such heroic resistance to the lure of the material world. Rather than heroic, it comes over as small minded and misguided. Her husband did not actually ask her to sing in his own praise, he just wanted her to recite poetry and let him into her world. She could have let him share in her devotion by selecting a less contrary song to sing. To the audience it seems that she needlessly antagonized him by unfavorably comparing him to Krishna.

If we stand back and look at the selection of songs for the movie, we can applaud Gulzar's choice to include one of the popular "Rāṇā" songs in which Mīrā defies the Rāṇā. In the contextualization, though, the song loses much of its subversive value. Gulzar drastically reinterprets the conflict with the Rāṇā. The song is not used to illustrate Mīrā's struggle with the courtly etiquette or in-laws' stipulations to liberate herself from such patriarchal rules. Rather it is used in the movie in a domestic scene between husband and wife where Mīrā sings the song to misguidedly tease her husband. One could say that in this case, Gulzar has domesticated her defiance against patriarchy.

Strident Mīrā: stained by the color of untouchable devotion

Mīrā continues to give offense to her husband, mostly in her carelessness about her public persona, and her total disregard for her husband's wishes. She adds insult to injury by becoming involved with the untouchable Sant Raidās. Here, the movie turns to the issue of caste and *bhakti*, which, as we have seen, has been so important in the "devotional" film, from early on. The scene revolves around Mīrā's song: *maiṃ sāmvare ke raṃga rācī* ("I'm dyed in the color of the dark one") (Gulzar 1979: 120–1). The contextualization may be the most ingenious and surprising interpretation of Mīrā's *bhajan*s in the movie. While it mainly focuses on caste discrimination, it also touches upon women's issues.

The movie ascribes the inspiration for this song to Raidās. Gulzar carefully sets up the meeting of Mīrā and the untouchable Sant Raidās as a transgressive one. First, she innocently accepts from him a musical instrument (*ektārā*) as a present. When Mīrā's husband finds out, he is furious and forbids her to leave the palace without his permission, but she defies him and goes out nevertheless to worship again. On the advice of Mīrā's enemies, he has her sent back to her paternal home. She arrives only to be turned away from home by her cousin-brother who is appalled that she would have defied her in-laws. Thrown out of both "homes," she now feels free to visit the low-caste Sant Raidās in his house. He is shown as engaged in the—for caste Hindus—repulsive work of coloring leather. At the same time, he is composing one of his poems, providentially on the topic of choosing one's path in the face of opposition (ibid.: 119). When Mīrā asks him for wisdom, he speaks in poetry again and answers with a line of the famous *dohā: ḍhāī ākhara prema ke, jāne so jñānī hoya* ("Just learn a couple of letters of the word love and be learned"). He chides her: she has love for God and that should be enough; there's no need for wisdom. He claims he has nothing to teach her and sends her on to the high-caste Tulsīdās instead. Then he notices that she got some stains of the highly polluting leather-paint on her sari. Mīrā ecstatically confirms: *maiṃ sāṃvare ke raṃga rācī* and thanks him for removing her doubt. Raidās resumes his activities, again reciting poetry to himself:

gaī kumati laī sādha kī saṃgata
bhagata rūpa bhaī sāṃcī
mīrā sāvare ke raṃga rācī
(ibid.: 120)
Gone are bad thoughts, when wise people are around,
She is molded in the form of a devotee.
Mīrā is dyed in the color of the dark one.

In effect, this contextualization ascribes joint authorship to the famous Mīrā *bhajan*, which she then sings while going off in the desert. The second line is: *loka lāja taja nācī, lāja śarama kula kī maryādā sar se dūra karī* ("I danced, careless about what people think; I forgot modesty, shame, and family name;" ibid.: 121). These words assume here a specific meaning: Mīrā has given up all caste rules for the sake of an untouchable guru. Similar interpretations exist in some circles of low-caste singers (Mukta 1994), and it is significant that this "bourgeois" movie chooses to follow suit. It is on this defiant note, with Mīrā singing this song, that the film is interrupted for the intermission.

Songs that work miracles, vows that work both ways

Elsewhere too, Gulzar contextualizes Mīrā's songs with relevance for women's issues. A good example is the song with refrain *pyāre daraśana dījau jāya, tuma bina rahyau na jāya* ("My love, show yourself, I can't live without you"; Gulzar 1979: 127).[15] This *bhajan* is normally interpreted as one of *viraha*, where Mīrā asks for a vision of Krishna. Gulzar gives it a literal twist: Mīrā is barred from *darśana* of the image in her favorite temple. She is undertaking a hunger strike to protest the closure of the temple. The director is working here with the traditional hagiographic motif of God's miraculous intervention in favor of the saint who is barred from his *darśana*. This song gains extra poignancy in the movie, where it is followed by a "miracle," where the closure of the temple is mitigated and Mīrā receives the much-desired *darśana*.

In order to make the scene relevant to his women audience, Gulzar has Mīrā's fast coincide with the widely popular *vrata*, or fast, of *Karvā Cauth*, when women fast for their husband's welfare and don't partake in food or drink till they see the moon rise (another cliché in the popular movie). However, Mīrā will break her fast only when she sees her divine husband's moon-face, thus her fast is in contrast to the one that ordinary women keep for their worldly husbands. The efficacy of both *vrata*s is confirmed, by means of what could be termed "a natural miracle": in a thunderstorm the temple doors catch fire and burn down so Mīrā finally gets the *darśana* she desired. At the same time, the *vrata* for the human husband comes true: when Mīrā swoons after this miracle, her husband romantically comes to the rescue on his horse and carries her back home (ibid.: 131).

Thus, Gulzar has subtly shifted the meaning of the song by fusing the hagiographic trope of the saint getting God's *darśana* notwithstanding opposition, with the scenario of *vrata* folk tale. Basically, *vrata* tales are promotional, in that they recommend the efficacy of the fasts that are associated with them. Such intertextuality between the devotional domestic milieu and the movies is far from new. Just the year before Gulzar completed the screenplay of *Meera*, [16] the movie *Jai Santoshi Maa* (1975, d. Vijay Sharma) was a hit, which was basically a creative adaptation of one such *vrata* tale (see Lutgendorf 2002). What is remarkable is that Gulzar has applied it to Mīrā's devotional songs, suggesting a devotional happy outcome, as well as a reconciliation with her husband. Again, we could call this a case of domestication of the *bhakti* saint's songs.[17]

Leitmotiv song 1: condemned by her own words

As mentioned, Gulzar uses some songs as leitmotiv: they come back in slightly different configurations in different contexts. The refrain of the very first of Mīrā's *bhajan*s, *mere to giridhara gopāla, dūsaro na koī* (Gulzar 1979: 68–9), is artfully echoed throughout the movie. The next instance we hear it is during Mīrā's wedding ceremony. The refrain is shown to play in Mīrā's head, washing out the "real" sound of the Sanskrit wedding recitations (ibid.: 97). Mīrā is unable to bear the contradiction between her avowed exclusive devotion to Krishna and her forced worldly marriage. She gets up and faints when her sari catches fire. Gulzar has managed to convey to his audience that this is the first real challenge to the young girl Mīrā's devotion by thus suggesting that she is undergoing an *agniparīkṣā* or trial by fire, to prove her colors.

Later in the movie, Mīrā is shown singing the same refrain at the height of her success, when the emperor Akbar comes to visit her in the company of the court singer Tānsen. Mīrā's devotion has meanwhile ripened through adversity and pain that she has suffered, as expressed in the addition of new stanzas to this song:

aṃsuvana jala sīṃca sīṃca, prema bela boī,
aba to bela phaila gaī, ānanda phala hoī
(Gulzar 1979: 141)
With the tears of my eyes, I've watered the creeper of love that I've sown.
Now the plant has grown and borne the fruit of bliss.

The words of the second stanza of the song allude to the context in the movie of Mīrā's isolation, after she has been sent away from both her marital and paternal home:

tāta māta bhrāta bandhu, āpaṇo na koī,
chāṃḍa daī kula kī kāna kā karihe koī
(Gulzar 1979: 141)
Father, mother, brother, relative, I have no one.
I've given up family honor, what can they do to me?

The third stanza reminds the viewer of an earlier scene where she had taken off her jewelry in disgust, and the one where she became Raidās's disciple:

cunarī ke kiye ṭūka, oṛha līnhī loī,
motī-mūṃge utāra, vanamālā poī
I have torn to pieces my shawl, I've wrapped myself in the ascetic's garb.
I've discarded pearls and coral, a simple forest garland I've made.

After this song, the emperor presents Mīrā with a gift of jewelry, which she promptly offers to her God. However, the emperor is the archenemy of her husband's family, and when it is found out that she has accepted gifts from him, she is accused of high treason. She is put on trial, and her case seems hopeless, as the judge is the *mahant* with whom she did not get along from the start. The accusations are not just about politics, they actually mainly evolve around her failure to carry out her traditional *strīdharma*, or woman's duty. Echoes of the same leitmotiv song reappear during the final trial.

In the beginning of the trial, she is informed of the death of her cousin-brother Jaimal at the hands of the same Akbar who applauded her song.[18] In response, she recites a combination of the second and third stanza of the same verse:

tāta māta bhrāta bandhu, āpaṇo na koī,
chāṃḍa daī kula kī kāna oṛha līnhī loī
(Gulzar 1979: 146; only
in the screenplay)

> Father, mother, brother, relative, I have no one:
> I've given up family honour, I've donned the ascetic's garb.

The reference to loss of natal family has now come true in yet a different meaning: her last kinsman has died. Mīrā is truly alone. The stanza underlines Mīrā's isolation. Compared to the earlier version, we note a slight change in the second half of the last line: "I've donned the ascetic's garb" instead of the defiantly rhetorical: "What can anyone do to me?" It is poignant that the earlier challenge is toned down. No longer can Mīrā dare anyone by saying: "What can they do to me?" Clearly the court, or at least the *mahant* is out to hurt her. All Mīrā can say here is that she has taken shelter in sainthood, she has wrapped herself in the ascetic's garb.

During the trial, also the refrain of the song comes back to haunt Mīrā. When the *mahant* asks her whether she considered anyone else her husband besides Bhoj, Mīrā answers: *jāke sara mora mukuṭa mero pati soī* "The one with the peacock-crown, that's my husband"). When pressed whether she committed bigamy, she recites: *mere to giridhara gopāla, dūsaro na koī* ("I call Giridhara Gopāla my own, and no one else;" ibid. 147).

To the audience it is clear: she is condemning herself. What started as a charming conviction of a young girl will lead to a criminal conviction in court. Her own words are turned against her. Mīrā gets to speak some good lines during the court case, which make her triumph in spirit over the *mahant.* However, the bottom line is that eventually, such strong emotions, when they clash with patriarchal values, are punished in grand public display. This is not a message that the women viewers are likely to miss.

During the night before Mīrā's verdict, Gulzar chooses to depict her singing appropriately the famous song: *galī to cāroṃ band huī, maiṃ hari soṃ kaise milūṃ jāya* ("The road is barred on all sides, how can I escape to meet Hari?") (ibid.: 154).

Typically the song is interpreted as that of a Gopī, locked in her in-laws' house, unable to go out for an adulterous rendezvous with Krishna. However, Gulzar adds a new meaning: he shows Mīrā imprisoned for her faith and indeed her fate is closing in on her. Gulzar gives the song a further subtle twist by showing a contrast between a calm Mīrā, acquiescing in her fate, and a restless Bhoj, pacing up and down, feeling trapped and unable to unite with his beloved. Maybe this song more aptly expresses his feelings rather than Mīrā's. There is a remarkable twist in the interpretation: Bhoj is the restless lover, rather than Mīrā.

This builds up to a final climax, where Mīrā is convicted and drinks, as expected, the poison cup. The director respects the traditional miracle story: he shows her unharmed, walking out of the confines of the court into the open, into the desert, with a large crowd of admirers following her. She enters her Krishna temple and disappears, while all that remains is her *iktārā* and the book in which her songs are recorded. It allows for her triumph in defeat in a subtle way, one that leaves the viewer questioning what this means and what Mīrā stands for. The movie is open-ended: it leaves possibilities open rather than closing them by over-determination: the sure hallmark of a good movie.

Leitmotiv song 2: love hurts

However, there is something else going on in the final song. Let us consider Gulzar's interpretation of Mīrā's famous song on which he will end the movie. It is the song in which she confesses her love is crazy and causes her unspeakable pain:

> *e rī main to prema divānī, merī darda na jāne koya*
> *ghāyala kī gati ghāyala jāne, ki jina lāgī hoya*
> O my, I am crazy in love. No one knows my pain.
> Only the wounded know the condition of the wounded, or those who've gotten hurt.

In the screenplay, Mīrā has sung this song before, when she was still a young, unmarried girl on her way in a boat to worship Krishna in her favorite temple. She was accompanied by her cousin-sister Krishnā and confidante Lalitā who made fun of her, teasing her about her love for Krishna. The scene is one of happy and care-free banter. However the tone changes when they arrive at the temple, which is on inimical territory, as it belongs to the Sisodiyās. The young women are arrested by the handsome Sisodiyā prince Bhoj who declares that they are trespassing on his land. Krishnā shows herself a true Rajputani, and grabs a guard's sword, ready to defend herself and her companions. We can tell that Bhoj appreciates her assertiveness, and he sets the women free, though not without a stern warning never to return. Clearly Bhoj has made an impression on Krishnā and she on him.

On the way back home, Mīrā sings her song again, and this time, Krishnā chimes in. This is Gulzar's subtle way of letting us know that she too has fallen in love. Mīrā adds a line: *jauharī kī gati jauharī jāne, ki jina jauharī hoya* ("Only the jeweler knows the jewel's worth, or who would be an expert;" Gulzar 1979: 77). All three girls burst out laughing; they interpret it with reference to Krishnā's newly aroused passion for Bhoj. Thus, Mīrā's *bhakti* is put in the same light as Krishnā's girlish first love. The song is set in a playful context of a young girl's awakening erotic love (*pūrvārāga*).

Charming as this may be, it undermines the seriousness of Mīrā's devotional love, equating it with an immature girl's first love. The broader contextualization of the song confirms this. The song comes just after the scene where a servant reports to Mīrā's aunt that Mīrā has gone to the Krishna temple on inimical Sisodiyā territory: "Queen Mīrā is a great Krishna devotee, Milady." Mīra's aunt voices the view that Mīrā went too far in her devotion: "I am a devotee too, but she has gone to the point of being crazy" (ibid.: 73). The voice of maturity clearly disapproves of the sentiment expressed in the song.[19]

This reflects a criticism of Mīrā's *bhakti* as overemotional and immature. As in the scene with the little turban, Mīrā's devotion is reduced to a girl's fancy for a particular image. While that device may make dramatic sense as an attempt of the director to focus Mīrā's devotion, it still has the unfortunate side effect of belittling it and casting it in the light of a girl's fancy for a doll. One wonders whether this was intentional. It might seem so in the light of another movie for which Gulzar wrote the script, *Guddi* ("Doll"; 1971). That movie revolves around a young girl outgrowing her infatuation with a movie star. Gulzar had an interesting scene where the immature young girl latches onto Mīrā's example as a rationale and model for her infatuation (Lutgendorf forthcoming). Gulzar may here well be expressing a personal assessment that romantic interpretations of Mīrā's devotion may potentially lead astray young girls into fantasy worlds with impossibly romantic lovers that impede them from the more realistic pursuit of founding a family with a suitable (though unromantic) husband. We see this concern echoed in the movie about Mīrā herself: she certainly fails at building a family with her husband.

This same song about Mīrā's crazy love is taken up again at the very end of the movie. Mīrā has been condemned to death. She drinks the cup of poison that is offered to her, and then walks off into the desert, a crowd of onlookers following her. As she goes, she sings again the song about the pain of love, that now has acquired new depth. After Mīrā's travails, the song resonates with lived-through experience. Mīrā's love has matured. Yet, it can be argued that Gulzar is working to undermine Mīrā's message. There are two new lines that had not been quoted before:

> *jo maiṃ aisā jānatī, prīta kiye dukha hoya*
> *nagara ḍhiṃḍhorā pīṭatī, prīta na kījo koya*
> Had I known this, that when you love, you'll reap sorrow,
> I would have announced on the drum: No one should love!

Even as she triumphs over death, Mīrā says that, had she known how love can hurt, she would have announced it loudly for all to hear. And Gulzar has her proclaim it now, for the public to hear. As the audience leaves the theater, these words hover on their lips and the question in their mind may well be: "would Mīrā not have done the same had she to do it over?" If these words encapsulate the message of the movie, it seems to be that excessive love is a dangerous thing, even if it is love for God: it comes back to hurt you.

Conclusion

In conclusion, we can say that the message is mixed. Gulzar is true to the hagiographic tradition, both in his telling the stories around songs, and redacting the songs to suit his purposes. At the same time, he also "updates" the songs in a profoundly modern way with reference to contemporary women's issues. While this may come over as feminist-friendly in some instances, there are also some missed chances, as when the defying "Rāṇā" song is "domesticated." Mīrā's devotion is shown to be excessive and to undercut her real-life happiness.

Thus the message is that she is not to be imitated by ordinary women, Mīrā is unique, no other woman can be like her or should follow in her footsteps.[20] In sum, we find at times that identification with Mīrā's voice is encouraged, at others distance is preserved. Whereas he is unambiguous on the caste issue (showing interesting interventions of Raidās in Mīrā's poetic oeuvre), Gulzar is less clear on gender equality. He shows both: advocacy of women's resistance to patriarchal norms, as well as reinforcement of the status quo.

Gulzar's movie does justice to Mīrā's songs through a sensitive and creative contextualization, and the device of having them "grow" as she matures in her *bhakti*. However, there is also an undercurrent of criticism. Mīrā's words are literally turned against her in the final trial. Even more significant is the way Mīrā's "last" song, which the audience comes away with humming, is left hanging "in the air." In short, Gulzar's recasting of Mīrā's songs reveals an ambiguity about the female *bhakti* saint and her potentially patriarchy-defying message.

It would be interesting to compare with the other Mīrā movies, as well as with the male-centered devotionals on this point. All movies seem to promote caste equality, but why is it that the message of gender equality is more ambiguous? Part of this element in Gulzar's movie may be attributed to the formula of the popular movie and the perceived audience expectation that the patriarchal status quo be maintained. Or it may be part of the way popular culture in general domesticates threats to the status quo. We can find a similar trend, for instance, in the comic strip version of *Amar Chitra Kathā* (Hawley 1995).[21] One can also go back in time and ascribe such changes to the interpretation of Mīrā that Gandhi promoted (Mukta 1994: 182–200). On the other hand, one may read this "domestication" also as typical for the seventies, in reference to the thesis that contemporary movies represent a defense of the sexual economy of the middle-class, upper-caste extended family (Prasad 1998: 170–5). Yet another element is the director's personal assessment of the dangers of romanticized love for leading young girls astray. A comparative study with other "devotionals" would help, as would a reception history of this fascinating and understudied sub-genre.

Notes

* I wish to thank the students of my advanced Hindi class in 2000 and 2002, with whom I read through the *Meera* movie script and Vasudha Dalmia for her response to the paper when presented at the 18th Annual South Asia Conference in Berkeley in February 2003.

1 Called "Saint Films" and discussed under that heading in EIC (204).

2 He had in fact earlier made a movie on the Tantric saint Gorakhnāth, called *Maya Machhindra* ("Illusion," 1932).

3 For this film's invocation of deity and saint "to provide an alternative vision of social conditions and political self-determination," see Vasudevan 2000: 152–3. In 1940 the same directors brought out *Sant Dnyaneshwar* on the thirteenth-century saint of that name, who wrote a popular commentary in Marathi on the *Bhagavad-gītā*.

4 However, the popularity of the Maharastrian saints extends to pan-Indian cinema, as witnessed by the Telugu movie *Bhaktimala* (1941, d. Haribhai Desai, who was himself Gujarati), in praise of the Varkari saints of Maharashtra (EIC 289) and *Chakradhari* (or *Panduranga Mahima*, 1977, d. V. Madhusudhana Rao), on the Marathi poet Gora Kumbhar (EIC 431).

5 Similar in inspiration was Vijay Bhatt's 1940 *Narsi Bhagat*, also built around the actor Pagnis (EIC 285). Another Gujarati devotional film with a clear socially revolutionary message was *Jogidas Khuman* (1948, d. Manhar Raskapur) about the bandit-saint of that name, who is portrayed as a Robin Hood figure (its enduring appeal is clear as it was remade twice (1962 and 1975; EIC 311). A similar theme comes up also in the 1971 *Jesal Toral* (d. Ravindra Dave), based on a folk tale of the conversion of a bandit by a devout woman (EIC 409). There was also a Gujarati *Bhakta Tulsidas* (1951; d. Manibhai Vyas). Its director later worked in Rajasthani and brought out *Baba Ramdev*, with the "devotional stars" actors Mahipal and Anita Guha in 1963). That movie too promotes the cause of uplifting untouchable castes (EIC 375).

6 Maybe we should also mention the Punjabi movie *Nanak Naam Jahaz Hai* (1969, d. Ram Maheshwari), made for the 500th anniversary of Nanak's birth, inspired by legends of Amritsar's Golden Temple, and featuring musical setting of the Guru Granth Sahib (EIC 400–1).

7 An early movie focusing on a woman-saint and depicting woman's domestic problems is a Prabhat Film *Sant Sakhu* (1941, d. Fattelal Damle and Raja Nene; with Hansa Wadkar in the lead role) on the Marathi saint-poet of that name. However, this movie is characterized as more a "family melodrama" than a "devotional" (EIC 291). Most of the movie seems to focus on the domestic oppression of the devout Sakhu, who in the end is saved through her devotion. The message seems to be that self-sacrifice and long-suffering submission to patriarchal structures, if coupled with intense devotion, will pay off in the end.

8 There have been several popular movies that, while not being "devotionals" strictly speaking, evoke and have been inspired by Mīrā's life. The most famous classic is *Jogan* (1950, d. Kidarnath Sharma), starring Dilip Kumar and Nargis (I am grateful to Gayatri Chatterjee for bringing this extraordinary movie to my attention). More recently, the theme is explicitly taken up in the title of the 1993 social *Meera ka Girdhar* (d. Vijay Deep) and 1992 romantic *Meera ka Mohan* (d. K. Ravi Shankar). Philip Lutgendorf has identified recurrent references to Mīrā, which he calls a "Mīrā trope" in other Bollywood movies (forthcoming).

9 On the popularity of these songs, see Martin 1995 and 1999 and Mukta 1994. It is not clear who this "Rāṇā" might be. It is one of the titles of the dynasty of Mewar, and as she was married into the Sisodiyā royal house, that seems fitting. Sometimes, this is interpreted as referring to her husband (as by Gulzar, see below), sometimes to her father- or brother-in-law. As her husband, Bhoj, never was the actual Rāṇā of Chitorgarh, it was likely someone else, but the identity of the "evil king" is under dispute.

10 In a sister-article, to be published in the volume edited by Theo Damsteegt and Diana Dimitrova, I focus on the analysis of the way the movie retells the Mīrā story by unraveling allusions to traditional hagiographic stories.

11 Thus we cannot agree with Kishwar and Vanita's assessment that the movie shrouds Mīrā in miracles and mysteries (1989: 101).

12 It was a big setback for the makers of the movie that Lata Mangeshkar refused to perform the songs and that Laxmikant Pyarelal consequently left them out, but they managed to ensure a wonderful score by Pandit Ravi Shankar (Gulzar 1979: 22–5).

13 Mīrā's wedding is portrayed in the movie as part of an enlightened rapprochement between her family, which is Rāṭhauṛ, and that of her groom, which is Sisodiyā. The two clans are portrayed as engaged in an age-old vendetta, but willing to forget the

past in view of the Mughal threat to Rajput independence. In the movie, the wedding takes place in tragic circumstances (see Pauwels, forthcoming b).

14 The song remains incomplete, but is continued in the next scene where Mīrā visits the temple near the lake (*śyāma mane cākara rākho jī, cākara rahūṃ bāga lagāsūṃ nita uṭha darasana pāsūṃ*). At this point the Sant Raidās passes by and Mīrā has shifted into another famous song (*mora mukuṭa pītāmbara sohe gala baijayaṃtī mālā, Vrindābana meṃ dhenu carāve mohana muralī vālā*; ibid.: 110).One variant of the second line of the incomplete song comes back later in the movie, in a more fitting context. When Mīrā protests the closure of her favorite temple and has incurred the wrath of her in-laws, she sings: *hari rūṭhyāṃ kumhalāsyāṃ ho māya* (124) "when Hari is angry, I'll shrivel up, o friend." The change in wording works very well in the context of her hunger strike, as she indeed seems to be withering away.

15 She also sings two other songs during the hunger strike, one in the morning, as she is sweeping the courtyard (*jāgo baṃsīvāre mere pyāre jāgo*, "Wake up, flute player, my darling, wake up," ibid. 125), and one during the thunderstorm (*bādala dekha ḍarī ho śyāma*, "Seeing the clouds, I grow afraid, Śyāma," ibid.: 126).

16 That is in 1976, apparently the writing was done between *Mausam* and *Kinara* (ibid.: 32).

17 While Mīrā returns to her in-laws after this incident, that is not the end of her familial troubles. Gulzar illustrates how her devotion gets her further in trouble with her in-laws through her songs, such as: *jo tuma toḍo piyā maiṃ nāhīṃ toḍūṃ re*, "Even if you break it off, my love, I will not give up our relationship" (Gulzar 1979: 139). The song comes right after Mīrā dreams that her Krishna *mūrti* is thrown in a well by her enemies and she wakes up to find her room locked up from outside. In the course of the song, Mīrā is shown as having somehow escaped the palace and traveling on pilgrimage as if in search of Krishna. This changes the interpretation of the song: instead of Mīrā sticking with her Lord in the face of his unfaithfulness towards her, or his trying to escape her, as the song on its own implies, here she is seen as steadfast in the face of persecution from her in-laws. (This famous song features in several "secular" movies, as analyzed recently by Booth 2000: 136–8). This song is followed by a rather triumphantly sung pilgrimage song: *karanā fakīrī phira kyā dilagīrī, sadā magana maiṃ rahanā*, "Let's take to the road as a mendicant, then there's no sorrow, just remaining immersed for ever" (Gulzar 1979: 139–40).

18 Jaimal Rāṭhauṛ of Meṛtā indeed fell at the defense of Chitor, as is well-known from historical sources. However, it is conveniently forgotten that he had earlier worked to regain his kingdom in alliance with the Mughals (see Pauwels, forthcoming a).

19 While this first occurrence of the song does not appear in the version of the movie I watched, the comment by Mīrā's aunt does. Similar mature disapproval of Mīrā's excessive devotion comes later in the same scene (also absent from my movie version). The boatsman who rows Mīrā and her friends to the temple, hears them talk about Mīrā's jealousy of Radha. He laughs: "Mīrā *dīdī* is jealous of Radha, like a co-wife. Women (*aurat-jāt*) are all the same!" (Gulzar 1979: 74). Finally, in a scene that is portrayed in the movie, the *pūjārī* of Mīrā's favorite Krishna temple chides her when she expresses impatience: "Does Krishna too sometimes come here? That's the one for whom I come looking here." He answers: "Devotees are the very essence of God, my daughter! You too are nothing but the embodiment of God. When the Lord was leaving Vrindāban, Radha approached him…" In panditic fashion, he starts to illustrate this with a story, but Mīrā disrespectfully cuts him short: "Don't mention Radha, Panditjī. Her, I… Devā says she is my co-wife." He wisely answers: "All God's devotees are the same, my daughter."

20 This attitude is also prevalent among high-status Rajput women (Harlan 1992).

21 The comic strip is actually based on a narrative from the thirties (Martin 2000: 173–4).

References

Hindi works: editions

Caturvedī, Ā.P. (1983) *Mīrā Padāvalī*, 7th edn., Prayāg: Hindī Sāhitya Sammelan.
Purohit, H. (ed.) vol. 1 1968 (1989: reprint), vol. 2 1975 *Mīrāṃ Bṛhatpadāvalī*, 2 vols, Rājasthān Purātan Granthmālā 96, Jodhpur: Rajasthan Oriental Research Institute.

Other references

Appadurai, A. and Breckenridge, C.A. (1995) "Public Modernity in India," in C.A. Breckenridge (ed.) *Consuming Modernity: Public Culture in a South Asian World*, Minneapolis, MN: University of Minnesota Press.
Booth, G. (2000) "Religion, Gossip, Narrative Conventions and the Construction of Meaning in Hindi Film Songs," *Popular Music* 19.2: 125–45.
Chatterjee, G. (2005) "Icons and Events: Reinventing Visual Construction in Cinema in India," in R. Kaur and A.J. Sinha (eds) *Bollyworld: Popular Indian Cinema through a Transnational Lens*, New Delhi: Sage.
Gulzar (1979) *Mīrā: Kathā, moṃtāj (montage), anusandhān aur paṭkathā*, New Delhi: Rādhākṛṣṇa Prakāśan.
—— (1983) "Interview, January 1982," in A. Vasudev and P. Lenglet (eds) *Indian Cinema Superbazaar*, New Delhi: Vikas Publishing House.
Harlan, L. (1992) "Abandoning Shame: Mīrā and the Margins of Marriage," in L. Harlan and P.B. Courtright (eds) *From the Margins of Hindu Marriage: Essays on Gender, Religion, and Culture*, New York: Oxford University Press.
Hawley, J.S. (1995) "The Saints Subdued: Domestic Virtue and National Integration in Amar Chitra Katha," in L. Babb and S. Wadley (eds) *Media and the Transformation of Religion in South Asia*, Philadelphia, PA: University of Pennsylvania Press.
Kishwar, M. and Vanita, R. (1989a) "Poison to Nectar: The Life and Work of Mirabai," *Manushi* 50–2: 75–93.
—— (1989b) "Modern Versions of Mira," *Manushi* 50–2: 100–01.
Lutgendorf, P. (2002) "Jai Santoshi Maa and Caste Hierarchy in Indian Films" and "A 'Made to Satisfaction' Goddess: Jai Santoshi Maa Revisited," *Manushi* 131: 10–16, 24–37.
—— (forthcoming) "The Mīrā-trope," in N. Martin (ed.) *Celebrating Mīrābāī, Hindu Saint for a Global World*, New York: Oxford University Press.
Martin, N.M. (1995) "Mīrābāī: Inscribed in Text, Embodied in Life," *Journal of Vaisnava Studies* 3.1: 5–44.
—— (1999) "Mīrā Janma Patrī: A Tale of Resistance and Appropriation," in N.K. Singhi and R. Joshi (eds) *Religion, Ritual and Royalty*, Jaipur: Rawat Publications.
—— (2000) "Mīrābai in the Academy and the Politics of Identity," in M. Bose (ed.) *Faces of the Feminine in Ancient, Medieval, and Modern India*, New York: Oxford University Press.
Mukta, P. (1994) *Upholding the Common Life: The Community of Mirabai*, Gender Studies, Delhi: Oxford University Press.
Pauwels, H. (2006) "Hagography and Reception History: The case of Mīrā's Padas in Nāgrīdās's Pada-prasaṅga-mālā," in M. Horstmann (ed.) *Bhakti in Current Research 2001–2003: Proceedings of the Ninth International Conference on Early*

Devotional Literature in New Indo-Aryan languages, Heidelberg, July 23–6, 2003, New Delhi: Manohar.

—— (forthcoming a) "Rāṭhauṛī Mīrā: Two Neglected Rāṭhauṛ Connections of Mīrā: Jaimal Meṛtīyo and Nāgrīdās," in N. Martin (ed) *Celebrating Mīrābāī, Hindu Saint for a Global World*, New York: Oxford University Press.

—— (forthcoming b) "Who is Afraid of Mīrābāī? Gulzar's Antidote for Mīrā's Poison," in T. Damsteegt and D. Dimitrova (eds) *Religion and Gender in Literature and Film.*

Sangari, K. (1990) "Mirabai and the Spiritual Economy of Bhakti," *The Economic and Political Weekly* July 7, 1990: 1464–75 and July 14, 1990: 1537–52.

Vasudevan, R.S. (2000) "The Politics of Cultural Address in a 'Transitional' Cinema: A Case Study of Indian Popular Cinema," in C. Gledhill and L. Williams (eds) *Reinventing Film Studies*, London: Arnold Publishers.

von Skyhawk, H. (2001) "Saint, Cinéma et dharma: Ekanāth et les intouchables au temps the V. Śāntārām," in F. Mallison (ed.) *Constructions hagiographiques dans le monde indien: Entre mythe et histoire*, Paris: Librairie Honoré Champion.

Part 4

Genre and themes from "Indo-Islamic" culture

6 Religious culture and folklore in the Urdu historical drama *Anārkalī*, revisited by Indian cinema

Alain Désoulières

Introduction: *Anārkalī* as stage play and film script

Anarkali is the quasi-mythical character of a slave girl in love with the Mughal imperial heir, Salim. The Prince passionately answered her love, but the Emperor (the father, Akbar), would not approve of such a debasing liaison. He had the poor girl walled alive while the Prince was kept away. The "romantic" drama takes place in Lahore, at the Mughal Court, supposedly in 1599. Legend has it that years after her tragic death, Salim, now the new (and still grieving) Emperor Jahangir, had a magnificent mausoleum built in her memory. This so-called Anarkali's tomb is still standing and very famous, as is Anarkali herself.

As far as the intrigue is concerned we have the "eternal triangle" of the couple of lovers plus the jealous rival. Akbar also symbolizes the intimate contradiction between the loving father and the caring statesman. The tragic end of the heroine is triggered by his opposing the intercaste marriage, but it also signifies the sacrifice of love for reasons of statehood. In short, this legend has all the makings for a successful drama or film.

The story of Anarkali was first written up as a historical drama in Lahore by Sayyad Imtiaz Ali Taj in 1922. It was not an immediate success. In his preface to the second edition, the author states that it was not appreciated by the theaters: they suggested changes that he did not like. The play contains very detailed descriptions of the locale and atmosphere of each scene, which was not easily created on stage, which may explain why it was refused by Indian troupes.

Imtiaz Ali may also have been ahead of his time. In the 1920s the historian of Urdu literature Ram Babu Saksena, was complaining about the lack of serious inspiration of Urdu drama, which he considered decadent and vulgar (1927: 350). According to him it lacked the proper dramatic serious national inspiration in its themes. The reason for the failure of the first version of Imtiaz Ali Taj's *Anārkalī* as a popular stage drama in the 1920s may be exactly that it was too serious a drama, and not vulgar enough. Imtiaz Ali seems to have written in response to Saksena. He was also reacting against two modern trends in Urdu drama: the prevalence of translations from English drama and of popular Parsi dramas that relied on Persian or traditional Hindu mythology (the latter called *nāṭak*). Imtiaz Ali opted instead for a historical drama.

Soon after the Lahore Cinema studios were created, Imtiaz Ali tried to have a film made. He was successful and Great Eastern Film Corporation produced *The Loves of a Mughal Prince* aka *Anarkali* (codirected by Prafulla and Charu Roy, starring Seeta Devi, EIC 251). Imtiaz Ali even acted the role of Akbar in the film. However, they were beaten by the Bombay studios that had also picked up the idea and story, and released another film *Anarkali* in 1928 (by Imperial, directed by R.S. Choudhury with Sulochana in the title role; remade in 1935; EIC 251). The Lahore film looked like a pale copy of the well-financed and well-distributed Bombay release (Gazdar 1997: 20ff.).

With the advent of the talking cinema in 1931, the Urdu stage drama, which specialized in historical drama, already affected by the (so-called) silent historical cinema, was in shambles. That is what prompted Imtiaz Ali, nearly ten years after his first version, in 1931, to rewrite and go to print: "considering the poor state of affairs in Urdu stage drama" (Taj 1931a: preface 5–7).[1] This time, the play was a success: it provoked many reviews and was constantly republished, not to speak of English translations and adaptations in Urdu (for example a versified adaptation), or other Indian languages. Moreover, his great story inspired quite a few films and television dramas. In this article we will refer mainly to the two best-known films, namely Nandlal Jaswantlal's 1953 *Anarkali* and K. Asif's1960 *Mughal-e-Azam.*[2] Even if neither acknowledges the original play, they are clearly influenced by it.

Thus the case of Anarkali illustrates the influence of Urdu literature on film, a contribution that is sadly sometimes forgotten by the modern film critics:

> Incidentally we would like to remind the reader of the importance of Urdu language and literature (Urdu legends, or *qissā*s, and novels) in the building of popular heroes in the Indian cinema, right from India's first talkies. Urdu films showing Muslim historicals and Muslim or Persian mythologicals played a very significant part in the making of Indian cinema. It is impossible to do justice here to so many poets and scriptwriters (like for example Sahir Ludhianvi) who worked very successfully for the Indian cinema.
>
> (Syed 1985: 489–93)

The *Encyclopaedia of Hindi Cinema*, though acknowledging Imtiaz Ali Taj's influence, does not classify *Mughal-e-Azam* as an "Urdu language film" (Arif 2003). However, it is indeed qualified as "Urdu film" by Rajadhyaksha and Willemen in their *Encyclopaedia of Indian Cinema* (1995), because of the influence of Imtiaz Ali Taj's drama.[3] The Urdu or Hindi label does not make much of a difference for the cinema directors, but it is an indication of the level and style of language, inspired by literature. "Urdu literature influenced films" or "Urdu literary films" seems to me a workable concept for classifying films.

It is fair to balance stressing the impact of Imtiaz Ali's work on cinema with pointing out that the influence goes both ways. As he rewrote his play, Imtiaz Ali did so with a view to attract filmmakers, as he says himself (1931a: preface 6). He included very precise stage directions, dialogues, descriptions, songs, and dances.

The case of Anarkali then illustrates the complex interactions at the interface of cinema and literature. This chapter explores first generally how Imtiaz Ali

Taj's *Anārkalī* exemplifies the genre of the historical drama and how that played in the films, focusing in particular on the tension between historical realism and popular entertainment. Further, I investigate in that light two crucial scenes in detail, namely that of the "reported kiss" and the final fatal dance scene.

Anārkalī: a historical drama by Sayyad Imtiaz Ali Taj

Sayyad Imtiaz Ali Taj's historical drama is divided in three acts (*bāb*): "Romance" or "Passion" (*iśq*), "Dance" (*raqs*), and "Death" (*maut*). Every act is subdivided into five scenes (*manzar*), and every scene bears a title that is actually the name of the precise places where the action is taking place (they are quoted in the list of scenes at the beginning of the printed drama). For example, the first scene of Act 1 is situated "between the Imperial Harem and the Lower Garden of the Lahore Fort." Such indications occur at the beginning of every scene, often introducing a precise description of the palaces and gardens. Thus we have a classical dramatic frame, one that respects the well-known rule of the three unities: unity of action in the tragic romance of the Prince Salim and the slave Anarkali (from the first meetings to the tragic end); unity of place in that the entire action takes place inside the Imperial palace of Lahore, and unity of time in that the whole drama is happening "during the Spring season of 1599" to quote the author (1931a: 9).

The play belongs in the genre of the historical drama, a modern prose genre that flourished in India, inspired by the European romantic and historical drama of the nineteenth century. In Europe as well as in India many historical feature films inherited from this literary genre as well as from the historical novel (naturally the historical novel also appeared in Urdu, for example with Sharar, who was also an historiographer of Lucknow).[4] The historical drama carries both light and serious dramas. It bears on a precise historical context, but may involve characters that are fictitious.

This genre has two constraints if it wants to achieve its aim, namely to convince and to seduce the reader; the first constraint is to be realistic enough, and the second one is to have a well-identified romantic and tragic plot. From the language point of view, it is obvious that realism must be achieved by using the appropriate historical terms and relevant registers of language. But witty dialogues and poetry (that become songs and dances in cinema), are also a must: they are powerful artistic factors that seduce the spectator.

There is a third element: to be successful on the stage (and on the screen), the historical drama must have popular religious and folklore features. These features were already there in the Parsi drama of Northern India, mostly in Urdu but not in a literary form. It may be the legend itself that borders on history, but also popular culture, religion, and characters that give some *couleur locale*, pleasing both the elite and the public at large. I will discuss each of these three elements in detail.

A Lahore legend: Orientalist interpretations of the "tyrant" Akbar

The historical drama writer is in need of a story that bears on a precise historical context in order to be realistic enough, and he has to work with a romantic and tragic plot, mostly with well-identified historical characters. With the myth of Anarkali, popular historiography of Lahore provided just that: its characters (except for the heroine) were authentic historical characters that had lived (and ruled) in Lahore. No wonder Imtiaz Ali Taj, himself an inhabitant of Lahore, chose this legend with its tragic, serious, and dramatic story.

There is an "Orientalist" aspect to the legend, as the story came to Imtiaz Ali mediated through Western travelers. In their travelogues, writers like Bishop Herbert, William Finch, and Edward Terry duly reported the legend. Their writings were featured in Foster's *Early Travels in India*: *Edward Terry and other European travelers of the Mughal era*, which was first published at Oxford in 1921, just before Imtiaz Ali Taj wrote his first version of his drama *Anārkalī* in 1922. He may have read Terry's *Voyage to East India* through Foster's anthology. On the other hand, the tales of the Western travelers were also eagerly quoted by local historians, as they loved to refer to Western sources, especially during the Victorian era, at the end of nineteenth century. Imtiaz Ali may have come across the travel reports that way.

The tragic end of the slave Anarkali walled alive by order of the "cruel" Mughal Emperor fitted well the Victorian and colonial ideology that needed to justify colonial exploitation by the promise of a civilized and peaceful rule, especially after the 1857–58 severe and cruel repression. However, the tale contradicted the well-known notion of Emperor Akbar's clemency and sense of justice. At the time he wrote the play and more so when he rewrote it without changing the plot, Imtiaz Ali must have been criticized for his choice to depict Mughal Emperor Akbar as an irate father and an inflexible ruler. However, invoking he had "studied Western drama for ten years" our author thought it best to stick to his somehow historical, tragic, and romantic tale. His hunch that it was still fashionable, especially in the booming cinema industry, may have inspired the decision to go in print, in spite of the opposition of the stage drama companies. He concludes his preface for his cultivated reader, or prospective cinema director, by explaining his preference.

> I do not know when and how this tale [Urdu *dāstān*] was invented. And the histories of Lahore that mention it do not say where they have taken it.[5] In the tale itself, there are several weak points, judging by internal testimonies that prevent the reader to make a solid judgment. But historians can discuss these points better than me. My drama is only concerned with [oral] tradition. I have been listening to the imaginary story of Anarkali from my childhood, thus the drama that my imagination saw in the pomp and splendor of the Mughal harem is the expression of this story of beauty, and passionate love with its failure as an unhappy end. So far whoever listened to my drama has this objection at this point: is this tragedy about Anarkali and Salim or is it about Akbar the Great? But Anarkali is such a heart-touching character that at the moment of choosing the name [and title] it was impossible for me to retain another subject.
>
> (Taj 1931a: preface 6)

It is not till the 1960s film version that the ending becomes "politically correct." Jaswantlal's 1953 *Anarkali* still sticks to the plot devised by Imtiaz Ali Taj with the same tragic outcome. However, K. Asif in his *Mughal-e-Azam* preferred a happy ending. Famously, he has Anarkali escape thanks to Akbar's clemency. This has been criticized:

> Again in his anxiety to show Akbar as a compassionate king, and to provide his film with a "happy ending," Asif changed the popular legend by letting Anarkali escape through the false bottom of the wall which opens into a tunnel. This defies the internal logic of the tragic situation.
>
> (Garga 1996: 175–6)

One could say that Asif finally gave in to the pressure that Imtiaz Ali had resisted so stubbornly, or that he at last managed to shake off the baggage inherited from the colonial period travelogues.

The sources of the story

Right in the introduction to the play, Sayyad Imtiaz Ali Taj cautions that "as far as [he] could investigate, [his] story has no historical base." However, he is careful to give his sources; presumably he thought it would interest his curious and cultivated reader, the intellectual Urdu speaking urban class of Lahore, which also included British residents.

> The tale (*dastān*) that is written in a frame in a wall of Anarkali's tomb by the Lahore Archeological Survey.... Anarkali (the pomegranate blossom), by which name the Civil station is called, was the title given to Nadira Begam, or Sharf-un-Nissa, one of the favorites of the Emperor Akbar. One day, while the Emperor was seated in an apartment lined with looking glasses, with the youthful Anarkali attending him, he saw from her reflection in the mirror that she returned Prince Saleem (afterward Jahangir) a smile. Suspecting her of a criminal intrigue with his son, the Emperor ordered her to be buried alive. She was accordingly placed in an upright position at the appointed place, and was built round with bricks. Saleem felt intense remorse at her death, and, on assuming sovereign authority, had an immense superstructure raised over her sepulchre. The sarcophagus is made of pure marble of extraordinary beauty and exquisite workmanship. It is, according to Mr. Eastwick "one of the finest pieces of carving in the world." On the top are inscribed the ninety-nine attributes of God, and on the sides is engraved the following Persian couplet, composed by Jahangir, her royal paramour:
>
> *tā qayāmat śukar goyim kard gār-e-khaviś rā*
> *āh gar man bāz bīnam rū-e-yār-e-khaviś rā*[6]
> Ah ! could I behold the face of my beloved once more,
> I would give thanks to my God until the day of resurrection.

> On the North side of the sarcophagus, below the ninety-nine attributes of the Deity, is the inscription—*majnūn salīm akbar* "The profoundly enamoured Saleem, son of Akbar," Saleem being the name of Jahangir when a Prince. The inscription shows how passionately fond Saleem had been of Anarkali, and how deeply her death had grieved him. It is the spontaneous outcome of a melancholic mind, the irrepressible outburst of an affectionate heart.
>
> (Taj 1931a: Preface 8)

But for the last sentence, and though he does not say so, this is literally taken from Sayyid Muhammad Latif's *History of Lahore*, from the section "The tomb of Anarkali" (1892: 186–7; translated from English into Urdu). Latif further elaborates on the later history of the tomb, under colonial rule with some architectural details, including the traditional inscriptions and chronograms bearing the dates of burial, and the date of completion of the monument. The date given in letters and figures is 1008 AH (1599 CE), which refers to the death of Anarkali. On the west side of the sarcophagus above the words "In Lahore," is another date, 1024 AH (1615 CE), which is the date of the building of the tomb. Akbar died on October 13, 1605, and thus the tomb was completed ten years after his death (Latif 1892: 187).

Imtiaz Ali Taj simply quotes the plaques and Persian inscriptions on the monument, without crediting Latif's work, but he must have read it, like every cultivated Lahori, fascinated by Mughal history as he was. Perhaps he did not need to tell his reader where the quote came from: everyone would know. Of course Imtiaz Ali Taj, who could read and write Persian very fluently, did not need Latif's work to read Persian inscriptions. However, Latif's work was a well-known historical source, along with the Lahore Archeological Survey.

Latif was also the author of an impressive history of Punjab, first written in Urdu and later on translated into English in 1889. There he does not mention the story of Anarkali. Latif's historical writings are usually well-documented with reference to Arabic and Persian sources. A few years later, when he relates the Anarkali story in his *History of Lahore*, he does not quote any Persian (or Indian) authority, only carefully noting the Persian inscriptions, translating them into English. The lack of Persian sources, as well as the absence of the story of Anarkali in his *History of Panjab* suggest that Latif was aware that it was but a local legend. We can speculate that he included it to please his English readership—he would not have been the first to do so—thus avoiding to contradict the doubtful testimony of European travelers, who themselves were relying on hearsay, and perhaps on local oral tradition.[7] This is not unlike Imtiaz Ali Taj, who was in search of a romantic tale to please stage-drama and cinema audiences.

The cinematic adaptations too feel the need to state clearly the legendary character of the love story. K. Asif characterizes it as a felicitous confluence of "history and legend" and Jaswantlal's foreword to the viewers states (in Urdu, Hindi, and English, a rare feature in the credit sequence): "The picture 'Anarkali' is based on a legendary romance between Prince Salim and Anarkali and has no foundation what so ever in history." That sounds like an echo of Imtiaz Ali's preface.

Further, the Urdu version of the trilingual foreword uses the same Urdu word (*dastān*) to qualify the story of Anarkali. As the credits role, the supposed monumental tomb of Anarkali is shown in the background, while a bard is singing the praise of Anarkali's fatal love. This is also reminiscent of Imtiaz Ali's preface. Though Imtiaz Ali Taj is not mentioned anywhere by name in the credits, he is the major inspiration behind how Jaswantlal framed his story.

Historical realism in setting and language

Imtiaz Ali was barely in his twenties when he wrote his first version of the drama. He had an intimate connection with the local legend, as he was from Lahore, living close to what is supposed to be Anarkali's tomb.[8] He was fascinated with Mughal and local history of Lahore. In those days there was still a strong tradition of Urdu and English local historiography, notably Latif's work, by which Imtiaz Ali was influenced a lot as we have seen.[9] For his second version, Imtiaz Ali Taj secured the help of two erudite local Lahori historians, Ghulam Abbas Sahib and Maulana Chiragh Hasan Hasrat, to proofread his drama, as he mentions in the preface of the second version (1931a: preface 7). This serves to reinforce his claim to historical realism.

Due to the loss of the first version of the play, we can only guess how Imtiaz Ali Taj revised his drama. We know he listened to some literary criticism. He may have expanded the descriptive passages of his play, which read like passages from an historical novel, particularly the first introductory descriptive passage about the royal garden and daily life in the women's quarters (Act 1, scene 1, 1931a: 11–12) and the presentation of Salim's palace and apartments with a luxury of colorful details (Act 1, scene 2, 1931a: 22–3).[10] These passages emphasize the *couleur locale*, and add to the realistic aspect of the play.

The realistic and picturesque description of the Mughal Palace goes well beyond the usual instructions for decor makers and stage indications. It first describes the landscape, has a slow approaching movement and enters the palace, and finally goes into minute details of the inner decoration and style, thus giving almost an indication for a camera movement. The description is replete with architectural technical terms. Combining technical/historical terminology with a well-structured description was a way to present to the reader a kind of reconstruction by means of literary description. Imtiaz Ali Taj knew the Lahore Fort very well and could have used descriptions of it in Urdu.

Another example of historical realism is the chosen time and place. Imtiaz Ali situates the story in the Punjab, where the Mughal Court is supposed to have sojourned,[11] and at the time of the Spring Festival, for which the author uses the Persian name, *Jaśan-e-nauroz.* Indeed, this was instituted by Akbar at the Mughal Court (see below).

In spite of all the attention to historical and archeological details, we should not forget that this is fiction and the buildings and palace described never existed in Lahore during Akbar's reign, but were built during Jahangir's reign. Imtiaz Ali Taj was certainly aware of this anachronism and we may take it as an intentional fake reconstruction of the past. In a similar approach, the successive film directors would reconstruct familiar Mughal buildings for their viewers, irrespective of whether they were actually built during Akbar's reign. In Jaswantlal's film, the Mughal architecture and interiors (in particular the sophisticated candelabras), including the great hall of mirrors, are close to what Imtiaz Ali Taj described. The same is true for K. Asif's *Mughal-e-Azam*. Similar observations prompted Salim Arif, in the *Encyclopaedia of Hindi Cinema*, to criticize the movie on grounds of lack of historical realism:

Authenticity versus effect

> This attitude towards historical characters and events resulted in films that violated authenticity for the sake of effect, of which K. Asif's *Mughal-e-Azam* is the best example. Based on Imtiaz Ali Taj's play *Anarkali*, *Mughal-e-Azam* had a predecessor in Filmistan's 1953 production of *Anarkali*. The same story with changed emphasis and excellent production values and performances, made *Mughal-e-Azam* a landmark in Hindi cinema.
>
> Though the *Mughal-e-Azam* characters have become a part of Indian cinema folklore, the film was anything but historically accurate in the manner of textual details, costumes, sets, and music. For instance, *thumri*, a nineteenth-century musical form is used along with *kathak* costumes in a court supposedly in the late sixteenth century India. Even the Sheesh Mahal (the royal bath of the actual queen) is enlarged into a dancing hall of the Mughal Emperor, Akbar. Anarkali could have been one of the numerous dancing girls of the Mughal harem; whether the Mughal Prince Salim fought his father over his beloved is not documented in history.
>
> (Arif 2003: 233)

Comparing the film directors' visions and the architectural approach in Imtiaz Ali Taj's Urdu drama, we may say that we have a case of historical reconstruction for romantic and popular intent. In a way, the directors stay true to Imtiaz Ali Taj's dramatic vision. Indeed, if we look at the introductory sequences of Jaswantlal's *Anarkali* with its typical Mughal-style arches of Anarkali's supposed tomb, with a storm agitating the palm trees or the décor of *Mughal-e-Azam* with the impressive Mughal Fort, its ever blooming gardens and inner decoration, we can see that Imtiaz Ali Taj's vision prevailed.

The author of the historical drama also has to make it sound authentic linguistically. The use of historical names and titles that fit the atmosphere of the drama make it sound real. Imtiaz Ali does this masterfully. A good summary is the initial list of *dramatis personae*, or cast of characters (simply called *afrād*, or "individuals"), where the author briefly names and defines the characters of his drama (1931a: 8). It is both a technical point and a way of immersing the reader into the Mughal historical atmosphere (for a full analysis, see Désoulières, 2007).

When he rewrote the play in 1931, Imtiaz Ali Taj must also have revised the poetic passages. Incidentally, two Persian ghazals included in the play do not mention Imtiaz Ali's *nom de plume* (or *ta<u>kh</u>allus*), "Taj." There is also a *gīt*, or song, and occasional quotations of Persian verses. The poetry is a minor aspect of the play, as all the dialogues are in prose with distinct registers of speech according to the social status of the different characters, but it is an integral part of the courtly decor and life style. Would Imtiaz Ali Taj let us believe that we are reading an "authentic" Hindi *gīt* and Persian ghazals from the end of sixteenth century?

What is left of Imtiaz Ali Taj's language and style in the films? This question is complicated by the fact that by 1960 we already have a cinematic tradition of its own for the myth of Anarkali. However, in general, film directors have retained most of the characters with their names and honorific titles. The use of appropriate names and titles according to the situation for the historical characters, whether in the court or in privacy, seems to have been well set by Imtiaz Ali Taj. This may be a reminiscence of the Parsi Drama historical tradition, but in any case the usage was adopted by the talking cinema. In his short article on Urdu Cinema, Siraj Syed (1985) says:

> Kamal Amrohi wrote *Pukar* in 1939 and, as parts of the dialogue, included a string of titles recited aloud in the palace whenever the Emperor entered the Durbar (*sic*). This was in high-flown Urdu and rightly so. They became and remained a highlight of the film to be repeated twenty years later with terrific impact in K. Asif's "Mughal-e-Azam."
>
> (Syed 1985: 489)

But Siraj Syed might have also quoted the film *Anarkali* by Nandlal Jaswantlal (1953) for the same highlight, and perhaps the preceding *Anarkali* feature films, which likely picked up the story inclusive the titles for the characters. Ultimately it is Sayyad Imtiaz Ali Taj's careful research that underlies these by now standard conventions in Urdu film dialogue.

Popular tale and folk traditions

The myth of Anarkali as related by Indian local historians and European travelers seems to have been inspired by local tales. Indeed Imtiaz Ali Taj claimed to rely mainly on "tradition." He refers to oral, and perhaps family traditions. As for the name of the heroine, Anarkali, it is consistent with "Indo-Islamic" popular culture. *Anār* is the Persian word for "pomegranate" and *kalī*, is a Hindi term for "flower bud." It seems that Imtiaz Ali's imagination was carried away by the poetic charm of the name: he almost says so when explaining how Akbar gave the poetic surname to the beautiful slave Nadira (Act 1, scene 1, Taj 1931a: 14). While Anarkali is inherited from the legend, Nadira is the realistic name invented by the author: *nādira* is a feminine Arabic adjective, meaning "the exceptional one." And again the name Anarkali, a metaphor by itself, is used for poetic and romantic effect in the mouth of Prince Salim (Act 1, scene 1, Taj 1931a: 30–1). In the list of characters, Anarkali's role is summed up as "a slave girl of the royal harem who caught the King's eye" which means a favorite, selected slave (*kanīz*, Persian word for "female slave"). The term does not imply that she is a courtesan, but her duties are to dance and sing, especially for the royal festivals. In both

Jaswantlal's and K. Asif's films we note the same features for Anarkali/Nadira, and she has exactly the same status and family within the harem.

As if to bring his legendary heroine to life, Imtiaz Ali Taj requested his friend and famous painter Abdur Rahman Chughtaï to enliven "his dead words" with a portrait of Anarkali, which provided a beautiful cover for his 1931 edition.[12] He remarks:

> My respected friend, the painter Abdur Rahman Chughtaï, who is the elegance and pride of India, has blended my dead words with his living touch of paint. Thus the printing of this drama has given me as much of happiness as if it had been represented on stage. Perhaps he [Chughtaï] may not think of it as such a great favor, but for me I take it as a subject of pride and honor. (1931a: preface 6)[13]

Figure 6.1 Anarkali portrait by Abdur Rahman Chughtaï; courtesy Mr Arif Chughtai. Printed with kind permission of Chughtai Museum, Lahore, holder of copyright to all Chughtai art material.

Imtiaz Ali Taj's choice of Chughtaï as an illustrator was particularly felicitous, as Chughtaï's style evoked to the reader both modern sensibility and sensuality of the 1930s, and the general aspect of courtly miniature painting art. Indeed the lack of perspective, the drawing technique, preceding the filling with colors, the turban and the attire of the young and beautiful Anarkali holding a flower (or cup; a typical attitude for Mughal princely portraits), all these traits tend to remind the reader of Mughal courtly miniature painting.

However some significant details defy the conventions of the genre and are distinctly modern. For one, many Mughal miniatures that represent women feature a classical landscape in the background. By contrast, we have a uniform background, the color of which matches the complexion of the heroine, studded with floral motifs, evocating both "Indo-Islamic" mosaics and Art Nouveau. Her face is seen in profile, and although her traits are very much traditional ones (by the drawing of her lips, nose and eyebrow), her jewelry is too elaborate for an Indian low-caste court dancer and it rather evokes Art Nouveau portraits. The same can be said for her long and elaborated hair locks, her turban, and the absence of any veil. In a nutshell this picture shows an eclectic mixture of Mughal portraiture traits with a modern sensibilities.

No wonder Imtiaz Ali Taj's would feel so happy and proud of this work of art, inspired by his writings. It encapsulates his stylistic attempt to blend realistic historical writing with romantic, modern, and popular tastes. The picture is an ideal representation of the crux of the drama. For him, that picture would serve to introduce his writings as potential script for film directors, somewhat like a cinema poster, at a time when he was refused by the Lahori stage companies. It would, as well advertise his work as an authentically Indian inspired, literary drama, following Saksena's recommendations for a new and creative Indian dramatic art (Saksena 1927: 360).

Apart from the main theme, Imtiaz Ali's work was indebted in other ways to popular tradition. One of his sources may have been the Punjabi popular legend of Sassi-Punnu, a story almost every educated child from Lahore knew.[14] The theme of the tale presents some striking similarities with that of Anarkali. Both are tales of impossible love foregrounding a frustrated (feminine) lover. Sassi is, like Anarkali the heroine and the unfortunate girl who becomes the victim of her love for a man who is incapable of defending her. In both tales, the heroine is from a humble family and punished by fate, for having dared to love a man who belongs to the aristocracy. In both tales, a key element of the plot is the intoxicating liquor used by the enemies of the unfortunate couple, to destroy and kill their love. Finally, both heroines are punished and killed for their audacious love by being buried alive: Sassi by a storm in the desert while she is desperately looking for Punnu, and Anarkali is walled by bricks on the Emperor's orders, while she is separated from Salim. This mode of execution is not, to my knowledge, recorded during Akbar's reign. Imtiaz Ali Taj may have received criticism for that detail, but, as he says, he remained faithful to the tale heard during his childhood.

Imtiaz Ali Taj knew his popular Punjabi tales: they were narrated within the family circle, read in Urdu (in his social milieu), and also played in *nāṭak*, or popular plays. Many of them would also inspire the Indian stage drama and, later on, cinema. Thus, it seems likely that popular tales have influenced the author's presentation of the legend. What is remarkable is his ability to balance his love for official Mughal history of Lahore (which he professes in his preface, quoted earlier) with the charm of popular tales.

Finally, throughout the play, the author interweaves the action with song and dance, often taken from folk genres current at the time. This phenomenon is best illustrated with a detailed description of the climactic *Jaśan-e-bahār* dance festivities (below).

We now have a more precise view of Imtiaz Ali Taj's literary design. He was writing what he thought would be a successful story, using popular and learned sources alike, within a serious literary and "historical drama." With the help of some local intelligentsia and a famous painter he republished his literary drama, not to have it played by the local stage drama company, but instead aiming for the movie industry. He tried to appeal to both the elite and popular audience, with a luxury of linguistic and historical details, as well as popular elements. The rest of the chapter will be a detailed demonstration of these aspects for two crucial scenes, one at the beginning of the romance, one signaling the dramatic end, one a dialogue, the other a dance sequence.

Case study 1. Dialogue in the harem: a reported kiss

As a case study, let us examine some features of one of the most famous dialogues written by Imtiaz Ali Taj, and find out what levels of language were used by the author and how it fared in the films. This dialogue, between the heroine Anarkali and her younger sister, Surayya, takes place at the end of the first scene of Act 1. The location is a secluded place of the women's quarter (the imperial harem). Anarkali, who is already the favorite dancer of the Emperor, and has also caught the eye of the Crown Prince, has retired alone most of the day.

> Surayya enters: a thirteen-year old, clever, cheerful, playful girl. Her features are better than Anarkali's, but she is not as charming. She has gained in wisdom by listening to the tales of the intrigues and plots of the palace. But because of her lack of experience and young age, she does not know the ways to dissimulate her wisdom.
>
> *Surayya:* So you are here, my dear Apa (elder sister) Nadira!
> *Anarkali:* So what, Surayya?
> *Surayya:* (in a loving tone) Oh come on, everybody is asking for you.
> *Anarkali:* (with a sad smile) Anarkali that was....
> *Surayya:* Why, Apa?
> *Anarkali:* Yes, that's the very word, why? (she gets up, intending to leave).
> *Surayya:* (putting her arms around her sister's waist) Why are you so silent, my dear sister?
> *Anarkali:* (smiling and dodging) Not so, my little one.
> *Surayya:* (playfully) The little one may agree, but Prince Salim may not agree, my sister.

Anarkali: (startled) The Crown Prince (*Sāhib-e-ālam*), you met him? When, today?

Surayya: (enjoying the situation) His Highness came to the Harem this afternoon. I met him on his way. Then he asked me: "Your Anarkali did not show up. Where is she today?" Before I could answer he said "Surayya, why is she so silent and staying away from everybody? Is it her habit or is it her condition these days only?" Then, taking my hand in both his hands with fervor, he told me "Surayya, please tell me, is she in the same condition, like me, these days?"

Anarkali: Then what did you tell him?

Surayya: I said: "That is also her condition these days, just like you." (Anarkali, losing her balance, sits on the stool). The moment he heard that he blushed and overwhelmed by happiness, he kissed my forehead.

Anarkali: (staring at her) Did he kiss your forehead?

Surayya: Yes and then his eyes were full of tears, and he went out quickly.

Anarkali: Oh my God, the Crown Prince's eyes full of tears. So whatever you said is true, Surayya?... (she pauses to think about it). Then what will be the result?

Surayya: (embracing Anarkali, and putting her mouth close to her sister's ear, as if she were going to tell something very important) Some day, my sister will become Hindustan's....

Anarkali: (putting immediately her hand on Surayya's mouth, being on the alert and listening with full attention) Shut up, Surayya, look, listen... (both of them are all ears, listening carefully—they pause for what seems an unlimited moment).

Surayya: There is nothing at all.

Anarkali: Alas, there was something... my heart is so oppressed. Surayya, somebody is talking in my ears: "Thou art a burnt star, Nadira." (pause) What a thing you told me! Why did I ask you, anyway!

Surayya: Listen, outside on the tree, what is he telling?

Anarkali: Oh the crow...

Surayya: You can now feel happy after this good omen (embracing her), my dear Apa!

Anarkali: (hugging her sister) My dear little Surayya.
(while kissing her cheeks again and again she kisses her on the forehead, and feeling suddenly embarrassed, she bows her head).

Surayya: (chattering) Why do you get so embarrassed, after kissing my forehead, Apa? Is it because the Crown Prince also did....?

Anarkali: (ashamed, evading her, sister) Oh I just forgot!

Surayya: (giggling) What a delightful way of forgetting.
(wherever Anarkali turns her face, Surayya stands in front of her in a playful manner. Finally, laughing all the way, she manages to cling to her sister. Anarkali is even more ashamed, and freeing

> herself from Surayya she runs away. Surayya also runs away, bursting into laughter).
> Curtain.
>
> (Taj 1931a: 20–3)

That is a typical scene where the heroine confides (or not quite confides) in her confidante, in this case her younger sister Surayya. Such a scene could be found in any classical European comedy. We also have at least two similar scenes in K. Asif's *Mughal-e-Azam* with the same characters. Indeed it is a conventional way of dramatizing a narration. First of all we have a short moral and almost physical portrait of the narrator/confidante, in fact a kind of "moral" stage direction, without using any concrete adjective, thus leaving the drawing of a physical portrait to the reader's imagination. This portrait, though shorter, echoes Anarkali's portrait, that has been given in the beginning of the play (in the second part of the first scene, Act 1). This occurs immediately before Anarkali's first lines, that is, before a rather simple and colloquial dialogue between Anarkali and her mother:

> Anarkali enters. A fifteen-sixteen year old girl with a delicate body, if it were not for a light red brightness, her *campak*-colored (golden) complexion would let us believe that she is sick. Her features are very different from what is understood as beauty as per the standards of poets. Should one take a look at her face, then the imagination tends to think of flowers. But if we are to refer to the surname [i.e. Anarkali] given to her by the Great Mughal, some people would say that more than the literal meaning, it is the beautiful combination of words that suits her better. Her wet eyes are radiant as if full of sorrows. And that is her main attraction.
>
> (Taj 1931a: 22)

This portrait where the reader's imagination is openly solicited, with the Urdu word *ta<u>kh</u>ayyul*, is indeed more concrete than Surraya's but again we hardly know anything real about Anarkali's physical appearance. The author alludes to traditional poetic metaphors to describe her: "*campak*-colored (golden) complexion," "wet eyes…radiant as if full of sorrows." This is balanced by the allusion to her surname *Anārkalī*, a given name that is not a real nom de plume, or *ta<u>kh</u>allus*, because a traditional *ta<u>kh</u>allus* would not combine Persian and Hindi words. Rather, the name qualifies her as a court singer, with a capacity for light poetry. Except for the phrase "delicate body" (*nāzuk andām*), hardly a realistic feature, rather a cliché, we lack a practical portrait with concrete descriptions for stage directions. It is therefore a poetic and literary level of language that the author uses.

Still, both portraits are drown with a subtle art of understatement, using negative constructions to describe Surayya's or Anarkali's physical beauty ("her features are better than Anarkali's, but she is not as charming," "if it were not for a light red brightness, her *campak*-colored (golden) complexion would let us believe that she is sick," and "her features are very different from what is understood as beauty as per the standards of poets"). We could call it an art of *litotes*. In both portraits the author hardly evokes physical beauty and relies on a terminology that belongs to a moral semantic field. This linguistic convention is akin to the tradition of Urdu ghazal and poetry.

Another notable feature of this scene is reported speech. Instead of the interaction between Surayya and Salim being played on stage, we hear through Surraya's monologue, the reported dialogue. The reported speech (the narrated dialogue) is followed by a short, direct dialogue between the two sisters with Anarkali expressing her conflicting feelings: anxiety and great joy at the same time. Importantly, the character Anarkali does not express her joy directly, it is all suggested by her silence or by her attitude, while her anxiety is directly expressed ("Anarkali that was...," and "the inner voice" that says: "Thou art a burnt star, Nadira"), as if to underline Anarkali's fatal destiny. Indeed, whatever could be good news, is either censured by Anarkali, putting immediately her hand on Surayya's mouth, or expressed by the crow, an ambiguous messenger of destiny. Again we note the understatement technique.

We note also the use of metaphors by the author of the stage drama. The poetic metaphor of the "burnt star" suits well the character of Anarkali who is supposed to be also a poet as well as a dancer, while the metaphor of the crow is rather a naïve one, and suits young Surayya, who is supposed to be a simpler and more popular character.

As far as historical realism is concerned, we notice the historical Mughal titles: *Śāhzādā Salīm* (Prince Salim) and *Sāhib-e-ālam* (the Crown Prince). Beyond these formal conventions, though, the language is mostly daily modern Urdu. After all, it is a teasing dialogue between two sisters.

While the scene may seem simple at first, in fact the author built an elaborated exchange of conflicting voices; at a first level we hear the two sisters, then, inserted in Surayya's lines, the reported dialogue between the Prince and Surayya, and later on, Anarkali's listening to her inner voice. To that inner voice, answers an external voice: the crow's voice, interpreted by Surayya as a good omen (a popular belief), but she is silenced by Anarkali and in any case her optimism is much weaker than the fatal metaphor used before "Thou art a burnt star, Nadira." This complexity is underlined by a subtle play with the personal pronouns: Anarkali's inner voice uses the intimate Urdu pronoun *tū* and Anarkali herself, being the elder sister, addresses Surayya with the same form, while Surayya addresses Anarkali as her *āpā* (elder sister) with the more respectful, yet familiar pronoun *tum*.

Then a short stage direction suggests an "indirect kiss" with Surayya's forehead as an intermediary, echoing the "reported kiss" of the reported dialogue. This "reported kiss" is underlined by a witty exchange between the two sisters playing on the word *bhūl* that can mean "forgetting" as well as "mistake." The whole thing is concluded by another short stage direction describing a happy hide-and-seek play between the two sisters. One may consider those stage directions as a metaphor: the love of the two sisters being an indirect way of showing a hide and seek play between the two lovers, Anarkali and the Prince, just as the witty dialogue between the two sisters about the kiss on the forehead.

But why such a complicated design in narration with an intricate dialogue peppered with moral stage directions, while we could have a direct (and romantic) dialogue on stage between the two lovers? First the hide-and-seek play between the two sisters used as a metaphor for a similar play between the two lovers is a way of avoiding a scene that might not have been allowed in Lahore theaters of those days. Similarly, at a time when kissing (even on the forehead), whether on the stage or on the screen was strictly forbidden, it was a rather nice way of evading censorship. Then, the reported speech, the abstract and moral vocabulary, the poetic and metaphorical language, and all those linguistic features suit the literary purpose and challenge of the author: to depict a forbidden romance.

In the film *Mughal-e-Azam* by K. Asif, we have a sequence that bears a great resemblance with this scene of the play. Surayya plays the confident and the go-between, for her beloved "Apa." The movie scene includes the hide-and-seek play, the reported speech and the "reported kiss" on the forehead with very similar lines, including the last one ("What a delightful way of forgetting"), with the same pun. Although the action that takes place before that sequence is different from that of the stage play, still K. Asif reproduced and quoted most of Sayyad Ali Taj's scene. What he leaves out is the "burned star" metaphor and the intervention of the crow, but he makes up by having two kisses on the forehead instead of one. We also have some kind of a pessimistic inner voice that warns Anarkali of her dreadful fate.

It is difficult to say why K. Asif included most of Imtiaz Ali's scene, but we can assume that both the witty aspect of it and the astute way of avoiding the censor's cut, while evoking a lover's kiss came in handy for the cinema director. Since that sequence is redundant for his film's story, we may also think that the director was paying homage to Imtiaz Ali's mastery of the art of dialogue.

Case study 2. The dance in the "Shish Mahal"

Both in Imtiaz Ali's drama and in K. Asif's *Mughal-e-Azam*, the Spring festival is the moment when the plot reaches an apex. It decides the fate of poor Anarkali; the plot closes in on her during the Nauroz celebrations within the Hall of Mirrors of the Imperial Palace.

The Spring festival

As noted above, in order to create a quasi-historical tone, at the beginning of every scene Imtiaz Ali Taj gives a very detailed description of its locale and atmosphere. This is well illustrated in the second act ("Dance," or *raqs*), the fourth scene ("The Hall of Mirrors"):

> *The Spring Festival in the Hall of Mirrors (śīś mahal) in the Fort (qilā) of Lahore:*[15] For the celebration of the Spring Festival (*Jaśan-e-nauroz*), the whole City (*śahar*) and Fort become the very reflection (*ainā bardār*) of the Mughal (*mughalīya*) pomp and magnificence. And wherever one may look, one sees intoxicated people, embraced by the pleasures and joys of springtime, quite forgetful of themselves. But in the imperial harem (*haram śāhī*), there is such a delightful coming and going with pomp and magnificence, that the eye is dazzled by its splendor. Golden tapestry (*zar bāft*) and silk

brocades (*kimkhwāb*) seem to put walls and doors on fire. Carpets (*qālīn*) from Iran and Turkestan would make the floor look like a garden. On the doors, curtains from China and Indochina (*Cīn-o-Macīn*) with beautiful pictures seem to keep the secret of some magic. Thanks to bushes of lanterns (*jhar fānūs*), round shade lanterns (*qamqama*), and chandeliers (*qandil*), the ceilings of the vast halls look like the sky of the world of poetry. In the large courtyard of the Harem Palace (*haram sarā*), it is not the agitation that prevails for the Weighing of the Emperor (*tulādān*) or other official ceremonies. However there is an extraordinary atmosphere of agitation. Novel and amazing displays of fireworks (*ātiśbāzī*) are ready. The performance is only waiting for the coming out of "the Shadow of God" (*Zil-e-Ilāhī*). Trusted servants (*muqarrabīn*) come one after another breaking the news of the arrival of "the Shadow of God." Whoever comes from inside [the palace], is surrounded by a crowd. Imperial ladies (*begameṃ)* and princesses (*śāhzādiāṃ*) looking like Aphrodite (*zohrā jamāl*) are dressed with nicely cut and light-colored shalwars covered by glittering robes (*pehwāz*). They are wearing priceless jewels (*jawaharāt*). One is covering herself with a fine linen (*śabnam*) stole, another one is adorning her head with an elegant turban with a plume (*kalghidār pagṛī*), they are looking like birds of Paradise (*koyal* from the Garden of Iram). They are all waiting very impatiently. Those who are tired are sitting. Some of them, hand in hand, are walking along in groups with a coquettish gait. Some are sitting in groups looking unconcerned, and exchanging laughs. In some groups they are playing charades and double entendre limerick (*pahaliyāṃ muqarniāṃ*), some exchange gossip and jokes. In another group some character is mocked (*sawang bharā jātā hai*, archaic instead of *sang bharnā*). And the spectators [all ladies] burst with laughter. In some places colorful dances are taking place, tambourines, drums, and tanpuras are playing. In another place evening rites are being celebrated and offerings are distributed.[16] Abyssinian, Turkmene, and Qalmuq women [imperial harem lady guards] are quite noticeable with their bright colored dresses. Slave girls (*kanīzeṃ*) are coming in a hurry, eunuchs (*khwājā sarā*) are running in all directions. One is calling someone, another is shouting at him. One is lifting a nape (*kh(w)ān*), somebody else is distributing betel nuts with cardamom (*pān ilaichī*), someone is serving sweet drinks (*śarbat*) to the noble ladies invited (at the harem). Outside, the musicians have taken hold of the whole Fort.

But the noises of such an agitation do not reach inside the palace of the Hall of Mirrors (*śīś mahal*). There, if at all there is some noise, it is only the sound of the pleasant melodies, like a gentle lullaby, played by the flutes (*surnā'ī*) and pipes (*śahnā'ī*) that reaches inside the palace. Here and there are fashionable illuminating candelabras, with one or several branches, and through the lamp shades elongated flames can be seen, some of them are straight, some of them convoluted; they may be white or with changing colors (*rangīn kafuri*). Amazing (*nighatbaiz*) clouds of rejuvenating (*ruh afzā*) amber perfumes are escaping from golden and silver incense burners.

(Taj 1931a: 81–2)[17]

This passage illustrates well Imtiaz Ali Taj's purpose of reconstructing the past as a realistic frame for his legend. The technical terms, though still present in modern speech, are to be understood within the "Mughal" context with a peculiar semantic marking; thus, the simple offering of betel leaf was almost a ceremony by itself, and therefore even the word betel, or *pān*, carries another meaning within the Mughal etiquette. The author knows that once he has instilled in the mind of the reader the curiosity for the "Mughal atmosphere" through the accumulation of material details in his description, then he has won his adhesion. The fact that some technical terms may be obscure for the reader does not matter, they are shrouded with "historical" aura. And the reader may either let his imagination work, or, if he is a stage drama or a cinema professional, his curiosity will be stimulated and his ability will be challenged.

In the economy of the drama, the "Shish Mahal" act is the pivotal moment of the plot: the destiny of Anarkali will be sealed because her "guilty and forbidden" love for the Crown Prince will be revealed by the mirrors reflecting her uncontrolled mimics during her Nauroz dance. To ensure this will happen, her rival has poured liquor in her drinking water. The author wants us to have the proper festival atmosphere and decor that will make a dramatic contrast with the prison where the unfortunate Anarkali is sent immediately afterwards.

Both films *Anarkali* and *Mughal-e-Azam* have retained those moments of glory and happiness with appropriate costumes and décor. At the same time, the film makers contrast the glory of Anarkali within the pomp of the Mughal Court with the sad and austere atmosphere of Anarkali's prison. Here too, Imtiaz Ali has a precedent with a shorter, but very realistic description in his third act (in the introductory text of second scene, called "Prison"). The situation of the heroine is perceived as all the more tragic because the author makes an exact counterpoint between the atmosphere and luxury of the harem and the Shish Mahal with the decor of the prison. No more laughter but cries, no more lights but penumbra and obscurity, and so on. What the playwright achieves with words is rewritten with the camera to the same effect. Such is the classical relationship between play writing and film script writing. But what is surprising is the fact that the filmmakers would not only borrow the main features and the heroine, they also try to reproduce the key episode, irrespective of the sad or happy end they opt for.

Dances and Hindu culture at the Mughal court

As the climax approaches we have dances, songs, and music, all described in detail by Imtiaz Ali. The happy celebration comes to a brutal end in Akbar's wrath, provoked by the audacious Anarkali. K. Asif chooses the *Jaśan-e-bahār* (the sixth day of the Persian month Farwardin) for a colorful scene. He introduces the ceremony with the customary "Indo-Islamic" court ceremonial and then we have "classical dance" followed by a song (*gīt*) where Anarkali openly rebels against her slavish destiny. An interesting point is that K. Asif would also choose the Nauroz celebrations within the Hall of Mirrors of the Imperial Palace. That religious festival was typical of Akbar's religious policy: he would blend different religious traditions in order to promote a general reconciliation between his feuding subjects.[18]

In Imtiaz Ali's drama we have a precise description of dances, the first one being a dance by a slave that evokes the separation of Radha and Krishna.

> The dancer enters the stage and (she) starts dancing. In the dance the feelings of Radha who is separated from Shyam are shown, as well as the very clear manifestations of her impatience while waiting for Shyam. During the dance, Ambar and Marwarid, two other slave girls of the imperial harem, come back. Dilaram, Anarkali's rival, is talking to them in a whisper. While keeping on dancing, the dancer comes close to Akbar and then signals to the eunuch who is standing near the "throne of the royal gifts." The latter takes a double shawl (*duśālā*) and presents it to Akbar. Akbar throws the shawl towards the dancer. She takes it and kneels down, bowing with her head, puts the back of her right hand on the floor and very slowly raises it to her forehead). [Then follow instructions from Dilaram to Ambar and Marwarid, as they are plotting Anarkali's disgrace and fall....]
>
> (Taj 1931a: 92)

Though rather brief this description of the dance has two implications: first of all it is a historical literary reminder of the Hindu background of most of Mughal court dances. And naturally the myth of the humble cowherdess overpowered by her love for Shyam (Lord Krishna), and being separated from Him, reminds the reader/spectator of Anarkali's rewarded, yet impossible love for Salim. So the use of popular (Hindu) mythology, often illustrated by dances, comes as a colorful metaphor of the drama's first act called *iśq*, or passionate love.

Then comes as second dance, the "dance of the two sisters," Zafran and Sitara (Taj 1931a: 94). The dance illustrates the relationship of two quarrelsome sisters. They sometimes unite or sometimes fight each other. But there is more quarrel than unity. After some teasing by putting the hand in the back of the other, and then embracing, followed again by rubbing cheeks, then some matter of dispute comes up. One has made quite a bad face while looking at her sister's jewelry. And the other replied by pulling a wry face in turn. Thus they fight just like hens. One pinches the other. The other pulls her locks. A fierce battle takes place. One loses and the other wins, and the winner laughs. As if to underline the metaphor for the rivalry of Anarkali and Dilaram, we learn through the dialogue that Anarkali herself has given a name to this dance. And for that she gets a reward.

The peacock dance

Above all we may note the description of the female peacock dance, or *janglī maurnī kā raqs*, which is clearly a metaphor of Anarkali's destiny (Taj 1931a: 96). This is the dance of the wild female peacock that has been encircled by the hunters, and whose male has been separated from her in the confusion. She wants to escape fearing for her life, but the love for the male draws her again and again. Full of fear she looks for her peacock. Her eyes wide open, stretching her neck she looks everywhere. But her quest is vain. She wants to call but because of her fear her voice does not go out of her throat. She stays standing and out of breath, she is shivering. The hunters are closing in at every moment. The terror is growing. Powerless, she runs away and comes back disappointed. Her coming and going becomes a kind of madness. A moment later love overpowers her. Without her male, life appears all blackness. Now approaches the moment of her death. She goes towards the hunters, offering her breast. An arrow pierces her chest, and the female peacock, victim of love, lies dead.

Imtiaz Ali notes the reactions of the protagonists at the completion of the peacock dance performed by Anarkali, which underlines the symbolic meaning of the dance: All are looking at the dance, fascinated. At the falling of Anarkali, several princesses rush out of their place. Quite worried Salim stands up. But after a small moment, Anarkali raises her head and salutes with a "kornish,"[19] and the fascination of the dance turns into offerings and praise.

This is a detailed description of the Peacock Dance, prevalent in Indian folk dance. The wild peacock is a common motif in popular Hindu folklore; the story of the female peacock killed because of her love for the male peacock may well be yet another avatar of the Krishna-Radha stories (Kirk 1972: 216ff.). In today's Punjab, peacock feathers are present in many shrines, Hindu, Muslim, and Sikh shrines alike. The peacock is also a symbol of royalty, perhaps from Maurya times and certainly in the Mughal Empire. This is embodied in the famous "peacock throne" of Emperor Shah Jahan, the *ta<u>kh</u>t-e-taus* crowned by a peacock studded with jewels with its wings opened. The peacock as the imperial symbolic bird, replaces the Persian Homa or phoenix (suggested by the very name of Mughal Emperor Humayun). In any case, the stage-drama viewer, may well assimilate the peacock fabula as a metaphor for the drama that is taking place within the Mughal family, even if the actual chronology is not respected.

With his careful description of the dancer's movements and attitudes, the author provides us with a short narrative, the message given by the traditional dancer's movements and mimics. We may surmise that it does not take long for a professional film dancer to identify and stage that kind of dance. No wonder that this "peacock dance" is taken up in the dance sequence in *Mughal-e-Azam*. However, in K. Asif's film, the dance ends with the dancer Anarkali offering to kill herself with a dagger out of sheer despair. At the moment of the symbolic death of Anarkali at the end of her dance, the big imperial fan, made out of peacock feathers falls. The camera shows the shapes and design of the thrones, evocating peacock tails or confronted peacocks. But to analyze the cinematic dance itself would take some more expertise, which is not within the scope of this chapter.

The dance and ghazal in Persian, uttered by the inebriated Anarkali, the detail of gestures, an awkward gait coupled with truncated Persian verses, also serve the function to provide a funny interval before the tragic end. All that is also echoed in Nandlal Jaswantlal's film, *Anarkali*, by a similar scene and a funny song. The song itself became a popular number.

More important perhaps to the writing technique of the drama is that we have here a metaphor of Anarkali's fatal destiny. She will be separated from her loving Prince, who can do nothing for her and she will die, a victim of her love. We may credit here Imtiaz Ali Taj for a very vivid description of a traditional dance and a very clever use of popular mythology. He is paving the way for cinema directors using the same fabula.

We find the same "wild female peacock" imagery also in other movies, for instance in a recent "historical" film, *Ashoka* by Santosh Sivan (2001). Not only do we have brief sequences of religious and folkloric costumed dances (featuring peacocks), but also clear parallel sequences: showing the quest of the lover for her paramour, along with brief sequences showing a peacock running away from the hunter's arrow. It is also no coincidence that, for historical fiction, Santosh Sivan uses a kind of Hindi heavily loaded with Sanskrit words and phrases. That compares well with the kind of Persian words and phrases used in the Urdu dialogues of both Imtiaz Ali Taj's stage drama and K. Asif's film. Indeed, Santosh Sivan is suggesting a kind of "Sanskritic" level of language to the viewer, who wants to be transported to Emperor Ashoka's times, just like Imtiaz Ali Taj's drama is supposed to help recreating, with some Persianized dialogues and Persian poetry, the atmosphere of Akbar's court. Santosh Sivan himself acknowledges his debt to the Anarkali story, in an interview published with the DVD I used, where he clearly states that he wanted to "make another *Mughal-e-Azam*" with a story of a Crown Prince and his unfortunate love, before he would become Emperor Ashoka.

In Imtiaz Ali Taj's drama and *Mughal-e-Azam*, the themes of the dances suggest the presence of popular Hindu culture at the Mughal Court. *Mughal-e-Azam* goes a step further in showing Akbar's wife, a Rajput princess, praying to Lord Krishna. We even see the imperial couple celebrating the birth of Krishna by swaying the cradle of the divine baby and feeding sweets to each other. Again, Imtiaz Ali Taj, in both historical and religious context paved the way for popular cinema, which naturally goes further.

Conclusion

Two important aspects are yet to be examined to complete the literary history of the drama and myth called Anarkali. First, I wish I could have been able to compare the first 1922 and the second 1931 version of Imtiaz Ali Taj's drama, but the first edition is not at hand. Second, there is a need for a detailed comparative study of the language of the characters, comparing those created by Imtiaz Ali Taj, and those created for the *Anarkali* and *Mughal-e-Azam* films. However, that would take a new series of annotated translations that could not be presented here. For now, we may credit Imtiaz Ali Taj for conceiving a plot based on the "eternal triangle," that is, the lovers and the jealous rival, acting within the framework of the impossible marriage, with supposedly historic characters out of a popular tale. No doubt Imtiaz Ali Taj also paved the way for the cinematic construction of the historical drama *Anārkalī* through his linguistic and stylistic efforts, with detailed technical descriptions and stage directions, well balanced by romantic and tragic notes, giving flesh to his "historic characters" by blending ceremonial "Indo-Islamic" titles and phrases with classical tragic monologues, and vivid dialogues.

More importantly, Imtiaz Ali Taj, fascinated by the popular legend of his childhood, had chosen to stick to the tragic end and the cruel castigation of the heroine, thus contradicting the popular image of Akbar's justice, as the Emperor is ultimately abiding by the *raison d'État*. Nevertheless, our playwright does not forget to present those diverse cultural and religious influences that characterized Akbar's Court, thus giving a Pan-Indian and universal décor to his drama. "Indo-Islamic" features are there, as well as Hindu mythology.

We may also say that the historical reconstruction presented to the viewer, in spite of the revision of his drama by two local historians, is designed in such a way that it also agrees with a more popular vision of the Mughal Court, perhaps awaking recent memories of the glamor of the Nawabs of Lucknow. Those recipes, as well as the skilful adaptation of a popular local legend into a romantic drama, were to be reenacted and amplified by popular Indian historical cinema, as well as television dramatic series.

Of course, not just the playwright Imtiaz Ali Taj, but also film directors, dialogue and song writers, dance and music composers, unforgettably dancers and actors, all contributed to the building of a new, living and yet mythical Anarkali. The infinite variations of the different plots, which yet conserve the basic characters and heroes, do typify what we can call "new mythology." Perhaps this new mythology, with characters like Anarkali or Umrao Jān Adā, (from Ruswa's novel) to quote only these two, represent the most outstanding contribution of literary fiction to a Pan-Indian, and now almost universal cinematic culture. To conclude this study, we would like to stress the idea that there is a noteworthy continuity between popular tradition, literary, as well as artistic creation, and new mythology.

Notes

1 Throughout the chapter, page numbers refer to the partly computerized reprint of Taj 1931a, which has the same text as Taj 1931b. The only difference is that Taj, 1931a has a color cover illustration by A. R. Chughtai and an Urdu-English glossary, while Taj 1931b has a black and white cover illustration from the 1953 Anarkali film and gives an appendix for the Urdu translation of the Persian verses, but has no glossary.

2 Another *Anarkali*, a Pakistani Urdu film of the 1970s is mentioned by Mushtaq Gazdar (1997) in his chronology of Pakistani cinema. There is also an old Pakistani *Anarkali* Urdu TV drama of the 1980s (partially inspired by Imtiaz Ali Taj's Urdu drama) and a fully colored remake recently (2003–04) in Pakistan.

3 Similarly, in an interview published by Nasreen Munni Kabir, the well-known film script writer and Urdu poet Javed Akhtar thought it wise to remind the public of the role of Urdu language and of the influence of Imtiaz Ali Taj in the making of the film Mughal-e-Azam:

N.M.K.: Were you ever tempted to write a Mughal social or a script for a historical fim like Mughal e Azam?

J.A.: Mughal e Azam is a fantasy, it has nothing to do with history. Jehangir had probably married many times and was married for the first time at eighteen.

N.M.K.: So Anarkali never existed?

J.A.: There is some grave in Lahore that's supposed to be Anarkali's.

There may have been some courtesan or singer who existed during Akbar's time by the name of Anarkali. That's about all. The idea of Jehangir falling in love with her and creating a rift between father and son is a story that was created by an Urdu playwright called Imtiaz Ali Taj (Kabir 1999: 72).

4 Maybe the most famous example is Ruswa's novel *Umrao Jān Adā*, first published in 1904. This story is set in the kingdom of Lucknow, and the heroine is not a historical

character as such, yet she has become a legend. Popular religious features and ceremony are quoted, and popular religious characters are also mocked. *Umrao Jān Adā* was also at the root of at least two successful feature films in Urdu (Désoulières 2000) and a recent big-budget remake by J.P. Dutta with Aishwarya Rai in the title role. Another case would be Premchand's novelette "The Chess Players," published in its Urdu version (*Śatrañj kī bāzī*) at about the same time as the first drama *Anarkalī*, *c.*1925. Arguably, this is a small historical *drama* with some dialogues. This was the only short story he wrote with a historical background, and it is precisely a post-Mughal one (the last days of the kingdom of Lucknow). It was also to become the theme of a famous film by Satyajit Ray. Unfortunately Premchand did not succeed in film story writing, and could not witness the cinematic adaptation by Ray.

5 Imtiaz Ali Taj must be alluding to Latif (1892) and Kannhya Lal (1884), to quote only the best-known ones. Possible sources of the legend, according to Munshi Muhammad ud din Fauq (in Naqush, Lahore Number, 1961: 265–9), are to be found in the reports of European travelers in India, which he refutes as doubtful testimonies. He also quotes a modern historian of Lahore, Muhammad Baqir.

6 Quoted in Persian by Latif with English translation (1892: 187). I have added the transliteration. The same applies to the second Persian inscription (below).

7 A revealing detail, as far as the ideology of Victorian local Urdu historiography is concerned, is that it almost always includes words, or entire paragraphs of praise for the British rule and the Empress of India, whether in Urdu or in English. We find this in Latif's *History of Panjab* (1889: 652, last paragraph), and also Kannhya Lal's *Tārīkh-e-Lahaur* (1884: passim). Incidentally, Kannhya Lal also quotes a brief tale of Anarkali, in his chapter on monumental tombs of Lahore.

8 Imtiaz Ali Taj lived close to the so-called Anarkali Civil Station. He signs his preface: Sayyad Imtiaz Ali Taj, 7 Railway Road, Lahore.

9 An excellent panorama of the cultural life of Lahore in those days, complete with a study of Persian and Urdu historiography of Lahore is to be found in the annual Urdu journal *Naqush*: Lahore Number (1962, recently reprinted), see Tufail 1962.

10 For more details, see Désoulières, 2007.

11 It needs to be said though that the presence of Akbar in Lahore at that precise time is not well documented.

12 Abdur Rahman Chughtaï (Lahore 1894–1975) in the 1920s executed large watercolor drawings in a modified [miniature] Bengal school style. By 1940, his painting was influenced by Mughal architecture, calligraphy, miniature painting as well as by Art Nouveau. Subject matters include Mughal Queens and Kings and episodes from Punjabi, Persian, and Indo-Islamic legends and folklore (*Encyclopedia Britannica*, s.v.). Chughtaï illustrated classics from Urdu literature, notably poetry by Ghalib and Iqbal.

13 The 1993 edition has the same cover, with the painting reproduced in color. The original picture is to be seen in Lahore Museum. But the Alhambra edition, which has a black and white cover (a still perhaps taken from the film *Anarkali* d. R.S. Chaudhury, 1935), does not reproduce the painting, and also omits this paragraph of the preface.

14 References are based on a current Urdu text published by *Nirālī Kitābeṃ*, Lahore, 1980, and oral Punjabi tradition.

15 I specify Urdu archaic terms that are all Indo Persian terms or lexemes peculiar to the Indo-Mughal referent reality.

16 The playwright does not forget the Hindu religious rites that were normally performed by the Hindu princesses of the harem.

17 Most of the objects and costumes evoked in this passage are indeed mentioned in an interesting study of Mughal Court material culture by Som Prakash Verma (1978), which was based on the observation of many miniatures and paintings. It is obvious that our author, in addition to the advice of intelligentsia of Lahore, was also influenced by miniatures.

18 The Persian Spring Festival, or Nauroz coincided with the anniversary of Akbar's accession to the throne. For a description of Nauroz honors in 1585, see for example Srivastava (1962: 330). "For geographical, cultural and linguistic reasons, Akbar perceived some

kind of affinity with the Zoroastrians who were of Persian descent and whose religion was the religion of the ancient kings of Persia, and consequently he took great interest in Mahyarji's [a Parsi priest coming from Gujarat] discourses..." (ibid.: 248). "The emperor put on the Zoroastrian sacred shirt and thread-girdle (sudreh and kusti), the outward symbols of the Parsee religion, introduced the Persian calendar from the beginning of the 25th year of his reign (March 1580), and also began to celebrate the Persian New Year's Day and other Parsee festivals (fourteen in number) from March 1582" (ibid.: 30–1, quoting *Muntakhab-ut-Tawarīkh* of Badayuni, and *Ain-i-Akbari*).

19 The "kornish" is a Persian style Mughal court salutation with the right hand and bowing low towards the king, often with three bows.

References

Editions of Anārkalī by Sayyad Imtiaz Ali Taj

Taj, S.I.A. (1931a; reprint, partly computerized, 1993 and 2003) *Anārkalī*, Lahore: Sang-e-mīl.

Taj, S.I.A. (1931b; reprint, computerized 2002) *Anārkalī*, Islamabad: Alhambra Publishing.

Other sources

Arif, S. (2003) "The Essence and Fabric: Authenticity Versus Effect," in Gulzar, G. Nihalani and S. Chatterjee (eds) *Encyclopaedia of Hindi Cinema*, New Delhi: Encyclopaedia Britanica (India).

Désoulières, A. (2000) "The Three Lives of Umrao Jan Ada," in V. Dalmia and T. Damsteegt (eds) *Narrative Strategies: Essays on South Asian Literature and Film*, Leiden: CNWS.

—— (2007) "Historical Fiction and Style: The case of Anarkali," *The Annual of Urdu Studies*, 22: 67–98.

Garga, B.D. (1996) *So Many Cinemas, the Motion Picture in India*, Mumbai: Eminence Designs.

Gazdar, M. (1997) *Pakistan Cinema, 1947–1997*, Karachi: Oxford University Press.

Kabir, N.M. (1999) *Talking Films, Conversations on Hindi Cinema with Javed Akhtar*, New York: Oxford University Press.

Kannhya Lal, H. (1884; reprint 1987) *Tārikh-e-Lahaur*, Lahore: Sang-e-mīl.

Kirk, J.A. (1972) *Stories of the Hindus: An Introduction through Texts and Interpretation*, New York: Macmillan.

Latif, S.M. (1889) *History of the Punjab* (translated from a previous Urdu edition), Lahore: New Imperial Press.

—— (1892) *Lahore, Its History, Architectural Remains and Antiquities*, Lahore: New Imperial Press.

Saksena, R.B. (1927) *A History of Urdu Literature*, Allahabad: Rām Narāin Lāl.

Srivastava, A.L. (1962) *Akbar the Great*, Agra: Shiva Lal Agarwala.

Syed, S. (1985) "Urdu Cinema," in T.M. Ramachandran (ed.) *70 Years of Indian Cinema, (1913–1983)*, Bombay: Cinema India-International Publication.

Tufail, M. (ed.) (1962; reprint computerized 2003) "Idara-e-Farogh-e-Urdu," *Naqush*, Lahore Number 92.

Verma, S.P. (1978) *Art and Material Culture in the Paintings of Akbar's Court*, New Delhi: Vikas.

7 From ghazal to film music

The case of *Mirza Ghalib**

Naseem Hines

Introduction

This chapter focuses on the way the Indian cinema and television industries present classical music and poetry from the "Indo-Muslim" world. The industry has contributed a lot to archive the Muslim contributions to North Indian (and Karnatic) classical music traditions. Its films present a memory of "Indo-Muslim" culture and civilization with its great personalities to the general public. However, its interpretations take some liberties and present the material in a distinctive way. I illustrate this with a case study of the nineteenth-century poet Ghalib's Urdu ghazals, as represented in a movie and a television serial.

In the arena of the Urdu literature, Ghalib (1797–1869) holds an important place. Indeed, he is the only poet on whose life and works a film *and* a TV serial have been made. There are films inspired by the life and works of other great Urdu poets, and ghazals of many Urdu poets have been used in popular cinema. For example, the life and works of Sahir Ludhianvi and Kaifi Azmi provided the impetus for Guru Dutt's *Pyaasa* (1957) and *Kaagaz ke Phool* (1959) and their poetry has been adopted for these films respectively. Also, Ismail Merchant's 1988 film *Hifazat*, based on Anita Desai's novel *In Custody* (1994), boasts Faiz's poems. However, it is popularly held that in such films, incidents are knitted together and presented in such a way as to create a composite picture based on several incidents in the lives of many Urdu poets. None of the above films explicitly mentions a single poet as inspiration.[1]

This chapter will focus on Sohrab Modi's 1954 Minerva Movietone film *Mirza Ghalib* and Gulzar's 1988 TV serial of the same name. Both directors are giants in the Indian cinema and television scene. I will first introduce each production, then outline how each takes its liberties with the story of Ghalib's life, and compare the two. Finally, I will discuss how the movies render Ghalib's ghazals. References to the ghazals will be to the recently reprinted so-called Nuskha-e-Khwājā edition, corrected by Ghalib himself (Sayyid 2000, which has his poems up to 1852). For later ghazals, I will refer to the edition by Malik Ram (1989).

Mirza Ghalib: *the movie*

In 1954, Sohrab Modi, stage and film actor and director famous for making historical movies, produced and directed the film *Mirza Ghalib*. A couple of

Modi's previous films had not done well at the box office, but *Mirza Ghalib* was a success and Modi once more came back to center stage. About the sensation this film created when it was first released, Firoz Rangoonwalla, in his *Indian Cinema: Past and Present*, writes: "Mirza Ghalib, . . . became the first Hindi film to get the President's Gold Medal" (1983: 126). Ramachandran, in his *70 Years of Indian Cinema*, calls the film a milestone and the "best feature film" of 1954 (1985: 641).[2]

The story for the film was written by no other than Saadat Hasan Manto, and the dialogues by Rajindar Singh Bedi. Celebrated for redefining and shaping the twentieth-century Urdu short story genre, Manto and Bedi are considered the titans of the Urdu literary tradition associated with the Progressive Writers' Movement that started in the 1930s.[3]

In most Indian films, the musical score is the most important component because it can play a crucial role in either making or breaking the film. The musical score of *Mirza Ghalib* is by the legendary musician, the late Ghulam Muhammad. Traditional musical instruments and compositions dominate. Talat Mehmood, and Muhammad Rafi are the playback singers for Ghalib (played by Bharat Bhushan). Suraiyya plays the role of Ghalib's beloved in the film and sings herself the ghazals assigned to her character. Suraiyya's singing for this movie is still regarded by some as the best example of ghazal singing in Indian Cinema. India's then Prime Minister, Jawaharlal Nehru, paid Suraiyya the ultimate compliment by telling her she had brought Mirza Ghalib to life (*Tumne Mirzā G͟halib kī rūh ko zindā kar diyā*, see http://www.upperstall.com/people/smodi.html last accessed 25 March 2007). We analyze the ghazals from the movie later in the chapter.

Mirza Ghalib: *the TV serial*

Gulzar's *Mirza Ghalib* debuted on the small screen in 1988. This serial of seventeen episodes provided the chief writer-director, time and opportunity to develop the story in considerable detail. The credentials of the TV serial are also impressive with Meraj, Ashfaq Ahmad, Ahmad Siddiqui, R.L. Mishra, Brajpal, and Chandra Prabha as associate producers, directors, and screen play writers. Interestingly, Kaifi Azmi was on the research team of both the film and the television series.

India Today in its TV column (November 30, 1988) covered the launch of *Mirza Ghalib* (which took place on November 10 1988): "His style of expression is really something else . . . beautiful picturization also of other aspects of the life of the famous poet" (*Andāz-e-bayān aur . . . jāne māne śāyar ke jīvan ke dūsre pahluoṃ kā bhī ¨k͟hūbsūrat citran*). According to this article, Gulzar was undaunted by the failure of two earlier historical serials, B. R. Chopra's serial based on the life of *Bahadur Shah Zafar*, and Muzaffar Ali's serial on *Jan-e-Alam.* As director of successful movies like *Mere Apne, Khushboo, Koshish, Aandhi, Angoor, Ijaazat,* and *Meera*, he got the prime time slot for his serial, even before fulfilling the qualifying requirements. Gulzar reportedly said that eighteen years earlier he had thought about making a film on Ghalib's life but decided against it. Now he considered the time right and television the right medium for this project.

The sources used are Altaf Hussain Hali's biography of Ghalib, Ghalib's letters, and the research of the famous poet Kaifi Azmi. Gulzar sees the series as a counterweight to the film *Mirza Ghalib*, which had been shown on Doordarshan. He stresses that there is more to Ghalib's life than what was portrayed in the film: "...much importance has been given to Ghalib's beloved without giving his wife her due importance in Ghalib's life as a sustaining and nurturing figure." Also, Gulzar wants to change the widespread notion that Ghalib indulged in drinking all the time.

The series was a success,[4] partly thanks to the acting talent of Naseeruddin Shah, who played the role of Ghalib and to the musical score by Jagjit Singh. The selection of musical instruments and the use of technology is less purist than the film. Chitra gave the playback for Ghalib's beloved, and Jagjit Singh scored the music and sang most of the ghazals picturized on Ghalib (some ghazals were sung by Vinod Sehgal). In a Zee-TV interview, Jagjit was introduced: "According to Gulzarji, after Ghalib himself, Jagjit contributed most to the success of the serial Mirza Ghalib."[5] In other words, the television serial not only created a sensation at its launch, but has continued to generate interest and is remembered even today with respect. It has now been released in a two-part DVD.

Different stories: the plot of movie and TV serial

Mirza Ghalib: *the movie*

The movie *Mirza Ghalib* explicitly addresses the issue of historical veracity at the very outset by means of a disclaimer. The film opens with a statement, "Many imaginary incidents and characters have been introduced in the film, therefore the film should not be received as a faithful historical account." Following this, a voice leads the audience to 1837 Delhi. We are told that after shining gloriously for 400 years, the bright star of the Mughal Empire was fading away fast. Nevertheless, even at this twilight, with the presence of the great Urdu poets, such as Shaikh Ibrahim Zauq, Balmukund Huzur, Hakim Momin Khan Momin, Mufti Sadaruddin Khan Azurda, Nawab Mustafa Khan Shefta, Hakim Aghajan Aish, and Muhammad Ali Tishna, the royal court of the last Mughal Emperor Bahadur Shah Zafar, an Urdu poet in his own right, was still shining brightly. This beginning marks the tone of the movie immediately as one of nostalgia for a glorious "Indo-Muslim" past.

In the very first few minutes, the audience learns that Ghalib, known as Mirza Nausha in his youthful years, had moved from Agra to Delhi where he lived with his wife Umraojan's father. Ghalib's father-in-law had introduced Ghalib to the circle of noblemen in Delhi, but was disappointed by his son-in-law's lack of progress. Thus, the relationship between the three of them was somewhat strained. In the following scenes young Ghalib leaves for the royal court to participate in a poetic symposium, *mushaira*, and his wife (Nigar Sultana) prays for her husband's successful debut, because finding a position at the royal court could spell the end of their financial difficulties.

> A *mushaira* was a gathering of poets, usually called together at the invitation of some prominent patron of literature, where each would recite his latest compositions. The proceedings were governed by well-known conventions, but within this conventional setting both appreciation and criticism could be frankly expressed—and in more than one way.
>
> (Russell and Islam 1994: 39)

According to the conventions, a *mushaira* begins with the junior most poet and culminates with the seniormost poet reading his poems the last. A lighted candle is placed in front of the poet who is reciting his poems; when his recitation is over, the candle is then placed in front of the poet next in turn. In a *mushaira* there can be several rounds, *daur*, of recitation. Usually, only a small group of senior poets, or those who are participating in the *mushaira* from some distance, continue to recite their poem in the final *daur* (for more details, see Naim 2004: 109–19).

Flying in the face of this tradition, in the film *Mirza Ghalib*, the *mushaira* begins with one of the courtiers reciting a ghazal of the host, Bahadur Shah first, in the presence of many poets, including his teacher and poet laureate Shaikh Ibrahim Zauq. The candle is then placed in front of Mufti Sadaruddin Azurda, followed by Lala Balmukund Huzur, Momin Khan Momin, and then Shaikh Ibrahim Zauq, respectively. Each of the poets is encouraged in the traditional manner of repeating the first lines of their couplets, a practice known as *misra uṭhānā*. Their presentation is supported with exclamations of appreciation coming from the audience. Ghalib's turn comes last; he recites his new ghazal: *Hai bas ke har ek unke iśare meṃ niśān aur*, or: "Their/her every gesture has another meaning" (Sayyid 2000: 103). Except for Mufti Azurda, and Nawab Shefta, this is not well received. This event is corroborated by Ghalib's letters. It is well known that "his verse came under criticism from the very start" (Russell and Islam 1994: 37–40).

Ghalib leaves the court unhappily, but on his way home, he hears a female voice singing one of his poems: *Nuqtah chīn hai g̲h̲am-e-dil*, or "The heart's sorrow complains" (Ram 1989: 150). He follows the voice to the singer Moti Begum's home, where he learns that she deeply appreciates his poetry. She is unaware of Ghalib's true identity and assumes that he was one of the noblemen invited at the *mushaira* at the Fort. Moti Begum wants to know all about Ghalib's debut, which she presumes to have been a triumph. Her appreciation works like a balm on Ghalib's hurt feelings. He leaves Moti Begum's house in a triumphant mood. Indeed, thanks to the intervention of Moti Begum, Ghalib will be brought to the attention of Bahadur Shah Zafar and come in the good graces of the Mughal Court.[6]

From this point onwards, the film turns into a romance between the singer Moti Begum and Ghalib. The third party in the love triangle is Hashmat Khan, the Sheriff of Delhi. He wants to marry Moti Begum and resents the fact that she loves Ghalib. Moti Begum's mother agrees to marry her daughter off to Hashmat in exchange for 2000 rupees. Distraught, Moti Begum sends a message to Ghalib with her servant. This comical character gets easily off-task and makes a stop at the local hashish-house, where he remains for days. By the time Ghalib receives Moti's message it is almost too late. Moti is about to commit suicide, but is discovered and stopped. When Ghalib rushes in with the money, the wedding procession and the groom Hashmat Khan are already at the door of her house. Ghalib hands over the money to the repentant mother, and leaves under the impression that he was too late. Moti Begum's mother, though, returns the money and the gifts to Hashmat, and calls off the wedding.

This incident is crucial to understand the depth of Hashmat Khan's wrath and warrants some detailed analysis. A traditional wedding procession (*bārāt*) is on its way to the bride's house. Hashmat Khan is wearing a *sherwani*, a long coatlike tunic, over a pair of white loose pants. His head and shoulders are bedecked in a *sehra*, a lacelike decorative mantle, made of jasmine buds and roses. Accompanied by his family, friends, and a musical band, riding a white mare, Hashmat Khan's wedding procession is passing through the narrow congested lanes. This is a moment of great honor and rejoicing for both, the groom and the bride's families and friends. Taking into consideration his social and administrative position in Delhi, being turned away in disgrace from Moti Begum's door at this moment has multiple implications. First of all, Hashmat's dream of marrying Moti Begum is shattered just when it is about to come true. To make matters even worse, he is turned back from his bride's house not only empty handed, but publicly disgraced. This is simply too great an insult to endure. It is not surprising at all to the audience when a furious Hashmat Khan swears vengeance.

In the following scenes, the film makes an effort to cover some of the main events of Ghalib's life that are well documented. For example, it portrays the relationship between Ghalib and his wife, which never recovers from the deaths of their children. Later they decide to adopt Arif, a nephew of Umrao Begum, but he too does not survive. Distressed, Ghalib begins to frequent the local gambling house. Around this time, gambling had been declared a social ailment and illegal in the Delhi area. Conspiring against Ghalib, Hashmat Khan succeeds in bringing up a charge of gambling against Ghalib, making him suffer disgrace. This incident has some roots in history:

> The full circumstances of the incident, which occurred in 1847, are somewhat obscure, and there are several conflicting accounts of it... Ghalib has himself given a brief account of this incident in a Persian letter: "The Chief of Police was my enemy, and the Magistrate did not know me. ... Although the Magistrate has authority over the Chief of Police, he behaved, where I was concerned, as though the Chief of Police had authority over him, and issued the order for my imprisonment. The Session Judge was my friend; he had always treated me with friendship and kindness, and in most companies where we met, had behaved quite informally with me; yet he too acted now as though he did not know me. An appeal was made to the higher court, but my case was not heeded and the sentence was upheld..." A contemporary

> newspaper reported: "Mirza Sahib has been sentenced to a fine of Rs. 200 and six months' imprisonment with hard labour."... The heavy sentence seems to have created a great stir in Delhi, and a good deal of indignation. The newspaper report already quoted continues: "When it is borne in mind that Mirza Sahib has long been a sick man on a strict diet... we are obliged to say that the distress and the hard labour will be beyond his strength to endure, so much so that his very life may be endangered.... It is contrary to all justice that, for a very ordinary crime, a talented noble-man whom the public honours and respects profoundly, should have to pay a penalty so drastic that it may well cost him his life."
>
> (Russell and Islam 1994: 66)

The injustice of Ghalib's punishment of imprisonment caused even Bahadur Shah to write a letter to the authorities appealing them to reconsider but to no avail. Ghalib was deeply saddened by this punishment because after this many of his friends and acquaintances turned away from him.

The next scene shows both Moti Begum and Umrao Begum visiting the shrine of the Sufi saint Hazrat Nizamuddin Aulia. Unaware of each other's identity they begin to talk to each other about the purpose of their visits. Soon Moti Begum realizes that she is talking heart-to-heart with none other than Ghalib's wife who is deeply disappointed over her husband's love for another woman. In deference to Umrao's pain, Moti decides to sacrifice her love for Ghalib. She moves to Mehroli where she lives in seclusion save the company of her mother and servant. When Ghalib gets out from jail, he disregards his wife who had come to welcome him, but rushes straight to Moti Begum's house. When he finds that she had moved away, he frantically looks for her, but when he finally finds her, it is too late. Moti Begum had pined away in Ghalib's absence, and he is just in time to have her die in his arms. Thus, Ghalib fulfills his earlier promise that he would come to Moti Begum, but under very tragic circumstances.

The final scene of the film is at the graveyard where Ghalib's wife has followed him. She puts flowers on Moti Begum's grave and leads her grieving husband back to their home. The film then, while tracing Ghalib's career from being an unappreciated poet thwarted by his rivals, to his rise as a star at the Mughal court, concentrates primarily on his tragic love affair.

Mirza Ghalib: *the TV serial*

The serial differs from the film on many interesting points. First, it foregrounds Ghalib as a poet: each of the episodes begins with Ghalib's famous couplet *Haiṃ aur bhī duniyā meṃ sukhanvar bahut acche, kahte haiṃ ki Ghālib kā hai andāz-e-bayān aur*, or "There are numerous men of letters in the world, but they say, Ghalib's style of expression is something else!" (Sayyid 2000: 105). The lines are in Vinod Sehgal's voice in a style of poetry recitation known as *tahtul-lafz* as opposed to *bā-tarannum*, or "with melody." Gulzar also ends each episode with a ghazal composed by Ghalib. Typically, the final ghazal is characteristic for the tone of the episode as a whole.[7]

The serial is presented as a flashback, as the musings of a gray-haired Ghalib who walks with the help of a cane in the opening episode. The first episode covers Ghalib's ancestry and early education.[8] We learn that Ghalib began writing poetry with the pen name *Asad*, or "lion," but later decided to change his pen name to *Ghālib*, "The Triumphant." We see him struggle with the ritual prayers. It is well documented by Hali and others that although deeply spiritual, throughout his life Ghalib had avoided conforming to the outward observances of Islam (Russell and Islam 1994: 35–8). We are also introduced to his relationship with his wife (Tanvi Azmi), which, though not smooth, still bespeaks the kind of intimacy that can develop only from years of mutual companionship, understanding, and appreciation. Importantly, we find out about his struggle to make a living. We learn about a "pension" from the East India Company that rightfully belongs to Ghalib (since his uncle had served as a military officer) and his first cousin Shams, but a distant relative is trying to establish his own claims as an heir.

At the end of this episode, we see young, self-confident Ghalib composing the ghazal:

> *Husn-e-māh garce bā-hamgām-e-kamāl acchā hai,*
> *Us se merā māh-e-khurśīd jamāl acchā hai.*
> (Sayyid 2000: 201)
> Though the beauty of moon at its zenith is good;
> Better is my moon; like the sun in beauty.
> Or:
> The moon is resplendent only once a month when it is perfect;
> but my moon is like the sun—radiant everyday!

This ghazal is light in mood, full of youthful self-confidence and optimism. That fits well the focus on young Ghalib, still fresh, young, naive, and inexperienced, believing that the system will work for him.[9] He is convinced that his "pension" is stopped only temporarily. When it is restored and arrears paid in full, all his financial difficulties will vanish. Unfortunately, the problems in his life compound, particularly those related to his livelihood.

In the second episode, Ghalib's childhood friend Bansidhar, with whom Ghalib remains friends throughout his life, is visiting him from Agra. Well aware of Ghalib's financial difficulties, he tries to help, but Ghalib does not accept it. Ghalib's wife, Umrao, is concerned about the company Ghalib keeps and his interest in wine and gambling. Umrao Begum also is very depressed because their children do not survive, but she turns to piety for solace.

Meanwhile, Bahadur Shah, at a ripe age, becomes the new Mughal King. Shaikh Ibrahim Zauq, the court poet and Bahadur Shah Zafar's teacher, asks one of his attendants to invite the local poets for a *mushaira* at the Fort. Ghalib's name is in the list one of the courtiers makes. When Ghalib receives this long-awaited formal invitation to the Fort, his family is ecstatic, confident that Ghalib will make a favorable impression and secure a position with a steady income. Ghalib recites his opening ghazal of his Diwan:

> *Naqś faryādī hai kis kī śokhī-e-tahrīr kā*
> *Kāghazī hai pairahan har paikar-e-tasvīr kā*
> (Sayyid 2000: 47)
> Against whose brilliant art does the picture complain?
> All bordered images wear parchment [pleading with their creator]

This is admittedly a multilayered couplet, which has been deemed "meaningless" by some critics (see Pritchett 2005). Ghalib himself feels compelled to explain that he had in mind a Persian custom to appear before the ruler wrapped in a paper robe to seek justice for a wrong. The implication is that like parchment, life itself is delicate and ephemeral. Like pictures in paper, God's creation is "bordered" within the frame of its physical bodies, human existence is short-lived. Thus, in the poet's fancy, the created complains to its Maker about the "joke" of its impermanence. This idea that life is ephemeral is expressed of course elsewhere, but never as masterly and densely as here.

The amazing thing about this couplet is how much is encapsulated within the two short lines of verse. To condense the idea in only fourteen words would surely be considered a remarkable feat by any literary standard. What makes the English translation daunting is that the Arabic word *tasvīr* can mean "image," "picture," and "statue;" similarly, the Persian word *śokhī* is best contextualized in the sense of "playing a trick, mischief, or a joke." Translating it as "brightness" or "brilliance" bypasses the original intended idiom. Compared to other ghazals, few attempts have been made to translate this poem. Gulzar surely made a good selection to explain Ghalib's failure at the court. His poetry was simply above the heads of his audience—as it is above the average television viewer.

Thus, like in Modi's movie, the very first ghazal Ghalib presents at the Red Fort bombs at the box office, so to speak. The audience takes its cue from Shaikh Ibrahim Zauq, the court poet, and is reluctant to praise this promising young poet from Agra. With a very heavy heart Mirza returns home.

In contrast to Modi's, Gulzar's Ghalib goes straight home. His household is disappointed at Ghalib's failure, especially his wife, who had spent the entire night praying for her husband's success at the recital. Clearly, their hopes of making a success of their lives in Delhi are not bearing fruits. Suspecting that the residents of Delhi will not let a poet who is not originally from Delhi become successful, Mirza's wife suggests that they return back to Agra. Ghalib responds that only immature people think that a petty issue like locality is important. In the series, then, Ghalib's lack of success is attributed to regional rivalry. Ironically, it was not far off when the common people of Delhi would accept Ghalib as one of theirs, and his couplets would be memorized and become the common idiom of Urdu speakers, but that time was yet to come. The episode ends as despondent

Ghalib composes: *Bāzīceh-e-atfāl hai duniyā mere āge*, "The world unfurls before me like a child's toy" (Ram 1989: 162).

The image here is that of a quilted version of modern board games.[10] In those days people used to carry with them a piece of cloth on which a game was either printed or embroidered (with a set of four cowrie shells to serve as dice and a few sets of flat pieces of different color glass, wood, or stones to serve as game pieces). This ghazal captures beautifully the episode's tone of growing disenchantment with the vicissitudes of worldly success.

The third episode begins with Zauq dictating one of his poems to a scribe. The next scene shows that Ghalib's *Diwan*, or complete collection of poems, is with a professional scribe. On its completion, Bansidhar is to take it to Lucknow and try to get it published. Ghalib's wife is expecting a child but Ghalib's financial circumstances have only worsened. He is still struggling to get his pension reinstated. The film and the serial both show that Ghalib visits gambling houses in hopes of changing his luck. Once, to Ghalib's chagrin, when he is coming down from the steps of the gambling house, the Sheriff notices him and warns that gambling has been declared illegal and that, if caught, Ghalib could go to jail.

In the fourth episode we see Ghalib celebrating Diwali by sharing food with non-Muslims, when he is chastised by the older residents of the neighborhood. Ghalib's cousin Shams gets the unsuspecting Ghalib to sign the document about his pension, which was supposed to be hand-carried to Commissioner William Fraser in Calcutta. Trusting his cousin, Ghalib signs the papers drafted in English, a language he cannot read. Soon after Ghalib signs the documents, to diffuse any suspicion, Shams gives Ghalib a sum of money on behalf of the Government. Jubilant Ghalib, hopeful that his pension will be reinstated, spends money on wine. Bansidhar returns back without securing an advance on Ghalib's *Diwan.* To make matters worse, Ghalib's newborn son does not survive. The episode shows Ghalib in deep distress. The two ghazals chosen for this episode are appropriately despondent in mood: *Dil hī to hai na saṅg-o-k͟hiśt* "It is only a heart, not stone or mortar!" (Ram 1989: 94) and one of Ghalib's personal favorites: *Sab kahāṃ kuch lālah-o-gul meṃ numāyā ho gayīṃ* "Not all, just a few became visible in the tulip and the rose" (Sayyid 2000: 145).

The fifth episode shows a very depressed Ghalib at Haji Mir's, the bookseller's shop, which he used to visit frequently. He is discussing with Mir Sahab that he may have no option but to move away from Delhi for better prospects, when he hears a female voice singing his ghazal: *Dil hī to hai, na sang-o-k͟hiśt.* Following the voice, he ends up at the apartments of the courtesan Nawabjan (Nina Gupta) who lives above Haji Mir's bookstore. Like in the film, in the serial also, initially, Ghalib shields his identity from the courtesan. She is reading a torn piece of paper with Ghalib's incomplete ghazal. Ghalib pretends that the ghazal was composed by a friend of his and completes the incomplete couplets for her. As he goes back to Haji Mir's shop, he is pleased that at least ordinary people in Delhi like his poems. In the next scene, Nawabjan prepares and presents the ghazal to her visitors with attractive gestures. The Sheriff of Delhi who is among her patrons is attracted to Nawabjan.

The sixth episode shows a restless and despondent Ghalib. He is composing a particularly heartrending ghazal, *Phir kuch ek dil ko beqarārī hai*, "Again the heart is a little restless..." (Sayyid 2000: 75), when Umrao Begum enters the room. In both, the film as well as in the serial, she shows understanding for her husband's disappointments in life, particularly when it comes to children, to the point that she suggests he should get married a second time. However, Ghalib would hear none of it.

The serial portrays Ghalib as sensitive to other people's needs regardless of their religion and social position. Another example is that he considers his friend Bansidhar's grandson as his own, and cares for his servants and their dependents as his own responsibility. He also supports his brother's family in Agra. He is portrayed as generous, not having the heart to send people away from his door. This is supported by Ghalib's letters. He wrote:

> I must support my family—a wife and two children; then there are the servants—Kallu, Kalian and Ayaz. Madari's wife and children are still here as usual; in short, it's as though Madari was still here. Miyan Ghamman had only left me a month when he came back. "I have nothing to eat." "Very well, my friend, you too can stay."
>
> (Russell and Islam 1994: 212)

Ghalib is portrayed as compassionate, clean-hearted and frank in his speech, and assuming that other people are like him.

The serial goes on to show that in the years that follow, Ghalib faces bad times. It is difficult for his servants to get on credit the items of daily necessities. His wife is unhappy with the way Ghalib spends his time. His younger brother in Agra goes mad and one day he appears at Ghalib's home in Delhi. Earlier, Ghalib's lawyer Hiralal had suggested that Ghalib should go to Calcutta in person to take up the matter of his income with the British authorities, but considering the matter of the expenses necessary for undertaking such a long journey Ghalib was still undecided. Now, grasping the urgency of the circumstances, Ghalib decides to leave for Calcutta to see Metcalf about his pension personally. He has to borrow even more heavily to complete his trip. Ghalib is gone from Delhi for almost three years, but to no avail. The matter of his income continues to remain unsolved. Back in Delhi, he is taken to court for being unable to pay off his debts. This incident is also shown in the film, and in both cases, Mufti Sahab, a friend and admirer of Ghalib intervenes and helps avert disaster temporarily.

In the course of his visit to Calcutta, Ghalib stops in Benares where he runs into Nawabjan's mother and asks about her. He tells her that he went to their house in Delhi to visit them. The flashback shows Ghalib, with a shawl on his arm, as he had promised her, finding nobody in the apartment except Nawabjan's servant. Ghalib learns from him about the abuse Nawabjan had endured at Hashmat Khan's hands. As he looks around the empty apartment, he sees written all over the mirrors and walls in red the first line of his own ghazal, *Iśq mujh ko nahīṃ, wahśat hī sahī* "If it's not love I feel, but ferociousness, so be it" (Ram 1989: 119).

Back in Benares, Nawabjan's mother tells Ghalib about the harassment they had suffered at Hashmat Khan's hands. She informs him that Nawabjan had waited to see him till her last breath, but now she is no more. She takes Ghalib to visit Nawabjan's grave where he spreads the promised shawl. The episode ends poignantly with the ghazal in Chitra's voice: *Yeh na thī hamārī qismat ki visāl-e-yār hotā*, "It was not in my luck to be united with my love" (Sayyid 2000: 67).

As a result of a conspired and preplanned raid in his house, the Sheriff of Delhi arrests Ghalib on the charge of running a gambling house from in his home (cf. Sadiq 1995: 636). Ghalib is appalled that matters would end up in such horrible circumstances. The couplets selected for the prison portion of the serial are presented in soft notes befitting the mood of the story line, with not too many musical instruments or fast moving melodies. Still, sometimes the selection of the poems seems inappropriate. For example, one of the ghazals played in the background of the prison scene begins with: *Dost g̲h̲amk̲h̲wārī meṃ merī sa'ī farmāeṃge kyā?* "In alleviating pain, will my friends help me out?" (Sayyid 2000: 65). In fact, this ghazal was composed before 1826. Moreover, it does not effectively represent his sentiments in imprisonment as the next *misra* (poetic line) of this couplet openly announces the poet's intention to inflict pain upon himself again as soon as the wound is about to heal. This does not fit the situation. Finally, the ghazal begins with a reference to *dost*, "friends," when there are no friends left. When Ghalib was sent to jail, most of his friends left his side. One of his later ghazals could have been more suitable, such as *Koī ummīd bar nahīṃ ātī*, "No hope bears fruit" (Sayyid 2000: 178).

Gulzar offers the interpretation that all of Ghalib's problems stemmed from the fact that he did not have any source of income. He was not financially savvy. He trusted the wrong people and thought that the old norms will continue to work when the times and tastes were changing very rapidly.

The series then turns to the horrors of the so-called Mutiny of 1857, when Ghalib's brother Yusuf Mirza was shot by a British soldier. The events are related to us in the dialogues of various minor characters such as Kale Sahab, the Sufi who was respected by Bahadur Shah. All these incidents can be corroborated by historical sources and with Ghalib's letters (see Russell and Islam 1994: 134–357). The serial ends by chronicling the brutalities after the repression of the uprising and Ghalib's demise. In the concluding episode, the series links up with modern times. One year after his hundredth anniversary, Indira Gandhi unveiled Ghalib's *Diwan*, the complete collection of his poems, and the Indian Government established the Ghalib Institute in Delhi, to support research on Ghalib.

The movie and TV serial compared

The film and the serial differ both in the treatment of Ghalib's life and the presentation of his works. In general, the film reduces Ghalib's life to a tragic love story, while the serial transcends that and gives a fuller picture of his life and works.

As regards the love story line, in the film, Moti Begum plays a crucial role in presenting Ghalib's poems to Bahadur Shah Zafar and is instrumental in gaining

Ghalib access to the royal court. The TV serial, however, does not make any claim that Nawabjan ever had access to the Red Fort, let alone played any part in promoting Ghalib's works at the Fort. The series shows Nawabjan performing for Hashmat Khan, the Sheriff, which Moti Begum never does in the film. Although we see in the serial that Hashmat Khan is jealous of Nawabjan's feelings for Ghalib, there is no mention of his intentions of marrying her, in contrast to the film's thwarted wedding when Ghalib comes to his beloved's rescue. In the film Moti Begum moves to Mehroli along with her mother and servant, but in the serial, she moves to Benares and the servant stays back in Delhi.

The relationship of Ghalib and his wife is portrayed similar in movie and serial.[11] The loss of their children plays a significant role in their estrangement. The serial deals with this aspect of Ghalib's life in greater detail than the film. Ghalib loves children and adopts Arif, Umrao's nephew, who also dies. This is a very important incident in Ghalib's life but the film does not cover it, and in the serial it is mentioned very briefly. Scholars consider the following poem one of Ghalib's most poignant ghazals in which he laments the passing of his nephew Arif: *Lāzim hai ki dekho merā rastā koī din aur*, "It is imminent that you wait for me for a few more days..." (Sayyid 2000: 107). Unfortunately, this ghazal is not selected for the serial.

Another point of difference is the role of the shrine of Sufi saint Hazrat Nizamuddin Aulia. In the film, this is where Moti Begum and Umrao Begum run into each other, but in the serial it is the site of a meeting of Ghalib and Nawabjan (see below). In both cases though, this meeting at a sacred place helps Nawabjan and Ghalib in the serial grow in their resolve not to give in to their passion, but instead to uphold the legitimacy of Ghalib's marriage.

Both film and serial report Ghalib's failed debut at the court. However, in the film, on his way back Ghalib meets Moti Begum and her appreciation of his poetry soothes his wounded pride, so he returns home in a triumphant mood. In the serial, Ghalib goes straight home and has to cope on top of his own also with everyone else's disappointment at his lukewarm reception at the Court. The conversation with his wife turns into an occasion to blame Ghalib's failure on the parochialism of Delhi's elite.

For our purpose the differences in the treatment of the ghazals are the most interesting. This is particularly striking for the ghazal, *Iśq mujhko nahīṃ*, or "this is not love I feel." In the film, this ghazal is quoted on a happy occasion at Mufti Sahab's house. Ghalib has been prevailed upon to recite one of his ghazals as he is so indebted to Mufti Sahab. Incidentally, Moti Begum is also present in the *zanana*, the women's quarters, because she was invited to perform and had accepted payment in advance.

The mood is light and festive. Standing behind the latticework of the window, the women in the household are watching the men from the inner portion of the house. At this point in the film, owing to a misunderstanding, Ghalib is under the impression that Moti Begum does not care for him. Ghalib is totally distraught as he tries his best to recite his poem, *Iśq mujhko nahīṃ*. As he stumbles over some words, Moti Begum spontaneously completes the lines aloud from behind the latticework. Ghalib recognizes her voice and is overcome by passion. Unable to continue any more, he excuses himself for feeling unwell. As he leaves, Moti Begum returns her fee and follows him. She catches up with him in the garden and in the course of their brief conversation Ghalib realizes that Moti Begum is still very much in love with him. He promises to visit her.

Let us compare how this ghazal is presented in the serial. Umrao Begum is expecting again and Ghalib goes to the shrine of Hazrat Nizamuddin Aulia to pray for the life of the unborn baby. Here, he runs into Nawabjan, who is visiting the shrine to pray for Ghalib's fame and success. Ghalib promises her that if her prayers were to bear fruit, he would visit her and bring her a shawl as a gift. They both part in horse driven carriages, each going their separate way. This episode is highly charged as the ghazal, *Iśq mujhko nahīṃ*, plays in Chitra's voice in the background.

In both instances, this ghazal is portrayed as expressing the sentiments of Ghalib and his beloved. In the serial, because the camera is on Nawabjan for a longer time and the ghazal is in female voice, it seems to be a cry from the depth of Nawabjan's soul. In the film Talat Mehmood recites the ghazal *tahtul-lafz* style. The tempo of the last couplet increases to express the intensity of Ghalib's feelings. The camera here focuses on Ghalib for a longer time. Thus, in the film, this ghazal seems to reveal Ghalib's heart more than giving voice to Moti's sentiments. This brings us to the next part of our investigation, the way in which Ghalib's ghazals are interpreted in the audiovisual media.

Ghalib's ghazals in movie and TV serial

Not only in the portrayal of Ghalib's life, also in presenting his poems in context, the directors bring their own interpretations. This section will discuss the selection and the contextualization of the poems, as well as the omission of lines from individual poems.

My argument is that both in the movie and the serial, the selection and placement of Ghalib's ghazals, coupled with the exclusion of some of the key couplets that determine the overall tone of the ghazal composition in question, change the understanding of these poems and reduce them to being merely instrumental in the progression of a love story. I will offer two illustrations to demonstrate how the selective exclusion of certain couplets completely robs the ghazal of its broader mystical meaning. Couplets with mystical meanings are excised in favor of those that can be interpreted as being romantic. The latter are more accessible and more suitable for general public consumption. However, in the process, one could argue, the very essence of the composition is taken away. This practice also provides a thematic unity in the song, whereas the ghazal genre allows for expression of completely different thoughts in each of its couplets.

Let us examine first the ghazal selection. Even with eight ghazals, the film is very tightly edited, and is not very long compared to other similar films that focus on "Indo-Muslim" history, literature, culture, and civilization, like *Anarkali* (1953),

Mughal-e-Azam (1960), *Pakeezah* (1971), and *Umrao Jaan* (1981). The following eight ghazals from the *Diwan* are in the film:

Dil-e-nādān tujhe huā kyā hai
(Sayyid 2000: 187)
O foolish heart! What is the matter with you?

Nuqtah cīn hai gham-e-dil
(Ram 1989: 150)
The pain in the heart complains.

Iśq mujh ko nahīṃ, wahśat hī sahī
(Ram 1989: 119)
If, what I feel is barbarity, not love; so be it!

Āh ko cāhiye ek umr asar hone tak
(Sayyid 2000: 117)
It takes an age for a wish to come true.

Yeh na thī hamārī qismat ke wisāl-e-yār hotā
(Sayyid 2000: 67)
It was not my fate to be united with my beloved.

Hai bas ke har ek unke iśāre meṃ niśān aur
(Sayyid 2000:103)
Her every gesture has another meaning.

Phir mujhe dīdah-e-tār yād āyā
(Sayyid 2000: 77)
I remember those tear-filled eyes again.

Rahiye ab aisī jagah calkar jahāṃ koī na ho
(Sayyid 2000: 159)
Now go and stay in a place where there's no one.

Compared to the conciseness of the movie, the stretch of seventeen episodes offers the serial greater scope to develop the story line and include more couplets and ghazals. Full count renders fourteen ghazals,[12] five of which overlap with the first five mentioned for the movie. In addition, the serial features the following:

Hazāroṃ khwāhiśeṃ aisī ki har khwāhiś pe dam nikle
(Ram 1989:170)
I have a thousand desires, each desire worth dying for!

Dil hī to hai, na saṃg-o-khiśt, dard se bhar na āye kyoṃ
(Ram 1989: 94)
It's only a heart not brick or stone, why would it not be moved by pain?

Voh firāq aur voh wisāl kahāṃ
(Sayyid 2000: 121)
What happened to that quarreling and reconciliation?

Bazīca-e-atfāl hai duniyā mere āge
(Ram 1989: 162)
The world unfurls before me like a child's toy.

Zulmat kade meṃ mere śab-e-gham kā jośhai
(Sayyid 2000: 177)
In deep darkness rages the passion of my night of sorrow.

Unke dekhe se jo ā jātī hai muṃh pe raunaq
(Sayyid 2000: 201)[13]
The radiance that shines on the face when I see her…

Kabse hūṃ, kyā batāūṃ, jahān-e-kharāb meṃ
(Sayyid 2000: 131)[14]
How can I say for how long I've been in this sorrowful world.

Sab kahāṃ, kuch lālah-o-gul meṃ numāyah ho gayīṃ
(Sayyid 2000: 145)
Not all, only a few have appeared in the tulip and the rose.

Na thā kuch to khudā thā, kuch na hotā to khudā hotā
(Sayyid 2000: 75)
When there was nothing, God was there. Had there not been anything, God would have still existed.

Even at the first glance it is very evident that almost all of the ghazals in common between serial and film express sentiments of love. Also with regard to the other ghazals featured, with a few exceptions, only romantic ghazals are included. In my opinion, this is the reason why out of the entire *Diwan*, a select number of ghazals finds its way in films, and is selected by ghazal singers, including Begum Akhtar, K.L. Sahgal, Noorjahan and Lata Mangeshkar: certain ghazals are popular precisely because of their romantic sentiments. Ghazals of high quality that express sentiments other than love, do not fit the bill at the box office and therefore must suffer complete disregard.

To go a step further, let us examine those ghazals that do make the selection. To make the lyrics seem more suitable for a romantic situation, a ghazal can be picturized in a manner that may differ from the intended emotion. Let us take the example of the depiction of the ghazal that begins with *Āh ko cāhiye ek umr asar hone tak*. The mood of this ghazal is pensive as it dwells on the serious side of life. In the movie, it is presented in the context of a festival. Instead of celebrating, Bahadur Shah is depressed and nothing seems to lighten his gloom. His wife Zeenat Mahal asks the maids in attendance to try to lift his spirits. Moti Begum dances and sings this ghazal of Ghalib. It pleases Bahadur Shah and he asks her for the poet's identity. Thus Ghalib owes a second chance at the Fort to Moti Begum. On close examination the words of the ghazal, seem to be most unsuitable to bring cheer to anybody, let alone a king who is already mournful. Nevertheless, in the film, Moti Begum is successful in drawing Bahadur Shah Zafar out of his melancholy! Similarly, the ghazal *Dil hī to hai na sang-o-khiśt* is also philosophical in character. Nevertheless, the serial gives it quite a carefree musical treatment. Nawabjan's dance and gestures are designed to please her patrons. To the discriminating audience, this kind of treatment of a serious, contemplative poem may seem out of good taste.

Thus we note a process that may be termed "romanticizing the ghazal." Another strategy is that within a given ghazal couplets that do not express romantic sentiments are excluded. One of the characteristics of the ghazal is that each single couplet can encapsulate a different thought, independent of each other. Thus, couplets of a single ghazal can address many different issues. In the Urdu ghazal tradition when all or a sequence of couplets focus on one single idea, it is an exception and there is a separate name for it: *ghazal-musalsal*, or "continuous ghazal." We note that in order to create a *ghazal-musalsal* from the "romantic" ghazals, couplets with mystical meanings are excluded.

Whereas typically a single couplet can be interpreted on a secular as well as a mystical level, there are couplets that defy dual interpretation. Unsurprisingly, we find that such couplets are excluded from the ghazals in the movies and TV, because they are inappropriate for the popular film's purposes.

To illustrate this point, we will analyze two of the ghazals common in the film and in the serial, and review those specific couplets that have been excluded from both. The first ghazal selected for the discussion, is one of the best known ghazals of Ghalib:

Dil-e-nādān tujhe huā kyā hai
ākhir is dard kī dawā kyā hai
Ham haiṃ muśtāq aur woh bezār
yā Ilāhī, yeh mājrā kyā hai
Maiṃ bhī muṃh meṃ zabān rakhtā hūṃ
kāś pūcho ki mudda'ā kyā hai
Jab ki tujh bin nahīṃ koī maujūd
phir yeh hangāmah ae khudā kyā hai
Yeh parī cehrah log kaise haiṃ
ghamzah-o-'iśwah-o-adā kyā hai
Śikan-e-zulf-e-ambarīn kyoṃ hai
nigāh-e-caśm-e-surmah sā kyā hai
Sabzah-o-gul kahāṃ se āye haiṃ
'abr kyā cīz hai, hawā kyā hai
Ham ko un se wafā kī hai ummīd,
jo nahīṃ jānte wafā kyā hai

Hāṃ, bhalā kar, terā bhalā hogā
  aur darveś kī sadā kyā hai
Jān tum par nisār kartā hūṃ
  maiṃ nahīṃ jāntā du'ā kyā hai
Maiṃ ne mānā ki kuch nahīṃ Ghālib
  muft hāth āye to burā kyā hai

The following English Translation is adapted from Matthews and Shackle (1972: 128):

O foolish heart! What is the matter with you?
  In the end, What is the cure for this pain?
I am eager and she is fed up,
  O God, what kind of a situation is this?
I also am capable of speech,
  If only she would ask me what I want!
When nothing exists except for You
  Then, Lord, what is all this commotion!
What kind of people are these with divine countenances!
  Nods, winks, and flirtations! What is all this?
Why these twisting, ambergris-perfumed locks?
  Why the glance from the collyrium-shaded eyes!
Where have the garden and the rose come from?
  What is the cloud and what is the breeze!
We expect commitment and loyalty from those
  Who do not even know what it means.
Do good unto others, good will be done unto you
  What else is the counsel of the dervish?
Gladly, I would sacrifice my life for you,
  I do not know what it is to ask for favors.
I agree that Ghalib is nothing,
  But if you get him for nothing, what is wrong with that?

The couplets number 5, 6, 7, 9, 10, and 11, are excluded from the film as well as from the TV serial. I argue that they were removed precisely because of their mystical nature. These couplets express the awe one feels looking at the wonderful world God has created. In particular, couplet 9 is didactic in tone and encapsulates Ghalib's idea of how a person should live his life in this world. When you sow good seeds, you will reap a good harvest. This did not fit the romantic context of either the film or the serial.

One could argue that film is a medium that relies on images, and corresponding images cannot be found easily for the excluded couplets, and that the selection of the couplets is made keeping in mind that the song should not exceed two and a half minutes or so in duration. Still, most audiences would agree that these couplets simply are not in sync with the kind of romantic situations expected in a common popular film production.

Let us now zoom in to see how the couplets that were selected for both movie and serial are picturized. In movie as well as serial, the ghazal above-discussed is assigned to Ghalib's beloved who is a singer by profession. In the film, she is portrayed by Suraiyya, whose gestures seem dignified compared to those of Nina Gupta's in the serial. In the serial, there is no doubt as to her profession as a courtesan. The difference in the portrayal of the very same ghazal in the film and the serial is remarkable because it is essentially indicative of the changing public tastes over the last quarter of a century.

The next ghazal for discussion is: *Āh ko cāhiye ek umr asar hone tak.* So popular is the first line, *misra*, of this ghazal, that people often quote it in every day life to express disappointment:

Āh ko cāhiye ek 'umr asar hone tak
kaun jītā hai terī zulf ke sar hone tak
Dām-e-har mauj meṃ hai halqah-e-sad kām nihang
dekheṃ kyā guzre hai qatre peh gauhar hone tak
'Āśiqī sabr talab, aur tamannā betāb
dil kā kyā rang karūṃ khūn-e-jigar hone tak
Hamne mānā ki taghāful na karoge, lekin
khāk ho jāyeṃge ham tum ko khabar hone tak
Partav-e-khur se hai śabnam ko fanā kī ta'līm
maiṃ bhī hūṃ ek ināyat kī nazar hone tak
Yak nazar beś nahīṃ, fursat-e-hastī, ghāfil
Garmī-e-bazm hai yak raqs-e-śarar hone tak
Gham-e-hastī kā Asad kis se ho juz marg 'ilāj
śam'a har rang me jaltī hai sahar hone tak

With this particular ghazal, much is lost in translation. Many connoisseurs of Urdu poetry firmly believe that certain couplets of Ghalib cannot be translated. However a functional English translation of this ghazal is as follows:

It takes an age for a wish to come true, who knows,
If one would live long enough to enjoy your vanquished locks.
A hundred crocodiles lie in the orb of every wave,
Let's see what a drop of water must endure before turning into a pearl.
Love requires patience, but desire is impatient,
In death, the heart will be red, but what to do with it until then?
Though I am sure that you'd rescue me right away from distress;
I am afraid that by the time you find out, it will be too late.

The reflection of sun teaches "annihilation" to the dewdrop;
  I too am here, till you recall me with a kind glance.
Life is short like the blink of an eye,
  When the flame flutters, the party is over.
Except death, Asad, what is the cure for the sorrows of life?
  But no matter what, the candle continues to burn till dawn.

Again, the same couplets are excluded from the film *and* the serial as well: 2, 5, and 6. Let us review the messages contained in these excluded couplets. Couplet 2 may sound cryptic to the untrained ear. It expresses the idea that nothing that is worth achieving in life comes easy. Pitfalls are numerous on the path to perfection. Patience is required to achieve anything meaningful. It takes a long time for a raindrop to transform into a pearl. This couplet proclaims Ghalib's philosophy of life, which is not a formula for instant gratification. Only hard work and perseverance can lead to success, that is, *if* you are lucky.

Couplet 5 is also philosophical in nature. As elsewhere, Ghalib contemplates the ephemeral nature of existence. The morning sun teaches the dewdrop a lesson of annihilation. The word *fanā* is loaded with the mystical meaning: " 'Fanā' is in the first place an ethical concept, that is, the renunciation of human qualities and increasing spiritualization; it is rather the return of the creature to the state 'as he was before he was' " (Schimmel 1992: 107). The lesson is that on the one hand, we must not forget that we are not here forever, at the same time, in life, we must strive for perfection. This indeed is deep philosophy encapsulated in a tiny couplet.

Couplet 6 is similar in mood to the previous one: a warning to mankind against the hollow fancies of this world. Human existence is no more than the blink of an eye: the moment the flame of the candle begins to flutter, the party is over. Compare this to a proverbial couplet similar in idea, attributed to poet-saint Kabir:

Pānī kerā budabudā, asa manus kī jāta
Dekhata hi chupa jāigo, jyoṃ tārā parabhāta
Human life, by nature, is like a hollow water bubble,
Even as you watch, it fades away like the morn-star.

My point is that the omission of couplets that are mystical and moral changes the very character of a poetic composition. As a result of these changes, the entire composition loses its metaphysical aspect and is reduced to being a mere love song. One could venture to say that thus transformed the poem is a mere instrument to fulfill the entertainment agenda of the celluloid world.

Conclusion

Film and television directors have contributed significantly to preserve a memory of "Indo-Muslim" culture. Simultaneously, they maintain an agenda to entertain through love stories. This has caused significant changes to the Urdu literature they present: the ghazal becomes "tailored"-to-entertainment needs through a "cut and paste" process. This is not without consequences: the culture it represents also becomes stereotyped.

We should not just blame the directors' entertainment agenda, though, the decline in understanding of Urdu poetry and its conventions may also have contributed to the exclusion of good couplets from the ghazals. Here, other factors come into play. Considering its rich literature, after independence Urdu education has not enjoyed the support it deserves. Support for regional language and literature falls to the Indian states, but despite the large number of Urdu speakers in India, no state is assigned to promote and support education in Urdu, not even Uttar Pradesh, the seat of Urdu learning and culture. Several recent articles raise the question of the future of Urdu literature in India, Pakistan, and elsewhere because Urdu education continues to experience neglect. More than a generation has passed since independence and the number of those who understand literary Urdu continues to dwindle (Askari 2004: 219). If "Indo-Muslim" culture reaches the general public only via the movies or television, its rich literature, philosophy, and cultural heritage will eventually dwindle. If Urdu education is not available to the public, its rich vocabulary, poetic conventions, and symbolism become less familiar. One can clearly foresee this in today's young people's demand for increasingly simplified Urdu in film lyrics.

Although most popular Hindi film songs include many Urdu words, yet, on close analysis one realizes that only a limited number of words, mostly of a romantic register, are repeated over and over again. By now, this set of words has become a part of the common film song vocabulary understood by most Bollywood patrons. This promotes the vicious cycle of remaining within the confinement of a certain core vocabulary and consequently Urdu literature continues to suffer.

In conclusion, I suggest that popular film and television's representation of Urdu literature brings with it a distortion. On the one hand, the changes make ghazals more accessible to the audience, by skipping lines from the poems to produce a unity of mood, and by changes in word choice from less Persianite to more Hindustani. Yet, through the selective focusing on the love story aspect and ignoring broader mystical meanings, the ghazal is also deprived of its purpose and identity.

In the *Special Edition* portion of the Yashraj productions of the DVDs of Guru Dutt's *Pyaasa* and *Kaagaz ke Phool*, Nasreen Munni Kabir, the leading scholar of Indian film, discusses the poetry component of older films. She makes the point that the poetry in the old films was not a filler to fill in the "song and dance" sequences of the film. In most cases these songs were not composed for a given film to suit a given situation. In fact many ghazals, nazms, and na'ats were composed by noted Urdu poets before they were incorporated in the films. The lyrics are really high-class poetry, contributing to the aesthetics and essence of the film. She identifies this as the secret of the continued appeal and longevity of the old film songs. I agree, but nevertheless one must be keenly aware of the fact that much is missing from the version presented in popular films, including parts that are worthy of being explored, enjoyed, and learned from. There is much more in the Urdu poetry beyond what meets our eyes and ears in "Bollywood." I conclude with one of Iqbal's couplets:

> *Sitāroṃ se āge jahān aur bhī haiṃ,*
> *Abhī 'iśq ke imtihān aur bhī haiṃ.*
> Beyond the stars, there are still other worlds;
> There are other fields to test man's indomitable spirit
> (Sadiq 1995: 453)

Notes

* The first draft of this chapter was written before I knew of the article by Alain Désoulières on Ghalib in film and literature. This study complements his, because my focus is on the ghazals rather than the story.

1 I am grateful to Shanta Benegal for stimulating conversations on this matter.

2 Surprisingly, this movie has not been high on scholars' radar. Dwyer and Patel (2002) and Barnouw and Krishnaswamy (1963) refer to Modi, but not to *Mirza Ghalib*. Tejaswini Ganti (2004) mentions neither. Many other works on Hindi Cinema have only one or two sentences about either the film or director.

3 For a detailed study of Manto's dramas and short stories on which the script was based, see Désoulières 2003. About Manto who wrote the story for the film, Alain Désoulières writes, "By his personal correspondence with his friends we know that S.H. Manto was fascinated by the very person of Ghalib, particularly at the end of his life. Apart from the two different short Urdu dramas with Ghalib as the main protagonist, Manto also wrote a short story relating 'an episode of Ghalib's life.' In addition, we know that Manto, who, after Partition, had to leave Bombay and lose the lucrative perspective of producing for cinema, intended to write for the cinema on Ghalib's life" (Désoulières 2003).

4 Gulzar has even been compared to Ghalib himself by the sarod maestro Ustad Amjad Ali Khan, who reportedly said when presenting him a lifetime achievement award: "Gulzar is a present-day Ghalib," see http://www.aiaua.org/projectindia/projectindia2.html (last accessed March 25, 2007).

5 The program, *Most Memorable of Sa re ga ma pa*, hosted by Shan, has been aired repeatedly on different stations, a taped copy is available from the author.

6 While there is a reference to a lost love in one of Ghalib's letters, there is no support for her intermediary role in introducing Ghalib to the Court.

7 In some of the early episodes, it seems as if Gulzar made an effort to select the concluding ghazal carefully to reflect the seriousness of Ghalib's circumstances. However in the later episodes he seems to have lost sight of this. It is actually disturbing that since the ghazals are placed at the end of the episodes, seconds after a new ghazal is introduced, the screen is obscured by the credits. Consequently, one gets a chance to enjoy only the musical aspect of a composition. One wonders whether this was intentional.

8 None of the episodes of the serial, which was initially available on video only, was numbered.

9 In fact this is a ghazal composed between May 1849 and August 1852 (see Sayyid 2000: 310). The director often takes such liberties with the chronology of the ghazals.

10 The meaning of the Persian word *bāzīceh* is "children's toy" (Aryanpur-Kashani 1986, qv), but it is given incorrectly in the serial. Ghalib explains this poem to his wife, glossing *bāzīceh* as "children's playground." This is not the only inaccuracy of this type: in one of the early episodes the scribe who is preparing the copy of Ghalib's *Diwan*,

explains to his wife that *harf-e-muqarrar* means "one who returns a second time." In fact it means "fixed letter" or "unchangeable character of script." Additionally, the ghazal he is quoting was composed between 1847 and 1852, thus added much later to Ghalib's *Diwan* (Sayyid 2000: 143).

11 The relationship between Ghalib and his father-in-law is portrayed differently, though. In the film it is a strained relationship, but in the TV serial, it is based on mutual appreciation, respect, and goodwill.

12 Only thirteen songs are featured in the CD *Ghazals from the Serial Mirza Ghalib.* Ten are sung by Jagjit Singh himself, one is a duet with his ex-wife Chitra, three ghazals are sung by Chitra alone, and one of the ghazals in the introduction portion, and the couplet which opens each episode is by Vinod Sehgal. Surprisingly, the most powerful ghazal of Chitra, *Iśq mujh ko nahīṃ, wahśat hī sahī*, did not make the cut. From the point of view of the emotion it carries in the context of the storyline, this ghazal is perhaps the best of the ones that came in Chitra's share. One suspects that this particular ghazal was excluded as a result of the strained relationship between Chitra and Jagjit at the time when the ghazals were being selected for the CD.

13 This is one of those instances when in the musical composition, the opening couplet, or *matla'*, of the ghazal is omitted. The opening *misra* of this ghazal is: *Husn-e-māh garce bā-hamgām-e-kamāl acchā hai*, "Though the beauty of moon at its zenith is good" (Sayyid 2000: 201). In the serial, the first couplet of this ghazal is recited without melody and is not connected with the ghazal as it appears in the CD. In the community of ghazal singers, it is a common practice to change the order of the couplets in between the *matla'*, and the signature couplet, *maqta'*. Yet, the first couplet is not often taken out as it is instrumental in finding the ghazal in question in its relevant *diwan.*

14 The real *matla'*, opening couplet of this ghazal is: *Miltī hai k͟hu-e-yār se nār iltihāb meṃ.*

References

Editions of Ghālib's works

Ram, M. (ed.) (1989) *Diwān-e-G͟hālib*, New Delhi: Ghalib Institute.

Sayyid, M. (ed.) (2000) *Diwān-e-G͟hālib: Nusk͟ha-e-K͟hvājah*, Lahore: Al Viqar Publications.

Other works

Anonymous (1988) "Kahte haiṃ ki Ghālib kā hai andāz-e-bayān aur," *India Today* November 30, 1988. TV Column. Delhi: Living Media India Ltd.

Aryanpur-Kashani, A. and Aryanpur-Kashani, M. (1986) *The Combined New Persian-English and English-Persian Dictionary*, Lexington, KY: Mazda Publishers.

Askari, M.H. (2004) "A Famine of Verbs," *The Annual of Urdu Studies* 19: 219–26.

Barnouw, E. and Krishnaswamy, S. (1963) *Indian Film*, New York: Columbia University Press.

Desai, A. (1994) *In Custody*, New York: Penguin.

Désoulières, A. 2003. "Images of a historical character: Mirza Ghalib," in T. Damsteegt (ed.), *Heroes and Heritage: The Protagonist in Indian Literature and Film*, Leiden: CNWS.

Dwyer, R. and Patel, D. (2002) *Cinema India: The Visual Culture of Hindi Film*, London: Reaktion.

Ganti, T. (2004) *Bollywood: A Guidebook to Popular Hindi Cinema*, New York: Routledge.

Matthews, D. and Shackle, C. (1972) *An Anthology of Classical Urdu Love Lyrics*, London: Oxford University Press.

Naim, C.M. (2004) *Urdu Texts and Contexts: The Selected Essays of C.M. Naim*, Delhi: Permanent Black.

Pritchett, F.W. (2005) "'The Meaning of the Meaningless Verses': Ghalib and His Commentators," in K. Hansen and D. Lelyveld (eds) *A Wilderness of Possibilities: Urdu Studies in Transnational Perspective*, New Delhi: Oxford University Press.

Ramachandran, T.M. and Rukmini, S. (1985) *70 Years of Indian Cinema*, Bombay: Cinema India-International.

Rangoonwalla, F. (1983) *Indian Cinema: Past and Present*, New Delhi: Clarion Books.

Russell, R. and Islam, K. (1994) *Ghalib: Life and Letters*, Delhi: Oxford University Press.

Sadiq, M. (1995) *A History of Urdu Literature*, 2nd edn, Delhi: Oxford University Press.

Schimmel, A. (1992) *Islam: An Introduction*, New York: State University of New York Press.

Part 5

Classics from colonial literature

8 Remembering, repeating, and working through *Devdas*

Corey K. Creekmur

No Hindu ever reads the *Mahabharata* for the first time.

A.K. Ramanujan, "Repetition in the *Mahabharata*" [1988] 1999

On the days that a letter from Devdas arrived, Parvati would look like she had grasped the moon in her hands. She would sit on the threshold of the staircase, and read the letter over and over, all day long.

Sarat Chandra Chattopadhyay, *Devdas* (1917, trans. Sreejata Guha 2002)[1]

Introduction

If only for the last century, no Indian ever sees *Devdas* for the first time. It is less convincing to assert that no Indian ever *reads Devdas* for the first time: while the stark novella by Sarat Chandra Chattopadhyay (1876–1938),[2] first published in Bengali in 1917 and soon translated into other major Indian languages, enjoyed a remarkable vogue and has endured for an often adoring audience, it is clear that the early adaptation of the story into a film by Naresh Chandra Mitra in 1928, and repeatedly thereafter by other filmmakers in both official and unofficial remakes, has ensured a deep familiarity more approvingly associated with ancient, sacred, and mythic rather than modern, secular, and popular texts. In contrast to the *Mahabharata* and *Ramayana*, the sweeping Sanskrit epics that still animate popular South Asian narratives, it may seem premature to identify the concise *Devdas* as a "classic," except in the careless way we label some texts "modern" or even "instant" classics. And since the term is usually offered as a designation of "timeless" literary value as well as a marker of antiquity, the celebration of *Devdas* as a "classic" in either sense certainly remains debatable or premature. *Devdas* is a story its readers have probably loved more than admired, and so critical estimations of the work (including its mature author's own apparently dismissive opinion of his early text) have had little negative impact on the tale's resonant and persistent appeal. As Meenakshi Mukherjee emphasizes, "Irrespective of the fact that serious present-day literary critics prefer to leave him [Saratchandra] alone, his highly durable grassroots popularity is a phenomenon of continuing cultural significance in modern India, proving adequately, if proof were needed, that despite surface differences there is a common Indian substratum of literary taste at the mass level" (Mukherjee 1985: 102).[3] If the power the story has exerted cannot finally be explained by the original text's intrinsic qualities, there is no denying its accumulated effect: since its appearance almost a century ago, *Devdas* has never been forgotten, in large part because it has never been allowed to collect dust, unlike other musty "classics" that are dutifully acclaimed but largely unread, and rarely remembered with affection despite their esteemed status.

To the contrary, *Devdas* is fondly recalled through its insistent *repetition*; like the inventive revisions that keep the *Mahabharata* and *Ramayana* vital, including through the modern mass media of comics, cinema, and television, each repetition of *Devdas* might be understood as a cultural readjustment to and of the basic story, with every return to the material an opportunity for the "timeless" story to serve the specific historical contexts that surround each of its reincarnations (see Nair 2002; Nazir 2002; Singhal 2002 for overviews of the story's retellings). In quite another cultural context—but in 1914, and thus close enough to the moment of *Devdas*'s birth to feel auspicious—Sigmund Freud described the repetition encountered so frequently in the psychoanalytic session as a means of psychic resistance: according to Freud, "the patient repeats instead of remembering, and repeats under the conditions of resistance" (Freud 1914: 151). Identifying for the first time what he famously termed the "compulsion to repeat" (*Wiederholungszwang*), Freud sought to explain the tendency of patients to repeat troubling past experiences in the present (especially in the relationship with the analyst, which Freud called transference) rather than "remember" them as past, which would allow the patient to "work through" (or interpret, and understand) them. While neglecting the valid and complex questions regarding the application of psychoanalysis to a South Asian context, I think Freud's early understanding of repetition (elaborated more controversially toward the end of his career) may at least help explain the manifest desire of Indian filmmakers and audiences to return to this story. *Devdas* is after all a rather miserable tale of its hero's dissolution and death, but its repetition might demonstrate either an urge to simply repeat rather than remember, or perhaps returns to *Devdas* are evidence of an effort to remember and slowly "work through," and finally move beyond, its meanings.

The steady production of versions of *Devdas* in the last hundred years at least encourages us to ponder its function as one of the central myths of modern India. Recourse to Freud's therapeutic concepts (designed of course to explain individuals rather than multifaceted cultures) might also lend a psychological perspective—perhaps appropriate given the mass-produced and mass-consumed fantasies of Indian popular cinema—to A. K. Ramanujan's more aesthetic and cultural explanation of the "certain kind of repetition" he identifies as "the central structuring principle" of the *Mahabharata*. (Ramanujan 1999: 163). In fact, in an apparent aside Ramanujan himself links a Freudian understanding of repetition to his own analysis of the repetitive form of the epic, in marked contrast to (as Western readers might expect) any of its characters: summarizing how the "replications" (or repeated actions) in the epic indicate "part of a total worldview," he notes that "experiences are not bound to one character. It's as if action is released from character. Furthermore, the same man undergoes an experience more than once—e.g., living incognito, or engaging in the dice game, almost rehearsing it once and playing it for real a second or third time—like a neurotic's compulsions to repeat, or certain 'autonomous complexes.' It's as if there's a kind of autonomy of action. Once set into motion, the act chooses its personae, constitutes its agents" (1789). By emphasizing the text's own compulsion to repeat, Ramanujan encourages the sort of "psychoanalysis of culture" Freud was both wary of and could not himself resist in his studies of "civilization." While Devdas might be identified as the very model of the modern, neurotic Indian (or at least of a Bengali stereotype), in part through his own compulsive drinking and his continuous abandonment of and unfulfilling return to his unhappy home, in what follows I wish to explore the persistent repetitions of *Devdas* the text—in at least a few of its key Hindi versions—rather than the character, who, as Ramanujan suggests, may simply be constituted by the repetitive structure that, across many reiterations and revisions, now exceeds and overwhelms him. In India, and in the transmission of popular culture through the South Asian diaspora, *Devdas* has been the vehicle of a continuous process of collective "remembering, repeating, and working through," even if this work has taken place in cinema halls rather than upon psychoanalyst's couches—disarmingly comfortable locations that were constructed almost simultaneously.

Adapting and remaking *Devdas*

Ramanujan's insights about repetition and the *Mahabharata* in part emphasize the cultural ubiquity of the story in South Asia, which might just as easily be encountered in oral, theatrical, or mass media forms before or indeed whether or not one ever actually "reads" it. Scholars have also emphasized that the epics do not survive in single, definitive texts, but have been sustained as palimpsests and alternate versions (See Lutgendorf 1992; Richman 1991; Richman 2000): contemporary consumers who are now adept at navigating DVDs featuring "extended director's cuts," "alternate endings," and "deleted scenes" are thus working with material closer to the heterogeneous form of ancient Indian texts than they perhaps recognize. Similarly, although the tragic triangle linking the self-destructive Devdas, his forbidden childhood love Parvati (Paro) and the reformed prostitute Chandramukhi has its ostensible origin in the 1917 novella, the story has since become one of the touchstones of popular Indian cinema, less through a "definitive version" than through continual repetition and variation. Again, the first, (now lost) silent adaptation starring Phani Burma, later a notable director himself, was filmed in 1928 by the prominent Bengali actor-director Naresh Chandra Mitra, but the first widely influential version was directed, perhaps simultaneously, in Hindi and Bengali for New Theatres, established in 1931 in Calcutta, by P.C. (Pramathesh Chandra) Barua, son of the Raja of Gauripur. (The films are usually identified as 1935 productions, but some sources state that the Bengali version was produced in 1936, and the Hindi version in 1939.)

Barua cast himself as Devdas in the Bengali version, and the legendary singing star K.L. (Kundun Lal) Saigal starred in the extremely popular Hindi version: because both Barua and Saigal also suffered from their character's alcoholism, the suggestion of a morbid identification with the role of Devdas has haunted later figures attracted to the story as well (on Barua and his influence, see Nandy 2001).

Devdas also exists in at least one Tamil (1936, d. P. V. Rao), Malayalam (1989, d. Ownbelt Mani), and two Telegu versions (1953, d. Vedantam Raghavaiah, and 1974, d. Vijayanirmala), as well as a Bengali remake (1979, d. Dilip Roy), though its most prominent versions following Barua's film are undoubtedly the remakes in Hindi by Bimal Roy (who had served as cinematographer on Barua's film) starring Dilip Kumar in 1955, and by Sanjay Leela Bhansali starring Shah Rukh Khan in 2002. Another recent Bengali version has also been released, suggesting that the story is extending itself into the current century. In addition to these many "official" versions of *Devdas*, the story and its tragic characters have also served as crucial referents for such major Hindi films as Guru Dutt's *Pyaasa* (1957) and especially his *Kaagaz ke Phool* (1959), which involves a dissolute director remaking *Devdas* as a film within the film. Guru Dutt is yet another key figure in Indian cinema whose tortured personal life unfortunately resonates with the tormented and self-destructive Devdas. Indeed, as Gayatri Chatterjee suggests, Devdas is the archetype of what she tentatively calls "the genre of the self-destructive urban hero" (Chatterjee 2003: 62) in Indian cinema. Among other films featuring this figure, a loose adaptation of Dostoevsky's *Crime and Punishment*, *Phir Subah Hogi* (1958, d. Ramesh Saigal) features Raj Kapoor in a rare Devdas-like role, whereas *Muqaddar Ka Sikander* (1978, d. Prakash Mehra), a more or less unofficial remake, forges the unexpected link between the early twentieth-century upper-class Bengali aesthete and Amitabh Bachchan's Emergency-era, working-class, angry young North Indian man (a point made by Nandy 2001; also see Creekmur 2005 for a discussion of the relation between Bachchan and earlier Hindi film heroes). Finally, the masochistic romantic relationships of *Devdas* are echoed in otherwise unrelated films such as *Anmol Ghadi* (1946, d. Mehboob Khan), *Awara* (1951, d. Raj Kapoor), and *Prem Rog* (1982, d. Raj Kapoor) that depict lifelong but socially thwarted passions between a young man and woman. Ashok Banker has suggested that Meena Kumari's character in the film *Sahib Bibi Aur Ghulam* (1962, d. Abrar Alvi) provides Indian cinema with its most notable female Devdas, a claim linking yet another star's troubled personal life with Indian cinema's most famous alcoholic (Banker 2001).[4] In short, the very model of the ardent lover whose desire is never consummated, the melancholic Devdas has spawned a school of sad heirs throughout the history of popular Indian cinema.

While the conventional terms available to discuss this body of films suggest two distinct modes of artistic transformation, all the film versions of *Devdas* after 1928 might be accurately identified as simultaneously adaptations *and* remakes; while this dual status for a text is not in fact so uncommon, each specific instance may complicate what is often taken to be an easily mapped relationship between an original and a copy. If, straightforwardly, the lost 1928 *Devdas* is the first adaptation, with the novel as its only direct predecessor, we might understand the more famous Barua versions to be not just later adaptations but also, and perhaps more significantly, remakes, works that refer not to a single origin but locate themselves in a series of texts. The fact that, following a somewhat common practice in the early sound era, two versions of the story were filmed by the same creative team in different languages (a common practice at the Pune-based film studio Prabhat, for instance) requires another category, the alternate-language version. Indeed, *both* of Barua's films are ostensibly remakes of Mitra's film, but alternate versions of one another: if remakes might be imagined as successive generations of a story, Barua's pair of films might be configured as twins; of course the complex relationships between generations as well as twins remain a source of dramatic tension in popular Indian cinema. Although adaptations (typically from literature or theater to film) and remakes (from film to film) are common as creative and commercial practices, the discipline of film studies has had surprisingly little to say about remakes (but see Horton and McDougal 1998), and only a bit more about adaptations, which have been most often praised or denounced in terms of their "fidelity" to their sources.[5] Most obviously, both kinds of text challenge the modern and Western aesthetic value assigned to originality itself, even if from time to time a remake or adaptation is deemed superior to an original. And while remakes might reward or disappoint a viewer familiar with an earlier version or versions of the narrative, most are made (unlike sequels) without the requirement of familiarity. Many film viewers encounter a remake without having actually experienced its source, and perhaps even without knowing that the text is a remake at all. Indeed, Bimal Roy, in a short essay on adapting Saratchandra to film, noted that "There is a great tendency in our country to judge such films by comparing them only with older film versions and never with the original classic on which it is based. How many film viewers care to read carefully what Sarat Chandra has written, when they go to see the film version of one of his stories?" (Roy 1994: 32). Despite his own recourse to an "original source" to fairly evaluate an adaptation, Roy's comments again indicate that the presumably straightforward relationship between any original and copy becomes tangled when a "simple" pair of texts expand into an unending series, as is the case with *Devdas*.

Recently, by questioning or simply ignoring the often simplistic demand of narrative fidelity—usually reduced to a demand not to alter story content and be inattentive to style—a number of critics have reinvigorated the discussion of adaptation, often praising examples that dare to adapt material boldly and creatively, with little conventional regard for a text's original status: the transformation of Jane Austen's novel *Emma* into *Clueless* (1995, d. Amy Heckerling), or Homer's *Odyssey* into *O, Brother, Where Art Thou?* (2000, d. Joel Coen) might be representative examples of successfully irreverent adaptations. However, the critical focus on adaptation has been largely limited to Hollywood or European examples and especially to adaptations of European and American novels, alongside a steady critical appraisal of cinematic adaptations of Shakespeare's plays. The few close considerations of adaptation in Indian cinema have focused, unsurprisingly, on the art cinema and its literary aspirations: Satyajit Ray's famous adaptations of works by Rabindranath Tagore, for instance, are commonly viewed as a creative dialogue between artistic giants working in their respective media (see Ghosh 2003 for a recent example). Adaptations into the popular mode of mainstream Hindi cinema of such works as R.K. Narayan's *The Guide* (1958) as *Guide* (1965, d. Vijay Anand) or Mirza Mohammad Hadi Ruswa's *Umrao Jān Adā* (1895) as *Umrao Jaan* (1981, d. Muzaffar Ali) are often taken less seriously, and typically viewed as at best semi-successful popularizations and at worst damaging trivializations of superior originals. Contemporary diasporic art films such as Deepa Mehta's *Earth* (1997) (also released as *1947*) from Bapsi Sidwa's novel *Cracking India* (1988, also published as *Ice Candy Man*) or Mira Nair's *The Namesake* (2007) from Jhumpa Lahiri's novel (2003) are more often implicitly aligned with the tradition of viewing Indian art films as serious if often imperfect adaptations of ambitious literary works. In the more "vulgar" realm of Indian popular cinema, many films are recognized to be copies—in effect pirate copies—of Western originals rather than legally negotiated, acknowledged adaptations, sometimes of multiple sources: for instance, Sanjay Gupta's thriller *Kaante* (2002), set and filmed in Los Angeles, is a relatively direct Hindi pastiche of *The Usual Suspects* (1995, d. Bryan Singer) and *Reservoir Dogs* (1992, d. Quentin Tarantino).[6] Such examples, hardly uncommon in popular Indian cinema, further complicate the relationships which available terms like "adaptation" and "remake" only partially clarify.

Within Indian cinema, moreover, the more typical and typically more complex examples often draw upon prior film sources *as well as* the Hindu myths that continue to animate many (though by no means all, as is sometimes overstated) popular films. For instance, perhaps India's most revered film, Mehboob Khan's *Mother India* (1957), is well-known to be a remake (with significant differences) of the same director's earlier but now more obscure *Aurat* (1940), itself inspired by the Hollywood film version of Pearl S. Buck's novel *The Good Earth* (1937), and more explicitly by her less familiar novel *The Mother* (1934). Stylistically, and in some thematic elements, the film is also indebted to the 1926 Soviet masterpiece *Mother* (directed by V.S. Pudovkin, from Maxim Gorky's novel) and King Vidor's leftist film *Our Daily Bread* (1934) (Chatterjee 2002). At the same time, like most versions of *Devdas* (as we shall see) *Mother India* draws directly upon the popular Hindu figures of Krishna and Radha (the name the main character played by Nargis shares with the goddess), among other allusions to Hindu mythology. Among the many other films inspired by *Mother India*, Amitabh Bachchan's breakout film *Deewaar* (1975, d. Yash Chopra) is commonly recognized to be a modern, urbanized remake of Mehboob's tale, with the dominant focus shifted from the mother-goddess to her rebellious son. Again, such complex cases, disallowing any easy categorization through the terms "adaptation" and "remake," may be more common than unusual in popular Indian cinema, and suggest how difficult it becomes to apply these terms comfortably to the considerable range of texts now designated by the title *Devdas*.

Repeating *Devdas*

Despite its many versions, the basic plot of *Devdas* has remained fairly consistent throughout its incarnations, and in bare outline it hardly explains the story's ongoing fascination. The rich Brahmin *zamindar*'s devilish son Devdas and the middleclass Parvati (affectionately called Paro) are childhood playmates who declare their love just before Devdas is sent away to Calcutta (or, in the most recent Hindi film version, England) for his education. After the young couple are reunited—Paro's playmate "Devda," the novel notes, becomes the more worldly "Devdasbabu" (27)—Parvati's family attempts to arrange her marriage to Devdas, but the latter's father rejects the union. Paro's family are lower in status, a trading family, and unfortunately neighbors, and the girl's insulted family responds by quickly arranging her marriage to a wealthy widower with grown children. Though promised to another, Parvati, in one of the story's now-famous set-pieces, risks her reputation by coming to Devdas alone in the night and asking him to save her from a loveless arranged marriage; the weak-willed Devdas hesitates, and decides that he cannot challenge his family and tradition. He is, however, distraught in his decision and, back in Calcutta, seeks to lose himself in drink and the seductive urban *demimonde.* His worldly college chum Chunilal takes him to a brothel, where he meets the prostitute Chandramukhi, who will fall in love with the glum young man who curiously pays yet seeks nothing from her. Three key events carry the story to its hopeless conclusion: Devdas writes Paro an insincere letter denying his love for her, which he attempts but fails to prevent from being delivered; before her wedding, Devdas, breaking a childhood promise never to strike Paro again, scars Paro's beautiful face (originally with a fishing rod), marking her with a symbol of his enduring love; finally, as he sinks into illness despite Chandramukhi's attempts to care for him after she abandons her profession, Devdas takes a last, aimless train ride across India. Finally, as he had promised, Devdas drags himself to the entrance of Parvati's home—to which she has been restricted—where he dies just before she is alerted to the presence of a stranger's body outside the gates that shut her inside as she runs to him. While providing these details may spoil the story for a first-time reader or viewer, my claim, again, is that most Indian viewers come to any telling of the tale with the plot well-known and its now-familiar, tableau-like highlights eagerly anticipated with each retelling. Suspense and revelation are not the pleasures offered by the narrative tradition in which *Devdas* is now embedded.

Devdas is marked as suddenly "modern" through his education and dress when he first returns from college; the novel outfits him in "foreign shoes, bright clothes, a walking stick, gold buttons, a watch—without these accessories he felt bereft" (22). More significantly, Devdas is something of a modern thinker, especially in his challenge to the idea of arranged marriage, his cigarette smoking (which in films replaces the novel's hookah), his addiction to the "Western" vice of alcohol, and in his bohemian attraction to the netherworld of brothels (vices aided by the cosmopolitan but irresponsible Chunnilal). As many critics have noted, the movement between the village and the city that abets the young man's descent is also fundamental to the historical experience of Indian modernity, and the consequent alienation from tradition. However, the young hero's perhaps attractive rebellion is offset by his continually emphasized weaknesses and grudging adherence to tradition: he is spineless, cruel, narcissistic, and a virtual Hindu Hamlet in his frustrating inability to act, especially when action seems most necessary. As Meenakshi Mukherjee wisely notes, because throughout his work Saratchandra "left the basic values undisturbed, he was permitted by his readers to critique certain other aspects of social behavior" (Mukherjee 1985: 106). The role of Devdas is then a complex one for a film "hero," at least in the decades before the "antihero" redefined the qualities of the popular protagonist in the 1970s. While many Hindi films celebrate the careful balance of tradition and modernity—for instance in recent films like *Dilwale Dulhania le Jayenge* (1995, d. Aditya Chopra) where previously opposed arranged marriages and love matches eventually align—*Devdas* dramatizes the inability of tradition and modernity to achieve balance: the home and the world—to evoke the paradigmatic title of Tagore's famous novel, adapted to film by Satyajit Ray—are in a sense this story's ultimate tragic couple.

The now-iconic figure of Devdas also might be read as the ritual sacrifice of the young Bengali Brahmin to gloomy European romanticism, depicting a sorrowful young Werther babu fully arrived in the subcontinent. As noted above, the appeal of that doomed figure, whose self-loathing might express a young audience's milder frustrations and inability to reconcile cultural demands and individual desires, continued at least into some of the manifestations of Amitabh Bachchan's angry young man, who nevertheless was more often motivated to fight back, even in vain, than to wallow in passive self-pity. For many, Devdas, no matter which charismatic star embodies him, remains a difficult character to like or admire, but who demands emotional identification rather than moral emulation: this ambivalent attraction may be exactly what was radical about the original character for generations of Bengali artists and readers. As a self-absorbed, selfish character who is by no means too good for this world, Devdas cannot adjust his damaged ego to what Freud called the reality principle; indeed, part of the figure's modernity is in his being defined and defeated by an individual ego rather than a class-or caste-based morality, a difference that makes traditional heroes unrealistic ideals rather than the type of young man one could actually imagine encountering on the streets of Calcutta in the early decades of the twentieth century. Whether the modernist figure of Devdas continues to retain its appeal and relevance for contemporary Indian audiences and postmodern, globetrotting Non-resident Indians (NRIs) will be central to evaluating the most recent version of the story.

Before undertaking that task, it will be helpful to outline the forms or levels of repetition that organize this most repeated of modern Indian narratives. The repetition that marks the story of Devdas in all its versions can be detected in large and small patterns, suggesting the intertwining of the work's thematic and formal significance.

First, as already emphasized, the repetitive, intertextual retelling of the story of Devdas through almost a century of adaptations and/or remakes makes it difficult and misleading to now consider any version of *Devdas* in isolation from its precursors or subsequent instances. Whatever dramatic force they once carried, the key moments in the story (Paro's arrival at Devdas's room, or his striking her) have accumulated significant meaning through repetition, often without significant variation. As noted earlier, even "unofficial" remakes of the story (such as the late films of Guru Dutt, or some of the Amitabh Bachchan vehicles) gain thematic weight through their allusions to the underlying model of the impossible triangle linking Devdas, Parvati, and Chandramukhi. At this level, repetition alone through the form of persistent retellings accumulates meaning for the story.

Second, the repetitive structure of the narrative itself, even without reference to multiple versions, is strongly marked by a literally redundant pattern of departures and returns that carry Devdas between his traditional village (associated with Parvati) and the modern city of Calcutta (inhabited by Chandramukhi), a circular action mirrored by the increasingly repetitive activity that embeds Devdas in the cycle of addiction. The original novella, often sparse in its descriptions, proceeds through a series of announced journeys and returns, whether bluntly noted "Several months passed. Devdas came back home after a long spell . . . Then the summer holidays came to and end. Devdas went back to Calcutta . . . In this manner four years went by" [21] or tersely declared: "Chuni, I am going home today" (42); "I have come back, Paro" (46). Such bare descriptions of often emotionally wrenching comings and goings, or arrivals and departures, culminate in the literally pointless train ride (itself fueled by Devdas's "return" to drink, and emphasized in most film versions by repetitive montage sequences of trains and signs identifying irrelevant destinations) that carries Devdas across India just before his death at the gates of Parvati's home. In short, the story of Devdas is itself an account of repetition, or repeated and thus often aimless actions that only conclude through entropic dissolution.

Finally, both the novella and the films rely on repetitive formal patterns in their particular organization of specific words, scenes, and shots: Sreejata Guha's recent English translation carefully renders this quality through persistent, indeed stylistically repetitive, reminders of mundane acts that become everyday rituals: "This was his daily routine . . ." (6); "She tried to repeat as much of the story as she could . . ." (6); ". . . Parvati went to the river every day to fetch water . . ." (45). Even Devdas's childhood promise to *not* repeat an action ("I . . . won't hit you ever again" [14]) is famously broken when he, again, strikes and scars Parvati before her marriage, a vicious (in Freudian terms, resistant) act designed precisely to disallow forgetting: "I have merely left a mark for you to remember our last meeting" (48). Even when finally realizing his other, later promise ("If it's the last thing I do, I'll come to you" [82]) Devdas seems more fated to repeat actions than to actually fulfill promises. His words are themselves unnecessarily redundant: "I will not come back to Calcutta ever again" (43). The films, typically constructed through conventional patterns of editing that impose narrative order on the sequence of individual shots, also often foreground rather than obscure such fundamental repetition, as I will demonstrate later.

Obviously many of the formal and narrative patterns that structure versions of *Devdas* are typical of the macrocosmic organization of narrative itself, or of the microcosmic rules of prose narration and narrative film editing (the latter especially emphasized by film theorist Raymond Bellour: see Bergstrom 1979). Rather than attend to these ubiquitous patterns that might simply link Indian examples to patterns found in most narrative texts, it makes sense to concentrate here on what may be identified as distinct forms of repetition associated more specifically with South Asian cultural practices and history. While the strongly emphasized pattern in *Devdas* of journeys away from and back home might be resonant in many cultures, what Mukherjee summarizes (with reference to the fiction of Saratchandra) as "the drift from village to city" (Mukherjee 1985: 107) generates a particular meaning for many of the most popular works of postindependence Hindi cinema, such as Raj Kapoor's *Shri 420* (1955) and well as more recent examples like Ram Gopal Varma's gangster film *Satya* (1998), which both begin with a young man's arrival in Bombay. Indeed, as an urban form itself, the Indian cinema has often recognized that its own existence depends upon the migration of a mass audience to the city, where cinema has been one of the more successful distractions from the difficulties of modern urban life. More recently, the symbolic and emotional significance of the corresponding return to the village, and even to India itself, has been a central concern in films like *Dilwale Dulhania le Jayenge* (1995, d. Aditya Chopra) and *Swades* (2004, d. Ashutosh Gowariker), both featuring Shah Rukh Khan as a globalized NRI who recovers his essential "Indianness" by returning "home." While hardly unique in this regard, *Devdas* may still be a touchstone for Indian narratives that rest upon movement away or back to spaces one desires and dreads. Indeed, *Devdas* might be said to explicitly embody a distinctly Indian "structure of feeling" that could be properly called "nostalgia," if that term can be used to retrieve its original designation of the pangs felt upon returning to a home long abandoned and changed (rather than the simple warm glow the term now often connotes).

However, *Devdas*, as already suggested, also undercuts its ostensible modernity through direct recourse to models from Hindu mythology, specifically the figures of Radha and her divine lover Krishna. Unlike films that simply replay traditional stories in modern dress, versions of *Devdas* invoke rather than reenact the story of this ideal couple, whose passion is intensified by their physical separation (*viraha*). As Mukherjee efficiently summarizes, "unfulfilled love as a higher value than fulfilled love can be seen as part of a mythic motif in India—Radha's separation from Krishna being the archetype. Union in marriage is a limited goal compared to the transcendence towards infinity achieved through perpetual *viraha*" (Mukherjee 1985: 104). Allusions to Radha's isolation from her lover provide a deep structure to the *Devdas* narrative, but are also typically provided on the text's surface through songs, drawing upon, as Mukherjee notes (citing Rajat Ray) "medieval Vaishnava poetry which moulded Bengali concepts of man–woman relationships through the Radha-Krishna myth" (Mukherjee 1985: 120).

Songs invoking this tradition not only speak Parvati's love out loud, even when, as in the novella "their meaning…passed Parvati by," (17) but also justify the socially unacceptable passion of the couple—recalling that the divine love between Radha and Krishna is "adulterous"—through analogy to not just a "classical" but a sacred source. Paro and Devdas cannot be unambiguously identified as avatars of Radha and Krishna: the fact that the Bengali youth are not divine is finally, brutally asserted, in contrast to the pure grief of *karuṇā rasa*, which is understood to be ultimately sublime rather than tragic (see Mukherjee 1985: 120). Their socially transgressive love nevertheless commands cultural approval, in part through audience sympathy, but perhaps more powerfully through the authorization granted by this elevated comparison. In what follows, more direct attention to aspects of the three most notable Hindi versions of *Devdas* will draw upon the elements summarized above, allowing us to again assess the relevance of the "working-through" of this persistent story across the past century.

Barua's *Devdas*

P.C. Barua's Hindi version of *Devdas* is not, unfortunately, readily available in good copies, though it fortunately survives from an era when most films are lost. This is especially lamentable since, with cinematography by the young Bimal Roy, it is clearly one of the most important films in Indian cinema history.[7] Modern audiences will tend to find Barua's film "primitive" and Saigal's performance stilted (with carefully enunciated Hindi that sounds quoted rather than spoken), but for its era the film is quite remarkable and formally inventive, using songs and voiceover dialogue, for instance, in ways that were innovative for early sound cinema. And many fans will attest that Saigal's "evergreen" songs have not lost their power and appeal. Unlike the novella, Barua's *Devdas* does not introduce his main characters as children, but as naïve young adults; Barua, in fact suggests that, the work's title aside, this is largely Paro's story, as she introduces and concludes the narrative, remaining to survive the unfulfilled life Devdas finally escapes. In all instances, the story of *Devdas* is really the story of the blocked relationships among three pivotal characters rather than focus on the male character.

Emphasizing such relations, critics often cite the film's use of parallel editing, most notable when, late in the story, Devdas cries out and the film cuts to Paro stumbling, then back to Devdas falling in his train car. Whether this device was Barua's innovation is hard to determine, but as a distinctly cinematic technique employed to suggest a "telepathic" connection between the separated lovers, such an "unrealistic" stylistic device remains powerful. While significantly reducing the many departures and returns summarized in the novella, the film highlights its structure by inserting transitional shots focused on the modes of transportation (especially trains, but also the evocative revolving wheel of a rustic cart) that convey Devdas out of and back into his village. Two sequences summarizing his journeys away are balanced by two sequences representing trips back: by the latter part of the film, this pattern has established itself as a structural motif and so at least one additional departure and return can be implied though direct cuts (assuming surviving copies can be trusted) to now-familiar locations: the audience, in effect, has learned to anticipate a pattern of repetitions that the film no longer needs to visualize explicitly. (At this point, of course, Devdas's drinking has intensified, so his repetitive addiction is matched by the film's noticeably increased pace of editing.) Finally, building upon a sequence with little emphasis in the original novella, the film condenses Devdas's aimless train travel across India by a series of shots of signs announcing different locations on the route: while each name identifies a different place, suggesting a linear series of trips that could be mapped, the shots and the signs they contain are otherwise the same and so, with none serving as a final destination, markers of pointless repetition. Barua's film—presumably the first widely consumed version of *Devdas*, despite the novella's popularity—incorporates the repetition at the heart of the story within its own formal organization, linking the repetitive rhythms of narrative cinema (most evident through the techniques of editing and montage) to the compulsive pattern that drives the sad tale.

Roy's *Devdas*

Perhaps the best known version of *Devdas* was produced in 1955 and directed by Bimal Roy, who had recently established himself as a notable Bombay-based director and producer working in a "Bengali" realist style with *Do Bigha Zameen* (1953). Most memorably, his version provides indelible performances by its major stars, Dilip Kumar, Vyjayantimala (originally from South India) as Chandramukhi, and Suchitra Sen (from Bengal) as Parvati. At first glance, Roy's version of the story seems subtle and naturalistic, with affinities to the then-emerging Bengali art cinema: the actors are restrained and convincing, and often placed in realistic locations rather than the studio sets that provide the stylized background for other versions. But closer examination reveals that Roy's film is formally intricate without calling attention to its techniques. Following the novella, but also picking up on what had by then become something of a tradition in popular Hindi films, Roy introduces his protagonists as children and will carry them to young adulthood through a transitional dissolve, in this case by focusing upon the richly condensed image of a closed and then open lotus in the river where Paro gathers water, an image that suggests the girl's "blossoming" as well as the cyclical revolutions (or repetitions) of nature, and with an object that moreover connotes the nation (and specific goddesses). (See Creekmur 2005 for a historical consideration of this technique.) Roy also makes careful, meaningful use of his restlessly moving camera throughout the film. When the boy Devdas calls Paro from her room by tossing stones at her window, a graceful crane shot travels with her from an upper floor to the gate where she meets Devdas below. Years later, when Devdas has returned from Calcutta, the shot replicates itself exactly without much fuss, so that the film style itself suggests a basic, enduring relationship despite the passing of years, and the embodiment of the characters by a different set of adult actors. Such repetition with a difference again demonstrates the necessary affinity between the content of this narrative and its narration: Devdas and Paro are no longer children, but their relationship—the structure that contains them beyond the social structures that keep them apart—remains exactly the same.

Another moving camera also underlines a key scene, when Paro and Chandramukhi—ostensible rivals but sisters in their doomed passion—view one another on the road. A pair of rhymed tracking shots of each women glancing at the other effectively unites them despite the social (and spatial) differences they embody: Roy's technique in fact accomplishes in the narrative's real space what the novella represents through Devdas's advanced delirium: "Thus it was Paro one day and Chandramukhi the next, presiding over his heart. Sometimes he had visions of both, side by side, as if they were the closest of friends. In his mind the two had become linked in the strangest of ways" (118). Notably, the first pair of shots (of Paro as a girl and young woman) effectively indicates the typical incorporation of the larger (natural and cosmic) cycles of repetition, collapsing the gap between past and present through a structural simultaneity that overrides the visible difference (the children are now adults) between the two scenes. The second pair of shots, linking rather than differentiating the two women, collapses not temporal distance, but the social hierarchy at the heart of the story's finally weak protest of tradition and convention.

Roy's film emphasizes that the tragedy of Devdas and Paro stems from the recognition that their love may be (like Radha's and Krishna's) timeless and eternal, but the world in which they live is emphatically and cruelly time-bound and fleeting. Similarly, the techniques that can formally align Parvati and Chandramukhi are offset by the social divisions that the narrative otherwise maintains. Through such subtle devices, Roy's version of the story seems to replicate and respect rather than challenge Devdas's own impossible position, torn between accepting and challenging traditions that ensure his unhappiness; the film cannot resolve its understanding that the past and the present are the same, but different; it appears that the "good girl" and the prostitute are alike, but cannot be compared. Experiencing this film as viewers, we recognize we have seen this shot before, even as we acknowledge that its content has changed. In Freud's terms, perhaps, Roy's version of *Devdas* brings us close to remembering the past we are repeating once again. However, even though it offered a vision of the recent past, the many echoes of *Devdas* in other films of the period, and afterward, suggest that the work's "older" anxieties and tensions still defined the postindependent present, officially progressive (in other words, Nehruvian) but of course—especially in popular culture—hopelessly addicted to the past as well.

Bhansali's *Devdas*

Most recently, Sanjay Leela Bhansali's extravagant 2002 remake of *Devdas* starring Shah Rukh Khan as Devdas, Aishwarya Rai as Paro, and Madhuri Dixit as Chandramukhi is said to have been the most expensive production in Indian film history. Although the original context for *Devdas* is early twentieth-century Bengal, the persistent return to the character and story throughout Indian popular culture suggests that they long ago became archetypes with broad, pan-Indian application and appeal. But Bhansali's film, presented as an explicit tribute to Saratchandra, Barua, and Bimal Roy, also may demonstrate that the relevance and appeal of *Devdas* is itself fading into the historical past: in Freud's terms, Bhansali's film may at last represent a "remembering" of the story as an artifact from the past rather than as an unconscious repetition in the present. If this version allows its audience—perhaps for the first time in large part defined by diasporic South Asians—to "work through" *Devdas*, this implies abandoning it for narratives that are currently relevant.

Bhansali's elaborate sets and costumes, in vibrant color and filling a wide screen, appear in vivid contrast to Bimal Roy's understated film, and render the historical past as a museum-like display: this version of early twentieth-century Calcutta does not suggest a historical recreation (which would seek to close the gap between past and present) as much as an attempt to construct an ideal rather than actual past: in the terms used for Indian film genres, this is perhaps the first version of the "social" *Devdas* rendered as a "historical." Notably, when Bhansali's Devdas returns to Calcutta in his Western clothing, his exceptionally ostentatious display seems designed to generate laughs: this, we recognize, is a hyperbolic version of past fashions, an exaggeration designed to underline the character's pretension but not to locate him in a realistic historical past. Put another way, this image of "modernity" no longer signifies, as it once did in versions of this story, the encroaching present, but it now represents a caricature of long past modernity we now find amusing and stylistically outdated. The casting of Shah Rukh Khan in the role is of course significant, as was the casting of the alcoholic singer K.L. Saigal or of Dilip Kumar, then known for playing melancholy figures: Shah Rukh Khan's comic narcissism and vanity, often associated with his displays of contemporary fashion, was a well-established feature of his screen persona when he took this role and this self-mocking quality renders his foppish Devdas more ludicrous than the character's earlier incarnations.

Although at its heart a rather simple story, Bhansali's *Devdas* allows the story to become operatic, or, less generously, overblown. To again employ Freudian terms, Bhansali's film at first seems defensive, obscuring the story's emotional core by plastering the surface of the film with gorgeous yet distracting details to create an opulent, extravagant spectacle, filled to the brim with vast sets and stunning costumes, often shot with breathless, rushing handheld (or Steadicam) shots of swirling action and blinding color. The soundtrack, as has become typical, also pounds away with thunderous beats at every emotional high or low point. As Anup Singh (2002) suggests, the director's aim seems to be to render the story's underlying strong emotions through the film's hyperventilating style as well as the situations of the characters. But this external abundance constantly threatens to overwhelm what might be understood as the story of internally tormented characters. Against its ostensible status as a "tribute" to the major figures who precede him, Bhansali may be unconsciously staging a kind of

Oedipal rebellion against his forebears, seeking to trump their restrained (perhaps repressed) efforts through an adaptation that overwhelms rather than acknowledges previous versions.

It is thus not just a longing for the "golden age" of Hindi cinema that makes Roy's version seem preferable to Bhansali's film: Devdas is, again, less a classical tragic hero than a modernist antihero, whose downward spiral does not occur in a mythic space, but in the historically specific modern world which, lowering the standards of genuine tragedy, can no longer support the grand gestures or heroic sacrifices of truly mythic heroes. The persistent echo of the divine yet erotic love of Krishna and Radha in the *Devdas* story is thus always as mocking as it is sustaining: while the devotion of Devdas and Paro may be unbreakable, they are after all not immortal gods, and so the world breaks them despite their passion, reducing them to the human status of the doomed Romeo and Juliet rather than elevating them to the realm of the eternal lovers of Hindu myth.

Whereas Roy's "modern" world (though located in the past) remained recognizable to his 1950s audience, Bhansali's film places its characters within a stylized modernity that is now so far in the past of contemporary audiences that it must be artificially overstated in a style associated with postmodernism, with the film's once meaningful historical setting taken over by the signifiers of the past, which compete with the story and characters for the audience's attention. The film is thus neither updated (by, for instance, making Devdas a drug addict rather than an alcoholic, or in the style of the "unofficial" remakes of the story, set firmly in their present, starring Amitabh Bachchan) nor genuinely historical, approaches which might have forced the audience to compare its present situation to the represented past. By creating a fantasy space with only slight reference to the real world or historical context—the film curiously avoids specifying its temporal location directly—the film constructs a fantastic vision of a romantic "Bengal" that may be as exotic for the film's (North) Indian audience as for its diasporic (and non-Indian) viewers. (Rather comically, the home of the "poor" neighbor Parvati is lavish, while Chandramukhi's brothel resembles a palace.)

Moreover, Bhansali's decision—unlike Saratchandra and Bimal Roy—not to depict Devdas and Paro first as children, except later, in brief flashbacks (with Devdas hardly depicted at all), tends to take the story out of a tradition—developed in part by earlier versions of this story and associated works in popular cinema—of presenting true lovers as recognizing one another even as children, whose passion never "grows up" or adjusts to the pressures of class, caste, or economic realities. While the childhood infatuation of Devdas and Paro is frequently described in dialogue, the avoidance of depicting the characters as children—in part, again perhaps, an effect of Shah Rukh Khan's prominent boyishness in his established screen persona—makes their lifelong love and Devdas's Krishna-like mischief (rather than passion) something we must trust upon hearing from others rather than something we are given to witness. The lifelong attachment of Devdas and Paro is grounded by the first section of Bimal Roy's film, whereas Bhansali trusts that mere reference to their childhood devotion will suffice. Removing the small history that Hindi films often dramatize by introducing characters as children and then later as adults finally seems emblematic of a larger decision to refer to rather than reconstruct history in this film. For Bhansali's *Devdas*, in other words, the past is neither repeated nor remembered: it has been "worked through" by being rendered irrelevant to both the present and memory of anything other than past styles.

As with each previous version of the story, this film's strongest moments are in small details and gestures, but the film itself seems to have been made with the mantra that "size matters" as it persistently boosts and trumpets many of its otherwise most delicate moments. While Bhansali's film was a commercial hit that played in major cinemas worldwide, its long-range impact seems less certain than previous versions of the story. The apparent attempt to make this the film to finally bring "Bollywood" to Western audiences also seems to have been a failure: curiously, the film's producers relied on a film steeped in a tradition known to virtually all South Asians in order to attract an audience that would be ironically coming to this material and these characters for the first time. If the echoes of this story are no longer immediate for globalized Indian viewers (despite their embracing of Shah Rukh Khan as their ostensible representative), they were simply unavailable to the non-Indian audiences the film was in part marketed to attract. Whether the myth of *Devdas* maintains its power into the twenty-first century remains to be seen, but one suspects that yet another version—probably in the now-established tradition of unofficial remakes—will be necessary to revitalize the tale for contemporary audiences, in the way that Bachchan's unexpected channeling of Devdas in some of his 1970s roles clearly shook up the norms of Indian popular cinema. In any case, the story of a young man who dies too young has seemed immortal for most of the twentieth century; ironically, his latest, most elaborate incarnation seems to hasten his legend's demise rather than sustain it.

Notes

1 All references will be to this translation of the novella. While the title of the novella should arguably be transliterated as *Debdas*, I use throughout the more familiar and widespread spelling for novel, films and the "*Devdas* phenomenon."

2 The author's name is sometimes rendered Sarat Chandra Chatterjee or Chatterji, among other Romanized variants, and in India he is commonly identified as Saratchandra, a convention I follow in this chapter.

3 On Saratchandra's unusual pan-Indian reception, see Satchidanandan 2003: 63–74; for a celebratory overview of his career and lasting influence, see Satyabrata Roy 1977.

4 Note that Saratchandra was not, as Ashok Banker mistakenly claims, the author of the source novel (Bimal Mitra's 1952 *Saheb Bibi Golam*).

5 For recent, innovative work countering this tendency, see Cartmell and Whelehan 1999; Hutcheon 2006; and Naremore 2000.

6 While its specific content is quite different, the foregrounded interlocking three-part structure and chaotic visual style of Mani Ratnam's *Yuva* (2004) is clearly derived from the Mexican film *Amores Perros* (Alejandro González Iñárritu, 2000) a hit on the international art circuit (and itself presumably partially inspired by the inter-locking

three-part structure of Krzysztof Kieslowski's widely seen *Three Colours* trilogy, 1993–94.)

7 A copy of the Bengali version starring Barua is said to have also survived, but to my knowledge is not accessible for viewing.

References

Banker, A. (2001) *Bollywood*, Harpenden, Herts: Pocket Essentials.

Bergstrom, J. (1979) "Alternation, Segmentation, Hypnosis: An Interview with Raymond Bellour," *Camera Obscura* 3/4: 71–103.

Cartmell, D. and Whelehan, I. (eds) (1999) *Adaptations: From Text to Screen, Screen to Text*, London: Routledge.

Chatterjee, G. (2002) *Mother India*, London: British Film Institute.

—— (2003) *Awara*, rev. edn, New Delhi: Penguin Books India.

Chattopadhyay, S. (2002) *Devdas*, trans. Sreejata Guha, New Delhi: Penguin Books India.

Creekmur, C.K. (2005) "Bombay Boys: Dissolving the Male Child in Popular Hindi Cinema," in M. Pomerance and F. Gateward (eds) *Where the Boys Are: Cinemas of Masculinity and Youth*, Detroit, MI: Wayne State University Press.

Freud, Sigmund (1914; 1958) "Remembering, Repeating and Working-Through (Further Recommendations on the Technique of PsychoAnalysis II) (1914)," in J. Strachey (ed.) *The Standard Edition of the Complete Psychological Works of Sigmund Freud*, vol.12, London: The Hogarth Press.

Ghosh, S. (2003) "Passionate Involvement: Love and Politics in Satyajit Ray's *Ghare Baire*," in P. K. Datta (ed.) *Rabindranath Tagore's The Home and the World: A Critical Companion*, Delhi: Permanent Black.

Horton, A. and McDougal, S.M. (1998) *Play It Again, Sam: Retakes on Remakes*, Berkeley, CA: University of California Press.

Hutcheon, L. (2006) *A Theory of Adaptation*, London: Routledge.

Lutgendorf, P. (1992) *The Life of a Text: Performing the Ramcaritmanas of Tulsidas*, Berkeley, CA: University of California Press.

Mukherjee, M. (1985) *Realism and Reality: The Novel and Society in India*, New Delhi: Oxford University Press.

Nair, P.K. (2002) "The *Devdas* Syndrome in Indian Cinema," *Cinemaya* 56/57, Autumn/Winter: 827.

Nandy, A. (2001) "Invitation to an Antique Death: The Journey of Pramathesh Barua as the Origin of the Terribly Effeminate, Maudlin, Self-Destructive Heroes of Indian Cinema," in R. Dwyer and C. Pinney (eds) *Pleasure and the Nation: The History, Politics, and Consumption of Public Culture in India*, New Delhi: Oxford University Press.

Naremore, James (ed.) (2000) *Film Adaptation*, New Brunswick, NJ: Rutgers University Press.

Nazir, Asjad (2002) "The Changing Faces of *Devdas*," *Eastern Eye* (5 July 2002) Emag: 8–9.

Ramanujan, A.K. (1999) "Repetition in the *Mahabharata*," in V. Dharwadker (ed.) *The Collected Essays of A. K. Ramanujan*, Delhi: Oxford University Press.

Richman, P. (ed.) (1991) *Many Ramayanas: The Diversity of a Narrative Tradition in South Asia*, Berkeley, CA: University of California Press.

—— (ed.) (2000) *Questioning Ramayanas: A South Asian Tradition*, New Delhi: Oxford University Press.

Roy, B. (1994) "Filming Sarat Classics," in Rinki Bhattacharya (ed.) *Bimal Roy: A Man of Silence*, New Delhi: Indus.

Roy, S. (ed.) (1977) *The Golden Book of Saratchandra: A Centenary Commemorative Volume*, Calcutta: All Bengal Sarat Centenary Committee.

Satchidanandan, K. (2003) *Authors, Texts, Issues: Essays on Indian Literature*, Delhi: Pencraft International.

Singh, A. (2002) "Sanjay Leela Bhansali's *Devdas* and the Intensity of the Self," *Cinemaya* 56/57, Autumn/Winter: 88–91.

Singhal, R. (2002) *Devdas: The Eternal Sage of Love*, Delhi: Pentagon Paperbacks.

9 The political aesthetic of nation and gender in Rituparno Ghosh's *Chokher Bali**

Mandakranta Bose

Introduction

Perhaps the least controversial attribute of a classic is its durability. The ability of a work of art to survive changing times and tastes seems to secure for it a permanent niche in the public sphere of the cultural tradition that gave birth to it. Not surprisingly, this durability also ensures the value of a classic as usable capital in the cultural marketplace, a commodity that can be profitably recycled. But the travels of a classic through time and across genre boundaries demand alterations that may affect not only the form and structure of the work in question but perhaps involve shifts in its ideological direction.

Two recent film renditions of classic works of fiction from India provide rich opportunities for tracking such shifts. As a student of the performing arts I am intrigued by the manipulations whereby Rabindranath Tagore's novel *Chokher Bali* and Sarat Chandra Chattopadhyaya's *Debdas* have been turned into films that not only attempt visualizations of verbal texts but effect systematic representations of gender and wealth.[1]

Although the center of my discussion here is *Chokher Bali*, I must confess that I am fascinated by *Debdas*. My connection with the novels is personal. They were my close teenage companions, as they were for virtually everybody I know of my generation of Bengalis, and their power over me has not weakened through the years. But I thought the passage of time had placed these treasures of an older world into the safe custody of fixed public response, turning them into classics. Not that classics are beyond question, but the reverence commonly granted to age tends to distance classics from living popular culture. This is certainly true of Rabindranath Tagore's *Chokher Bali*, a story that is read today by few readers other than Bengali literature majors, though known by name to the average Bengali because of Rabindranath's mythic status. Like most literary classics *Chokher Bali* lives only among a cultural minority, and even that elite group seems unaware that Rabindranath's novel was actually made into a film long before Rituparno Ghosh's effort.[2] This was a black and white film made in 1938 by Satu Sen, with such stage and screen luminaries as Chhabi Biswas as Behari, and Suprava Mukherjee as Binodini,[3] but is no longer available, which prevents any comparison with Ghosh's work and the possibility of expanding its context.

Saratchandra's *Debdas* has fared far better and is to some extent an exception to the generalization I made above.

Devdas

If ever there was an Indian classic on celluloid, it is *Devdas*. Its literary success has been phenomenal. Published in 1917 in Calcutta, it became a hit across India, editions quickly selling out and the Bengali text translated into several other Indian languages. We might note that this success had as much to do with Saratchandra's already established name across India as a spokesman of social protest, the underclass and forbidden love. It was particularly the last theme that *Debdas* celebrated, with great success because it did so without extending explicit approval of deviance and without seriously questioning dominant morality.

The first movie version, a silent film in black and white, was made in 1928 by Naresh Mitra. The talkie version was soon to follow in the form of a double remake in 1935. One was in Bengali, the other in Hindi, both directed by Pramathesh Chandra Barua, who played Devdas in the Bengali version, while the Hindi version had K.L. Saigal in the title role. Some twenty years later a similar feat was repeated by Vedantam Raghavaiah, who made a Tamil as well as a Telugu version in 1953. Within two years of this, in 1955, Bimal Roy made one of the most successful versions in Hindi with Dilip Kumar as Devdas, Suchitra Sen as Paru and Vyjayantimala as Chandramukhi. A second Telugu version followed in 1974, directed by Vijaya Nirmala, and in 1979 appeared a Bengali *Devdas* directed by Dilip Roy, with Soumitra Chattopadhyaya as Devdas, Sumitra Mukherjee as Paru, Supriya Chaudhuri as Chandramukhi, and film idol Uttam Kumar as Chuni Babu. Finally, on July 2, 2002, overshooting all conceivable limits of fantasy, Sanjay Leela Bhansali burst upon the Bollywood heavens with his multibillion rupee Hindi *Devdas*.

Money is impossible to ignore when we talk about Bhansali's film. The statistics are so overwhelming that the cost itself seems to constitute the film's claim to attention. The film's publicists bludgeon us with figures, making reckonings in crores, not lakhs: it is "perhaps the costliest set of [*sic*] made in the history of Hindi Cinema."[4] Just one structure, Chandramukhi's house, cost Rs. 12 crore, and the total cost is entirely beyond my comprehension or memory. When you think about these vast amounts you begin to suspect that money does not just make the film, it *is* the film. A golden light casts a constant glow over buildings and people, sometimes enriched by the filter of acres of stained glass, reflecting off the masses of jewelry the women wear all the time. The opening shot shows Devdas's family home, an incredible confection of marble that "mansion" or "palace" fail to describe. Paro's (as the name is pronounced in the film) supposedly humbler home has vast water features, stained glass panels of no evident function, and at least one indoor tree complete with a white dove. As for her husband's home, the word "palace" hardly describes anything so profligate in its colonnades and turrets. The people in this world of prodigality are its fit representatives with their well-fed bodies, whether we are looking at the nubile young dancers or at the rolls of fat in the exposed back of Devdas's mother in the opening scene. No speck of dust is allowed to spoil this hallowed ground of grand passion and grander sacrifice. The costumes "speak," to quote a heading on the film's website, of the director's notion of the proprieties of class and wealth, as in the fedora, topcoat, silver mounted cane, and cigarette in a long holder that stamp "London-returned" all over Devdas.

The fictional world Bhansali has constructed has met with tremendous success. Audience appreciation, as tallied from internet responses on three popular websites in 2004, averages 7.41 out of a possible 10.[5] Why it does not score a perfect 10 is not clear to me from the spectator reviews I have read, all of which are ecstatic about sets, costumes, acting, dancing, and above all about the human drama of an epic love and loss. Clearly, I would be wrong in giving it something in the negative numbers, because the film is not the novel and it is not right to apply the standards of Saratchandra's romantic naturalism to Bhansali's aesthetic of fantasy. What is more, as I ponder my minority response against the general approval of the film, I realize that it is a fantasy that feeds upon powerful yearnings in the modern Indian consciousness. What could these be?

It is tempting to answer that the film provides the escape of fantasy to audiences weary of the daily grind of Third World life. But this catchall explanation will not do because it does not explain the film's huge appeal for the upwardly mobile Indian middle class and NRIs, who seem to be the most vocal admirers (their chorus of adulation facilitated by their command of English and ownership of computers). The display of wealth is unquestionably a draw but it seems to me that the film's visual rhetoric negotiates self-valorization on a deeper level. The equation between wealth and status has been a common paradigm of Indian cinema (and perhaps of most cinematic traditions) but it seems to have become an indispensable part of national (and nationalist) self-assertion in recent time, as Patricia Uberoi has observed in her study of the 1994 Bollywood superhit *Hum Aapke Hain Kaun*. Citing Rustom Bharucha's 1995 article "Utopia and Bollywood," Uberoi points out that "in terms of its sets, props, and costumes, the film is a veritable parade of fetishized middle-class status symbols.... The two homes on display, including that of the less prosperous professor, were much admired by my companions,... Viewers were for the most part very appreciative of all this opulence" (Uberoi 2001: 319–20). This could well be a description of Bhansali's *Devdas* in its construction of self-approval.

Mansions, rich clothing, and jewelry are only the obvious expressions of wealth, and the film never tires of iterating these commonplaces. But the film also reinforces them through less obvious tactics. For instance, why does the camera expose Devdas's mother's fleshy back? Answer: fat signifies wealth. How come Paro's home is filled with dozens of young women, obviously family dependants? Because, prosperity is proved by numbers. Why is Durga Puja, a strictly seasonal celebration, performed as a daily ritual? Because elaborate religious observances signify the moral right to prosperity. Here, at one stroke, the film brings together the economic and religious idealizations that are increasingly defining Hindu self-perception in our times, and does so in a matrix of breathtaking spectacle that creates an aesthetic to answer needs that are as political as they are commercial.

Commercialism is the last word one would want to use about Rituparno Ghosh's *Chokher Bali*. As we move from *Devdas* to *Chokher Bali*, it is tempting to see them as polar opposites. Bhansali's extravagance is countervailed by Ghosh's minimalism, the fantasy of *Devdas* by the realism of *Chokher Bali*. *Devdas* proudly flies the banner of Bollywood entertainment while *Chokher Bali* seeks legitimation as a putative art film. *Devdas* cost uncountable crores, *Chokher Bali* a miserly two-and-a-half. Against the chorus of audience approval for *Devdas*, Ghosh's film scores a sorry 6 out of 10 in the only tally I can find on the web.[6]

Tagore's *Chokher Bali*

The high seriousness of Ghosh's film rendition of *Chokher Bali* is integral to its heritage. Written in 1903, *Chokher Bali* was, as Rabindranath himself says in his introduction to *Chokher Bali* (Tagore 1961: 212), part of a very specific discourse that had been initiated by Rabindranath's elder contemporary Bankimchandra Chattopadhyaya in his novel *Bishabriksha* (The Poison Tree) and enhanced by Rabindranath's own works, *Nashtaneer* and *Ghare Baire*. Bankim's novel recounted, as did many of his other works, how women's lives revolved exclusively around men's needs and how male desire destroyed life and love. In Rabindranath's treatment this theme of women's subjection to the world acquired an undercurrent of anguish at India's colonial subjection, varying in emphasis in different works, sometimes barely noticed but never absent. In *Chokher Bali*, as in Rabindranath's other stories, this complex probing of experience that is at the same time emotional and political demands on the reader's part a cerebral engagement beyond surface empathy, severing it from the conditioned expectations of romantic love stories. Because it does not provide opportunities for unambiguous moral or social judgment, Rabindranath's *Chokher Bali* resists marketability. The main lines of the events Rabindranath narrates and the characters he imagines will bear this out.

Set in the opening years of twentieth-century Bengal, *Chokher* Bali is the story of four young men and women. One of them is Mahendra, whose mother, the wealthy widow Rajlakshmi, wants him to marry her friend Harimati's beautiful and educated daughter Binodini. On his refusal, and that of his close friend and virtual sibling Behari, Binodini is married off to another man, only to be widowed soon. Mahendra's reluctance to marry is, however, overcome when he sees his aunt Annapurna's niece Ashalata, the bride chosen for Behari, and rushes to marry her. Besotted with Ashalata, Mahendra neglects his medical studies and alienates his mother, who brings Binodini from her lonely village home to live with the family. Ashalata is naïve, barely literate, and domestically inexpert, but loyal and affectionate, and she is overawed by Binodini's beauty, sophistication and efficiency. But she is won over by Binodini's friendliness and they become "sois," or bosom friends as each other's ritually named *chokher bali*, or "sand in the eye."

Fascinated by Binodini's grace and cultivated nature, Mahendra falls in love with her even as he agonizes over betraying his wife's trust, especially as Behari warns him against surrendering to his passion for Binodini, whom Behari sees as a conniving enchantress. Leaving home only intensifies his passion, particularly when he receives love letters purportedly from Ashalata but clearly composed by Binodini, who plays out her own fantasy of imagining herself in Ashalata's privileged position. She relishes the sense of worth that Mahendra's attention gives her and the power it brings her over him, but is also put off by his treachery to his wife and actively repulses what she sees as weak-natured infatuation. In contrast to Mahendra, Behari stands out as a man of integrity and loyalty, on whom both Binodini and Ashalata come to depend during Rajlakshmi's illness when Mahendra stays away from home. In his envy Mahendra accuses Behari of being in love with Ashalata, who is shocked and avoids Behari. Binodini is attracted to Behari, but blaming her for Mahendra's foolishness, he turns away from her. All four principals in the story now find themselves marooned in individual misery and estranged from one another. Rejected by Behari, Binodini allows herself to be taken away on a long and aimless journey by Mahendra, whose romantic overtures she continues to rebuff, as much because she has no respect for him as because she hopes someday to come across Behari on her travels. This arid relationship eventually drives Binodini and Mahendra back to Calcutta, where his mother Rajlakshmi lies dying, attended by Annapurna, Behari and Ashalata, whose inner strength has been brought out by her betrayal. She forgives Mahendra but their reconciliation restores neither their passion for one another, nor his authority in the family, in which he is now a nonentity. Understanding Binodini's pain and integrity at last, Behari offers to marry her but she declines, choosing instead to seek exile in Benaras with Annapurna and leaving Behari to devote himself to serving the poor.

It is not hard to understand why *Chokher Bali*—I am speaking of the novel—cannot compete with Harlequin romances. Nothing much actually happens in it and it is neither driven by sensational action, nor by purple rhetoric. Unlike Bankim's *Bishabriksha*, Rabindranath's story has no tempests of weeping, no death by fire and poison, not even the scent of illicit sex. All that is gripping in the story takes place in the inner world of the characters. Even so potentially catastrophic an event as Binodini's decision to leave home in the company of Mahendra, turns out not to be an elopement at all and leads to no climax of tempestuous passion. It does not even slam the doors of her family in her face forever. Nothing is resolved in terms of concrete action and if there is any decisive movement in the story, it is towards a clarity of self-discovery that leads to resolute affirmations of self-worth. How is such a story to be retold on film without breaking down into mere postures of passion? What material action will anchor the inner drama visually? Is it any surprise that the solitary attempt to film the story before Rituparno Ghosh came along (in 1938, when Tagore was still alive) failed to make a mark on the Bengali cultural scene?

Ghosh and Ray: Intertextuality

The context for the reincarnation of *Chokher Bali* as a film directed by Rituparno Ghosh and released in October 2003 is not simply that of Rabindranath's apotheosis as the ruling spirit of Bengali letters. Nor must the film be placed solely within the context of Rabindranath's reflections on women's self-discovery that I have mentioned above, particularly his treatment of the theme in *Nashtaneer* and *Ghare Baire.* More specifically, the film is one in a distinct line of cinema set by Satyajit Ray when he made *Charulata*, his version of *Nashtaneer*, in 1964 and followed up with *Ghare Baire* in 1984. Ray's work on Rabindranath is not of course limited to these but they represent the thematic continuity that Rabindranath himself notes. It is a reasonable assumption that in filming *Chokher Bali*, which by the way is carefully billed as Rituparno Ghosh's retelling of Rabindranath's novel, Ghosh has deliberately tried to follow Ray, first, by choosing a story about a woman's gradual recognition of autonomy denied, and second, by bringing out resonances between women's quest for self-determination and India's political struggle. Not surprisingly, Ghosh sometimes echoes Ray's technical touches as well, as for instance, in showing Binodini training a pair of binoculars from an interior to sweep over the external world, as Charu does in *Charulata*. Ray's visual style comes to mind again when we see Binodini's binoculars and Ghosh's camera panning the ghats of Benaras in shots reminiscent of the early Ray film *Aparajita*. I may in passing compare the use of binoculars in *Chokher Bali* and *Devdas*. Ghosh essentially replicates Satyajit Ray's play with binoculars in *Charulata*, where Charu observes the world from her closed, aristocratic interior through opera glasses. In *Chokher Bali* the instrument becomes Binodini's eye on the world when she shuts herself up inside a houseboat on the Ganges in Benaras; Rabindranath's text has no such action. In *Devdas*, Bhansali arms both Paro and Devdas's grandmother with large binoculars to spy upon one another's house, despite their easy accessibility to both, apparently because of their insatiable and stereotypically feminine curiosity, as suggested by their gestures. Bhansali's invention may simply be an accidental parallel and typical of his prodigality with things: instead of one binocular, he provides two. Again, this may be accidental. But Ghosh's little touch is too close to Ray's as a metaphor to be an accident, particularly as Ghosh's admiration for Ray is well known.

Given this kinship it is hard not to speculate that the making of the Rabindranath films by Ray and Ghosh resulted from a similar reading of the world. Even though their particular worlds are separated by time, it might be argued that they are intimately linked by the same public discourse on selfhood, identity, gender, and nationalism, differing in intensity and extent but not in its basics. It is also hard not to think that Ray showed Ghosh the way to dramatize interiority, reaching for the inner landscape through the visual metaphor of domestic interiors. But where Ray stops short of drawing an explicit parallel between women's self-affirmation and India's, Ghosh works relentlessly to construct a political allegory by stretching the theme of liberation from the wife bound to her husband to the nation bound to its foreign masters. Ghosh's preoccupation is understandable because the discourse of liberation is no less important today than it was when Ray made *Charulata* in 1964. One aspect of its importance, to Ghosh's advantage, is that this discourse of liberation, particularly the liberation of women, is a very marketable commodity in today's political climate.

In my view, the currency of that discourse and the immediacy of its themes explain why a story so lacking in what Rabindranath mockingly called *ghatanar ghanaghata*, or "thunderous action," should find a reteller now. The issues explored by Ray have in fact gained momentum since his time and are much more in the public eye. Self-defining action and self-determined identity are integral to the modern consciousness, which sees all relationships, private or public, as political. Equally important is the rhetoric of that modernity, which urges everyone to assert selfhood. This climate of expectation not only supports legends of liberation, but also insists on them. Can a socially sensitive director, or a commercially canny one for that matter, afford not to turn to *Chokher Bali*?

Realism and glossing desire

Rituparno Ghosh possesses a sensibility finely tuned to the moral and political subtext of *Chokher Bali* and hones it further by drawing upon current debates and scholarship on gender, politics, and history. The list of consultants he acknowledges in the film's credits is a who's who of Calcutta intellectuals. Historical authenticity marks his work in every step, in his sets, costumes, locations, idioms of speech, custom and manner. This concern for authenticity has raised questions for some viewers. One of them, the gifted stage actor Shaonli Mitra, wrote a long essay in the November 2, 2003 issue of the Bengali biweekly magazine, *Desh*,[7] questioning the fit between the film's claim of historicity and its portrayal of social customs, such as the unobstructed access that Behari and Mahendra have to the private quarters of the young women. She is also troubled by Ghosh's construction of the material world of the film, which she views as a tasteful but falsifying idealization of the lifestyle of wealthy Bengalis in late-nineteenth-century Calcutta. These objections, limited as they are to the film's surface, can be set aside fairly simply. Rabindranath's original story places the men and women in easy and unquestioned proximity and does so in a believable way by linking them in sanctioned familial relations of brother-in-law and sister-in-law. What Mitra considers an invasion of women's spaces is part of the original novel's narrative design.

The issue of realism is in fact a trivial one when we limit it to material objects or social customs. Much more interesting to the question of realism and of profounder import to what we understand to be "real," is the gloss Ghosh puts on these objects and the spin he puts on the events that take place both in the social world and within the characters. "Gloss" is the right word in this context because Ghosh's is a superlatively glossy production without being blindingly flashy like Bhansali's *Devdas*. Abheek Mukhopadhyay's camera casts a warm, red-brown glow over the entire film, turning bodies, furniture, landscape into an intimate and desirable presence that pulsates with life. Ghosh's film is almost obsessed with the human body, bringing the spectator's eye into virtually tactile closeness with the gorgeous limbs of the actors. From the opening shot through the entire play, the camera lingers over bare limbs, particularly the smooth arms and shoulders of Aishwarya Rai (as Binodini) and Raima Sen (as Ashalata). In showing these women wearing nothing under their sarees, the director is of course faithful to contemporary women's practice, but he certainly capitalizes on that historical fact to eroticize his characters. Even as he draws a tasteful veil over nudity, his very reticence heats up the suggestibility of the scene. The strategic use of the body as a sexual signifier is particularly striking in the picnic scene where Behari, played by Tota Raychaudhuri, wades into the garden tank to pick lotuses and the camera lovingly dwells on his muscular brown back, as Binodini watches in fascination. The gaze of desire in this case is Binodini's, and purposefully so identified by Ghosh. His interpretation is evident from his choice of narrative emphasis between the two opportunities that Rabindranath's text provides for sexualizing the picnic, although Rabindranath himself does not seem aware of that. First, Mahendra's wife Asha, delighted "like a wild doe at escaping from the brick prison of Calcutta" (Tagore 1961: 252), joins Binodini in taking a long bath in the garden tank. This obvious opportunity for the idealized portrayal of bathing women (a long established motif in post-Ravi Varma painting) is left untouched by Ghosh. The second, barely present opportunity in the text is Binodini's command *to Mahendra* to take a bath and get ready for lunch (ibid.: 253). It is by Ghosh's textual intervention that Mahendra is erased from the scene, which turns to *Behari's* body instead and makes it available for Binodini's contemplation. The sexual charge that affects the scene is entirely Ghosh's invention. The plot manipulation is not subtle but obvious here, as is the fact that the theme of sexuality that preoccupies Ghosh is established as much by visual maneuvers as by overt narrative intervention.

The pattern of narrative intervention is by no means discreet. Ghosh's sexualization of the story is open and even heavy-handed in his representation of the relationship between Binodini and Mahendra. Ghosh's rendition repeatedly shows their encounter developing into withdrawals into private spaces barred from the spectator's gaze. In Rabindranath's text, the possibility of sexual encounter is not merely avoided; it is specifically repudiated. Binodini repeatedly repulses Mahendra, for instance, when he goes to her room at night in chapter 32, only to be struck by the "lightning" that flashes from her eyes (ibid.: 308). She declares her love for Behari and putting her arms around his neck offers him her lips as the one sign of acceptance she desires before leaving him forever: "For one moment, they were motionless and the room silent." Then they take their leave from one another (ibid.: 317). In Rabindranath's story, the terrible irony for Binodini is that Behari, whom she loves, will not even at this moment of revelation enter into what society declares to be an illicit relationship, while Mahendra, whose infatuation disgusts her (ibid.: 325), is only too keen to do so. Lacking any means of support, she is forced to live in a house rented by Mahendra, but refuses to let him live there. Later, she decisively rejects him in a house by the Ganges in Allahabad, where on a moonlit night she adorns herself with flowers awaiting a fantasized reunion with Behari. Imagining that she is waiting for him, Mahendra approaches her only to be repulsed again, and to be told that it is Behari for whom Binodini is looking as she wanders the length and breadth of India with Mahendra (ibid.: 365–6).

None of the emotional energy sparked by Rabindranath's systematic deferral of sexual fulfillment finds room in Ghosh's film. Instead, we see Mahendra and Binodini getting into a clinch, slamming bedroom doors behind them, going for a ride in a carriage and pulling down its shutters, and shutting themselves up in the bedroom of a houseboat on the Ganges at Benaras. In case the spectator does not get the point, Ghosh puts on Binodini's bare shoulder a raw love bite, and just in case the spectator still does not get it, he makes Asha question Binodini about it. Rabindranath makes the reader's imagination work to create sexuality; Ghosh makes the imagination redundant.

Why a director as talented as Ghosh should walk on such heavy feet is an interesting question. The bulk of the film shows his delicate and light touch, an eye both for the telling detail (such as Binodini's teacups) and metaphoric vista (the ghats of Benaras), a finely tuned ear for the rhythms of passion, and a wry humor (Mahendra and Asha in bed after their wedding). The work he gets out of his actors is phenomenal, unfailingly responsive to the varying needs of social occasion and personal feeling. Who could have thought that the Aishwarya Rai who assumes the postures of suffering in Bhansali's *Devdas* could be the same Aishwarya Rai who embodies the substance of suffering in *Chokher Bali*? Substance is something that Ghosh excels in revealing in his actors. All the characters he puts on the stage are believable and multidimensional persons, each suggesting depths beyond their surface actions. Every part and aspect of Ghosh's work on the film is carefully designed and every effect precisely calibrated. The overt sexualization of the story must then be part of his design.

The visual rhetoric of nationalism

To understand that design, we must consider the second major theme of the film, the theme of national liberation. As I have said before, the personal liberation of women and the political liberation of the nation run parallel in *Chokher Bali* in an allegorical relationship expressed as a plot of two contests, one seeking release from the harness of gender and the other from that of colonial subjugation. The colonized character of turn-of-the-century India is carefully underscored in the film, beginning with the opening shot of Binodini who is speaking to her British mentor in English, surrounded by objects of British domesticity. An English woman, presumably a missionary, comes to Rajlakshmi's house accompanied by an Indian assistant to spread the Lord's word and education for native females, only to faint from the heat, to the wonder and disgust of Asha. Mahendra wears faultless British apparel and holds medical consultations with an English doctor in measured tones. Evidently, this is part of his identity as medical student, which stands revealed as a colonial construction, for modern medicine was a British import to India, an unambiguously Western construction of knowledge, and its pursuit a signifier of the colonized native. This postcolonial critique is neither pressed far, nor is any response to colonial hegemony foregrounded. The growing struggle for independence does not touch any of the characters, although Behari dedicates himself to the service of the country, as he does in Rabindranath's original. But his patriotism, in the film as in the novel, is charity, not resistance, and never progresses beyond serving the underprivileged to combating the colonizer. While the historical moment of nationalism is one of the realities of the film, it exists there more as a static experience than a dynamic process. The film's narrative does not unfold to reveal any action in the arena of national struggle. Yet, the film ends with one of Rabindranath's best known nationalistic songs in praise of Bengal as the motherland while we are told that Bengal was partitioned into two in 1905.

This abrupt turn to an overt political address to the audience is most perplexing. How is the legend of a nation violated connected with what had seemed so far to be the story of a woman's painful search for self-authentication? The only way to unite them is as complementary parts of a political allegory in which the subjugation of the nation is inscribed upon women's bodies and minds. This equation, one that is fast becoming a tired cliché of contemporary liberal discourse, is obvious enough but it is debatable how effectively it validates the argument at the core of the political allegory. The film's persistent invocation of sexuality might add up to connote Binodini's need for and attempts at self-determination, which could be parlayed into a metaphor of India's struggle for independence and pain at its denial. But to work effectively, a metaphor needs to be a two-part construct. Ghosh's treatment misses out on filling out the woman-nation, gender-politics tropes, first because the nation is hardly visible and second because the politics never progresses beyond personal power struggles in the family. The allegory is also weakened by Binodini's unexplained disappearance before the narrative ends, in a decisive departure from Rabindranath's conclusion. Is she on a journey to self-realization somewhere? Is she utterly lost, a victim to inexorable social forces? If Binodini equals the nation, is the nation then also sunk without trace? If this is the answer, then it falls into an inexplicable repudiation of the left-liberal axiom that individuals may die but nations struggle on through suffering and loss. This makes the politics of Ghosh's *Chokher Bali* suspect and makes me wonder whether the film really works towards political perceptions or merely towards political postures. I question whether Ghosh has the crises of gender and nation in his sight or the performance of gender and nation. The material texture of his work—the lighting, the close-ups, the lyrical music—effectively turns the hard experience of personal crisis into romantic melancholy of great aesthetic impact, but an impact that releases no political energy. Instead, it leaves the film's narrative and ideological processes unresolved.

Conclusion

How shall we explain the vacuum at the center of what appears to be a purposeful, even proselytizing reconstruction of a (minor) classic? As I have noted above, Ghosh systematically runs the stories of Binodini and India in tandem, but the promised allegory remains arbitrary, claiming legitimacy not by building up an argument but by asserting the priority of self-determination as an axiomatic truth. Ghosh's *Chokher Bali* is nowhere near Bhansali's *Devdas* in creating wish-fulfilling fantasies of wealth and sex, but it nonetheless feeds the romantic cult of the unconquerable spirit of the disempowered. Both films exploit emotional and social themes that sell well, cutting across class strata and appealing as much to the desire for opulence as for feel-good political positions. In other words, the directors of *Chokher Bali* and *Devdas* have remade their originals to suit present times. Yet this process of reconstruction by the director performing as *auteur* has not obliterated the core of emotional experience imagined by the original authors in either work. On the contrary, both novels have survived the passage of time and the makeover of genre in engaging with contemporary consciousness. Stunned I may be by Bhansali's extravagance, and wary of Ghosh's political correctness, but I still sense Saratchandra and Tagore sitting in the wings watching their stories cross over from print to celluloid. Whether you like the directorial interventions of Bhansali and Ghosh or not, you can see in their work how classics resonate with times other than their own, live beyond their own worlds, and provide the next with frameworks for self-reflection.

Notes

* Much of this chapter is the result of discussions with Tirthankar Bose. I gratefully acknowledge his help and advice.

1 I have used Bengali orthographic practice in transliterating the title of Saratchandra's work as *Debdas*, but *Devdas* for Bhansali's film as in the film's title.

2 I infer this from the lack of any mention of the earlier movie in the debate over Ghosh's film in the media after its release.

3 The full record of this film is in the Internet Movie Database (www.imdb.com/title/tt039090974).

4 See the film's official website (http://devdas.indiatimes.com).

5 User ratings are on http://www.imdb.com/title/tt0238936 (accessed April 2004): rating 7.2/10; on http://www.planetbollywood.com/Film/Devdas (accessed April 2004): rating 7.54/10; on http://film.guardian.co.uk/Film_page/0,4061,749274,00.html (accessed April 2004): rating 7.5/10.

6 Ratings from www.imdb.com/title/tt0390974 (accessed April 2004).

7 Perhaps the most influential cultural arbiter in the Bengali-speaking world.

References

Chattopadhyaya, B.C. (1952) "Bishabriksha," in J.C. Bagal (ed.) *Bankim Racanabali*, vol. 1, Calcutta: Sahitya Sansad.

Chattopadhyaya, S.C. (1985) "Debdas," in S. Sen (ed.) *Saratsahityasamgraha*, Calcutta: Ananda Publishers.

Mitra, S. (2003) "Chokher Bali," *Desh*, November 2, 2003.

Tagore, R.N. (1961) "Chokher Bali," in *Rabindra-Racanabali*, *Birth Centenary Edition*, vol. 8, Calcutta: Government of West Bengal.

Uberoi, P. (2001) "Imagining the Family: An Ethnography of Viewing *Hum Aapke Hain Kaun*," in R. Dwyer and C. Pinney (eds) *Pleasure and the Nation*, New Delhi: Oxford University Press.

Part 6

Agenda-driven literature

10 Lyrically speaking

Hindi film songs and the progressive aesthetic

Ali Mir

Īśvar Allāh tere jahāṃ meṃ, nafrat kyoṃ hai jaṅg hai kyoṃ?
Terā dil to itnā baṛā hai, insān kā dil tang hai kyoṃ?...
Is duniyā ke dāman par, insane ke lahū kā rang hai kyoṃ?...
Dil ke darvāzoṃ par tale, tāloṃ par ye zaṅg hai kyoṃ?
O Ishwar, O Allah, why this hatred, this war in your world?[1]
Your heart knows no bounds, why then are the hearts of humans so small and petty?...
Why is the garment of the world stained with human blood?...
Why are the doors of hearts locked, why are these locks rusted?

Setting the stage

So goes the hauntingly beautiful song from the 1998 film *Earth*. Written by Javed Akhtar and set to music by A.R. Rahman (and incidentally, put to good use by Gohar Raza as the recurring theme of "Evil Stalks the Land," a documentary on the 2002 Gujarat violence), the song is obviously an homage to another one that was written earlier by Sahir Ludhianvi:

Khudā-e bartār, terī zamīn par, zamīn kī khātir ye jaṅg kyoṃ hai?
Har ek fatah-o zafar ke dāman pe, khūn-e insān kā raṅg kyoṃ hai?...
Jinheṃ talab hai jahān bhar kī, unhīṃ kā dil itnā taṅg kyoṃ hai?...
Saroṃ meṃ kibr-o-ghurūr kyoṃ hai, diloṃ ke śīśe pe zaṅg kyoṃ hai?
O great God, why do people of your earth wage war over land?
Why is the garment of every conqueror stained with human blood?...
Why are the hearts of those who desire the whole world so small and petty?...
Why are their heads swollen with pride and arrogance, why are the mirrors of their hearts rusted?

Do these two songs represent bookends of a line that ran from Sahir through Kaifi Azmi and Majrooh Sultanpuri to Javed Akhtar? Is there a generational continuity of progressive sentiment that Urdu poets deployed in the arena of popular culture through their Hindi film lyrics? After all, one can, without much effort, recall a number of progressive film songs written by the Urdu poets of the Progressive

Writers' Association (PWA). In order to answer these questions, I bought books of lyrics, crosschecked with online databases and asked friends to tell me about the progressive songs that came to their mind. Surprisingly, the search yielded a far smaller output than I had first imagined. Nevertheless, there is a story to be told here, a narrative to unfold, a lesson or two to be learned.

The centrality of song in Hindi cinema

The deployment of songs to propel a narrative has a long and varied tradition in India. Many of the country's popular art forms have used this technique for a long time: the traditions of Kutiyattam and Kathakali from Kerala, Jatra from Bengal, Nautanki and Ramlila from North India, Tamasha from Maharasthra, Terukuttu from Tamil Nadu, Burrakatha in Andhra Pradesh, Yakshagana from Karnataka, Bhavai from Gujarat, Ojapali from Assam, Lila from Orissa and of course, the various enactments of *Rāmāyaṇa* and *Mahābhārata* (Thoraval 2000: 50).

The early Parsi theater, the precursor to Indian cinema also had its share of songs. As Javed Akhtar says in an interview with Munni Kabir, in a play about Marcus and Helena set in Rome, for instance, Helena pining for her love would burst out into a song: *Piyā more āj nahīṃ āye* or "My beloved hasn't come today" (Kabir 1999: 51). The original plays of the likes of Agha Hashr Kashmiri were subsequently adapted into Hindi cinema. Here is a typical dialogue from *Asīr-e-Hirs* ("Prisoner of Greed"). The dialogue is between Chengiz Khan and his love, Naushaba:

N: *Pyār se ek savāl hai* (I have a question for my love.)
C: *Farmāiye vo kyā khayāl hai?* (Pray, what are you thinking?)
N: *Kumhār jo miṭṭī kā khilonā banātā hai, vo kis kām ātā hai?* (The clay toy a potter makes, what good is it?)
C: *Us se dil bahlāyā jātā hai. Agar vo kisī ke hāth se chūṭ jāye, yā ṭhokar se ṭūṭ jāye, to kumhār to sakht malāl hogā.* (It is to amuse one's heart. But if it slips through one's fingers, or is broken by a careless foot, the potter will be very sad.)
N: *Kyoṃ aisā khayāl hogā?* (Why would he feel so?)
C: *Kyoṃki us śakhs ne kumhār kī mehnat barbād kar dī* (Because the person has destroyed the potter's effort).
N: *Wāh wāh, subhānallah. Khūb bāt irśād kar dī.* (Wonderful! The Lord be praised. That was beautifully said). (Ibidem)

Given this history, it is no surprise then that Indian cinema took so easily to including songs as a form of theatrical narrative.

The history of Hindi film lyrics actually predates the talkies. The standard practice during the Silent Era was to provide musical accompaniment to the film from the orchestra pit. Each movie theater had its own band of musicians that played along with the film itself. The first instance of playback singing seems to have occurred in 1921 for the movie *Bhakta Vidur*. Vidur's wife, spinning a charkha, mouthed the words of a song that was lip-synched for the audience by a live singer in the theater (the audience sang along, often demanding encores). By the time the first talkie, *Alam Ara*, was released in 1931, songs had taken center stage in Indian cinema (according to one account, *Alam Ara* had 55!).

Songs and the independence movement

The use of Hindi film lyrics as a means of articulating a progressive sentiment was, not surprisingly, intertwined with the freedom struggle. While some film screenings in the North used the interval between the changing of the reels to lead the audience into singing nationalist songs, the deployment of lyrics to propagate resistance was first popularized in the South. Daring filmmakers in Tamil Nadu and Andhra Pradesh defied the British censors by using the poems of the banned revolutionary poet Subramanya Bharati (1882–1921) in films, sometimes without credit, for example, *Navayuvan* ("Modern Youth," 1937); *Menaka* (1935); *Adrishtam* ("Fate," 1939); *Naam Iruvar* ("We Two," 1947). Hindi cinema, initially cautious, soon followed suit. The 1936 film *Janmabhoomi* ("Land of Birth") was one of the first to have an explicitly nationalist song (written by J.S. Cashyap): *Jai jai jananī janmabhūmi* ("Hail to the land of our birth").

One lyricist who consistently wrote patriotic songs for films was Ramchandra Narainji Dwivedi, better known simply as Pradeep, whose most famous song is probably this one from *Jagriti* ("Awakening," 1954):

Āo bacco tumheṃ dikhāyeṃ jhāṅkī Hindustān kī.
Is miṭṭī se tilak karo, ye dhartī hai balidān kī.
Vande Mātaram, Vande Mātaram.
Come children, let me offer you a peek into Hindustan.
Adorn your foreheads with its soil, for this is the land of martyrs.
I bow to the motherland, I bow to the motherland.

Writing first for Bombay Talkies, Pradeep soon joined the newly created Filmistan, whose first film *Chal Chal Re Naujawan* ("Walk On, Youth," 1944), scripted by the PWA writer Sadat Hasan Manto, included a song extolling the unity of Hindus and Muslims:

Manzil sabhī kī ek hai, rāheṃ alag alag,
Voh ek hai, par apnī nigāheṃ alag alag:
Mandir meṃ hai Bhagavān, voh masjid meṃ Khudā hai.
Kisne kahā Hindū se Musalmān judā hai?
Bolo Har Har Mahādev, Bolo Allāh-o-Akbar!
Though our paths are different, our destination is the same,
There is but one God, just different ways of looking at Him:
In the temple He is called Bhagavān, in the mosque, Khudā.
Who says that Hindus and Muslims aren't but one?
Say Har Har Mahadev, say Allahu-Akbar!

In the 1940 film, *Aaj Ka Hindustani* ("Today's Indian"), directed by Jayant Desai (featuring Miss Rose, Prithviraj, Ishwarlal, Sitara and comedian Charlie),[2] Prithviraj, playing a nationalist, is picturized walking through his village singing:

Carkhā calāo behno, kāṭo ye kacce dhāge,
Dhāge ye kah rahe haiṃ, Bhārat ke bhāg jāge!
Carkhe ke gīt gāo, duniyā ko ye sunāo:
Carkhā calānevālā, Gāndhī hai āge āge!
Spin the spinning wheel O sisters, and as you cut these threads,
Listen as they say that India's destiny has awakened!
Sing songs of the spinning wheel and tell this to the world:
That the charkha spinner Gandhi leads us all!

Some of the songs that were written during the Quit India movement consciously pushed the censor-imposed bounds of acceptability. The opening song in *Kismat* ("Fate," 1943), written by Pradeep and composed by Anil Biswas, had the following chorus:

Āj Himālay kī coṭī se, phir ham ne lalkārā hai:
Dūr haṭo, dūr haṭo āī duniyāvālo, Hindustān hamāra hai!
From the peak of the Himalayas, we defiantly announce:
Get out O foreigners, for India is ours!

Gautam Kaul, in his interesting book *Cinema and the Indian Freedom Struggle*, documents an anecdote about how the censors were hoodwinked into thinking that the reference to "foreigners" in the song was about the Japanese army and not the British. *Kismat* was first released in Kanpur at the Imperial Talkies. The British authorities received information that this song was being played repeatedly on public demand. Officer Dharmendra Gaur, the brother of Vrajendra Gaur, author, lyricist and screenplay writer of many films, was sent to investigate. A detention order under Section 26 of the Defense of India Rules had been readied to arrest Pradeep. Dharmendra Gaur reportedly saw the film four times, but filed a report saying that another line in the same song, *Tum na kisī ke āge jhuknā, German ho yā Japāni* ("Do not bow before anyone, be they German or Japanese"), demonstrated that the song was not anti-British. *Kismat* ended up running for 186 weeks at Roxy Cinema in Calcutta. Other lyricists such as Pandit Narendra Sharma (*Hamari Baat*, "Our Story," 1943), Qamar Jalalabadi (*Chand*, "Moon," 1944), D.N. Madhok (*Pehle Aap*, "You First," 1944), Zia Sarhadi (*Badi Maa*, 1945), and Gopal Singh Nepali (*Amar Asha*, "Eternal Hope," 1947) took heart from this, and penned freedom songs with increasing frequency.

Gramophone records served the purpose of popularizing film music beyond the cinema halls. Since the recordings were not of a great quality, the lyrics were printed on cheap booklets and distributed with the records. The British administration banned several of these songs, but the booklets circulated freely carrying the word around.

Independence unshackled filmmakers from the limitations placed by the censors on patriotic songs and lyricists celebrated. Songs like the one from *Ahimsa* ("Nonviolence," 1947): *Āzād ham haiṃ āj se, jailoṃ ke tāle toḍ do*, or: "We are free from today, let us break the locks of our jails" and from *Majboor* ("Helpless," 1948): *Calā gayā gorā aṅgrez, ab kāhe kā ḍar*, or: "The white British have departed, what do we have to fear now?" became more and more common.

Songs and progressive movements

In the meantime, the PWA was gathering momentum. This radical movement breathed a new life into cultural production and rapidly gained popularity. Not surprisingly, the medium of cinema was seen by the PWA as a space for intervention. The mood of the nation allowed members of the Association to make inroads into the film industry and leftist writers were soon writing scripts and stories for large film studios, exposing the large movie-going audience to socially conscious ideas.

Another institution that had a considerable impact on the evolution of Indian cinema was the *Indian People's Theatre Association* (IPTA), the cultural wing of the Communist Party of India (CPI). Launched in 1943 "to defend culture against Fascism and imperialism," IPTA worked towards the development of an avant-garde culture in India, largely in theater—its primary field of engagement—but also in the arena of cinema.

A large number of the country's cultural intelligentsia—actors, directors, screenplay writers, journalists, lyricists, musicians and technicians—came together to produce work that was in line with their politics of social justice. Writer-director Khwaja Ahmed Abbas, cinematographer-director Bimal Roy, director Chetan Anand, music composer Salil Choudhary, poet-lyricists Sahir Ludhianvi and Majrooh Sultanpuri, and actors Balraj Sahni and Utpal Dutt were all linked to IPTA.

K.A. Abbas, a cofounder of the IPTA, made *Dharti Ke Lal* ("Children of the Earth," 1946) from a story by Krishan Chandar, a film that examined the Bengal famine in a documentary-like fashion. Mohan Bhavnani's *Mazdoor* ("Laborer," 1934) was inspired by IPTA's play "The Factory" and based on a story by Premchand. It was one of the first of its kind, and offered a realistic portrayal of the plight of industrial workers. Chandulal Shah's *Achhut* ("Untouchable," 1940) was a film focusing on the theme of untouchability; Mehboob Khan's *Manmohan* (1936) critiqued the patriarchal order; *Jagirdar* ("Feudal Landlord," 1937) questioned the issue of land ownership; and *Hum Tum aur Woh* ("I, You, and the Other," 1938) was about a woman who seeks sexual and emotional comfort through an extramarital relationship. All these films challenged existing social norms in a probing fashion.

While writers and directors belonging to the Progressive Writers' Movement made a number of films that exhibited a political consciousness and a desire to precipitate social change, it took a while for the Urdu poetry of the movement to enter the arena of film lyrics. Although Sahir Ludhianvi made his debut in 1941 (in *Naujawan* "Youth") and Majrooh Sultanpuri in 1946 (with *Shahjahan*), their early lyrical output belonged to the traditional genre of love-poetry.

For reasons that are too complex to go into in detail, the leading Hindi poets of the time had shied away from writing film lyrics. The leadership of the Hindi poets was at that time dominated by an orthodoxy that insisted that its members refuse to degrade their art by writing for popular cinema or theater in the *bazaari* language of Hindustani. As Yogendra Malik points out "literary traditions in Hindi tended to be dominated by Hindi revivalism, nationalism and romanticism" (Malik 1988: 115). The leading Hindi writers and poets of the time frowned upon socialism as "an alien philosophy unsuitable for the Indian context as well as upon popular culture as a medium for their work" (ibidem).[3]

The Urdu poets on the other hand were more than eager to explore this new medium of expression. Kaifi Azmi, Majrooh Sultanpuri, and perhaps most significantly, Sahir Ludhianvi started writing for cinema and dominated the landscape of its lyrical production for the next few decades. Other progressive poets such as Shailendra, Ali Sardar Jafri, Jan Nisar Akhtar, Neeraj, and Gulzar joined the fray in due course.

Progressive lyrics come of age

The decade of the 1950s proved to be the time when progressive lyrics came of age. This was the period dominated by the auteurs of Hindi cinema, the moviemakers with a vision. K.A. Abbas, Bimal Roy, Raj Kapoor, Kamal Amrohi, and of course, Guru Dutt sought to use cinema as a pedagogical tool and a space for constructing social critique. Their expression found a cause in the failure of the free nation to fulfill its promise of an egalitarian society with justice for all citizens. As the euphoria of independence dissipated, and as people understood that the end of British occupation did not mean the end of their misery, disenchantment with the Nehru government grew.

Some like the IPTA poet, Prem Dhawan, who had written *Jhūm jhūm ke gāo āj*, or "Swing and dance today," celebrating the exit of the British, continued to urge the youth of the Nehruvian era to engage in the process of nation building:

> *Choṛo kal kī bāteṃ, kal ki bāt purānī.*
> *Naye daur meṃ likheṃge ham mil kar nayī kahānī.*
> *Ham Hindustānī, ham Hindustānī!*
> Forget yesterday, yesterday is gone.
> We shall write a new story for the new times.
> We Indians, we Indians!
>
> (from *Hum Hindustani*, "We Indians," 1960)

But, for a whole host of others, Nehru became the symbol of the betrayal of the promise of independence. As Rajadhyaksha and Willemen point out, this was a period reflecting "the emotional and social complexities affecting the artist when the reformism associated with Nehruvian nationalism disintegrated under the pressure of industrialization and urbanization creating the space for Indian modernism but also generating social dislocation" (EIC 93).

Sahir strode on to this stage like a giant, writing songs for movies like *Nayā Daur* ("The New Age," 1957) and *Phir Subha Hogi* ("Morning Will Come again," 1958) in a manner that was in keeping with his reputation as a revolutionary poet.

Sāthī hāth baṛhānā, sāthi hāth baṛhānā!
Ek akelā thak jāyegā mil kar bojh uthānā,
Sāthī hāth baṛhānā!
Comrades, lend your hand!
One alone will tire soon, let us bear this burden together,
Comrades lend your hand!

Miṭṭī se ham lāl nikāleṃ, moti lāeṃ jal se,
Jo kuch is duniyā meṃ banā hai, banā hamāre bal se.
Kab tak mehnat ke pairoṃ meṃ daulat kī zanjīreṃ?
Hāth baṛhākar chīn lo apne sapnoṃ ki tasvīreṃ,
Sāthī hāth baṛhānā
We are the ones who extract rubies from the earth, pearls from the sea,
All that is of value in this world has been created by us.
How long will labor be chained by those who own wealth?
Reach out and snatch that which you have always dreamed of.
Comrades, lend your hand!

Pyaasa ("Thirsty," 1957), of course, is the movie that is best remembered as Sahir's vehicle. A Guru Dutt film about a struggling poet coming to terms with postindependence India, the story gets its radical edge mainly from its songs. The poet-protagonist of the story, after an agonized search for meaning, offers this disdainful take on the current times:

Ye mahloṃ ye takhtoṃ ye tājoṃ kī duniyā,
Ye insān ke duśman samājoṃ kī duniyā,
Ye daulat ke bhūke rivājoṃ kī duniyā,
Ye duniyā agar mil bhi jāye to kyā hai?
This world of palaces, thrones and crowns,
This world of societies that hate humanity,
This world of traditions hungry for wealth,
Even if one obtains this world, so what?

And as the poet, played by Guru Dutt himself, wanders through the red-light district and observes the desperation that forces women to sell their bodies, he sings a song that is a minor reworking of a poem that Sahir had written earlier (called *Cakle*, or "Brothels"), the opening line of which went: *Sanākhān-e-tasdīq-e-maśriq kahāṃ haiṃ?* or "Where are those who are praise the purity of the East?"

The story goes that Nehru had given a speech in which he had remarked "I am proud of India." Guru Dutt asked Sahir to work this line into the refrain of the song. The result was:

Ye kūce, ye nīlām-ghar dilkaśī ke,
Ye luṭte hue kārvān zindagī ke,
Kahāṃ haiṃ, kahāṃ haiṃ, muhāfiz khudī ke?
Jinheṃ nāz hai Hind par, vo kahāṃ haiṃ?
These streets, these auction houses of pleasure,
These looted caravans of life,
Where are they, the guardians of selfhood?
Those who are proud of India, where are they?

This taunt was followed by a harsh indictment of the national leadership:

Zarā mulk ke rāhbaroṃ ko bulāo!
Ye kūce, ye galiyāṃ, ye manzar dikhāo!
Jinheṃ nāz hai Hind par unko lāo!
Jinheṃ nāz hai Hind par, vo kahāṃ haiṃ?
Go, fetch the leaders of the nation!
Show them these streets, these lanes, these sights!
Call them, those who are proud of India!
Those who are proud of India, where are they?

Censorship

This mode of filmmaking soon ran into problems. The censor board, now under the control of the Indian government, kicked into gear, reflecting the government's hyper-sensitivity towards any reference to people's struggles, particularly in the cause of socialism. Director Ramesh Saigal was asked to delete a line from his movie *Kafila* ("Caravan") which went: "The caravan of the people of Asia is on the move." Sahir's line *Paise kā rāj miṭā denā* "End the rule of the wealthy" was axed from another film. Pradeep's song from the film *Amar Rahe Yeh Pyaar* ("May This Love Be Forever," 1961) was deleted in its entirety, presumably because of the lines:

Hāi! Siyāsat kitnī gandī!
Burī hai kitnī firqabandī!
Āj ye sab ke sab nar-nārī,
Ho gaye rāste ke ye bhikhārī!
Alas! How dirty are the politics of the time!
How despicable this sectarianism!
Today, all these men and women,
Have been turned into beggars!

The lyrics of *Phir Subha Hogi* were considered so radical that two songs from the film were banned for a while. One was:

Āsmān pe hai khudā aur zamīn pe ham,
Ājkal vo is taraf dekhtā hai kam.
Kis ko bheje vo yahāṃ khāk chānne?
Is tamām bhīṛ kā hāl jānne?
Ādmī haiṃ anginat, devatā haiṃ kam!
God is in the heavens while we are here on earth,
These days, He does not pay us much attention.
Who can he send here to sift through these sands,
To figure out the condition of these teeming masses?
For there are too many people, not enough deities.

And the other was a parody of the famous Iqbal poem, *Sāre jahān se acchā Hindostān hamārā*, "Our India is better than the rest of the world":

Cīn-o-Arab hamārā, Hindostān hamārā,
Rahne ko ghar nahīṃ hai, sārā jahān hamārā!
China and Arabia are ours, so is India,
Yet we have no home to live in; the whole world is ours!

Jitnī bhī bilḍingeṃ thīṃ, sethoṃ ne bāṇṭ lī haiṃ,
Fūṭpāth Bambaī ke, haiṃ āśiyāṃ hamārā.
The wealthy have distributed all the buildings among themselves,
While we are left to take refuge on the footpaths of Bombay.

These songs reflect a disenchantment of the urban poor with the state. The ban came into effect around the time of the second parliamentary elections and was not repealed till 1966 (Kaul 1998: 179).

After independence, the Indian government maintained monopolistic control over its radio broadcasting. When B.V. Keskar succeeded as the Minister of Information and Broadcasting in 1952, he decided to ban the broadcast of film music on All India Radio, considering it simultaneously too vulgar, too Westernized and too steeped in Urdu, choosing instead to promote light classical music. Most listeners simply tuned over to Radio Ceylon or Pakistani stations, both of which were broadcasting Hindi film songs. In 1957, film music was back on All India Radio on a new channel called Vividh Bhārtī. It is probably fair to say that most Hindustani-speaking Indian households had their radios perennially tuned to this station.

Since the only medium through which the public got to hear film music was the radio, station programming determined the songs that the public listened to. Popular demand, expressed through write-ins to programs like *Man Cāhe Gīt* ("Favorite Songs"), began to play a significant role in the kind of music that was heard on the airwaves, and therefore in the kind of music that was produced.

New trends

Eventually, the social sensibility of the 1950s and early 1960s lost its appeal, shrinking the space available for progressive cinema, and consequently progressive lyrics. There were two major reasons behind this.

The first was the break-up of the studio system in the 1960s, a phenomenon that changed the rules of the filmmaking game rather significantly. Serious, socially conscious cinema gave way surely but steadily to popular entertainment and the space provided by the studios to the maverick filmmakers, writers, and poets withered away. The growing urban population, which formed the largest chunk of the viewing public, gravitated towards escapist films seeking perhaps to forget their frustrations. Opulent sets, well-choreographed songs, and a formulaic script were the order of the new day. As Aruna Vasudev puts it, the films that were produced were mostly "absurd romances packed with songs and dances, made like fairytales with a moral" (quoted in Thoraval 2000: 50).

The second reason for the decline, as Peter Manuel elaborates in his fine book *Cassette Culture* (1993), was the advent of the portable cassette players. The early ones arrived in the country in the late 1970s in the hands of the guest workers returning from the Gulf. The fetishization of the cassette player (everyone wanted to have one) symbolized the changing aspirations of the middle class and its freshly discovered consumer power (which was beginning to be unleashed by the newly instituted policies of economic liberalization). With foreign collaboration now a possibility, new tie-ups like Bush-Akai, Orson-Sony, BPL-Sanyo and Onida-JVC started manufacturing cheap cassettes. Sales of recorded music consequently went up from $1.2 million in 1980 to $12 million in 1986 and over $21 million in 1990.

Bourgeois democracy, thus unleashed, paved the way for what can be called the Age of Bappi Lahiri. Foot-tapping, easily consumable, and subsequently disposable tunes became the order of the day, and banal lyrics were welcomed:

D se hotā hai Dance
I se hotā hai Item
S se hotā hai Singer
C se hotā hai Chorus
O se Orchestra!
I am a Disco Dancer!!
D for Dance,
I for Item,
S for Singer,
C for Chorus,
O for Orchestra!
I am a Disco Dancer!!

The allegedly anti-establishment films of the "Angry Young Man" days did not provide much scope for progressive writing either. I say "allegedly" because there was nothing really anti-establishment about this cinema; all it did was to promote the image of an alienated, disillusioned youth who sought vigilante justice by taking the law into his own hands. One might even argue (perhaps a bit uncharitably) that *Sholay* ("Flames," 1975), possibly the biggest blockbuster produced in India and a film whose influence can still be seen on Indian cinema, is essentially a story about two mercenaries fighting subaltern dacoits on behalf of the feudal *thakur*, or landlord, of the village. Songs in these films were used merely to interrupt the narrative and to provide some light moments. Rhyme became the handmaiden of the tune, and relatively meaningless lyrics fit comfortably in this setup:

> *Koī hasīnā jab rūṭh jāti hai, to aur bhī hasīn ho jāti hai.*
> *Station se gāṛi jab chūṭ jātī hai, to ek-do-tīn ho jāti hai.*
> When a beauty gets upset, she becomes even more beautiful.
> When a train leaves the station, it departs from sight.

Even the likes of Sahir were reduced to writing love songs of, shall we say, dubious merit (such as the one in *Trishul* that went: *Gapuci gapuci gam gam, kiśiki kiśiki kam kam*); his light and frothy songs in *Deewaar* (*Kah dūṃ tumheṃ ya cup rahūṃ dil meṃ mere āj kyā hai?* "Should I tell you what is in my heart, or shall I remain silent?") were in popular demand while the only semi-progressive song he wrote for the film (*Dīwaroṃ kā jaṅgal jis kā ābādī hai nām,* "This forest of walls that we call a city" was left on the editing table.

Ironically, the one space that could have provided refuge to the progressive poets, the so-called parallel cinema movement, did not open up its doors to their lyrics. Songs were seen as an unnecessary impediment to the narrative. In an attempt to produce a cinema of calculated, purposeful naturalism that anxiously sought to distance itself from the *bazaari* Hindustani of commercial films, the alternate filmmakers adopted a self-consciously Sanskritized Hindi, as is evident even from the titles of the films by Shyam Benegal, Govind Nihalani, and others: *Ankur* ("Seedling"), *Nishant* ("Night's End"), *Manthan* ("Churning"), *Bhumika* ("Character"), *Aakrosh* ("Anguish"), *Ardhasatya* ("Half-truth")...

Music overwrites the lyrics

A further wrinkle was added to the development of film lyrics with the emergence of A.R. Rahman whose genius captured the nation's imagination with a fresh brand of music that was a breathtaking amalgamation of classical Hindustani and Carnatic *rāga*s, syncopated jazz rhythms, meticulous orchestration inspired by his Western classical training, and complex changes of tone and tune. His musical scores for South Indian films were such huge hits that these movies were dubbed in Hindi and re-released for a wider audience. The unfamiliar actors and the crude dubbing were more than offset by the wild popularity of the music. Lyricists were brought in to write fresh words for the songs and operated under the constraint of trying to write songs that would provide an acceptable level of lip synchronization.[4] The subordination of the lyrics to the tune and lip-synch became so overwhelming that we were treated to gems like *Strawberry āṅkheṃ* ("Strawberry eyes") and *Telephone dhun mein haṃsne vālī* ("The one who laughs like a telephone ringing").

This about-turn was quite dramatic since, at least until the 1980s, most lyricists were poets in their own right and first wrote out the words to the song based on the requirements of the script and then handed them over to the composers who set them to a tune. In an interview, a disgruntled Kaifi Azmi complained bitterly about the new trend of lyricists being asked to fit words around already composed musical scores "*Ye to vahī bāt huī*," he said "*ki kisī ne kahā ki ye khabar khudī hai; is size kī lāś le āo!*" ("It is like being told that a grave has already been dug and now an appropriately sized corpse has to be found to fit in it").

The most successful lyricist of today, Javed Akhtar, says that the emphasis is now on the tune and it is up to the songwriter to find the right words, and just as importantly, the appropriate sound that works for the melody. The following comment by Akhtar in an interview with Munni Kabir is interesting in and of itself, but also points to the diminishing importance of the words vis-à-vis the sound.

> The meaning of the words is important but so is their phonetic effect. Ultimately the song is being written to be sung. So it should *sound* extremely good... What I'm going to say might sound very strange, but every sound has a certain visual effect. If you take "j": now "ja" has a sparkle that is very white. While the sound of "cha" also has a sparkle, it's somehow yellow or golden. "Ta" sounds like throwing a ball on a solid floor. But if you throw the ball on wet ground, then you get the sound "tha". If you hit the ball against a hollow wooden wall, you'll hear a "dha". Sounds create different images in your mind. Like "dha" is a sticky sound, "gha" is a dense sound, "ga" is clean.
> (Kabir 1999: 123)[5]

Despite the constraints under which he writes, Javed Akhtar does produce the occasional lyric that reminds one of the time that once was, when Hindi film songs pressed the cause of social justice, a time that seems to have long gone:

Fūṭpāthoṃ ke hūṃ rahnevāle, rātoṃ ne pālā ham voh ujāle,
Ākāś sar pe pairoṃ tale, hai dūr tak ye zamīn,
Aur to apnā koī nahīṃ, aur to apnā koī nahīṃ.
Bacpan meṃ khele gham se, nirdhan gharoṃ ke beṭe,
Phūloṃ kī sej nahīṃ, kāṃṭoṃ pe ham haiṃ leṭe.
Dukh meṃ rahe sau gham *sahe, dil ye kahe.*
Roṭī jahāṃ, hai svarg apnā vahīṃ.
We are the pavement dwellers, we the light that has been sheltered by the nights,
Our companions are the sky ahead, the ground beneath our feet,
And none else, none else
Our childhood spent playing with sorrow, sons of poor houses:
Our beds made not of flowers, but thorns.

We live with unhappiness, suffer sadness, and say with our heart:
That our heaven is where we can find bread.
(song from Yash Chopra's *Mashaal* 1984)

Conclusion

Peter Manuel, describing the Frankfurt School's analysis of popular culture, writes that "modern capitalism operated through the acquiescence of a depoliticized, alienated and generally stupefied public. The mass media (and in Adorno's thought, popular music), played essential roles in legitimizing the status quo by stultifying critical consciousness, commodifying and disarming oppositional art, and promoting consumerism and the myth of a classless society" (Manuel 1993: 9). In this context, the media function as "manipulative instruments" that seek to promote the voices of those who are comfortable with the status quo while delegitimizing the voices of those who challenge and subvert the relationships of power and domination in inequitable social systems. It is no surprise then that the content that is produced in Hindi cinema, including its lyrics, tends towards escapist fantasies and commodity fetishism played out in chimerical dreamscapes.

At the same time, it is important to remind ourselves that popular culture is a site of contestations, negotiations, mediations, and rearticulations, a space where hegemonic and oppositional values symbolically and explicitly engage one another. This chapter then, is partly the mourning of that which has passed, but it is also an attempt to remind ourselves that the current struggles for social justice have a history, and a celebration of those who helped produce it.

In the movie *Kabhi Kabhie* ("Sometimes," 1976), Sahir wrote a song, that anticipates the end of his period as a poet:

Maiṃ pal do pal kā śāyar hūṃ,
Pal do pal merī kahānī hai,
Pal do pal merī hastī hai,
Pal do pal merī javānī hai.
I am a poet of a brief moment or two,
My story is a passing one,
My life is ephemeral,
My youth, transient.

Kal aur āyeṃge naghmoṃ kī khiltī kaliyāṃ cunne vale,
Mujh se behtar kahne vāle, tum se behtar sunne vale.
Kal koī mujh ko yād kare, kyoṃ koī mujh ko yād kare?
Masrūf zamānā mere liye, kyoṃ waqt apnā barbād kare?
Maiṃ pal do pal ka śāyar hūṃ.
Tomorrow, there will be others harvesting the blooming buds of fresh songs,
Others who will write better than I could, others who will listen better than you can.

Who will remember me tomorrow, why should anyone?
Why would this busy world waste its time on me?
I am a poet of but the moment.

But Sahir did more than just write in and for the moment. He not only left behind an oeuvre that still plays on our radios and stereos, but also inspired a whole lot of others like Shailendra, Hasan Kamal, Javed Akhtar, and occasionally, even the not-quite-progressive Anand Bakshi to follow in his footsteps. Listening to a tape of songs from the 1971 movie *Dushman* ("Enemy"), with lyrics by Anand Bakshi, I did a double-take when a song (*Dillī kā Qutub Minār dekho, Bambay śahar kī bahār dekho*; "Look at Delhi's Qutub Minar, look at Bombay's spring") suddenly sprung the lines:

Logoṃ ko paise se pyār dekho!
Zālim ye sarmāyādār dekho!
Look at how people love wealth!
Look at the oppressive capitalist!

The word *sarmāyādār* stands out because it is a legacy of the progressive poets, their contribution to popular vocabulary. Its explicit use reminds us of the time when lyrics and poetry were defined by the PWA, and when film songs thought it appropriate to unselfconsciously critique the disproportionate accumulation of wealth by a few (the *sarmāyādārs*).

Perhaps because he recognized his influence, or perhaps merely in hope, Sahir, in a rare moment of self-assertion, added a coda to his *Kabhi Kabhie* song, that in our opinion, is an apt comment on the generation of PWA poets:

Maiṃ har ek pal ka śāyar hūṃ,
Har ek pal merī kahānī hai,
Har ek pal merī hastī hai,
Har ek pal merī javānī hai.
I am a poet for all times,
My story is forever,
My life, unending,
My youth, eternal.

Notes

1 Ishwar is one of the ways Hindus refer to God; Allah is the Muslims' name for God.

2 As an aside, it is interesting to note that Hindi film comedians often chose to take on Christian names such as Johnny Walker, Polson, Charlie, Johnny Lever; but that is another story.

3 See also Kesavan 1994: 244–57. Kesavan also talks about the influence of Hindi literary stalwarts such as Bharatendu Harishchandra, Pramath Nath Mitra and Thibo Babu in the role Hindi writers played in the domain of popular culture.

4 The instructions given to these lyricists included ones like "write this verse without using the 'm' sound" since saying anything with "m" in it required the lips to come together and would interfere with the lip-synch of the song.

5 This logic presumably leads Akhtar (in our opinion, an outstanding lyricist) to write songs like: *Āp kitne sweet kitne nek ho; Birthday kā jaise koī cake ho*, or: "You are so sweet and virtuous; Just like a birthday cake." Sweet, OK. But a *virtuous* cake?!

References

Kabir, N.M. (1999) *Talking Films: Conversations on Hindi Cinema with Javed Akhtar*, New Delhi: Oxford University Press.

Kaul, G. (1998) *Cinema and the Indian Freedom Struggle*, New Delhi: Sterling Publishers.

Kesavan, M. (1994) "Urdu, Awadh and the Tawaif: The Islamicate Roots of Indian Cinema," in Z. Hasan (ed.) *Forging Identities*, New Delhi: Kali for Women.

Malik, Y. (1988) "Socialist Realism and Hindi Novels," in C. Coppola (ed.) *Marxist Influences and South Asian Literature*, New Delhi: Chanakya Publications.

Manuel, P. (1993) *Cassette Culture: Popular Music and Technology in North India*, New Delhi: Oxford University Press.

Thoraval, Y. (2000) *The Cinemas of India (1896–2000)*, New Delhi: MacMillan.

11 *Dharmputra* and the Partition of India*

Cecilia Cossio

Introduction

The Partition of British India in 1947, with the creation of two nation-states—India and Pakistan—has been the bloodiest and most traumatic event in the history of this part of the world. Bloody, for the number of victims it caused, counting the dead and the displaced; and traumatic, for the suffering, social laceration and hate that followed, leaving an infected wound that has proved difficult to heal. It is generally accepted in Indian historiography that Partition was in no small measure caused by Muslim separatism, the political interests of the Muslim League and its leader Muhammad Ali Jinnah, *Qa'id-e-'azam* ("supreme leader" of the Muslims) from the late 1930s. However the publication in 1985 of Ayesha Jalal's book on Jinnah breathed new life into the "revisionist theory" that sees the events of 1947 more as the fruit of the intransigent policy of the Indian National Congress than of Muslim separatism (Roy 1993). It is not our intention to review the history of Partition, but only to reaffirm that the question is still foremost in people's mind as we study how it is treated in literature and film.

The partition in Hindi literature and cinema

The sociocultural effects of the division of the country are also reflected in the body of narrative literature written in Hindi, Urdu, Panjabi and Bengali. Alok Bhalla, editor of a short story anthology on the theme (1994), observes that these works present similar characteristics, including the memory of a common and shared history. The ways of life of the villages or small cities reveal feelings of closeness and interrelation between the different communities even if they are not happy utopian communities free of friction. Moments of conflict are recognized and recorded, but the experience of life appeared secure enough to permit society to activate mechanisms for the containment of tensions. Since the narrative memory does not recognize religious-based community separation in the everyday life of pre-Partition India, these works manifest in general a sense of extreme bewilderment in the face of the events and an inability to understand the collective madness that was unleashed. Practically no text identifies any (historical or social) reason for the separation and the massacres, and they are not held to be the consequence of an ancient hatred between Hindus and Muslims or between Muslims and Sikhs (Bhalla 1999: 3120–1).

Compared to the literary works on the Partition, the cinematographic production appears less rich at first. One reason may be that since the medium of cinema seeks to reach a vast and diversified audience, caution is called for in broaching such a delicate issue. Moreover, filmmakers have to work within restrictions imposed by a rigid censorial control. The first films that attempted to tell the story of the event or some aspect of it appeared more than a decade after 1947: for example, *Chalia* (1960, d. Manmohan Desai), which dealt with the tragic aspect of the abduction, rape, killing and suicide of women during Partition. A decade later, in 1973, *Garm Hava* ("Hot Wind," d. M.S. Sathyu) was released, the first film that dealt with the situation of the Muslims who remained in India. Finally, in 1988, Govind Nihalani, who fled Karachi after Partition, made a television film, transmitted in serial form: *Tamas* ("Darkness"), based on the novel of the same name by Bhishm Sahni (who in the film plays the role of an old Sikh). It was the first Hindi cinematographic work that dealt in a direct—not idealized, disguised or figurative—manner with the tragic events of 1947. After the destruction of the Ayodhya mosque by Hindu extremists on December 6, 1992, other films on similar subjects have begun to appear, as expressions of the "new cinema:"[1] *Mammo* (1994, d. Shyam Benegal); *Naseem* (1995, d. Saeed Akhtar Mirza); *Train to Pakistan* (1997, d. Pamela Rooks); *1947–The Earth* (1998, d. Deepa Mehta); *Karvan* ("Caravans," 1999, d. Pankaj Butaliya); and *Pinjar* ("The Cage," 2003, d. Chandra Prakash Dvivedi).[2] In these films we find the same features as in the literary works: dismay in the face of an event that appears to lack any historical and social motivation, madness that transforms "normal" people into bloodthirsty beasts, a sense of bewilderment, an inability to understand a world that has suddenly become alien, and the memory of a time now irrevocably lost, a time that was not always peaceful and harmonious but familiar, consolidated, and secure. Thus, Partition returns to the screen forty years after the event, precisely when Hindu extremism seems to have struck a chord in some strata of the population. It is perhaps this phenomenon that has induced sensitive filmmakers to return in time and present a drama that itself seems to be striving to return: the historical film often projects upon the past the problems and fears of the present, in an effort to comprehend them.

Dharmputra, novel and film: synopses

Dharmputra, published in 1954, is a rather short novel (176 small-sized pages in the edition consulted, Catursen 1985; henceforth: DhP), divided into 42 chapters, written by a particularly prolific author, Acarya Catursen Shastri (1891–1960).[3] The title signifies "a son taken in and brought up according to *dharma*," where *dharma* stands for the code of right religious, ethical, and social behavior of the Hindus; but a translation closer to the true meaning of the story is "son by faith." The *Dharmputra* of the novel is, in fact, a son raised as a Hindu, who discovers he is a Muslim during Partition, that is, at the very moment when the tension between Hindus and Muslims reaches its climax. Inspired by this novel, noted filmmaker Yash Chopra made his film of the same name in 1961.[4]

Novel

The events take place between the first noncooperation campaign (1920–22) and 1947. The novel starts as a luxury automobile pulls up in front of the office of doctor Amritray and an elderly Muslim, elegantly dressed, gets out. The man introduces himself: he is Nawab Mushtaq Ahmad Salar Jang Bahadur, an old friend of Amritray's father. The reason for his visit is his granddaughter Husnbanu, who is pregnant, but betrothed to Nawab Vazir Alikhan. Amritray fears that the old man is going to ask him to perform an illegal operation; instead, the Nawab, in the name of the friendship that bound him to the doctor's father, asks him to bring up the baby as if it were his own, promising to provide the child with a substantial income. Amritray is stunned, but after speaking with Husnbanu, whose beauty and personality deeply impress him, he decides to accept the proposal, which is accepted also by his wife Aruna, who has not yet borne children.

The birth of the child, Dilip, takes place in Mussoorie, at the Nawab's summer residence. Back in Delhi, the Nawab gives a party to celebrate the birth of Amritray's son, grandson of his dearest friend. He also announces his intention to give the child half of his own wealth. There is a complication: Amritray has fallen in love with Husnbanu, who herself is not indifferent, but after a painful conversation they will be brother and sister. After a last farewell to the child and to Aruna, with whom she has established a deep bond, Banu departs to get married. A sterile destiny awaits her: her husband turns out to be impotent and afflicted with leprosy.

The years pass and Dilip now has two brothers, Sushil and Shishir, and a sister, Karuna. They all study at the university, but have different inclinations. Sushil is a communist, Shishir a Congress member, while Karuna is interested only in humanity. Dilip is a member of Rashtriya Sangh. His parents prepare to arrange his marriage with Maya, daughter of Ray Radhakrishna, a well-known lawyer with progressive ideas, but Dilip categorically refuses: he will never marry a woman educated abroad, daughter of an impure family that does not observe *dharma* and treats foreigners and Muslims as equals. He even offends his potential father-in-law by bringing up questions of caste (Ray Radhakrishna had been expelled from his caste long before for having gone to England to work). Maya wishes to avenge the offense, but the meeting between the two young people is fatal for both: they fall in love. Unfortunately, by this time relations between the two families have cooled.

Meanwhile, World War II reaches Asia. The Congress does not intend to support the war alongside Britain; in August of 1942 Gandhi launches the Quit India movement, demanding that the British withdraw from the country. Thousands of nationalists and the entire Congress leadership is arrested. The communists, who have been backing Britain since Russia entered the war, are considered traitors to the national cause. Shishir is arrested, and so is Dilip after publicly inciting his companions to fight the British to restore *dharma*. The two brothers are briefly reunited in jail, but Dilip is transferred to another prison, where he strikes up a warm friendship with other prisoners. After his release, Dilip throws himself into political activity in order to avoid thinking about his beloved Maya, who in her turn continues to love him. When Aruna learns of this, she is prepared to arrange the wedding, but Dilip is unable to open up with her.

Just then, after twenty-eight years, Husnbanu, now widowed, returns to Delhi to live at Rangmahal, the palace of her deceased grandfather. In all those years, there had been no contact with Amritray's family, so as not to disturb their peace. Now Banu renews her ties with her "brother" and "sister," but does not want to meet her son. Meanwhile the Partition of the country comes into force. In Delhi too there are violent clashes between Hindus and Muslims. Dilip participates with a crowd of companions and heads for Rangmahal to burn it down. However, Amritray and Aruna reach the palace, ready to defend Banu. The fire rages and Dilip manages to rescue everyone, but he is seriously injured. When he regains consciousness, he is able to speak with Maya and reveal his feelings to her. Banu does not have the courage to meet him, so Aruna reveals the truth to Dilip. After three painful days, Dilip goes to meet his real mother and ask her forgiveness. Fearing that the revelation can hold grave consequences for the family of his adoptive parents, he decides to move away with Banu, despite Amritray's and Aruna's attempts to dissuade him. Only Maya is able to persuade him to stay. In the final pages of the book, Amritray and Aruna on one side, Ray Radhakrishna and his wife on the other, welcome the guests to the wedding of their children, Dilip and Maya, while Husnbanu extols the virtues of the bride and groom.

Film

The film is divided in two parts. The first part starts, as the novel, with a luxury automobile pulling up in front of the office of doctor Amritray (Manmohan Krishna). An elderly Muslim gentleman gets out, the Nawab Badruddin (Ashok Kumar), who was a close friend of Amritray's father. With him is his daughter Husnbanu (Mala Sinha), Amritray's "sister." The reason for their visit is Banu's pregnancy. Amritray recalls the extraordinary friendship between his father and the Nawab and the deep affection that ties him to Banu. Together with his wife Savitri (Nirupa Roy), he decides to raise Banu's child as their own.

The child, Dilip, is born at the Nawab's summer residence in Shimla. Back in Delhi, at the birth celebration he arranged for his friend's grandson, the Nawab announces he will give half of his own wealth to him. Subsequently he decides to make a pilgrimage with his daughter. While traveling, they encounter Banu's lover, Javed, who, unaware of her pregnancy, had left Delhi after the Nawab's refusal to consent to the wedding. Now it is the Nawab who asks him to accept Banu as his bride. Everything seems to be going well, and Banu becomes pregnant again. Then fate strikes: a fall down the stairs makes her lose the child, as well as the possibility of having other children. The family decides to build a "bridge" joining the two houses (located across the street from one another) so that Dilip can go from one to the other without danger.

Meanwhile the strength of the national movement grows in the country. During a demonstration against the British, Nawab Badruddin is killed by the police. Javed and Banu leave Delhi and go to live abroad.

The second part of the movie starts with the return of Javed and Banu. India has profoundly changed, Hindus and Muslims have gone their separate ways and the phrase *Hindū-Muslim bhāī-bhāī* ("Hindu and Muslim: brother to each other") has been superseded by two others: *Allahu-akbar* ("Allah is great") and *Jay Bajraṅgbalī* ("Victory to Bajrangbali"). But the relations with Amritray and Savitri have not changed: they are still one single family. Banu meets Dilip (Shashi Kapoor), but he takes his distance: he has become a radical Hindu—an unbearable fact in the eyes of his "parents." His siblings, Sushil, Sudesh and Rekha, affectionately make fun of him for his manias.

Dilip does not want to marry Mina (Indrani Mukherjee), the only daughter of a lawyer-friend of the family, because she studied abroad for two years, and thus has become impure. Banu and Savitri, with Rekha's help, try to bring the two young people together. They meet at the university, where Dilip chants ones of his poems for independence, and again at Rekha's house; Dilip's poetry and a walk in the rain are decisive. The families plan a big wedding, though under a cloud of growing tension between Hindus and Muslims.

At that point, Partition comes into force and there are bloodbaths in Delhi. Javed is wounded and Amritray has him brought to his home for treatment. Dilip has gone off to take on the "enemy" and has been thrown out of his family home. He incites his companions to burn the Muslim house linked to his house by the terrace-bridge. However, Amritray and Savitri block his way: they have come to die with Banu. In these circumstances, Savitri feels obligated to reveal the truth to Dilip. He is dumbstruck. Then, fearing for the life of his four parents, he switches sides and confronts his ex-companions, at which point the police arrive to disperse them. Mina had called the police. She has come to be with Dilip, be he Hindu or Muslim.

Relations between the characters in the two narratives

Present throughout the film are the features of the Partition narrative as outlined above: the memory of a shared history and dismay in the face of the successive social breakup. This is less evident however in the novel. Here, close relations are created only between Amritray, Aruna, and Banu. The closeness of their fathers is only mentioned indirectly. Amritray does not recognize the Nawab, even if his father has always spoken of him; the Nawab has to introduce himself to him and remind him of his friendship with his father and his own generosity in having borne the young man's medical school expenses abroad. The two men always remain distant.

In the film, by contrast, Amritray greets the Nawab warmly, calling him *cācājān* ("uncle," "father's brother," with the suffix of respect and affection, "life" or "dear"). Furthermore, three flashbacks that follow throw light on moments of a long and affectionate association.

First flashback: Amritray is looking at a photo of his father and the Nawab engrossed in playing chess; the photo comes alive and the two men smoke and laugh, pulling each other's leg. Amritray arrives and announces he has been promoted with top grades; the two men show joy and pride; the Nawab gives the young man a handful of money to celebrate the result.

Second flashback: The Nawab consoles Amritray, embracing him: "Today your father has not died, today my friend has died. And as long as I live also Gulshanray, your father, will live." He himself will fulfill his friend's wishes and send Amritray to medical school abroad. He concludes sadly: "Today my world has become a desert! He was my only friend and now he is gone."

Third flashback: It is the festival of *rakṣā-bandhan*, when sisters tie a sacred thread or *rākhī* to the wrists of their brothers (real or chosen). Banu comes looking for Amritray to tie on the *rākhī*, asking for a reward. Amritray wants first to receive a sweet from her, then he gives her a coin. "Finally I've had something from this stingy brother!" Banu says, laughing; and Amritray: "Crazy girl! You have everything. The meaning of the *rākhī* is that a brother would give his very life to protect his sister." Banu looks at him affectionately: "My big brother!" and runs away happily.

This last scene underlines the difference in the relationship between Amritray and Banu in the two narratives. In the novel, Amritray is subjugated by Banu's personality and beauty: only with pain and hardship does he manage to return to a serene life with his wife. In the film, the very first scenes inform the spectator that the two grew up as siblings together and share a strong affection. This affectionate bond between the two families—and not a request by the Nawab—is what determines Amritray and Savitri's decision to keep the child. In the novel the decision appears as an act influenced by Banu's charm, on the one hand; on the other, as a sort of blackmail/transaction: "I was your father's friend, I paid for your studies; now you become the *dharmpitā*, or 'adoptive father,' of the child, and I shall give substantial wealth."

The episode of the birth celebration of the child in the two texts similarly highlights the difference in the relationships. Let us compare the Nawab's address to the guests:

Novel

> This is doctor Amritray, the son of my friend Bansgopalray. Ever since he was a child I have considered him as a son. Bansgopalray and I had no problems of religious difference. We were intimate friends. It was I who insisted on sending Amritray abroad and I paid his study expenses. Now that he has had a son and Bansgopal is not here to participate in this joy, I do it in his place and this joy I feel is not only external, it is in my heart. And I shall prove this to you now. If Bansgopal were alive, he would do the same. (. . .) I have no intention of presenting an example of friendship to the world, or of showing off Hindu-Muslim brotherhood; I look only to the love in my heart, the emotion

> and the duty. And today I divide my wealth in two parts, one part I give to my granddaughter, princess Husnbanu, and one part to my friend's son, to this little angel.
>
> (DhP 19–20)

Film

> Dear friends, we have invited you here for the names-giving ceremony of doctor Amritray's first son. You know about the ties that bind us. The friendship between me and Gulshanray, his father, was held up by people as an example. Some elderly people affectionately used to make fun of us calling us Laila and Majnu.[5] There are no longer friendships like that today. Whether the times or men are to blame, I wouldn't know. Perhaps times have changed. Perhaps with the increase in machines, men too have become machines. Or perhaps today men for whom affection and friendship are the most precious thing are no longer born. Or perhaps men no longer have need of affection and friendship. But I do need them. Out of the affection and friendship that tied me to Gulshanray, today I have wanted this ceremony for Amritray's son. I have no intention of holding up examples of friendship or of repeating slogans such as "Hindu and Muslim: brother to each other." The accounts of life are settled with life.... I want to announce in front of all of you that my wealth will be divided in two parts. One part will go to my only daughter, Husnbanu; the other part will go to Amritray's son, Dilip.

The two speeches are similar only in appearance. In the first case, the Nawab *informs* the guests of a deep friendship between men of different religions, in the name of which a donation is made that otherwise would be rather strange. In the second case, the Nawab not only *reminds* the guests of the time of a deep friendship well-known to them all, but emphasizes how the changing times make those relationships of intimate closeness increasingly rare: the reference to Hindu-Muslim brotherhood appears almost as an addition, required not by the fact that the two men were of different religions but only by the changing of the times, which shifts the focus from men as subjects to the attributes or adjectives of men (machine, Hindu, Muslim).

The normal practice of intercommunity frequentation of the past is recalled also in the novel, but in a different tone than in the film.

> At that time Pakistan had not yet been created, neither were there conflicts between Hindus and Muslims. In Delhi, the verses of Zafar, Ghalib, Zauq and Mir [famous Urdu poets] were heard in every alley.... The Hindus were true Hindus and the Muslims true Muslims. But this did not compromise the mutual feeling of brotherhood. They frequented one another's homes, they ate and drank together. When a Hindu visited a Muslim's home, the host carefully instructed his servant: "Go to the *tamolī* [betel seller], have him

> prepare some *pān* [betel] and bring it here as is fitting." And the *pān* arrived wrapped in fresh leaves, hanging from a string, not touched by the Muslim servant.
>
> (DhP 28–9)

Similarly, on the occasion of Banu's wedding, in which Hindus and Muslims participate, the food preparation and consumption is separate for each community, also because—as the author informs us—the Nawab enjoys a vast network of relations with Hindus and Muslims and considers it his duty to respect the convictions of each (DhP 29). In the film, the fact of the two families, that is, Hindus and Muslims, eating together seems altogether usual. In the novel, the portrait of Indian society of the time appears more realistic, at least as far as the more traditionalist classes are concerned. Here, intercommunal dining is shown as exceptional, revealing the intimate and affectionate bond between the characters.

Both film and novel include a scene where Banu and Amritray's wife eat together from the same tray. This scene is more intense in the novel, where the sense of "transgression" is deeper, especially for Banu. She appreciates the greatness of Aruna's heart, which dares to challenge dogmas of purity and impurity in the name of a higher relationship (DhP 147). In the film, Savitri unconcernedly picks up a morsel of the food they are sharing and puts it into Banu's mouth. Banu is surprised at first, but immediately reciprocates. The "sin" is liquidated with nonchalance by Savitri, who with a shrug of her shoulders asserts the socially constructed character of religion.[6]

In the film, the son of Muslims is welcomed as one's own son, for whom there never arises the slightest feeling of "difference." Dilip, even when he becomes a Hindu extremist and thus very far from Amritray and Savitri's way of thinking, will always be seen and loved as a flesh-and-blood son. In the novel, by contrast, there are a number of occasions when Amritray and Aruna have an acute sensation of Dilip's "otherness," with a sentiment that in some way they transmit to him. The distance manifests itself especially when the question of Dilip's wedding is most urgent. Amritray is concerned about the deception they would perpetrate against another Hindu family by proposing a Muslim husband, thus "contaminating" an innocent girl. On the other hand, the truth would be no less traumatic: not only for Dilip, but also for their own family which, with regard to Hindu society, would be impure for having raised a Muslim as their son. This attitude is consistent with the premises of the narration and with social reality. In the film, this problem simply does not occur; it is only Dilip's refusal that angers his parents.

The revelation of the truth too takes on different importance in the two narratives. In the novel, this part covers a period of six days, narrated in the final chapters (37 through 42). The moment of greatest intensity is the meeting between the three parents and Dilip. Here, the mutual relationships seem deeper than elsewhere; also Amritray and Aruna's affection for Dilip appears more sincere, precisely when they seem to deny him: "I want to shoot Dilip, that devil of a son" (DhP 164). Only then does Banu understand that this young man is her son.

And Aruna confirms: "It is truly Dilip, sister, look at him for the last time and for the first time." Then, crying, Aruna embraces her and invites her husband to shoot. To save his parents, Dilip will also save Banu and the two Muslim servants. Later, Aruna will reveal the truth to him: "When he had heard her out, Dilip . . . did not respond. He did not cry, did not get excited, was not shaken, did not move. . . . he remained as relaxed as before, without a gesture, without a word, without movement, like a stone" (DhP 177–8). And so he remains for three more days, while the rest of the family is in anguish for his possible reaction. In the end, Dilip goes to recognize and embrace his mother. His intention of departing with her, to keep Amritray's family from suffering socially, is derailed by Maya's words: "They say that even the gods of stone are pleased by true adoration and grant the desired pardon, but you have shown yourself to be more pitiless than a stone; and why shouldn't you, you are not Hindu, so how could the greatness of a Hindu divinity come alive in you!" (DhP 183). Dilip, defeated, entrusts himself to Maya: "Maya, take this life of mine, it is yours. Come, let us go to greet my mother" (DhP 184) and together they go to touch the two mothers' feet.

In the film, the revelation has greater dramatic intensity, since it is concentrated in a much shorter span of time, which takes up and condenses chapters 37 and 40 of the novel in a sequence of three scenes, broken up by a scene of devastation. The first scene is the encounter on the terrace-bridge of Amritray, Savitri, and Banu with Dilip, who has come to tear down that symbol of union. It includes the revelation. The second scene shows Dilip's reaction, surrounded by the entire family. Dilip is devastated by the discovery, because his entire world has been shattered: "You have put the shroud on my living body," he says in desperation; "The fire I have set with my own hands today will burn me." In the third scene, Dilip confronts his ex-companions and Mina intervenes. It will not be the sorrowful reassurances of the four parents that relieve him but the words of Mina, to whom he had said that he no longer had a name. "I did not fall in love with your name," Mina replies, "it was with you I fell in love, it is you I love."

The path to Partition in the novel: epic of conquest, epic of resistance

Both novel and film incorporate historical parts about Partition and the events that led up to it. In the novel the historical episodes are at times integrated into the narration, but more often presented separately, nearly as a parenthesis or even as a separate chapter. These are historical-didactic essays or comments, redundant with respect to the story. The author situates the story at the watershed of World War II, which divides the world into two parts: the capitalist countries, led by "old conservative fatties" whose catchword is "economy;" and the "democratic" (*janvādī*) countries, led by the new generations whose catchword is "labor" (DhP 67). At the head of the latter we find the young Soviets who thought that after they had defeated Fascism they would have liberated men throughout the world from slavery. Young people all over the world looked to this work of the young Soviets with veneration. In the hearts of millions of the world's youth their name burned like letters of fire. Meanwhile, the Anglo-American bloc wanted to drown the world in a river of blood once again. The dollar-king of America now resounded with the same slogan that the German Fascists had been repeating until yesterday. And now was the hour of decision for the destiny of the world's people. There were only two roads before them: to be free, or to be slaves of Anglo-American imperialism (DhP 68).

Also in India communism is asserting itself, but since the British are in command its sympathizers are kept under surveillance.

Being communist was considered an unforgivable sin, something like being traitors to the state. But "the progressive youth did what they held right to do, fearing neither gallows nor prison. In fact, they had already come to be feared by the government" (DhP 69).

The nearly two pages on the communist movement and on the two blocs are not particularly important for the rest of the chapter (three and a half pages), apart from communicating the narrator's thoughts on the question; the history of the world and of the country are tied into the story of the novel through the diverse inclinations of Amritray's children: Dilip is connected with militant and anti-Muslim Hinduism, Sushil is a communist and Shishir a Gandhian Congress member.

In 1939, when the war begins, India, as part of the British Empire, is involved, but the Congress decides not to support the war. At this point we have another historical-political chapter (24) relating the events that will lead to Gandhi's Quit India Resolution, with the slogan "do or die" (August 1942). This is unquestionably an important moment in the story, but the presentation is conspicuously didactic. The narrator recounts with full particulars, all the facts—or his interpretation of them—about the events in Europe and the repercussions on the various members of the nationalist movement: the apparently unstoppable German advance; the difficult position of the British; the Congress led by apathetic old men, incapable of a coherent political line; the vital energy of Subhash Chandra Bose, his flight to Germany and reappearance in Burma; the Japanese advance on Singapore; the British, American, and Australian soldiers in India; the famine of 1943; the "burning arrow" ("do or die") shot by Gandhi, followed by the "August revolution" (DhP 106–8). Only in the following chapter, after this "history lesson," are the events tied into the plot of the novel: Shishir takes part in the August revolt and is arrested, followed by Dilip who spurs on the revolt among the Rashtriya Sangh sympathizers. At this point, the author (like the nationalists) loses sympathy for the communist movement because Russia enters the war alongside the Allied forces, that is, the Anglo-American imperialism whose intention it is to "drown the world in a river of blood." The Indian communists, represented by Sushil, as they are tied to the Soviet decisions and line up on the same side, become stigmatized as traitors.

> [The communists] had become supporters of the English. They raised their voices against the Congress. Questions of equality and socialism had been left behind and diplomatic maneuvers had led them astray from the straight and narrow path. ...For this reason the communists were boycotted

> everywhere and were considered traitors, backstabbers. . . . Not even the English trusted them. . . . A people as intelligent as the English understood at once that those who betrayed the trust of their own country would most certainly have betrayed also theirs.
>
> (DhP 112–13)

A few chapters later we find another "history lesson": an essay on Subhash Chandra Bose and Jawaharlal Nehru. Subhash, a controversial figure for his war choices (siding with the Axis forces), but much loved by the people, is depicted in a positive light. Nehru, on the other hand, is not only portrayed negatively as an ambiguous personality, self-important, but also irresolute, submissive to Gandhi and to party discipline to the point of betraying his principles. This critique is barely tempered by a generic acknowledgment of his anti-imperialist stance (DhP 122–6).

The author examines the reasons for the antagonism between the different communities prior to Partition, and, quite conventionally, places the blame primarily on the British. They are held responsible for the division of the nationalists into three branches: Congress, led by Nehru; the untouchables, under the leadership of B.R. Ambedkar (1891–1956); and the Muslims, headed by Jinnah. Still, the person considered mainly responsible is Jinnah, who is quoted saying "We are neither brothers of the Hindus, nor their companions. We have a separate nation of our own, with separate interests" (DhP 153). According to the author, while Jinnah was able to represent Muslim interests in an exclusive and imperious manner, Congress was unable to do the same for the Hindus, since it was a national body. Muslim separatism is attributed to Islam itself, which is seen not only as a religion, "but is a political and social organization erected on the foundations of religion. In this regard, it was very different from the Hindu religion and from Hindu sentiments" (DhP 153). Precisely for this reason, the organizations that represent the Hindus, such as Hindu Mahasabha, are feeble in the defense of their own community; but more blameworthy still is Congress, which allows the Muslim minority to gain an equal footing in the negotiations: "By definition, Congress was a national association and recognized Hindus, Muslims, Christians, Parsis, all as a single nation, but in reality the representatives of these communities were not the representatives of a single nation. Particularly the Muslims who, considered a minority up to a few years earlier, were becoming equal partners" (DhP 135). They were seen to have a double advantage: they could negotiate both as the Muslim League and as Muslim members of the Congress. "This means: what is mine is mine, but also a part of what is yours is mine" (DhP 154).

This assessment agrees generally with the accepted narrative of the struggle for independence, but with a strong Hindu coloring. In this view, the common struggle is undermined by the particular interests of the Muslims (and by the untouchables) who refuse to belong to the single homeland and want to manage their slice of inheritance on their own—a bigger slice than is their due. Congress is forced to give in, it is handicapped by being a "national" body albeit with a Hindu majority. However, the narrator asserts that the Hindu religion regards the heart and is not the base of a political and social structure! That slice, nonetheless, does not sate the appetite of the Muslims, who unleash the reign of terror. Blame for the massacres before and after Partition is placed in no uncertain terms on Pakistan alone, that is, on Muslims *tout court*.

> Pakistan had unleashed unrestrained behavior and in the twinkling of an eye in western Punjab and eastern Bengal the bazaar of clash, theft, fire, rape and murder was running wild. From all over reports of killings and depredations were pouring in; in the twinkling of an eye this chapter of the killings took on such vast proportions that it was without equal in the history of the human race. The pen is unable to describe now the demons' plays. Layalpur, Mintagumri, Shekhupura, Lahore and Gujranvala were strongholds of the Sikhs. The Sikhs were forced to flee them or die terrible deaths. In the bazaars of Lahore and Calcutta the flames of terrible fires shot up into the sky. The cries of pain of innocent women and children, of old people and youths, the sobs of the dying, resounded in the houses, in the alleys, in the bazaars, in the hospitals. From Calcutta the terrible flames of the fire reached Noakhali, Bihar, Allahabad, Bombay and Delhi.
>
> (DhP 154–5)

The narrator does not mention how the aggressive and conservative Hindu component in Congress that had increased considerably in the 1920s, played a decisive role in widening the rift with the Muslim League, particularly after the 1937 provincial elections. Nor does he mention the role played by Hindus and Sikhs in the massacres. He combines the "Direct Action Day" of August 16, 1946 (the Calcutta massacre, with equally bloody responses in other parts of northern India) with the massacres that took place in Delhi after August 15, 1947, when the refugees brought news of the tragedy on the western border. Thus, the pages of *Dharmputra* paint a picture of Muslims armed to the teeth, long prepared for an uprising to conquer the city.

> The ambitions of the Delhi Muslims to repopulate the Mogul throne, drowned in wine and devoured by the fire of lust, in the deserted Red Fort, began flying as if they had put on wings.... Rifles, munitions, cannons, pistols, bombs, radio transmitters, everything was ready in the secret residences of Delhi.
>
> (DhP 155)

Between August and September of 1947, Delhi becomes the theater of bloody retaliation of Sikhs and Hindus against the Muslim inhabitants. Gandhi deserves most of the credit for the—however fragile—pacification, risking his life with a hunger strike to death, and finally ending up assassinated by Hindu fanatics. Several Delhi Muslims were forced to flee their homes to seek shelter in refugee camps that had been set up for them in some areas of the city (the largest were at Jama Masjid, Purana Qila, and Humayun's Tomb), where they lived in misery, aided only later on by the Indian authorities, barely recognized as Indian citizens (see Qidvaī 2000 and Pandey 1997, 2001).

The Delhi clashes—as interpreted by the author—are the part that is best integrated in the fictional events of the novel. Dilip takes part in the "battle of Sabzimandi," one of the neighborhoods most deeply involved in the riots. There is also a description of the procession of the Muslims, refugees in their own city, towards the refugee camp of Humayun's Tomb. At the surface, there is human commiseration, but the author can barely suppress a triumphant jubilation.

> But the Muslims' strength was broken and, frightened, they began to flee. Conquering Hindustan became a dream, reaching Pakistan became difficult. . . . Files of Muslims, with children and relatives loaded onto carriages and carts, cars and horses, with sad and frightened eyes, giving Delhi and the Red Fort looks of pain, left their homes and went towards Humayun's Tomb. In the city, Sikh refugees and young people of Rashtriya Sangh roamed boldly like tigers in the wild. After seven hundred years they saw these days. This Delhi was in truth a city of Muslims. The language, color, wealth, grace and urbanity of this place—everything was Muslim. For seven hundred years the Hindus, in semislavery, had rested their forehead on the threshold of Delhi. They [the Muslims] were leaving, leaving this very Delhi, like a lush garden, giving it looks of pain, seeing the Hindus, the age-old slaves, roaming like tigers through its rich streets.
>
> (DhP 160–1)

The novel does not present the events of Partition as a terrible consequence of political contraposition, but as the final act of an ancient war, unleashed by the Muslims to subjugate India. The massacre is not between desperate individuals, inhabitants of a single country, though of different faiths. Rather, they appear as the settling of accounts between two peoples: the foreign aggressors, the Muslims, who seven centuries earlier had swooped down to subjugate the Indian people, the Hindus, who were now driving them back. This reading of Indian history—of Hindu resistance against Muslim aggression—is derived from the Hindi historical narrative that developed between the end of the nineteenth and the beginning of the twentieth century (and has not gone out of style, if we consider the campaign for the destruction of the Ayodhya mosque). Such a reading is, to say the least, debatable and insulting. It establishes a false kinship between the Muslim invaders of the past (Turks, Afghans, Moghuls, and others) and the Muslim Indians of 1947, most of whom are descended from Hindu converts. Many of the Delhi Muslims, like millions of other Muslims in India, had chosen to be citizens of independent India, but ended up being at best second-class citizens.[7] The ending of the novel confirms this. Dilip's discovery of his Muslim origin, does not change his ideas on the relations of Muslims with India; hence he now cannot but feel he belongs to a community that is guilty of the "semislavery" in which it held the Hindus for centuries and that now, defeated, has to accept a condition of inferiority. Dilip is fortunate and will be able to enjoy privileges granted by magnanimous "victors," but in disguise: the truth remains buried in the circle of the families involved.

The path to Partition in the film: Congress-Nehruvian imprinting

The film gives us a different vision from the very first scene. The story begins in 1925, a few years after the first noncooperation campaign, which was a moment of great closeness between Congress and the Muslim League. By 1925, relations between the two organizations had deteriorated, but there were still some traces of their previous shared intents. That is what the director focuses on when showing images of a march for India's independence with slogans such as "Long live the revolution" and "Hindu and Muslim: brother to each other." A voice-over comments, establishing the guiding thought for the narration:

> The earth of this country is our mother. This earth is our shroud. For her we have sworn to die. Hindus and Muslims are the expression of a single reality, they are the name of a single culture, of a single civilization. Hindus and Muslims are two sons of a single country, who have the same destiny of life or of death, who share the same joy and the same pain. Hindus and Muslims were one, are one and will remain one. Hindus and Muslims are brothers, both ready to die for their homeland.

After this, the fictional story unfolds. After the building of the terrace-bridge between the two houses, we return to general politics. It is the time of the second Satyagraha campaign (1930–34), but the division between the two communities is growing deeper and deeper. The film shows an assembly of citizens, most of whom are Muslim, conservative and socially upper-class, with British representatives as guests. They distance themselves from the "disorders" created by common "delinquents" in the name of revolution and of independence and profess their loyalty to Britain, which all Indians should support. Although the name is not mentioned, the assembly embodies principally the Muslim League, portrayed in a Nehruvian interpretation, as an association linked to elitist community interests, not representative of the Muslim Indian population and, therefore, antinational. In the scene, Nawab Badruddin takes the word.

> The man who refuses to be the son of his own mother cannot be the son of anyone else. The man who betrays his country cannot be anybody's friend. The political voice that today calls the revolution a revolt you have already heard in 1857, when the war of liberation was fought.[8] People like you gave the name of treason to that war. The struggle against the chains of slavery is called treason and rebellion. Also that which you today call riots and disorders are declarations of freedom. ... I am descended from those whose corpses covered with wounds lie on the battlefield and you from those thieves who grew rich by selling their shrouds. You are the traitors, you are the vipers nurtured in our bosoms, more dangerous than the English for our country.

The Nawab will later participate in a demonstration for the boycotting and burning of foreign goods. While inciting the crowd to take down the British flag and replace it with the Indian tricolor, he is mortally wounded. He falls clutching the flag and murmuring "Long live the revolution! Hindu and Muslim, brothers to each other…" Thus perishes the symbol of a struggle that united Indian people of all communities, represented by Congress. It is not fortuitous that the character, who openly condemns the policy of the Muslim League and the ultraconservatives as relying on the foreign rulers to defend their own interests against the people's struggle, is himself a Muslim.

As in the novel, in the film too the historical commentary is presented almost parenthetically, often as a voice-over underlining the progression of action. For instance, in the sequence that separates the first part of the film from the second, the narrative points to the responsibility of the British in the Hindu-Muslim clash.

> Fifteen years have passed since the death of the Nawab Sahab. After his death Javed and Banu went abroad, while many political changes came about in India. The English were greatly concerned about Hindu-Muslim unity and sought new ways to fracture it. Seeing that power was about to slip through their fingers, they gave new impetus to the policy of "divide and rule." The result was that Hindus and Muslims began to take their distance from one another. Ancient time-honored bonds began to break.…The voice of Hindu-Muslim unity was suffocated by the noise of the cry "Allah is great" and "Victory to Bajrangbali."

The political and social changes are noted with dismay by Javed when he and Banu return to India just before Partition. He recalls the days of brotherhood and remarks on the shortness of human memory. The same sentiment resounds in Amritray's words: "People used to say 'Hindu and Muslim: brother to each other'; now all we hear is 'Hindi Hindu Hindustan' and 'we will take Pakistan.'" The clouding of the memory of a common history drives the events towards the dramatic outcome of Partition. Now the parenthesis has the face of a Congress leader who evidently represents Nehru, by now resigned to accept the inevitability of what is about to occur.

> If some Muslims who yesterday loved all of India today love only a part of it, never mind. If their love has been shrinking, so be it. Also brothers become divided. If they want to go and live on their own, let us let them go.…If they want the country to be divided, well, let it be divided!

While the novel fuses Jinnah, the League, and the Muslim population into a single guilty bloc, the film narrows the field to "some Muslims." In this, it follows the conventional Congress-inspired vision: Congress as a national and secular body, sole representative of the *entire* Indian people, is forced to accept the will of a minority to detach itself from the common homeland. This acceptance is a necessary evil to avoid greater evils and to obtain independence in the near future.

The words of the nameless Nehru-like character lead directly into the following scene, in which Dilip is arguing with his brothers Sudesh and Sushil. We see two views on the Muslims in collision, one sectarian and one secular, with the dooming possibility of accepting Partition as the lesser evil in the background.

Dilip: No, it must never be divided! . . . Bhārat belongs to Hindus. If Muslims don't want to live with Hindus, they may go. And if they don't go on their own, we will compel them to leave!

Sushil: . . . Bhārat belongs to all those who consider it to be their nation. The question is not the division of the country, it is a question of independence, of bringing this age-old slavery to an end. If we want to get rid of the British, we will have to stop this fighting among ourselves.

Dilip: And you will stop this fighting by dividing the country?

Sushil: If this is the way to get rid of our enemy, this is what we'll do.

Dilip: This country has been ruined by thinking like yours and people like you. Whatever the Muslims demanded, you kept on giving it to them. If it weren't for you, Muslims wouldn't have had the courage to confront us.

Sudesh: And if it weren't for you, Muslims wouldn't have demanded a separate nation. This idea of a second nation, of Pakistan, came to them because of Hindus like you. You consider Muslims untouchables, you've never considered them as equals.

Dilip: Certainly not! They have continued to work against Hindu *dharma*. They spread Islam with the sword!

Sudesh: Rubbish! British propaganda! . . .

Sushil: . . . Muslims ruled over India for hundreds of years. If they had used the sword, there wouldn't be a single Hindu left.

Dilip: Don't you know your own history? They destroyed thousands of temples to build mosques. But they could not vanquish the inner strength of Hindu *dharma*!

Sudesh: What is this *dharma* you are always talking about? There has been so much bloodshed everywhere in the name of religion, so many millions of innocent people killed. And you are still not satisfied! Religion is the most despicable thing today. It's all rubbish!

Dilip: One more word against *dharma* and I'll kill you!

On the one hand, the dialogue places part of the blame for the separatist intentions of the Muslims on intolerant Hindus such as Dilip, who refuse to recognize Muslims as full-fledged Indians. At the same time, it denies the popular belief about foreign Muslims who came to India to spread Islam with the sword, separating the invasions of the past from the social reality of contemporary India.

While in the novel no Muslim is portrayed as a patriot, and the Nawab is described as part of a vanishing aristocratic world, in the film the Nawab is the most fervent nationalist, the only character to give his life for the Indian cause. The last pages of the novel are devoted to the felicitous conclusion with reconciliation of all characters, interpreting Partition and the departure of the "vanquished" Muslims as a sort of happy ending for Indian—Hindu—history. The film, then, is worlds apart from the literary text, denouncing the clashes between the communities as the fruit of a wrong-headed policy of opposing interests.

The visual representation of Partition is resolved in the manner of popular cinema with a song. "Who are the dead, without name and without religion? Not men of two enemy countries, but sons of the same land." Later, Dilip imagines a world without religion, where only humanity has value. Mina agrees, "if there is no place for humanity here, we shall go elsewhere." Once again, parenthetically and as an epilogue, the Congress leader intervenes. We hear his voice, but the image shows Nehru in a newsreel of the independence days.

> No one will be forced to leave. This land belongs to those who consider it their motherland. What has occurred and is still occurring in the name of religion is for us a source of shame. Religion that makes man an enemy of man is not a true faith. What has blemished us is not religion, but those who mock religion using it for their own ends. Brothers, too, may be divided, but not with the sword; blood must not be divided from blood with the sword. We are all children of the same mother. And that mother is the land of our birth, our motherland. Humanity alone will be able to help the motherland, love alone will be able to save it. Hindus and Muslims are the two mainstays of this bond of civilization that is the bridge that unites them. And even when everything has collapsed, that bridge stands firm and will do so for ever.

The final shot is of the terrace-bridge, a symbol of Hindu-Muslim unity. The unity has been presented as fact ever since the first scene. It is interpreted as a social reality that has taken shape over centuries during which originally different cultures have lived together, have been modified and amalgamated by their reciprocal contact. A social reality that even this great collective tragedy cannot—or ought not—change. India, so the film asserts, is still the place of Indians, of whatever religion they may be. To sanction this union, Dilip and Mina, a Muslim and a Hindu, with the public approval of all, become man and wife. This conclusion is rather idealistic, for the epoch of the story and also for 1961, the year of the film's release. In fact, the film was a critical but not a popular success. Its failure at the box-office may be due to the position on Partition it expresses (however orthodox in general terms), but perhaps even more so because of the happy ending of a love story beyond acceptable limits. Had Dilip been killed in the confrontation with his former companions, or Mina while trying to save Dilip (a common filmi solution for love stories involving a couple "at risk," that is of different caste or communities, etc.), the response of the public, moved by the sacrifice, might have been warmer.

An unconcluded conclusion

Compared to the secularism of the film, the sectarian spirit of the novel—fifty years after its publication—actually appears closer to the current mood of a country where militant Hinduism enjoys widespread approval. Catursen's text in fact gives us very little of those elements which Alok Bhalla identified as common in Partition literature; it presents itself, rather, as an epigone of earlier historical narration, dominated by the epic of (Muslim) conquest and (Hindu) resistance. The film, in fact, takes the book as nothing more than the cue for quite a different story, whose nucleus rotates around something more subtle, ambiguous, and elusive. What the novel ignores is briefly touched on—but intensely felt—in the film: the theme of personal individuality with respect to social identity.

Notes

* This chapter is a revised translation of an Italian paper by the same author: '*DHARM-PUTR* e la partizione dell'India', *Annali di Ca' Foscari*, XLI, 3 (Serie orientale 33) 2002: 211–37). We are grateful for the permission to translate the article in English. Throughout the chapter, we spell consistently *Dharmputra*, as in the official Romanized spelling of the film, used here also for the novel.

1 This cinema too is the result of a "Partition," officially dating from 1969. The rationale was to distinguish it from the popular (or commercial, as it is often simplistically termed) cinema.

2 Recent films on Partition also include *Gadar: Ek Prem Katha* ("Rebellion: A Love Story," 2001, d. Anil Sharma), which tells the story of a Muslim girl, Sakina, left behind in India while her family is attempting to reach Pakistan. She is saved by a young Sikh, Tara Singh. They fall in love, get married and have a child. Later on, Sakina and her parents get in touch once again and Sakina goes to Pakistan to meet them. Her father is not willing to send her back and wants to marry her off to a (politically important) friend of his. Tara and their child arrive in Pakistan to bring Sakina back with them. While attempting to reach India, Sakina is seriously wounded by her father, who finally repents. This is a remake of a Punjabi film based on a true story, *Shaheed-e-mohabbat Boota Singh* ("Martyr in Love, Boota Singh," 1998, d. Manoj Punj). While in the earlier film there is a greater balance in the responsibility of both sides, the newer movie displays anti-Pakistani (and, indirectly, anti-Muslim) feelings, as has become common in many more recent films. In this respect, *Gadar: Ek Prem Katha* represents a dissonant voice in the filmography of Partition. By contrast, *Khamosh Pani* ("Silent Waters," 2005), a Pakistani-European coproduction made by a Pakistani director, Sabiha Sumar, warmly recalls the shared history common to the majority of Indian Partition films.

3 Born in the village of Chandaus, Bulandshahar District (Uttar Pradesh), Catursen studied Sanskrit and traditional Ayurvedic medicine in Benares and at Maharana Sanskrit College in Jaipur. He started writing when he was barely twenty and his vast output includes narrative, poetry, drama, history, politics, philosophy, and medicine. His novels include: *Amar abhilāṣi* ("The Eternal Yearning One," 1933); *Mandir kī nartakī* ("The Temple Dancer," 1939); *Vaiśālī kī nagarvadhū* ("The Courtesan of Vaishali," 1948, considered his masterpiece); *Ālamgīr* (1954); *Somnāth* (1954); *Sonā aur khūn* ("Gold and Blood," 1960). Catursen has also written some 450 short stories, many of them on historical subjects (on Catursen, see Kapūr 1965).

4 Born in Jalandhar (Punjab) in 1932, Yash Chopra started out as an assistant to his elder brother Baldev Raj (b. 1914), film producer and director, known simply as B.R. Chopra, a highly influential personality in the world of Indian cinema. Yash began directing on his own in 1959, with *Dhool ka Phool* ("Flower of Dust"). An independent producer since 1974, he has established himself as a major filmmaker; in 2002 he received the prestigious Dadasaheb Phalke Award. His most successful films include: *Kabhi Kabhie* ("Sometimes," 1976); *Deewar* ("The Wall," 1975); *Trishul* ("The Trident," 1978); *Silsila* ("The Affair," 1981); *Chandni* (1989); *Dil to Paagal hai* ("The Heart is Crazy," 1997); *Veer-Zara* ("Veer and Zara," 2005). He also produced the hit film *Dilwale Dulhania le*

Jayenge ("The Courageous will Take Away the Bride," 1995), directed by his son Aditya Chopra (on Yash Chopra, see Dwyer 2002).

5 A popular Arabian tale is about the romance between Qais and the beautiful Laila. Her father refuses to give her in marriage to the young man, who has gone crazy (Majnu) with love. When Laila dies, Majnu, too, dies on her grave.

6 In the novel this episode takes place much later, when the two women meet again after 28 years: "Laughing, Banu said: 'If you let me, bhābhī [sister-in-law], I will touch it. I would like to put a morsel in your mouth.' 'Heaven save me from such a disgrace! If you touch it, it becomes poison. As soon as I eat it I will die.' Aruna, frowning, took a piece of the cake and put it in Banu's mouth, after which Banu forgot everything and incessantly started feeding Aruna and Aruna did the same with her" (DhP 147).

7 On the situation of Muslim Indians after 1947, see Hasan 1997.

8 The Nawab refers to the anti-British revolt of 1857, called "Mutiny" or "First War of Independence," depending on one's political stance.

References

Bhalla, A. (ed.) (1994) *Stories About Partition*, 3 vols, Delhi: Harper Collins.

—— (1999) "Memory, History and Fictional Representations of the Partition," *Economic and Political Weekly*, October 30, 1999: 3119–28.

Catursen, Ā. (1954; 2nd edn 1985) *Dharmputra*, Delhi: Rajpal and Sons.

Dwyer, R. (2002) *Yash Chopra*, London: British Film Institute.

Hasan, M. (1997) *Legacy of a Divided Nation: India's Muslims Since Independence*, London: Hurst.

Jalal, A. (1985; 2nd edn 1994) *The Sole Spokesman: Jinnah, the Muslim League and the Demand for Pakistan*, Cambridge: Cambridge University Press.

Kapūr, S. (1965) *Ācārya Catursen kā kathā sāhitya*, Aminabad: Vivek Prakāśan.

Pandey, G. (1997) "Partition and Independence in Delhi: 1947–48," *Economic and Political Weekly*, September 6, 1997: 2261–72.

—— (2001) *Remembering Partition: Violence, Nationalism and History in India*, Cambridge: Cambridge University Press.

Qidvaī, B.A. (1990; 2nd edn 2000). *Āzādī kī chāv meṃ*, New Delhi: National Book Trust.

Roy, A. (1993; 4th edn 1999) "The High Politics of India's Partition: The Revisionist Perspective," in M. Hasan (ed.) *India's Partition: Process, Strategy and Mobilization*, New Delhi: Oxford University Press.

Conclusion

Heidi Pauwels

We have journeyed a long way, studying adaptations of the classical epics, creative reworkings of classical Sanskrit drama, reverberating echoes of medieval devotional *bhajans*, *gīts* and ghazals from Indo-Islamic culture, rousing socialist songs from the 1930s and beyond and film versions of novels from the colonial and postcolonial period.[1] Each of the chapters we have read is rich in its close reading of individual films and comparative analysis. Now it is time to ask what are the general lessons that we have learned from this exploration in the world of North Indian popular cinema and its connections with literature.

Modernity of the medium and period-specificity

First, we have found that there is no easy way to generalize how classics are being recast. North Indian popular cinema is not homogeneous. When we compare different films inspired by the same literary sources, we find complex processes at work. We cannot sum this up in an easy formula. The cliché that "Bollywood" plays it conservative and the sub-argument that it represents an endless rehash of the epic texts does not hold water. We cannot say that what is going on in popular cinema is "old wine in new bottles," a superficial dressing up of tradition in modernity's clothes. There is not one "Bollywood" way of adapting literature, but a remarkable multiplicity that is a testimony to the creativity of the directors, writers, and their crew. Movie versions of the same "text" may be progressive or conservative, diametrically opposite in their conclusions, as illustrated by Lutgendorf's and Aklujkar's chapters, which find conservative and transformative versions of the epics. When we look at the transformation from book to movie of a novel with what seems to be a quite chauvinist Hindu approach, *Dharmputra*, we have to conclude that the film is much more "secular," and goes beyond the sectarianism of the book. In short, we cannot speak about a hegemonic Bollywood ideology at work when classics are presented on celluloid.

Second, in the absence of a formula, we may attempt to unravel a narrative, to write a history of North Indian popular film adapting fiction. If we pay attention to the historicity of the films, that is, break up this diversity along the lines of periods in which the films are made, we may be able to distinguish certain common traits for different periods. Again, things are not that simple. We definitely do not have evidence for a triumphant march of egalitarian values and democratic ideas, certainly not for gender issues. Sometimes matters seem to be quite the opposite, a trend that goes downhill in more recent movies. Munni Kabir has pointed out that there is a big difference in the production climate of the 1950s as opposed to now (Kabir 2004). At that time the production unit operated like a family, with the director as the enlightened patriarch; this led to a situation in which the director's vision was central and one could speak more of the director as an author. Now there is less of a team spirit and more fragmentization of the job, as a consequence of which the director has less authorship. Kabir sees a change of the work atmosphere from a more "secular" one with the director as a benign patron for his workers, to a more distant, professional and "modern" one, which also shows division along communal lines. This evolution is mirrored in a change of themes from "secular" socialist themes to the capitalist fantasy of wealth and religious respectability. The latter trend becomes particularly marked since the 1990s feel-good movies, starting with *Hum Aap ke Hain Koun…!* (on the consumer- culture aspect of which, see Uberoi 2000).

Mir notices a similar phenomenon with the disappearance of the progressive element once so strong in film lyrics, and its being overwritten by the musical score. Such differing emphasis creeps in also in new versions of old movies based on literary sources, such as in particular *Devdas*, which has lost much of its religious reform agenda in its recent remake in favor of an extravaganza of "feel good," as noted by both Creekmur and Bose.

Still, we need to qualify this generalization about periods. Movies from different periods may be remarkably similar in their treatment of the literary source. Thus, Hines, studying Ghalib, finds that the movie from the mid-1950s and the TV serial from the late 1980s share many features, including a tendency to reduce Ghalib's complex ghazals to fit the love-song format.

If we flip the coin and look at treatment of the same literary source in contemporary movies, we find even there diversity. Lutgendorf and Aklujkar have each compared movies from the same period (1980 and 2000 respectively) and found that, though these films came about in the same historical climate, they represented diametrically opposite ideologies. One may look for explanations in differences of register, positing a scale of more folk and more artsy movies, as Lutgendorf does, yet, he hastens to qualify that we cannot speak about a strict dichotomy. Aklujkar also alerts us to the fact that what may seem a more "traditional" and straightforward remake of epic material may include "interpolations" with a progressive agenda, such as the feminist-nationalist interlude in one song of *Sampoorn Ramayana*. Thus, even one movie can incorporate subversive and reactionary elements in the same breath. This is also illustrated by Pauwels' analysis of Gulzar's *Meera*, which shows elements of protest as well as reinforcement of patriarchal status quo. What we can conclude is that in any given period, there is still scope for a rich diversity of readings and for confirmation as well as contestation.

The gender issue

The previous two points anticipate already our answer to the "woman question". We cannot unproblematically conclude that the modernity of the medium of film entails a unidirectional move towards a more "democratizing" interpretation of cultural icons, in particular with regard to women. It may be tempting to posit a development parallel with Hollywood where feminist critique seems to have led to transformations in themes and foregrounding women characters since roughly the 1970s. Yet, this volume demonstrates that such is not unequivocally the case for India. Aklujkar discusses one recent movie, *Lajja*, that seems to exemplify a trend of freeing women from the shackles of patriarchy, yet she also contrasts it with another contemporary movie, *Hum Saath Saath Hain*, that works to affirm the subjugation of women to the patriarchal family. She concludes that both movies in the end find compromises and refrain from opposing women and patriarchy.

We should also keep in mind that the tendency to contest patriarchal treatment of women in traditional texts is not limited to the medium of film. *Lajja* is not new at all in its protest against Sītā's plight. Medieval vernacular versions of the *Rāmāyaṇa* also reject Rāma's treatment of Sītā (Hess 1999). So maybe it is not the modernity of cinema that is responsible for the contesting voices, but cinema is the medium for a long-standing tradition of questioning and self-relativation (see Richman 2001).

We need to guard also against the cliché that the medium of film leads to reducing women to sex-objects due to an overemphasis of the erotic and exploitation of sexual potential of literature. In her analysis of the opportunities for erotic treatment provided by the text of *Choker Bali*, Bose shows that some opportunities are taken, but others not. We might well infer that a more fruitful question to ask would be why this is the case for some instances and not for others.

The whole issue of the perceived sexism of the popular Indian movie has been revived of late. Interestingly, even Indian feminists that previously have not minced their scornful words for "Bollywood," seem to have turned around. The feminist magazine Manushi recently carried a provocative article, which started out thus: "'Bollywood is much more complex and a far greater agent for positive social change than is acknowledged by those who claim to represent the high culture of India,' says Madhu Kishwar" (Kishwar 2003). This begs comment. Our volume certainly illustrates the complexity of the issue. To what extent the Indian popular movie can be said to actually be an agent for positive change is a question that awaits further analysis. Again, collaboration between different disciplines will be necessary, especially anthropologists need to be invited to take up the topic.[2]

Film by the book

Returning to our focus on literature, we need to make another point. Whatever the filmmaker's agenda, there is no doubt that his (rarely her) "reading" of literature becomes highly influential. In this way, the film becomes a master-reading, so to speak, often criticized, yet even if so, setting the agenda of the debate around the book. Thus it is doubly important to understand that even the "master's" reading is not the first one, it is dependent upon others. What is often suppressed is the process of transmission between the text and the film. Critics who care to compare tend to jump from the "original" straight to its transformation on the screen, as if there were no intervening line of transmission.

Maybe the most important realization that runs through this book is that "the text" never comes to the film maker "pure." It is mediated through different perspectives, including orientalist and postcolonial ones. This is in particular the case for the Sanskrit literature of the Great Tradition, which, as Chatterjee so eloquently describes, has come mediated through orientalist lenses. As she points out, the director of the movie *Shakuntala*, Shantaram, though influenced by these romantic castings of the heroine, still "talks back to the empire," by accessing different sources, including the "epic" Shakuntala, that is the version as told in the *Mahābhārata.* Aklujkar has made us aware of the rich tradition of Marathi and other vernacular stage performances of the Sanskrit *Mṛcchakaṭikam*, which fed into Girish Karnad's movie production. Again it would be a mistake to assume the film is derived "straight" from an original text.

We find a similar phenomenon of Indian stories coming filtered through orientalist perspectives in *Mughal-e-Azam.* The play from which the movie is ultimately derived reworks the Anarkali myth that had come mediated through Western travelers' reports intent on characterizing the Mughal rule as "tyrannical." By giving the story a new twist in his happy ending, the filmmaker, K. Asif manages to bypass this "mis-characterization" of the clement Akbar as tyrannical and to correct for the Western generalization. He thereby restores Akbar's memory as tolerant and forgiving, implicitly repressing the British self-serving sweeping theory of "Muslim misrule."

The movies inspired by the epics too come mediated through long performance traditions. Lutgendorf makes clear how each of the two movies he analyzes partakes in the characteristics of one broad stream of more "popular" and "elite" theatrical forms respectively. He points out that the revival of the *Mahābhārata* on the screen may have to do with a theatrical wave of stagings of Dharmavīr Bhāratī's Hindi play *Andhā Yug.* Aklujkar too mentions inspiration from theatrical conventions on *Rāmāyaṇa* films. Thus, it would be a fallacy to simply compare the "word on the printed page" and see how it is transformed into on the screen. That would be skipping a few stages—notably the *stage*—and neglecting the complex transactions that occurred on the road in between.

A similar phenomenon can be noted for the depiction of songs. One of the contributions of the volume lies in going beyond plot and narrative, but looking in detail at the popular movie songs. Like the stories, songs too have many layers of transmission. They can come from the prestigious locales of "high art" performances, or via communal singing in the temple, at the Sufi shrine, or during folk celebrations, or via popular cassette culture, or all of the above and some more. In the process, mixing and matching goes on and different layers of meaning are thus acquired. We could propose to balance the attention in film studies to "interocularity" with "interaurality": songs and stories have been heard before in different spheres of life. Part of the appeal of popular movies is that they activate memories of what has been heard in other "registers." The scholar's task is to carefully analyze this process. Hines, Mir, and Pauwels have made only a modest start, focusing on the lyrics.[3] Much more work is needed here, especially input from (ethno-)musicologists and scholars of folk music would be able to advance the field.

This gets us well beyond the naïve film critique where everything revolves around the value judgment of the "faithful" adaptation. There is more going on than mere re-presenting or misrepresenting. As our analyses in this book show, films can affirm, deny, contest, "update"—all of the above in one breath. They can infuse tired old themes with new life, and/or draw legitimacy and hijack literature for their own purpose. Sometimes, the most interesting adaptations are the most agenda driven. They can be said to be most "authentic" in the sense that they contribute their own emotion. The agenda of remake itself is not an exclusively modern phenomenon, but one of all times. Indeed, "fidelity to the original" is not a requirement of the South Asian tradition, in the case of for instance, the epics or *bhakti* lyrics. The epic stories can said to be less an "Ur-quelle" or "original source" than a matrix of meaning, within which many contemporary speakers, including movie directors work to construct their own identity.

Creekmur also points us to studying variants between different prints of same movie, such as director's cut, post-censorship board cut. Mir has discussed what the censor board cut from the progressive lyrics he studied. Lutgendorf alerted us to the problem of low-quality prints of movies as available on the commercial DVD market. Pauwels points to discrepancies between the screenplay as published and the movie as commercially available. This sets us on track for the future to identify another way in which textual studies can usefully contribute to film studies. Movie versions can be read with lessons learned from textual criticism in mind. This goes further than the stereotypical Ur-quelle-Stammbaum model, which has long been superseded in textual studies. New models take into account the intrinsic value of different versions and what they reveal about the particular circumstances in which they came about.

Self-referentiality of film

We have noticed again and again that popular Indian cinema is very explicit about its literary sources and its ways of dealing with them. We have run the whole gamut of self-representation of the film: as a book, as was the case with Bimal Roy's *Devdas*, which opens with a shot of the frame of the book, over Sohrab Modi's *Mirza Ghalib*, which self-consciously states it takes its liberties with Ghalib's story, to Gulzar's *Meera*, which in the film itself shows the "original composition context" of Mīrā's songs and interestingly, outside of it, elaborately discusses the director's interpretations of the Mīrā story in the foreword to the published screenplay.

This is complicated by a simultaneous inter-referencing of movies that have taken their cue from the same literature. Thus we find a thick web of audiovisual quotations. The *Devdas* "series" as discussed by Creekmur is an obvious example of this phenomenon. In an interesting reversal, Mandakranta Bose shows how Ritwik Ghatak's choice of a source text by Tagore can be read as a reference to Satyajit Ray who did many Tagore filmings. Not only does the movie carry visual references to Ray (such as the binocular motive), but the very choice of the source text of the novel signifies actually a tribute to the artistic film director. The good movies set the themes for generations of filmmakers to come. To fully appreciate the new films one has to understand them against this broader—and often forgotten—background.

The awareness of issues of such intertextuality within the film itself may be more outspoken in the Indian popular cinema than it is in Hollywood. Lutgendorf draws our attention to the ironic self-consciousness of the characters in the movie *Hum Paanch* that they are playing out the *Mahābhārata* once again. He also notices that such is not the case in the more realistic *Mahābhārata* movie version *Kaliyug* with its more Hollywoodish self-forgetfulness of the main characters.

Often, such multiple intertextual references go beyond the connoisseur's delight and carry a special significance. In the film *Lajja*, the episodes where Vaidehi gets involved in the life of the actress Janaki abound with such playful references. Janaki compares Vaidehi to Karisma Kapoor (whereas the audience of course savors the fact that the actress actually playing the role is Manisha Koirala) and they both attend a movie with Shah Rukh Khan and whistle at him in the dark cinema hall. Such "film-within-a-film" references are part of the delight of Indian popular cinema, an inside joke for the connoisseurs, so to speak. More significantly, there is also the "play-within-a-film" dimension: at the time of their first meeting, Janaki is playing the role of Anarkali, not in Imtiaz Ali's drama, but in the famous scene of the movie *Mughal-e-Azam*, with the song *Pyār kiyā to ḍarnā kyā*, or "What's there to fear if one has loved?" This proves to be prophetic, as indeed Janaki has loved (and is pregnant by) one of her fellow-actors and will face the dire consequences of love outside marriage. Outside the drama, Anarkali/Janaki will have to defy the jealous director Purushottam, who was playing "Akbar," and who tries to break up her romance with the other actor. Sadly, he succeeds. There is no subterranean tunnel to help this Anarkali out in Rajkumar Santoshi's movie, and her fate seems to be to be "buried alive" in an asylum for the mentally disturbed. Finally, there is the "audience within the movie" feature. In *Lajja*, in the scenes where Janaki defiantly tries to change the *Rāmāyaṇa* performance she is enacting, we see that the audience does not like it and starts rioting. This may well be a bitter irony on Santoshi's part, predicting the fate of his own film. Indeed, his predictions came true. *Lajja* was declared to be a subversion of the *Rāmāyaṇa* by the Shiv Sena, which tried to have it banned. And, as Aklujkar points out, just like in the movie, where the rioters burn posters of the actress playing Sītā, BJP workers in Bhopal burned posters of Madhuri Dixit in her role as Janaki playing Sītā, as well as effigies of the director. From this example we see that the self-reflective dimension of the Hindi movie is multilayered and complex and can range from the superficially amusing to deeper ironic. In order to unearth such references, we need scholars well-versed in film studies and popular culture, willing to take he time to articulate the rich web of allusions they perceive in these seemingly straightforward movies.

The stigma of inauthenticity

Related to the problematic of the film's position vis-à-vis the source text, we see over and over again the haunting question of realism of the period represented. Ever-lurking seems to be the reproach of "inauthenticity," of misrepresenting the epoch depicted. Critics are often keen to point out anachronisms or other "slips" of the directors. We saw this come up as a point of criticism for Ghosh's *Chokher Bali* (Bose's chapter), as well as for *Mughal-e-Azam* (Désoulières). In the latter case, even the author of the play of which the film is derived, took care to imbibe his work with an aura of authenticity, as Désoulières shows in detail, with reference to décor, costume, and customs, as well as the language used—although be it a nineteenth-century reconstruction of the sixteenth-century Mughal court. If Ghosh's film trots out in its credits the names of specialists and consultants to ensure the viewer of the authenticity of his movie, Ali Taj claimed in his preface to have had his work checked by two well-known Lahore historians and experts. He is well aware that the plot of his play itself, the story of Anarkali, is a legend, which is not corroborated by historical evidence. Still, he takes great pains to ensure that his portrayal of the period is authentic.

On the other hand, when working in the genre of the "devotional," no such demands of authenticity are made, rather the opposite, the historical approach may be punished as "inauthentic" in a different way. Thus complained Gulzar, who blamed the initial failure of his *Meera* on his "historical" rather than "devotional" treatment of the Mīrā story. In his view, the audience disliked his attention to psychological veracity rather than melodramatic effects. The weight of historical detail was felt to distract from Mīrā's devotion, which should have been the main point.

In any case, both the historical costume drama and the devotional movie are understudied. This is a pity, as both reveal interesting reappropriations of history and of saints of the past, preoccupations similar to other contemporary modes of writing popular history. Désoulières does not address this explicitly, but his chapter raises interesting questions in that regard. What is remembered, what is forgotten? What sources are privileged? It pays off to look in detail at the language used, which may be carefully and lovingly reconstructed, with some unexpected "modern" twists and anachronisms. Most importantly, which issues are taken up and which points are neglected? This may reveal something about the agendas of the moviemakers and their times. Why is it that the devotional movies stress the socially progressive stance of *bhakti*, whereas they seem to promote a status quo for gender issues—as Pauwels implies? How is it that a 1960s movie writes a more progressive history of Partition than the 1954 novel, which Cossio studies? Linguists, scholars of religion, and above all historians could usefully contribute to these questions.

Turning the tables

We also note an interesting reversal. The adaptation from literature to film becomes a two-way affaire: moving not just from book to movie, but back, Importantly, as is the case in the West, the release of a movie boosts the sale of book. It can even inspire new translations of the book, as is the case with *Devdas* (the first complete translation of the book came out in 2002, as Creekmur informs us in his chapter), and foster a renewed interest through critical studies of the novel in relation to the book. This in turn will influence the next remake of the movie. A similar phenomenon can be recognized in the case of poets made by cinema, such as Sahir Ludhianvi, who acquired fame through Guru Dutt's movies, which in turn sparked interest in his poetic work. Hines stressed the contribution of Bombay cinema to keep the memory alive of great Muslim contributors to Indian music, such as Ghalib. Movies can bring new life to "Dead Poet Societies," so to speak.

This draws attention to a related phenomenon of reversal apparent in postcolonial literature from the last few decades, namely, that movies become reference points in literature. Here we step outside the boundaries of this book, referring to the successful Indian English authors, such as Salman Rushdie and Vikram Seth. Their novels abound with references to films and the world of movie stars, both explicitly and implicitly. We could speak of a typical postcolonial hybridity, because at the same time these novelists incorporate much from the venerable Indian tradition. Vidyut Aklujkar has previously (1993) written on how Rushdie transformed stories from the classical Sanskrit treasure house of stories, *Kathāsaritsāgar.* The example of Rushdie shows how the film based on the classic turns itself into a classic and goes on inspiring new artists in and beyond the world of popular Indian film.

Final conclusion

There are multiple paths from literature into film. We have to be careful not to privilege one over the other. The interchange is not just one-way street. It is marked by happy hybridity. Films can be both solemn or joyously playful celebrations of literature—as well exemplified in the aptly titled *Utsav*, discussed by Aklujkar—and the other way round. There are no hard and fast borderlines. It is more useful to think in terms of porous surfaces, with ideas, characters, plots, images, songs and snatches of dialogue floating around freely.

At the end of the day, the main lesson is that things are always more complex than they seem. An earlier subtitle for this book was "classics *on* celluloid," which might suggest, a simple projection onto the screen of literature, a one-way transposition from one medium to another. Instead, we find again and again that closer analysis will unearth myriads of complex interrelations. The new subtitle "recasting classics," foregrounds the process, which is complex. Literature often comes to film mediated through drama and subsequently through other films. We have studied a few cases in which the "original" text is forgotten and comes via other films, most strongly maybe with *Mughal-e-Azam* and Taj Ali's *Anārkalī*. Creekmur has eruditely pointed the way to some of the intricate webs of meaning woven in North Indian popular cinema, including *Devdas*. And then we noted that the world of films influences literature in turn.

We have only just started the task of distinguishing between the different layers that make up the seemingly simple movies of "Bollywood." Mainly, we have come to realize that is important to do so in order to avoid ascribing elements acquired early on in the process to the final stages and to get sensitized to what precisely is preserved, what is foregrounded, what is neglected, or what is erased at which stage of the process. If we do not bring our scholarship to bear on these issues, we run the risk of misinterpreting themes and plots to the period of the film, whereas they find their origin in an earlier period when the literature that inspired it was written or composed. There remains much work to be done.

Notes

1 In bringing together such different types of literature, the interesting thing is that these literatures typically are approached in different literary modes: much research has been done on differences of literary disposition versus oral disposition. Sometimes this is summarized that in the former there is an "interiorization" of the reader-text relationship, while in the latter this is "externalized" with declamatory style, music, and so on. (Vasudevan 2000: 9). Interestingly, by reworking these different genres into movies, the literature comes to be approached in yet a different, visually predominant way, which we could say is closest to the "oral disposition."

2 A wonderful start has been made by Gopalan's analysis of the "lady avenger" films of the late 1980s and early 1990s (2002: 34–59) and for the study of masculinity, by the anthropological work of Steve Derné (2000).

3 Note also Daisy Rockwell's recent analysis of Guru Dutt's experiments in film song picturization, with reference to poetry by Ludhianvi and Kaifi Azmi (2003: 109–24).

References

Aklujkar, V. (1993) "Haroun and the Sea of Stories: Metamorphosis of an Old Metaphor," *Commonwealth Novel in English* 6:1–2.

Derné, S. (2000) *Movies, Masculinity, Modernity: An Ethnography of Men's Filmgoing in India*, Westport, CT.: Greenwood Press.

Gopalan, L. (2002) *Cinema of Interruptions: Action Genres in Contemporary Indian Cinema*, London: British Film Institute.

Hess, Luida (1999) "Rejecting Sita Indian Responses to the Ideal Man's Cruel Treatment of His Ideal Wife," *Journal* of the American Academy of Religion, 67.1: 1–32.

Kabir, Munni (2004) "The Wisdom of Mehboob Khan, Bimal Roy, Raj Kapoor and Guru Dutt," Unpublished Presentation for the Symposium, Classics on Celluloid, in Seattle, April 2.

Kishwar, M. (2003) "The Idea of India: Bollywood as India's Cultural Ambassador," *Manushi* 139. Online. Available HTTP: <http://www.indiatogether.org/manushi/issue139/idea.htm> (accessed September 2006).

Richman, P. (2001) *Questioning Ramayanas: A South Asian tradition*, Berkeley, CA: University of California Press.

Rockwell, D. (2003) "Visionary Choreographies: Guru Dutt's Experiments in Film Song Picturisation," *South Asian Popular Culture* 1.2: 109–24.

Uberoi, P. (2000) "Hum aap ke hain koun . . .!" in R. Dwyer and C. Phinney (eds) *Pleasure and The Nation: The History, Politics and Consumption of Popular Culture in India*, Delhi: Oxford University Press.

Vasudevan, R.S. (ed.) (2000) *Making Meaning in Indian Cinema*, New Delhi: Oxford University Press.

Index

Note: Page numbers with *f* refer to pages with photographs or illustrations

www.ingramcontent.com/pod-product-compliance
Lightning Source LLC
Chambersburg PA
CBHW071503110726
47908CB00003B/713
9780415576604